Medicine & Society
In America

Medicine & Society
In America

Advisory Editor

Charles E. Rosenberg
Professor of History
University of Pennsylvania

AUTOBIOGRAPHY

OF

SAMUEL D. GROSS, M.D.

WITH

SKETCHES OF HIS CONTEMPORARIES

EDITED BY HIS SONS

IN TWO VOLUMES

VOL. II

ARNO PRESS & THE NEW YORK TIMES

New York   1972

921
G 878
v. 2

Reprint Edition 1972 by Arno Press Inc.

LC# 71-180576
ISBN for Vol. I: 0-405-03980-8
ISBN for Vol. II: 0-405-03981-6
ISBN for set: 0-405-03953-0

Medicine and Society in America
ISBN for complete set: 0-405-03930-1
See last pages of this volume for titles.

Manufactured in the United States of America

AUTOBIOGRAPHY

OF

SAMUEL D. GROSS, M.D.

IN TWO VOLUMES.

VOL. II.

AUTOBIOGRAPHY

OF

SAMUEL D. GROSS, M.D.,

D. C. L. OXON., LL. D. CANTAB., EDIN., JEFF. COLL., UNIV. PA.,
EMERITUS PROFESSOR OF SURGERY IN THE JEFFERSON MEDICAL COLLEGE
OF PHILADELPHIA.

WITH

SKETCHES OF HIS CONTEMPORARIES.

EDITED BY HIS SONS.

IN TWO VOLUMES.

Vol. II.

PHILADELPHIA:
GEORGE BARRIE, PUBLISHER.
1887.

PRINTING-OFFICE OF THE PUBLISHER

CONTENTS OF VOL. II.

SKETCHES OF SOME DISTINGUISHED CONTEMPORARIES.

CHAPTER XIII.

CHAPTER XIV.

AUTOBIOGRAPHY.

AUTOBIOGRAPHY

OF

SAMUEL D. GROSS, M.D.

CHAPTER I.

JANUARY 1st, 1878.—Another year has gone, one which but for my loneliness would have been one of the happiest of my life. Christmas brought me many sweet letters and little tokens of affection from my young friends, especially in the form of bouquets and baskets of flowers, so expressive of good taste and refined feeling. Who does not love flowers? I know of nothing which is so well calculated to lift up the soul to God as their cultivation, which I consider almost a divine occupation. My older daughter and her husband with their three children have spent the Christmas holidays with me, and have contributed much to my happiness. The father, B. F. Horwitz, returned this afternoon with his two clever boys, leaving his wife and daughter, a dear, loving child of ten years, to keep house for me for a few weeks. My health is excellent, and my aptitude for work was never better.

The profession during the last two months sustained a serious loss in the death of Dr. Paul F. Eve, of Nashville, and of Dr. Edward Hammond Clarke, of Boston, the former one of our best surgeons, and the latter one of our most prominent physicians. With both of these gentlemen I was personally acquainted, and fully appreciated their high character. In connection with the death of these two men, I cannot refrain here from referring to the sudden demise of my young friend, pupil, and assistant, Dr. Theodore Horwitz, who died in December, after an illness of a little over two days, at the age of twenty-one years, at the opening of a life which gave every promise of being brilliant. He was ambitious, industrious, and studious, with a high sense of the honor and dignity of his profession. He was particularly fond of surgery, but was well versed in the branches of a medical education. Long before he became a student of medicine he followed me in my operations both in private practice and at my college clinics; and when at length he began his studies as a regular matriculate, his progress was sure and rapid. His examination for graduation received the praise of the Faculty. Soon after, he was elected resident physician of the Philadelphia Hospital, standing at the head of the list in a competitive examination of twenty-one candidates. After the close of his term of service he reëntered the college, where at the time of his death he was one of the assistant demonstrators of anatomy, and a member of my clinical staff. He was a zealous student, kind-hearted, genial, and agreeable in his manners, a faithful instructor, an excellent son, a high-toned gentleman. To these qualities he added a lofty sense of morality and great respect for religion. I feel it to be my duty to make this record of my young friend's character, and to hold him up as an example for the imitation of those whom he has left behind.

New Year's day, 1878, being Tuesday, Mr. Henry C.

Carey spent the evening with me in playing euchre, as has been his wont for some time past. For a while he ran ahead of me, a circumstance which never fails to put him in the best possible humor, which is not always the case when he is badly beaten. We played altogether twelve games, and came off even. "I will not," said he, "play another game this evening, lest I be conquered." As he rose from his chair to leave, I said, "Mr. Carey, who are the great women you have ever known in this city?" "I can recall," was his reply, "only three of any considerable celebrity in their day, and I am not certain that they deserve to be called great—Mrs. Meredith, Mrs. Rush, and Mrs. Gilpin. These were all noted for their hospitality and for their faculty of entertaining their friends, as well as strangers. There are," he added, "no such women now. I do not know one who is their equal, or who can be compared with them. The present race is frivolous and insipid. The men," he said, "are no better. There is no literary talent among them; they are tradesmen and shopkeepers. The Wistar Party consisted of members of the American Philosophical Society, and comprised men of distinction in the different professions. The Saturday Club, which succeeded that party, is made up of all sorts of men. The Binneys, the Ingersolls, the Duponceaus, the Whartons, the Merediths, the Peterses, the Chapmans have disappeared, and there are none to fill their places. There is no one to take my place at my Sunday evening reunions. We have no historians, no poets, no novelists—no writers, in short, of any great merit in any branch of literature. Philadelphia has gone to the d—l." The literature most worthy of Philadelphia, at the present time, is in the department of medicine, which is universally acknowledged to be equal to any in the world.

On February 5th, 1878, I received the following telegram from my friend and old pupil, Professor David W. Yandell, of Louisville : "My father died this morning of pneumonia.'' The news, thus briefly announced, fell heavily upon my heart, for I had known Dr. Yandell long and well, and had for him a warm and affectionate regard. For fifteen years we had been colleagues in the Medical Department of the University of Louisville at a time when that institution had one of the ablest Faculties ever brought together on this continent. Dr. Yandell was a native of Tennessee, the son of a prominent physician, and a graduate in medicine of the University of Maryland in the days of Davidge, Potter, Hall, and De Butts. The first course of lectures which he attended was in the Transylvania University, at Lexington, in which he soon afterwards became a celebrated teacher of chemistry, first as an assistant of Dr. Blythe, and finally as his successor. He occupied this chair until 1837, when, along with two of his colleagues, Cook and Short, he went to Louisville, and was appointed to the chair of Chemistry in its University, in the organization of which he took a most active and useful part. He held this position until the retirement of Professor Charles Caldwell, when he was transferred to the chair of Physiology. In 1859 he left Kentucky and settled at Memphis, and connected himself with the medical college in that city. At the opening of the civil war he devoted himself zealously to the hospital service, and distinguished himself as a humanitarian. While in this service he spent his leisure hours in the study of divinity, was licensed to preach, and in 1864 was ordained pastor of a Presbyterian church. After three years spent in this office he returned to Louisville, where he devoted the remainder of his life to literary and scientific pursuits, to the practice of his profession, and to the promotion of the interests of the church, of which he was during his whole life a devout member.

Dr. Yandell was the recipient of many honors from his professional brethren. In 1872 he was elected President of the Louisville College of Physicians and Surgeons, and in 1877 President of the Kentucky State Medical Society. His name is indelibly associated with the progress of medicine in Kentucky. He was of an active, restless disposition, a warm friend, and a fearless enemy. The many controversies in which he was obliged, as a member of the medical faculty of the University of Louisville, to engage, in defence of that institution when assailed, as it often was by those who were striving to obtain chairs in it, showed him to be a man of great powers as a thinker and a writer. His pen could be dipped alike in gall or in honey, as the occasion might demand. He had a deep, black, penetrating eye, betraying his remote Italian descent, a soft, pleasant voice, agreeable features, a tenacious memory, and a kind word for every one. He seldom forgot a man's name, face, or history. He was six feet high, with a slight stoop and an inclination of the head to one side. Finally, he was a tender and devoted husband, a loving father, a good neighbor, and an upright citizen. His two sons worthily wear his mantle.

Of these sons, the younger, Dr. Lunsford P. Yandell, is a fine specimen of manly beauty with the manners of a courtier. He was at one time a classmate of Dr. Austin Flint, Jr., and of my son Dr. S. W. Gross in the University of Louisville, in which he now ably fills the chair of Materia Medica, Therapeutics, and Clinical Medicine; and he is well known as one of the editors of the Louisville Medical News.

Of Dr. David W. Yandell, who occasionally addresses me in a letter full of interest and affection as his " Dear Master," what can I say that shall be worthy of his varied talents and of his big noble heart? The Professor of the Science and Art of Surgery and Clinical Surgery in the University of Louisville, he is distinguished as a didactic lecturer and as a bold and skilful operator. Indeed there are few men who are better equipped than he for the multiform and arduous duties of the clinician. In private life he is devoted as husband, father, friend ; in the social circle his brilliant conversational powers, his inexhaustible fund of anecdote, his wide reading, and his apparently endless resources make him on all occasions a charming companion ; while his quick, vigorous intellect and rare powers of eloquence would have admirably qualified him for the career of a lawyer or a politician, if he had chosen to devote himself to the cares and turmoil of public life.

The delicate, tender words of love and sympathy that fall from his pen, like drops of dew from a fragrant flower stirred by the sighing of a summer wind, frequently give place in his journal, The American Practitioner, to an able caustic review, or to a true but scathing exposure of wrong-doing, which causes many an offending medical brother to regret the publication of an ill-written book, or the performance of an action worthy of the just resentment of the editor. Truly, indeed, do these sons tread in the footsteps of their father.

On February 7th Dr. J. B. S. Jackson, of Boston, spent the evening with me. I wanted him to take a room in my house, but he declined. He was very agreeable and chatty, full of professional enthusiasm and of general information. He is one of nature's noblemen, modest, unassuming.

February 28th.—I have just delivered the last lecture of my course, and feel thankful that this labor, so wearing and exacting, is once more at an end—especially thankful that my health has been uninterruptedly good, and that I did not miss a single lecture during the entire session, although I appeared before my class regularly six times a week. Indeed, I do not think I ever taught better or with greater force and enthusiasm than I have this winter. The class was very large, numbering five hundred and ninety-eight, and representing almost every State and Territory in the Union, as well as a number of foreign countries. Everything passed off harmoniously. Two hundred and three candidates received the degree on the 11th of March. Dr. Wallace delivered the valedictory, in which he had the bad taste to attack the social position of English physicians, much to my regret, because what he said was not true. The more exalted grade among them have, as physicians have among us, the *entrée* to the best society in Great Britain.

I received my degree in medicine in March, 1828, and this may therefore be considered as the anniversary of my fiftieth professional birthday. Inclusive of three years spent in preliminary training as a medical student, embracing two courses of lectures, I have now been in the profession fifty-three years—a long life in any pursuit whatever. Medical education has engaged much of my thought and labor; and if the medical schools of the country had been true to the cause, and had properly seconded the efforts which I, in common with others, made, the standard would long ago have been placed upon a pinnacle commanding the admiration of the profession and the respect of the public. I thank God devoutly for the mercies He has shown me during this long period of my life!

Fifty years! What mighty changes have taken place in the world during that time! The arts and sciences have been revolutionized. When I entered the profession it was overspread with a mantle of darkness. It is true great progress had been made in every direction; but theories, conjectures, and uncertainties were the characteristics of the day. Hardly anything was definitely settled. Physiology and pathology were conjectural branches of the healing art. Chemistry was in a rudimentary, transitional state. Hygiene and state medicine had no existence. Toxicology and medical jurisprudence were occult arts. Surgery and medicine were the merest arts, without any scientific associations or connections. Midwifery and gynæcology were in a crude condition. Disease was by many regarded, not as an aberration of function, or perversion of health, but as a sort of undefinable entity engrafted upon the system, from which it was necessary to expel it, often with violent remedies, more injurious to the patient than the malady itself. Therapeutics, indeed, had been more labored than advanced. Very little was certainly known respecting the action of medicines upon the system. The text-books were of an inferior order, and medical literature had made little progress. All these things are now happily changed for the better; and we may flatter ourselves that we have laid, deeply, broadly, and firmly, the foundation of a great temple of medicine, the superstructure of which, however, it will take ages to erect and beautify.

It may here be appropriate to speak of friends which during these long years of my professional life have ever cheered me with their companionship, and have been to me a source of comfort in dark days of trial and affliction, for nothing apart from my immediate family has afforded me greater happiness than my library. I have always been passionately fond of books, and have spent money freely in their purchase. As may well be supposed, it was a source of profound grief to me, upon leaving Philadelphia in 1829, to be compelled to part with most of my books, medical and miscellaneous, to enable me to pay off a few pressing debts. It was not until years had elapsed that I was in a condition to make purchases again. Gradually, however, my collection expanded, and when I left Louisville for this city, in 1856, my library contained nearly, if not quite, four thousand volumes. Of these nearly two thousand were destroyed the following winter in the burning of the University of Louisville, in which they had been placed for safe keeping. This disaster was irreparable, and the effect which it produced upon me it is scarcely possible to overstate.

My medical library now numbers upwards of five thousand volumes. It is particularly rich in works on surgery,

and in medical journals, although of late years I have
fallen behind in periodical literature, owing to its enormous extent and costly character. In surgery I have a
great number of monographs, and the principal systematic
treatises, systems, and cyclopædias in the English, French,
German, and Italian languages. Of the books of the
Fathers of Surgery I have nearly every one, some in the
original languages, others in translations. My collection
of works on military surgery, medicine, and hygiene, without being extensive, is very respectable. The most valuable of them by far are the magnificent volumes entitled
Surgical Reports of the Army, issued from the office of the
Surgeon-General, and kindly presented to me by that distinguished officer. These were drawn up by Dr. George
Otis and his assistants, and comprise a body of facts on
military surgery without a parallel, and reflect the greatest
credit upon the nation.

The best collection of the Fathers of Medicine and of
Theology, until a comparatively recent period, owned by
any one man in this country, was that of the late Dr. John
Redman Coxe, for many years Professor of Materia Medica
in the University of Pennsylvania. After his death these
works, many in rare editions, were sold under the hammer.
The opportunity of securing the medical part of the collection was not seized by the Philadelphia College of
Physicians on the plea of the want of funds. For the
same reason Dr. La Roche's collection of works on yellow
fever was allowed to be scattered. Such conduct showed
great remissness and want of enterprise on the part of the
heads of that institution. The theological collection fared
somewhat better. Many of the works were bought for the
Princeton Library and for the Theological Seminary in
West Philadelphia, but not a few of them found their way
into private hands. Of the medical works I bought myself
a considerable number. Having left an unlimited bid with
Messrs. M. Thomas & Son, I received from them a note in

the morning after the first day's sale desiring a personal interview. The purpose of the interview was to inform me that some of the books had brought a very high price. The works of Paracelsus, for example, in two volumes, had been knocked off to me at fifty-four dollars. "Who," I asked, "is my competitor?" "Young Coxe, a grandson of the late owner of the books," was the reply. As I was going up-stairs we met. I said, "I am told you were very anxious last night to obtain the works of Paracelsus, and as the price is higher than I had expected, they are, if you wish them, at your service." "I am obliged to you; I will take them." In less than five years, during which young Coxe died, the two volumes were again in Thomas's rooms, and I now bought them for seven dollars. Such is the fate of books! For a German edition of the work bought some time subsequently I paid twenty dollars.

The miscellaneous part of my library has been well selected, and comprises a number of the best works on general literature, history, and biography in the English language. The fact is, I have more books, professional and miscellaneous, than I have room for. Bookcase after bookcase has been put up, and yet my books are scattered everywhere over the floor.

If I had the leisure I know of nothing that would afford me greater pleasure than to spend a few hours regularly every day in my library in studying the older medical authors and writing commentaries upon them, and comparing their doctrines and practice with those of recent authors. I should regard such labor as a genuine luxury. Increased interest could readily be imparted to it by accompanying such commentaries with biographical sketches of the writers. There are many excellent kernels of useful knowledge to be found in these ancient tomes. I am not one of those who believe that our ancestors were fools. They were as wise in their generation, according to the knowledge which they possessed, as we are in ours. If their works lie on the shelves and are now rarely read, their fate is no worse than that of their successors will be, for every professional work is, as a rule, short-lived. I do not recollect the time that books did not afford me pleasure, food for reflection, or genuine instruction. They have often solaced me in affliction, stimulated my ambition, and inspired me with hope and confidence in my efforts to do good. They have never scolded me; and if they have sometimes put me to sleep, it was because I had been previously fatigued. I thank God for books and for the privilege of enjoying them. Seneca says, "Leisure without books is the sepulchre of the living soul."

My miscellaneous reading has been somewhat extensive, but too desultory to be of much value to me. I have always felt deeply interested in biography and travels. History, too, has a great fascination for me. Of novels I used to be very fond, especially those of Bulwer and Cooper.

I left Philadelphia this morning, May 31st, to attend the meeting of the College Association and of the American Medical Association next week at Buffalo, taking in Niagara by the way, which I visited for the first time in 1826 while a medical student, and again in 1853 in company with my entire family. My present visit is made in company with my two daughters, who are a constant source of happiness to me. The Falls have not materially changed since my last visit; but Table Rock has disappeared. The American Fall presents more of an excavated, horseshoe appearance, and the Canada Fall is much more depressed in the centre, giving it a somewhat hollow outline. The new Suspension Bridge is a beautiful structure, and many improvements are to be seen immediately around the Falls. Extortion is met everywhere; one cannot move in any direction without a heavy tax upon one's purse. A passage across the bridge costs twenty-five cents, and a drive through the so-called park on the American side two dollars. Of late years the number of visitors is said to have materially diminished on account of these rascalities.

On Monday, June 3d, I rode to Buffalo and attended the meeting of the College Association, founded in 1876 in this city for the improvement of college discipline and for other purposes, prominent among which is the object of bringing the different medical schools of the country under one regularly organized system or uniform mode of action. About thirty schools were represented. The sessions were, for the most part, dull and uninteresting. In the afternoon I offered a series of preambles and resolutions, prefaced by some pertinent remarks, in which I stated that, in my opinion, the time had arrived when all the schools of the country, high and low, should unite upon three courses of lectures as indispensable prerequisites to graduation. With this view one of the resolutions provided that the colleges should hold a meeting at some convenient time and place, at which they should send two delegates, namely, a member of the Faculty and a member of the Board of Trustees, with full power to act. The resolutions, after some discussion, were unanimously adopted, with a recommendation that the meeting should be held during the latter part of the week preceding the session of the American Medical Association, and at the same place. If this plan does not succeed, I know of no other that will. The meeting of the schools without the sanction and co-operation of their respective governing powers is worse than idle. That plan was tried sufficiently, first in 1867 at Cincinnati, and in 1869 at Washington City. Whatever the result of the meeting may be, it is certain that the decision of the great question involved in the resolutions is merely a matter of time, and that in the near future. A change in our curriculum of instruction is absolutely demanded, not less by the public than by the profession, and the sooner it is effected the better.

The American Medical Association met June 4th, Dr.

T. G. Richardson, of New Orleans, in the chair. The
attendance during the week was large—nearly six hundred
—embracing some of the best men in the profession. The
president's address was "appropriate, well-timed, and
suggestive," as one remarked. A great deal of excellent
work was done in the Sections, and there were evidently
an increased earnestness and interest manifested in the
proceedings. The Association was in good working condition. The meeting was harmonious, and a decided
success. Some of the public entertainments surpassed
anything witnessed before. This was especially true of
that given by Mr. Bronsom Rumsey, a wealthy gentleman,
living in a large mansion, surrounded by spacious grounds
with trees and shrubbery, and traversed by a pretty little
lake furnished with boats. Chinese lanterns were suspended in every direction, and Bengal lights imparted an
Oriental aspect to the scene. Professor White also entertained the Association elegantly at his handsome residence
on Main Street. All the prominent ladies of Buffalo were
present, and, by their beauty, intelligence, and tasteful
toilets, added greatly to the enjoyment of the occasion. A
delightful entertainment, accompanied with dancing, was
given on the previous evening by the Buffalo Club at their
house on Delaware Avenue. Many of the wives and
daughters of the members of the Association attended
these agreeable and costly reunions, which form so characteristic a feature of the annual meetings.

I must not forget to mention that during this meeting a
backwoods doctor, as he was shaking hands with me,
asked, "Is Doctor Eberle still living?" I promptly replied,
"If he is, it is not in this country, for he died in 1838,
nearly forty years ago!" I do not know whether this man
was a professor in a medical school or not.

June 12th.—I had an urgent invitation to attend, to-day,
at the Boston Music Hall, the anniversary dinner of the
Massachusetts Medical Society, but was obliged to decline

it, as I returned, fatigued and exhausted, only three days before from Buffalo. This invitation has been repeated annually for three successive years, and I am extremely sorry that it has not been in my power to meet my kind New England brethren at the festive board, as I had the assurance from the anniversary chairman, Dr. Peter Pineo, and his predecessors of an enthusiastic welcome.

On June 28th I went to New York to attend a reception of Dr. Nathan Bozeman, an old private pupil, given to Dr. T. G. Richardson, also a private pupil contemporary with Bozeman, and to myself. The evening was intensely hot, and therefore less enjoyable than it otherwise would have been. About sixty medical gentlemen of the one hundred and twenty or one hundred and thirty invited were present, chiefly New Yorkers, with a few from Brooklyn and Jersey City. Most of my old friends were out of town. The occasion was one of unusual hilarity; the supper was elaborate; and at eleven o'clock the company separated. The oldest man present was Dr. Alfred Post, a veteran member of the profession. He is a nephew of the celebrated Wright Post, a skilful operator, and was my successor in 1851 in the chair of Surgery in the University of New York.

The heat this morning, July 4th, is horrid, the thermometer running into the nineties in the shade. The flies adhere to one's face and hands with the tenacity of adhesive plaster; and the noise from the discharge of pistols and fire-crackers is deafening. No proclamation has been issued to prevent this nuisance, so destructive of the comfort of sick and nervous persons everywhere in our city, and attended with the loss of so many eyes and fingers, if not also of much life and property. I have long been of the opinion that the observance of the Fourth of July as a holiday is a national evil; and I deeply regret, in common with many good citizens, that it is not abolished. Far better would it be if people attended to their regular occupations instead of indulging in dissipation, in which drunkenness and disorderly conduct generally form a conspicuous part. The mischief that is done to morals is incalculable; and, if accurate statistics could be obtained of the accidents destructive to limb and life which occur throughout the length and breadth of the country on this day, the mind would recoil with horror from the ghastly result. But, it is said, "This observance is necessary, because the Fourth of July is the birthday of our independence, and because it serves to keep alive a spirit of patriotism among our people, especially among our young men." This is the sheerest nonsense. True patriotism requires no such stimulus or incentive. The occasion is always sufficient for the hour. In view of the many fires which occur on this day from the effects of cracker-shooting, our method may properly be called the Chinese method of spending it.

July 5th.—The papers this morning are filled with accounts of yesterday's accidents. In a conversation, at a dinner party a few years ago at Mr. George W. Childs's with Lord Houghton, that gentleman, with some feeling, expressed the opinion that the celebration of the Fourth of July as a national festivity ought to be abolished on political grounds, as tending to keep up ill feeling between Great Britain and the United States! I cannot think it has any such tendency. Nevertheless, for the reasons I have assigned, I wish that it should cease to be a national holiday.

July 7th.—I was consulted, a few evenings ago, respecting the health of General Preston, my old Louisville friend, by his son, Mr. Wickliffe Preston, who now resides in New York. Two months ago the General suddenly lost the sight of his left eye from the spontaneous rupture of some of the vessels of that organ, resulting in a destructive effusion of blood. The effect of such an occurrence upon a mind already over-sensitive can easily be imagined. I take a greater interest in the condition of General Preston because he was one of my earliest Kentucky friends, and was for nearly ten years my next-door neighbor. I met him socially for the first time in the summer of 1841, at the home of the late Mr. Robert J. Ward, at a dinner given to him and Mrs. Preston, then recently married. The entertainment was a very agreeable one, and I recollect how every one was struck by the appearance of the groom and his bride—two noble specimens of a man and a woman, tall, well-formed, and very handsome; in fact, regal in bearing. Young Preston soon showed himself to be a fluent and attractive talker, and a man of high culture; and his wife, a daughter of Robert Wickliffe, of Lexington, familiarly known as the "Old Duke," was not far, if at all, behind him in these respects. Subsequently I saw a great deal of Mr. Preston; and when, some years afterwards, he became my immediate neighbor, the intimacy between our families became warm and lasting. The last time I saw him was in 1875, when, for two days, my son, A. Haller Gross, and myself were his guests at Lexington. I need not add how pleasantly the time passed in the bosom of this charming family, where all vied with one another to contribute to our comfort, and how reluctant we were to quit their hospitable roof. A princely style pervaded the establishment, graced by a wife and four daughters that would do honor to any household. General Preston is the descendant of an old and influential Virginia family, a native of Louisville, Kentucky. He was a graduate of the Cambridge Law School when Judge Story was at the head of its Faculty. His earlier education was obtained at Bardstown and at New Haven. He served as Lieutenant-Colonel in our war with Mexico, and subsequently for two years as a member of Congress. On the dissolution of the Whig party he became a Democrat; and in 1859 was appointed Minister to Spain by President Buchanan. During the Rebellion he exerted all his powers in favor of the Confederacy, and acted during nearly the entire period of the war as a Brigadier-General. He possesses uncommon intelligence and great personal popularity, and has fine powers as a stump orator, so necessary to political success in the West and South. Since the close of the war, he has lived in complete retirement; and my impression is that his political disabilities have never been removed.

General Preston, on his way from the West to Spain, stopped for a few days with his family in Philadelphia. On the evening before their departure, Mrs. Gross and I gave them an entertainment, attended by many of our friends and some distinguished strangers. General and Mrs. Preston were, as might have been expected, very popular at the Court of Madrid.

July 8th.—This is my seventy-third birthday—three years of life beyond the age allotted by the Psalmist. My health is perfect. While my friends are dying off around me, I am spared, simply, as I suppose, because my body, despite my age, is in a comparatively sound condition, and because I take care of it. My two daughters sent me pleasant letters, abounding in tender expressions, and accompanied by trifling presents. My grandchildren also sent me sweet letters. My daughter-in-law and sister-in-law each marked the day with a bouquet. And my two sons—well, they have each kissed my forehead, emblematic of their affection and devotion. I ought to be happy, but am not. There is one above all the rest, who is absent, and who was always my great comforter. With proper care I may live to see another birthday. We will see.

Mr. Bloomfield H. Moore, an old friend, has just died. He was a self-made man, and therefore all the better for that. He was highly cultured, refined, and intelligent. He had a strong inclination for scientific pursuits, and was a great reader. He was a very useful citizen, prosperous in business—that of a paper manufacturer—and liberal in the distribution of his wealth. His library was large and well-selected, comprising many, if not all, the standard literary works of America, England, and France. His wife is the well-known Philadelphia authoress, whose writings have made her name favorably known at home and abroad. Mr. Moore had travelled much, was a fluent talker, and had a mind so well stored that he was at all times a most agreeable companion. The immediate cause of his death was pleuro-pneumonia. He died in the fifty-ninth year of his age.

This evening, in conversation with an old friend, Mrs. C., long a resident of St. Louis, I was reminded of a visit I made to that city in 1842, and again in 1854, the latter during my attendance as a delegate at the meeting of the American Medical Association. On my first visit I made the acquaintance of a man who had possession of the medical and obstetrical, and in part also of the surgical, practice of St. Louis. Indeed, such was the confidence reposed in his ability, judgment, and sagacity among all classes of citizens, that it was deemed unfashionable for any one to be sick without the aid of Dr. Carr Lane. I am not certain from what State he came—probably from Virginia. Whatever the fact may be, he had long been a resident of St. Louis, and had become identified with its prosperity at a time when it stood in need of friends and competent advisers. Everybody knew Dr. Lane, and his patients loved him, the women and children in particular. Tall and commanding in appearance, with a bland, benevolent countenance, he was the personification of a good, kind-hearted man, in whom there was no guile or deceit. He literally carried his heart in his hand. His manners, however, were without polish, and his speech was often bluff, like that of one who thoroughly appreciated the strong hold which he had upon the community. With the profession of St. Louis generally he was not popular; and there were not a few among the younger members who did not hesitate to sneer at him. This was perhaps not surprising when it is remembered that Dr. Lane was destitute of scientific information, that he never read a medical book, and that he was a mere routine practitioner of the old school; and yet his success in the sick-room, and in dealing disease heavy blows, must have been great; otherwise he could not have been the popular physician he was, or have sustained himself for so many years, as he assuredly did, in the esteem and affection of the people of St. Louis. There must have been great and deserved merit somewhere—a natural gift, so to speak, of prying into the secrets of disease, and great readiness in applying suitable remedies for its subjugation. Such men are uncommon. But it has been my lot to meet with several examples; and I have invariably remarked in them certain traits of real cleverness, apart from their manners, to which their success was largely due as practitioners. They are usually tender-hearted, good nurses, agreeable talkers, and warm sympathizers. They rule by kindness. Radcliffe and Abernethy ruled by rudeness, associated, it is true, with great talent.

One of Lane's peculiarities was a habit of rummaging the rooms of his patients in search of something to eat or drink. Indeed, it seemed to be an idiosyncrasy with him, appearing at all times, in season and out of season, and the act was often performed apparently without consciousness of what he was doing. It was upon one of these occasions that a patient, who had often witnessed these freaks, determined to play a trick upon him. The visit took place early in the forenoon. "Mrs. H., have you taken your medicine?"—a big dose of calomel and jalap prescribed the evening before. "No, doctor; but I intend to take it presently." At this moment the doctor espied a glass upon the mantel partially filled with jelly and containing the cathartic medicine. The mixture disappeared in an instant. For two days no doctor was seen, and much discussion was indulged in on account of his protracted absence.   When at length he re-appeared he looked pale and haggard, and apologized by saying that he had been seized, soon after he left the lady's room, with a severe attack of cholera morbus.   The lady, now quite recovered, laughed heartily, saying, "It served you right."   "Served me right!   What do you mean?"   "I mean it served you right for swallowing my dose of physic in the jelly-glass upon the mantel day before yester-day."   Lane left his patient's house wiser than he entered it.   He was appointed by President Buchanan Governor of New Mexico, but he remained only a short time on duty. During the war he strongly sympathized with the Southern people, and finally died, pretty much as he had lived nearly all his life, in poverty.

A very different kind of a man from Carr Lane was Dr. William Beaumont, of the United States Army, whose ac-quaintance I made during my first visit to St. Louis, where he was then stationed, in connection, if I mistake not, with Jefferson Barracks, and engaged in a somewhat active prac-tice.   He enjoyed a wide reputation, founded mainly upon the elaborate experiments which he had performed, some years previously, upon digestion in the person of Alexis St. Martin, a young Canadian, who had received a gun-shot wound in the region of the stomach, which left, when healed, a large fistulous opening in the wall of the abdo-men communicating with the organ.   The results of these experiments were published in 1838; and as I had writ-ten a favorable review of them for the Western Journal of the Medical Sciences only a short time before my visit, my reception was perhaps a little more cordial than it otherwise would have been.   However this may be, I found in Dr. Beaumont an agreeable gentleman, suave and interesting in conversation, with great enthusiasm for his profession, and admiration for its successful culti-vators.   The only thing that marred the pleasure of

this and other interviews was his deafness, which compelled him to use an ear-trumpet, and the listener to raise
his voice to a fatiguing pitch. Dr. Beaumont was a man
of small stature and delicate frame, with a darkish, sallow complexion, imparting to him a somewhat unhealthy
appearance. He was at the time fifty-seven years of age,
and looked old. An active life, attended with the many
exposures incident to an army career, had made serious
inroads upon a constitution never strong or robust. Lebanon, Connecticut, in 1785, had the honor of giving birth
to this distinguished savant. His death occurred at St.
Louis in 1853.

The experiments of Dr. Beaumont made his name favorably known to men of science throughout the civilized
world. They were the first efforts, upon a large scale,
to place the subject of digestion with different articles of
food and drink upon a practical and scientific basis; and
it is therefore impossible to award too much praise for the
patience with which, through a series of years, and at
much expense, they were conducted. The government, it
is true, contributed a certain sum towards this object; but
the amount was inadequate, and Beaumont had to draw
largely upon his own purse. The work of Dr. Beaumont
was translated into the different languages of continental
Europe, and it is still quoted with approbation by all writers
on Physiology. Indeed, the facts which it has developed
in relation to the process of digestion are invaluable.

I was glad to meet, on this occasion, a former pupil of
mine, Dr. Charles A. Pope, who, after having attended a
course of lectures in the Cincinnati College, took his degree in the University of Pennsylvania, and then went
abroad, spending two years in pursuit of knowledge,
chiefly in Paris and Vienna. On his return from Europe,
in 1841, he settled at St. Louis, where, at my instance,
he was appointed Professor of Anatomy in the Medical College of that city. On the death of Dr. Prather,

a few years afterwards, he was transferred to the chair of Surgery, a position which he ably filled until he went to France with his family in 1867. For twenty-five years Pope was the principal surgeon in the Western metropolis, enjoying a large and lucrative practice, performing numerous operations, and attracting patients from all the adjoining States. He was well educated and accomplished, tall and slender in form, with a handsome face, a genial disposition, and agreeable manners. He rose rapidly to distinction in his profession, and in the esteem and affection of his fellow-citizens. No physician or surgeon of St. Louis ever enjoyed in a higher degree the good opinion of his professional brethren or of the public at large. His success was due not so much to his address or manners as to the fact that he was an innate gentleman, a man of high tone, to use an American expression, of sterling integrity, and well versed in the art and science of medicine. Such qualities could not fail to inspire public confidence. As a teacher Pope occupied a high rank. I never heard him lecture; but he had the reputation of being a good talker, easy, and free from ostentation in his delivery, and always full of his subject. His demonstrations were models of elegance and precision. He spared no pains or expense to illustrate his surgical courses. His museum was rich in models and preparations, not a few of them the productions of his own hands or of the hands of his pupils. His medical library comprised the choicest works in medicine and surgery in the English and foreign languages. In 1854 he built for himself a palatial residence in a recently settled part of St. Louis, and furnished it in splendid style. Early in his professional life he married Carrie, only daughter of Colonel O'Fallon, one of the most opulent men at that time in the West. This connection brought him additional influence, and raised him, apart from his practice, into independent circumstances. Instead of inducing him to relax his efforts, the marriage

only served to inspire him with increased energy and
ambition. Three children, a son and two daughters, were
the issue of this alliance. In 1867 this man, still young,
was happy in the possession of a very remunerative practice and of numerous and warmly-attached friends; happy
as a teacher in a highly respectable school in great degree
the creation of his own talents and exertion; and happy
in the enjoyment of every worldly good. It was at this
juncture that he was lured from his fascinating home
and many friends. Early in June, 1868, I found him
in furnished apartments on the third floor of an elegant
house in one of the most fashionable streets of Paris, engaged in playing chess with a young lady. He received
me with open arms, and showed every mark of attention
to my dear wife, my son, and myself during our month's
sojourn in the gay metropolis. But I soon saw that he
was out of his natural element. He had occasional fits
of despondency, felt himself out of place, and longed to
be back in the harness in a city where he had achieved
so many triumphs. In St. Louis he was Pope indeed;
in Paris he was nobody. I left Paris towards the end
of June, and never again met him. In the spring of
1871 he revisited St. Louis, called thither by business
affairs, and was caressed and feasted by his old friends.
On his return to Paris it was noticed that he was at
times melancholy and abstracted. The fits of despondency gradually increased. One day, as he was returning
from the Bois de Boulogne, he felt, as he himself told his
family, an almost irresistible inclination to throw himself
under the wheels of the carriage. Soon after this, one
afternoon, as he was sitting at the bedside of his invalid
wife, holding her hand in his, and conversing about the
vanities, vexations, and disappointments of human life,
he suddenly went into an adjoining room, and there, horrible to relate, terminated his existence.

Such was the sad end of this gifted man, of which the

late Dr. Linton, a former colleague of his, wrote me a full account within a short time after its occurrence. I have always thought, and in this opinion Dr. Linton agreed with me, that Pope would never have committed this rash act if he had remained at his post in St. Louis. It is not unlikely, from what I have learned since his death, that there was some hereditary predisposition to insanity in his family. He was a native of Huntsville, Alabama, where he was born in 1818. During his pupilage at Cincinnati, Professor Willard Parker and myself were associated in private teaching. I must not forget to add that Pope, in 1854, was elected President of the American Medical Association at its meeting in St. Louis—a high compliment for one so young in the profession, but well merited. He contributed a number of valuable papers to the periodical press, and was for a time one of the editors of the St. Louis Medical Journal. He translated from the French a monograph on the Use of Water in the Treatment of Surgical Affections.

In 1854, during my second visit to St. Louis, I attended the meeting of the American Medical Association, sent thither as a delegate by the University of Louisville, in which I was then Professor of Surgery. I went down the Ohio in company with Dr., now Professor, Joseph Leidy, the late Dr. George W. Norris, and the late Professor Joseph Carson, whom I had entertained the previous evening at my house. Upwards of two days were spent upon the river, there being at that time no direct railway communication between the two cities. Dr. Jonathan Knight, of New Haven, who had been elected President the previous year, was expected to preside over the meeting; but, as ill luck would have it, he could not come, and his place was filled by the first vice-president, Dr. Usher Parsons, of Providence. Unfortunately, Dr. Parsons was quite destitute of a knowledge of parliamentary proceedings, and hence lamentably incompetent. Great confusion arose in consequence, and for a while the scene was most disgraceful. In the midst of this confusion Mr. John J. Crittenden, then on a visit to St. Louis, entered the hall, and at once loud calls were heard from every side that he should take the chair. This, however, only increased the excitement: first, because Mr. Crittenden was not a doctor or a member of the Association; and secondly, because just then great prejudice existed against him for the reason that he had recently been engaged in defending Matt Ward, the slayer of young Butler. Order was at length restored, and the business of the meeting proceeded with, entire harmony prevailing during the remainder of the session. To show the prejudice that existed in the Association against every one who had any connection with the Ward trial, I may state that I was assured by a number of my friends that I would have received the nomination for President if I had not served as a witness on the occasion. I may add that this feeling against Mr. Crittenden widely pervaded the country, and lasted during the greater part of the remainder of his life. How unjust it was is proved by the fact that the Kentucky statesman was powerless in the matter. As the intimate and lifelong friend of the Ward family it was impossible for him to decline to act as counsel for the defence. I was equally helpless. I had long known the family, and was on the closest social relations with them.

The fate of this young man is well known. He was married, and lived on a plantation in Arkansas. During the war some Confederate troops were encamped near his residence. One day, while walking out, he was mistaken for a Federal soldier, shot, and instantly killed. I knew Ward well; and a more gentle, inoffensive man I never saw. I am sure nothing was further from his mind than to kill Butler, but he became excited during the interview, and, allowing his feelings to get the better of his judgment, committed the rash, unjustifiable act. Butler him-

self was a kind man, and the chastisement which, as his
teacher, he inflicted upon Ward's brother had not been at
all severe, and was no doubt well merited.

Cape May, July 15th.—I am at my old quarters, the
Stockton. I see some familiar faces, but, with the exception of ex-Secretary Robeson, none of any prominence.
Mr. Robeson is decidedly fat, with a rubicund complexion ;
and he has evidently maintained his physical status notwithstanding his immersion for three weeks in the stifling
atmosphere of the Camden court-house while trying to
defend Hunter, the famous murderer.

July 18th.—The morning newspapers are filled with accounts of the excessive heat which is now passing, in the
form of a wave, over this country, and with a degree of
violence heretofore without a parallel. The thermometer
in many places in the shade ranges as high as 103°, and in
the sun from 115° to 118°. The loudest wail comes from
St. Louis, where the mortality from sunstroke within the
last few days has reached the appalling figure of upwards
of two hundred. Other Western cities, too, have suffered,
but not to the same extent, and the fatal cases have proportionably been much less numerous. It is supposed that
the heat at St. Louis was greatly intensified by the large
quantity of dust with which the air in that city is always
surcharged in dry weather, many of the streets being mac-
adamized with porous limestone. Possibly other causes
may be in operation. It is now pretty generally admitted
that dust has certain highly inflammable qualities, and
that to its combustion, under certain conditions, are due
what are known as spontaneous fires. How these isother-
mal waves, which often pervade an entire country, are
formed, must for the present remain undetermined. The
chemistry of the air exhibits many unsolved problems—
far more than our philosophy has dreamed of.

CHAPTER II.

I WENT to town this afternoon, July 21st, to look after my patients. I found a card from the Committee of Reception of the British Medical Association inviting me to attend the meeting of that celebrated body at Bath, England, on the 6th of August. This act of courtesy vividly recalls the great pleasure I experienced and the hospitality heaped upon me at two former meetings of the Association. In the evening I received a call from my old friend, Dr. Kimball, the celebrated ovariotomist, of Lowell, Massachusetts. He is on his way home from California, and complains loudly of the fatigues of his journey, especially of his visit to the Yosemite Valley. He is a man of medium stature, with sharp, angular features, and is somewhat reserved in his manners. He was at one time a professor of surgery in one or two of the New England schools, enjoys a high reputation as a practitioner, and has performed ovariotomy nearly two hundred times. Much of the success of his cases is due, he thinks, to the fact that he always employs well-trained nurses for his patients. He is upwards of seventy years old.

Cape May, July 26th.—Our hotel is crowded with visitors, driven from their homes by the late excessive heat. To-day the weather is delightfully cool, and the thermometer in Philadelphia is at 70°. Here one is obliged to wear thick winter clothes to keep warm. Among our guests are three men of note—Archbishop Wood, of Philadelphia; General McClellan, Governor of New Jersey; and Mr. Montgomery Blair, the gentleman who introduced the resolutions in the legislature of Maryland which led to the appointment of the so-called Potter Committee to inquire into the Louisiana election frauds. The Archbishop has fully recovered from his late severe illness, and is looking remarkably well. He is accompanied by the Bishop of Harrisburg, Right Rev. Dr. Shanahan, a clever and amiable gentleman, and by his secretary. "Little Mac," as he was familiarly dubbed by his soldiers, looks thin, old, and careworn. While studying medicine with his father, Dr. George McClellan, I used to pat his white head and give him candy, never dreaming that he was destined some day to be the commander-in-chief of a great army and to occupy so large a space in the public eye. He presents none of the outward characteristics of a great man, although he has undoubtedly high military ability. He might have achieved immortal renown as a soldier if he had possessed one-half the dash of his father, who was really a great surgeon. The reinforcements for which he waited never came—and so his opportunity was lost. He is surrounded by politicians, and is evidently manufacturing capital for the Presidential campaign of 1880. He is accompanied by his charming wife, a daughter of General Marcy, U. S. A., and his two children—a daughter of "sweet sixteen," and a good-looking son of twelve. A shaggy little pet dog, bearing the illustrious name of Samuel Jones Tilden, completes the party.

Montgomery Blair is a tall, gaunt-looking man, belonging to that class of politicians who are bitter and unrelenting towards their opponents. His appearance is somewhat Catalinish, although he is affable in conversation, and is really a clever gentleman. He has been long in office, and is regarded as an honest, upright, conscientious man. He would not hesitate to accept the nomination for the Presidency if tendered to him. Mr. Blair was for nearly four years Postmaster-General under Mr. Lincoln, and was a very efficient officer. This afternoon, at my request, he entertained me with a lengthy account of the present depressed condition of the country. He is inclined to think that the trouble is mainly due to official corruption and high taxation—not to over-production, as is so generally believed.

A telegram has just reached this country announcing the death of my good old friend, Professor Karl Rokitansky, of Vienna. He was my senior by nearly one year and a half. About three years ago he retired from the University of Vienna, which he had served so long and so well, to seek rest in retirement. Alas, his death has shown how short this rest has been! A brief sketch of the life and character of this great man will be found in another part of this work. His loss will be mourned by the medical profession everywhere.

Rokitansky, notwithstanding the numerous high and responsible positions which he occupied for so many years, and the great services which he rendered to science, the profession, and the State, died comparatively poor. In view of these circumstances, the government, besides continuing his pension to his widow, conferred upon her a "special donation," so as to place her beyond the possibility of want.

Cape May, August 1st.—I have been sitting at my window this morning looking at two noble dogs running to and fro upon the beach, plunging into the water, and evidently enjoying themselves hugely. The circumstance vividly brings to my mind the extraordinary fondness now displayed by young unmarried and even married ladies for dogs. One cannot walk along a fashionable street in any of our cities without encountering some of these young women leading a pug, either with a delicate chain or a silken cord, apparently happy in the thought that her less-favored sisters will be sure to regard her with envy. If, as occasionally happens, she is joined by a big puppy, this feeling is proportionably increased. I like dogs well enough. They have their uses; they are of service in the chase; they keep off burglars from one's premises; and a smart terrier will catch rats; but of what use an ugly pug is passes my feeble comprehension. Of all the disgusting sights that meet the eye there is to me none more revolting than that of a refined-looking woman kissing and fondling the nasty creature, taking him to bed with her, holding him on her lap while eating her dinner, or taking him out in her carriage. But there is no accounting for tastes. A poodle, it is said, was the only creature for which that fool of fools, Beau Brummel, had any genuine affection. When his dog was taken sick, his canine physician told him that he must be bled. "Bled!" said the Beau in horror. "I shall leave the room. Inform me when the operation is over." When the animal died he shed tears, supposed to have been the only tears he ever shed, and buried himself for three days in his chamber. He declared he had lost his best friend—probably he meant his only sincere and disinterested friend. We hear of Englishmen having immense kennels, trained for hunting; but the only lady of whom history makes mention as having had more than one hundred dogs at one time was the Duchess of York, who, to complete her happiness, added the puppy Brummel to the list! I recollect reading of an English countess who contracted hydrophobia from letting her poodle lick an ugly wart upon her face; and numerous cases have been reported of late years in which this frightful disease was induced by the bite of a pet Spitz. Some people make pets of cats.

Robert Liston, the celebrated Scotch surgeon, used to drive through the streets of London with a black Maltese cat in his carriage; and not long ago the newspapers stated that a daredevil of a fellow was daily fondling a pair of young tigers! The canary-bird is a common pet. I have one of these little creatures that has afforded me a great deal of happiness. "Dicky," as I call him, is so tame that he will come to me on call, perching himself on my shoulder, running round my neck, sitting on my finger, and eating out of my mouth. The mocking-bird is a detestable creature, screeching in the night when everybody wants to sleep; and as to the parrot, it is a pity it was ever born. The young crow is easily tamed, but is a great thief, carrying off everything it can lay its bill upon, and concealing it so well as to render its recovery difficult. The rook is dull and stupid, with many of the qualities of the crow. The reed-bird has a harsh note, and its long, dangling legs give it an ungainly appearance. The partridge and the robin have nothing to recommend them as pets. Birds in confinement are incessant feeders, and yet, despite this bad habit, so well calculated to induce dyspepsia, many of them are long-lived. The bullfinch is easily domesticated, and capable of forming a strong attachment to its keeper. The late Mr. Madeira, a well-known cutler of this city, had a cockatoo which was supposed to be upwards of sixty years of age at the time of his master's death. "Crocky" was a beautiful bird, and could say as distinctly as any one, "How d' ye do? Good-by."

While speaking of dogs and birds I am reminded that my practice has not always been confined to the human subject. One day during my residence at Louisville I was sent for in great haste to visit a lady at some distance from my house, and when I reached her I found to my surprise that it was not she who was sick but her dog, whose eye was hanging out upon the cheek simply by the optic nerve in consequence of a wound inflicted half an hour before in a fight with a big mastiff. Immediately, though not without some difficulty, I replaced the organ, and the little favorite recovered without an untoward symptom or the slightest apparent impairment of vision. The lady, who was frightfully agitated at the thought of losing her only companion—for, although she was married, she had no children—was unbounded in her expressions of gratitude.

On another occasion, also during my residence at Louisville, a lady sent me a note, begging me most urgently to see her at once, as her favorite chicken had broken his thigh. I applied the necessary dressings, but as the poor bird was restless and self-willed the limb did not recover without considerable deformity, and the consequence was that I lost caste as a veterinary surgeon. Had the case gone to court I verily believe I should have been seriously damaged in reputation. The lawyers would have had a fine opportunity to *peck* at a doctor.

Cape May, August 6th.—A Mr. Leggett, a highly respectable citizen of Pittsburgh, dropped dead in his room at the Stockton Hotel this morning, immediately after his return from taking a bath in the sea. Apoplexy is supposed to have occasioned his death. Such a euthanasia is in striking contrast with death produced by a lingering disease, in which the body is completely metamorphosed by emaciation and the mind rendered peevish and fretful, if not seriously weakened.

I was greatly shocked, two evenings ago, by the appearance of my old friend and former fellow-student, Dr. Washington L. Atlee, who during the last three months has lost nearly one hundred pounds of flesh, and who has for a number of weeks been literally hovering over the grave, deadly pale, unable to turn in bed, harassed with nausea and vomiting, racked with pain, and suffering with insomnia and every kind of distress incident to cancer of the kidney, the ruthless malady under which he is supposed to be laboring. God defend me and mine from such a death! Is it not a terrible affliction for one who has all his life been engaged in doing good to his fellow-men, and who has never consciously committed any serious immoral act?

For the last three weeks I have been daily sitting at the same table with a clever-looking young lady without knowing her name. Upon inquiry I find it to be Roby; and upon further inquiry I learn that she is a daughter of the well-known Dr. Joseph Roby, a teacher of anatomy, who, after having been a professor of that branch at the Bowdoin Medical College, Maine, at Dartmouth, New Hampshire, and at the University of Maryland, died about twenty years ago in Baltimore, leaving behind him an excellent reputation. I never met with Dr. Roby, but had a high appreciation of his abilities. One of his peculiarities was that, while he could discourse most eloquently upon anatomy, he never looked his class in the face, or took his eye off his subject. Another was his reticence. When excited, however, he could converse pleasantly and intelligently upon almost any subject. These peculiarities were impediments to his popularity, and he never acquired much practice in consequence. It is to be regretted that no sketch of his life has been published. He was a native of New England, and died comparatively young, leaving his family, consisting of his wife and a son and a daughter, poor.

The name of Roby brings to my mind that of another professor of anatomy in the University of Maryland, whose acquaintance I made in 1828, shortly after I received my medical degree. I refer to Dr. John Wells, whose early death was much regretted. He was introduced to me by a fellow-student of mine, Dr. John Butler, afterwards the distinguished superintendent of the lunatic asylum at Hartford; and I shall never forget the favorable impression made upon me by the young teacher, who, although he had only recently left the lecture-room, was apparently on the high road to fame. He was neatly dressed, conversed with fluency, and had delightful manners. I almost envied him his position. The horizon of his life seemed to be gilded with sunshine. Alas! how little we know of the future! Soon after the close of the first session of his connection with the University of Maryland, during which he had won popularity as an able and attractive teacher, he was taken ill, and in a short time was numbered with the dead.

August 16th.—I left Cape May this afternoon in company with my son-in-law, Mr. B. F. Horwitz, his wife and daughter, after a sojourn at that delightful summer retreat of nearly five weeks, during which I bathed in the sea nearly every day. My health is decidedly improved; indeed, I may say, it was never better. Nearly the whole of every morning I spent in my private room, engaged in writing reminiscences of my professional contemporaries, of whom I find that I have sketched not fewer than eighteen. Lounging about on the piazzas of my hotel, talking nonsense, or worse, listening to women's gossip, I detest. Occasionally I enjoyed a game of euchre, frequently coming off victorious. Only during two evenings was I annoyed by mosquitoes, those plagues of Cape May, Atlantic City, and of some of the other places of resort along the Jersey shore.

August 22d.—A calamity befell me three days ago. As we were taking our seats at the breakfast-table, the bottom of the cage of my canary-bird Dicky fell out, and we have not seen the poor fellow since. Of course he is lost. I feel quite melancholy at an accident which has deprived me of the society of so sweet and innocent a companion.

Poor Henry Armitt Brown died yesterday after a protracted illness from typhoid fever, induced, there is reason to believe, by the bad sewage in the neighborhood of his residence. Such events are not uncommon in every community, and they will continue to occur until proper measures are adopted against the development of preventable diseases. The Prince Consort of Great Britain perished from this cause; and the Prince of Wales came very near losing his life, some years ago, in consequence of a severe and protracted attack of typhoid fever occasioned by the bad sewage at Sandringham. Mr. Brown was thirty-four years of age at the time of his death, which is deplored as a national loss. He was a graduate of Yale College, a lawyer by profession, and a man of great talent and high culture. As an orator, he had—with the exception perhaps of Mr. Dougherty—no equal in Philadelphia, and no superior in this country. Had he been spared, he would have been distinguished in the councils of the nation, and achieved an enduring reputation. When such a man dies, the public may well drop a tear upon his grave, and unite in expressions of warm sympathy for his bereaved family.

August 31st.—General Preston, my old Louisville neighbor, left me this afternoon after he and his son had been for two days my guests. His object in visiting me was to consult me respecting his health. After a thorough examination, I find no disease about him whatever. All he needs is absence from the cares of business, and change of air, scene, and food. He is a man of diversified knowledge, general, literary, and scientific. His memory is prodigious, and it was a great pleasure to listen to him and Mr. Henry C. Carey, whom I had invited to join him at dinner, as they discussed political economy and other subjects of interest. He went away saying that he had spent two of the happiest days of his life under my roof.

On September 11th I attended the funeral of my old friend, Dr. Washington L. Atlee, who died on Saturday, September 7th, after a painful and lingering illness, caused by malignant disease of the left kidney, which he bore

with the philosophy of a martyr and the patience and
resignation of a Christian. For more than a year his
health had been gradually failing; and, although he was
still actively engaged in his professional duties, often
making long, rapid, and fatiguing journeys by day and
night, it was apparent to his family and friends that some
deep-seated malady was slowly sapping the foundations of
life, and leading him on to an irresistible destiny. He
was one of the most emaciated human beings I ever saw;
and yet amidst all this decay it was pleasant to see his intellectual powers preserve their vigor almost to the very
last moments of his life.

My acquaintance with Atlee began in the autumn of
1826, when, as students of medicine, we entered together
the office of Dr. George McClellan. He formed one of
a group of fourteen or fifteen young men, some of them
of great promise, and nearly all refined, educated, and
well-bred gentlemen. Atlee was tall, handsome, and full
of ambition, with a highly inquisitive mind, constantly
in search of knowledge and of new truths. There were
few questions propounded by his preceptor which he did
not readily answer. In the lecture-room he was one of
the most attentive of listeners, always in his place at the
right moment, and always orderly and courteous in his
demeanor. He had little to say to any one. It was evident that he was an earnest, thoughtful young man,
who had a proper sense of the importance of his work
and of the profession of which he was destined to become
so bright and useful an ornament. At the close of the session he retired to the office of his brother, Dr. John Atlee,
of Lancaster, and did not resume his attendance upon the
lectures until the autumn of 1828. He graduated the following spring. The next fifteen years of his life were
spent in the active pursuit of his profession, first at Mount
Joy, and afterwards at Lancaster, his native city. During
this time he devoted much attention to the study of

botany, and made a large collection of plants, now in the possession of the Pennsylvania College, at Gettysburg. He also delivered courses of lectures on hygiene and natural history, and assisted in founding several useful local institutions for the improvement of the public. In 1844 he was appointed Professor of Medical Chemistry in the Pennsylvania College of Philadelphia, and soon after broke up his residence at Lancaster. After eight years of hard work in this school, with little more than a nominal income, he severed his connection with it, his practice having by this time become sufficiently extensive to occupy all his leisure. In 1853 he competed successfully for the Prize Essay of the American Medical Association. He was an extensive contributor to the medical press, most of his papers having reference to the diseases of the female generative organs. His last essay, if I mistake not, was one on Fibroid Tumors of the Uterus, read before the Gynæcological Section of the International Medical Congress, convened at Philadelphia in September, 1876. His earlier discourses and papers embraced a great variety of topics, medical, pathological, therapeutic, educational, and scientific, and afforded evidence of unflagging industry and of a well-trained mind. His work on the Diagnosis of Ovarian Tumors forms a valuable contribution to American medical literature, based as it is upon a large personal experience running through a period of many years.

The fame of Dr. Atlee, however, will mainly rest upon his labors in the field of ovariotomy, in which, after the inventor of the operation, Dr. Ephraim McDowell, of Kentucky, he was the most conspicuous figure. His efforts began at a comparatively early period of his professional career, and he lived, notwithstanding the clamors raised against him, to see the operation established upon a permanent basis. At the time of his death his cases amounted to nearly four hundred, being greater than those of any

other ovariotomist on this continent, and next in number
to those of T. Spencer Wells, of London. The opposition
which he encountered in these labors was often of the most
rancorous character. Not unfrequently, indeed, the term
woman-murderer was applied to him. Two men of great
reputation as obstetric practitioners were loud and unsparing in their denunciations. One of these lived long
enough to recant, and to express his sorrow at his conduct;
the other, naturally full of prejudice, died in his erroneous
convictions. In 1875 Dr. Atlee read an address before the
Philadelphia County Medical Society, as retiring president,
in which he depicted in glowing terms the struggles and
triumphs of ovariotomy in his adopted city. I was present
on the occasion, and was surprised at the mild and courtly
manner in which he treated his adversaries. One could
not fail to perceive that he had been a martyr to the
cause which he had for many years so nobly upheld and
defended. What his success as an operator was I am unable to say, as no record of his cases has thus far been
published. There is, however, reason to believe that it
was fully up to the general average; that is, about two
and a half in three cases. One great disadvantage under
which he labored was that many of his patients, living at
a great distance from his home, could not receive his personal supervision during the after-treatment, a matter of
such vital importance in all great operations. A goodly
number of cases doubtless slipped through his hands from
this cause. As an operator in his specialty he possessed
great skill. The whole procedure was conducted with consummate ability. He carefully assigned to his assistants
their respective duties, and as soon as the patient was thoroughly anæsthetized everything progressed in an orderly
and systematic manner. The only instruments generally used were an old but sharp scalpel, a probe-pointed
bistoury, scissors, forceps, and a curved needle. Like
Desault, he knew that simplicity is the perfection of an

operation. It is said that he kept a pretty full record of his cases, which will doubtless be published by his family, and thus serve to augment his fame.

Atlee took a deep interest in the welfare of the American Medical Association, of which he was at one time one of the Vice-Presidents. He was a frequent attendant upon its meetings, having made his last appearance at Chicago in 1877. He was President and one of the founders of the Philadelphia County Medical Society, and of the Medical Society of the State of Pennsylvania. At the time of his death he was a member of the Council of the American Gynæcological Society. In his intercourse with his professional brethren he was, it has been alleged, not always fair; but of this I know nothing from personal observation, although we repeatedly met in consultation; and I feel assured that the statement is not supported by facts. There are always captious and fault-finding men whose great aim in life seems to be to misrepresent, if not to slander and vilify, their superiors. Atlee had many warm friends in and out of the profession, and was the idol of his family. His funeral was largely attended, and it was evident that the many women present, both at the house and in the cemetery, had lost a counsellor who in the hour of their suffering had afforded them substantial aid. His practice for many years was extensive, and must have been lucrative. He rarely went into general society, and my impression is that he disliked entertainments or large social gatherings. At the time of his death he was seventy years of age. The life of Atlee is full of interest; for it shows how a man, if faithful to himself and to his calling, may surmount weighty obstacles and attain wide reputation. To him do the women of this continent owe an everlasting debt of gratitude as an ovariotomist.

The history of ovariotomy, for many years Atlee's specialty, is one of great interest. As already stated, its originator was Dr. Ephraim McDowell, born in 1771, a native of Virginia, but a resident of Danville, Kentucky, where his first operation was performed in 1809. The woman survived thirty-two years, and in the meantime gave birth to a son, whom I knew well during my residence at Louisville. His cases, as I was the first to show, amounted altogether to thirteen, of which an account of only eight was published during his lifetime; while the remainder, after a tedious and troublesome correspondence, were ferreted out by myself, as may be seen by reference to my History of Kentucky Surgery, prepared for the Kentucky State Medical Society, and published in its Transactions for 1852. McDowell's earlier operations were received with great disfavor both at home and abroad. Dr. James Johnson, the editor of the London Medico-Chirurgical Review, was particularly severe in his criticisms, casting doubts upon the veracity of the backwoodsman and denouncing him as an unscrupulous surgeon. Mr. Lizars, of Edinburgh, was the first, in the year 1823 if I mistake not, to perform the operation on the other side of the Atlantic, and, although it was unsuccessful, it served to direct the attention of the profession in different parts of the world to the subject. The operation however did not receive fair play until it was practised on a large scale by Clay, Brown, Bird, Walne, and T. Spencer Wells, of England, and by the two Atlees, Kimball, and Peaslee, of the United States. The labors of these men have served to establish it as one of the great resources of surgery in a department of female complaints which were for a long time regarded as utterly irremediable. McDowell died in 1828, without, probably, having dreamed that he had achieved immortality as the father of ovariotomy. Doubtless he was a bold surgeon; but his history shows that he was a humane man, and that he took a deep interest in his patients. He ranked high as a general practitioner, and enjoyed an enviable reputation as a lithotomist. He was not a cultured man. He wrote indifferently; and this perhaps was one reason why the publication of his earlier cases made so bad an impression upon the profession. Efforts have been made for some time past to raise a suitable monument to his memory. In 1875, at the meeting of the American Medical Association at Louisville, Kentucky, I contributed one hundred dollars towards the object.

September 14th.—Dr. W. J. Little, an eminent physician and surgeon of London, arrived this evening from New York, to be, by special invitation, my guest for several days. Fortunately my son-in-law, Mr. Orville Horwitz, his wife, and eldest daughter Florence arrived the previous day, so that it will be comparatively easy for me to entertain him. At the same time their presence will greatly increase his comfort and enjoyment. I met Dr. Little for the first time at Oxford, in 1868, and subsequently in London, where I received some attentions from him. His reputation as an orthopædic surgeon had long been familiar to me. He is sixty-five years of age, tall and slender, with a fine, open countenance. He is a great talker, very genial and intelligent, and has a well-cultivated mind. He is in love with our country, although as yet he has seen little of it. I was invited a few days ago to meet him at a dinner given to him by Dr. Detmold, of New York, but was unable to go on account of professional engagements.

Dr. Little's reputation, however great as a general practitioner, will mainly rest upon his labors as an orthopædic surgeon and upon his success in introducing the operations for clubfoot and analogous distortions among his countrymen. Being himself a sufferer from equino-varus and partial paralysis, he became an enthusiastic follower of Stromeyer, the inventor of subcutaneous tenotomy, and published paper after paper to illustrate the value of the new procedure. He graduated in the University of Berlin in 1837. He availed himself of Stromeyer's personal skill in his own case, notwithstanding that he had been strongly advised by his professional friends at home and abroad not to submit to his treatment. Finding himself greatly benefited, he returned to the Prussian metropolis, and with the aid of the celebrated surgeon, Johann Friedrich Dieffenbach, introduced the operation into Germany. He thus became the apostle of subcutaneous tenotomy throughout the world. In 1839 he issued his treatise on Clubfoot and Analogous Distortions, which was followed in 1853 by a more elaborate production, entitled The Nature and Treatment of Deformities of the Human Frame. These treatises are only a portion of his publications. Nearly all of them, however, had reference to his early and favorite studies. He was the founder of the Royal Orthopædic Hospital of London, the first institution of the kind ever established, and was for some time one of its physicians. He is a member of many medical societies, foreign and domestic, Surgeon to the London Hospital, and a Fellow of the Royal College of Surgeons—well-deserved honors.

Saratoga, September 18th.—I arrived at Saratoga this afternoon in company with my daughter, Mrs. Orville Horwitz, and her husband. The United States Hotel, where we are stopping, is crowded with Unitarians, who are holding what is called their Biennial Conference, made up of delegates from all parts of the Union. Among them are many men of distinction, such as E. Rockwood Hoar, the President, the Rev. Dr. James Freeman Clarke, the Rev. Dr. Bellows, Edward Everett Hale, George W. Curtis, the Rev. Dr. Everett, and Ralph Waldo Emerson, the philosopher of Concord, Massachusetts. Emerson is accompanied by his daughter, Miss Emerson, a tall woman, past middle age, dressed in a speckled calico gown, with a blue sash hanging like a long streamer down her back, presenting altogether a grotesque appearance, exciting general attention and comment. Mr. Hoar is a handsome man, with a fine face and a good head, and makes an excellent presiding officer. He is an easy speaker, with a

good deal of dry humor. The address of Mr. Everett and
that of Mr. Curtis, the only ones I heard, were admirable,
well written and well delivered. The former was on the
new ethics of Unitarianism; and the latter on political
morals, or civil service reform—a subject which had long
engaged the study of Mr. Curtis. The discourse delivered in June, 1877, by the Rev. Dr. Clarke, I did not
hear, but it was widely circulated on the occasion, and I
read it with great care. Its title was, Why am I a Uni-
tarian? This tract gives a satisfactory idea of Unitarianism. Clarke is a strong man, an able, lucid thinker, and
whatever he says upon the subject is worthy of consideration. He explicitly states that Christ is not God, but a
mere man who approaches nearer to God than any other
human being that has ever been created, and who is, consequently, in some sense divine. The more nearly we
come up to Christ in our work and conduct, the more
nearly we attain human perfection and God's approval.
Dr. Clarke does not believe in the Trinity, and he boldly
asserts the fallacy of the doctrine of everlasting punishment, regarding it as a thing utterly inconsistent with our
conceptions of the wisdom and goodness of God. Like all
rational men, he sees God in everything:

> "All are but parts of one stupendous whole,
>   Whose body Nature is, and God the soul;
>   That, changed through all, and yet in all the same;
>   Great in the earth, as in the ethereal frame;
>   Warms in the sun, refreshes in the breeze,
>   Glows in the stars, and blossoms in the trees,
>   Lives through all life, extends through all extent,
>   Spreads undivided, operates unspent; . . . .
>   To Him no high, no low, no great, no small,
>   He fills, He bounds, connects, and equals all."

Dr. Clarke is not very clear regarding his assumption
that the Bible is an inspired book. His meaning, if I cor-

rectly interpret it, is that the Bible was not a direct inspiration of Deity, but that whatever it comprises of good is an emanation from God, just as all other good works are, and that, therefore, it is worthy of man's holiest respect and veneration. "The very fact," says he, "that it has withstood the assaults of so many ages, and the false interpretations and misrepresentations of its friends, shows it to be no ordinary book, but that it merits our fullest acceptance and our closest study." I believe God to be just and merciful, without any of the attributes that disfigure and disgrace our feeble, finite natures, and that whatever happens takes place through the agency of laws inherent in matter from all eternity. All diseases, epidemics, and accidents are the result of a violation of these laws, and of our own ignorance, crimes, or misdemeanors. God cannot be said ever to have killed or wilfully afflicted any human being. It has never, as is so often stated, pleased God to remove from this earth any mortal man. People die because the machinery of life is worn out or broken down. God does not take the life of a parent, a child, a brother or sister for the sake of bringing the survivors to repentance, or nearer to Himself. To entertain such a belief is an imputation upon the goodness and wisdom of the great Being who is the author, the governor, and the preserver of the universe. Theologians belittle themselves when they talk thus flippantly about matters which they cannot comprehend.

September 25th.—The American Gynæcological Society, instituted three years ago, is now holding its third meeting in the hall of the College of Physicians of this city. It consists of fewer than fifty members; but among them are included the names of some of the best medical minds of the country, such as D. Humphreys Storer and Lyman of Boston; Kimball of Lowell; Fordyce Barker, Thomas, J. E. Taylor, Emmet, and Bozeman of New York; Wilson and Howard of Baltimore; Busey of Washington City;

Byford of Chicago; Reeve of Dayton; Parvin of Indian-
apolis; White of Buffalo; and Ellwood Wilson, Penrose,
Goodell, and Albert Smith of this city. There were also
some young men present, many of them of more than
ordinary promise. The number of members is limited to
sixty. J. Marion Sims, and Battey, of Georgia, were not
in attendance. The rules for admission are stringent.
The applicant must be a man of more or less note, and
must present a dissertation upon some gynæcological subject. At the annual meeting his claims are duly considered by the council of the society. This year there were
five aspirants, of whom only one, Dr. Bozeman, of New
York, was successful. The papers read before the meeting were mostly of singular excellence. A volume of
Transactions is published annually. Dr. Fordyce Barker
was its first president. The society during the last year
lost two of its most illustrious members in the death of
Edmund Randolph Peaslee and W. L. Atlee. It is impossible to overestimate the importance of such a body of able
and scientific men engaged in a common cause.

September 29th.—Dr. and Mrs. James R. White, of
Buffalo, dined with me to-day. They are pleasant, intelligent people, and I was glad to have it in my power to
pay off an old score in the form of a fine luncheon given
to my dear wife and myself at their residence in 1853.
Dr. White is Professor of Obstetrics in the Medical College
of Buffalo, and enjoys a high reputation as a gynæcologist,
and as an obstetric practitioner. He has contributed many
excellent papers to medical literature, and he is the author
of several novel and valuable methods of treatment. He
is a tall, well-built, fine-looking man, an honor to his profession. He took his medical degree in my Alma Mater in
1834, and almost immediately afterwards settled at Buffalo,
where he soon became prominent as a practitioner.

Professor White, in his remarks at the table, related an
interesting incident which occurred in the practice of the

late Dr. Charles Alfred Lee, a warm personal friend of mine, which proves the influence of the mind upon the body in disease. An elderly woman, of the humbler class of society, called upon Dr. Lee with the request that he would examine her case, and, if possible, relieve her, saying that she had been sick for several years and had derived no benefit from the advice of other physicians. After having made a careful investigation of her case, he wrote a prescription, and told her to mix with the ingredients a pint of water, taking a tablespoonful three times a day for a week, at the end of which she would, he had no doubt, be well. Before half the week had elapsed she returned, declaring that she was perfectly cured, and that she had come to thank him for his advice. "How did you take the medicine?" "Well, as you told me, I tore the paper up as finely as possible, and then mixed the pieces with a pint of water, stirring the mixture well, and taking a tablespoonful three times a day. I thank you, doctor; I am quite well."

This anecdote reminds me of an incident related by Swift as having occurred in a clergyman's family at Yarcomb, England. A servant being suddenly taken ill, the family physician prepared a bolus from the medicine-chest, at the same time wrapping up in the paper the brass grain-weights used in weighing drugs. He left both on the table. Instead of taking the bolus the man swallowed the paper and weights, saying, when the mistake was discovered, that he never should have succeeded had he not cut them into smaller pieces, "and he thanked God that, though the dose was rather rough and sharpish, he had got it all down."

Dr. Lee was a physician of not a little note in his day. Born in Connecticut in 1801, he graduated at Williams College, and took his degree in medicine at Pittsfield, Massachusetts, in 1825. He was a man of active intellect, a hard worker, and for many years a Professor, chiefly of

Medicine and Materia Medica, in different schools. He assisted in founding the Medical College of Buffalo, and the New York Medical College, long since defunct. He was for a while editor of the New York Journal of Medicine. He made many valuable contributions to medical literature, edited Copland's Medical Dictionary and enriched it with valuable notes, and took an active interest in the treatment of the insane. He was a tall, handsome man, with a large head and a keen brown eye, and was a ready talker and writer. I saw Dr. Lee for the first time in July, 1832, during the terrible visitation of the Asiatic cholera in the city of New York. Lee and Roe had charge of the Greenwich Street Hospital; and I need hardly add that they treated me with great courtesy, and extended to me every facility for carrying out the objects of my mission. Roe was short-lived, while Lee attained a happy old age, dying in 1872.

November 3d, 1878.—This is Sunday, and at two o'clock this afternoon, my regular dinner hour on the Sabbath, I shall receive Mr. George W. Callender, along with Dr. Levis, Professor W. H. Pancoast, my son Dr. S. W. Gross, and a few non-professional friends, to make merry over a saddle of venison, a pair of canvas-back ducks, and a glass of champagne. The visit of Mr. Callender to this country has been heralded for some time, both at home and abroad, and I should not be at all surprised if he felt somewhat vain in consequence. In reality, however, he has something to be proud of, for he is a surgeon and practitioner of merit, a true representative member of the British medical profession, and as such worthy of any attention we can bestow upon him on this side of the Atlantic. He has fairly earned his titles. For many years he was assistant surgeon to St. Bartholomew's Hospital, an office which he vacated some time ago for that of one of the chief surgeons of that institution, and lecturer on anatomy in its medical school. Early in life he published

a treatise on Femoral Hernia, and he has been a liberal
contributor to the medical press, especially to the Transactions of the Medico-Chirurgical Society of London, and
to St. Bartholomew's Hospital Reports, of which he has
been for some time one of the editors. He is also the
author of several articles in Holmes's Surgery. All his
writings display ability and strong common-sense, based
upon a large practical experience and accurate observation. His manners are bland and dignified, and as a companion he is highly agreeable. He is receiving much
attention, not only from the profession, but from our citizens generally, and everybody with whom he is brought
in contact is pleased with him. At New York and Brooklyn, as well as in this city and in Boston, he was entertained by some of the most distinguished men in the profession. It is delightful to witness such attentions; for,
apart from the fact that every respectable foreigner is entitled to consideration on his own account, they have the
effect of bringing men into closer relations, and of thus
establishing a pleasanter feeling between the medical profession of Europe and America.

St. Bartholomew's Hospital is, next to the Hôtel Dieu
of Paris, the oldest institution of the kind in the world,
having been founded by Rahere in 1123. Among the
surgeons associated with it in modern times, the names
of John Abernethy, Edward Stanley, Sir William Lawrence, and Sir James Paget stand preëminent. It was
while engaged upon the performance of his duties at this
hospital that Abernethy missed the opportunity of being
knighted. George IV., "the first gentleman" in the kingdom, while Prince of Wales, suddenly came to the conclusion one morning that he would have a wen removed
which had long disfigured his forehead; and as Abernethy
was at the time the most prominent surgeon in London,
he despatched to him one of his friends, a nobleman,
with the request that he would bring him at once to

the palace to perform the operation. Abernethy's reply was characteristic: "Tell the Prince that I am obliged to meet my class at St. Bartholomew's, and as soon as I can get off it will afford me pleasure to attend to his wishes." The indignant Prince sent word that he did not need the surgeon's services. Mr. Astley Cooper was immediately called in, removed the tumor, and soon after received the honor of knighthood, which contributed not a little to his introduction to the nobility, and to the largest income perhaps ever enjoyed by any professional man in Great Britain, his receipts for a number of years having averaged upwards of one hundred thousand dollars. It is worthy of note that the Prince at the time of the operation showed some wit. When asked what the nature of the tumor was, Cooper said, "It is a steatome." "Well, then," said the Prince, "I hope it will stay at home." Abernethy was beyond question one of the greatest surgeons of his day in Great Britain, an admirable teacher, an able writer, and a masterly observer. He was a great wit, and many anecdotes are related of his eccentricities. Having attended a very respectable widow lady in a severe illness extending through a number of weeks, he became much interested in her only daughter, who nursed her mother with the most tender devotion. It was Saturday evening when Abernethy made his final visit. Taking the young lady aside, he said to her, "I have witnessed your devotion and kindness to your mother. I am in need of a wife, and I think you are the very person that would suit me. My time is incessantly occupied, and I have therefore no leisure for courting. Reflect upon this matter until Monday." Monday came, and it is hardly necessary to add that the young lady became Mrs. Abernethy.

Edward Stanley, who died only about fifteen years ago, wrote what was long regarded as the best work on the diseases of the bones in any language. It was illustrated by a beautiful atlas, and was republished soon after its appearance in London by Lea & Blanchard of this city in 1849. My impression is that, notwithstanding its many excellences, it had but a very limited circulation, although it was highly appreciated by all our better educated surgeons. It was the first systematic and elaborate treatise upon the subject since the appearance of the work of Boyer in 1803.

Lawrence was well built, with a lofty presence and a noble bearing. He was a learned and judicious surgeon, but not a great operator. According to my notion, he was the best medical writer of his day in Great Britain. His treatise on Hernia and that on the Eye are models of pure English, while the subjects discussed in them are treated in an exhaustive manner. As reflecting the science and practice of abdominal and ophthalmic surgery of the period in which they are written, both are immortal productions. His lectures on Physiology, Zoology, and the Natural History of Man, delivered before the Royal College of Surgeons of London, and afterwards published in book form, met with much opposition on account of their alleged irreligious tendencies, and excited much discussion and bitter criticism, in which his old master in surgery, Mr. Abernethy, took a leading part. Much of this feeling, not a little of which grew out of misapprehension and wilful misrepresentation, gradually disappeared, and Mr. Lawrence lived long enough to witness the prevalence of more liberal sentiments on the part of the profession and the public. The honors of knighthood were conferred upon him only a few years before his death. For a long while he lived, some six or eight miles from London, in an elegant villa, embowered in shrubbery, adorned with statuary and paintings, enriched by a fine library, which was the abode of a generous hospitality. He was particularly fond of entertaining American visitors.

Sir James Paget, now consulting surgeon, laid the foundation in St. Bartholomew's of his great work on Surgical

Pathology. He was long one of its internes, and was a frequent and elaborate contributor to its famous Hospital Reports. Mr. Savory and Mr. Holden are members of the regular surgical staff, and are both surgeons of distinction.

January, 1879.—Death has been busy in the medical profession of Boston since the beginning of the new year, having gathered to their homes two of its best-known physicians. My old friend, Dr. John B. S. Jackson, after a brief illness was the first to go ; and Dr. Jacob Bigelow followed on the 10th, at the age of ninety-three years. On the evening spent by Dr. Jackson at my house, not quite a year ago, I little thought, as I pressed his hand and bade him good-night, that I should never see him again. Younger by at least a year than myself, he seemed to have lost none of his elastic and sprightly nature, and looked as if he were destined to run into the eighties. But the machinery of life suddenly broke down, fortunately unattended by much suffering. My acquaintance with Dr. Jackson began in 1839, during a visit which I made to Boston in search of a publisher for my Pathological Anatomy. We were then both young men, full of ambition and enthusiasm, deeply interested in similar studies ; and it was this circumstance, no doubt, which served to draw us more closely together, and to establish those kindly relations and warm sympathies which terminated only with his life. Many letters passed between us, some of a purely friendly nature, others on matters of scientific investigation ; and our meetings were always of an affectionate character. He had the simplicity of a child and the enthusiasm of the philosopher. He was warm in his attachments, true as steel, an ardent searcher after truth, and a correct interpreter of nature. He had a solid rather than a brilliant mind, and a tenacity of purpose which impelled him to make thorough work of whatever he undertook. His dissecting-room was his constant companion, where he quietly worked out the great problems of pathological science, and laid the foundation of those two great museums of which the profession of Boston is so justly proud, and with which his own name is indissolubly associated. What John Hunter accomplished for morbid anatomy in London, John B. S. Jackson accomplished for morbid anatomy in Boston. Of the microscope he made but little use. He had implicit faith in his scalpel, and was not a little distrustful of the revelations of an instrument which has been productive of vast differences in results in the hands of different observers. Hence histology, which has made such marvellous strides during the last quarter of a century, formed no part of his studies. He belonged to the school of Bichat rather than to that of Schleiden or of Virchow. He accumulated a vast amount of original matter; for Boston and its vicinity, I might say almost the whole of Massachusetts and the immediately adjoining States, were tributary to his workshop. For many years hardly any specimens of interest or importance failed to reach his hands for examination. He thus became, if I may coin a new word, the post-mortemist of all his professional brethren for hundreds of miles around. The vast treasures thus gathered together now enrich the Warren Museum in Harvard University and the cabinet of the Boston Society for Medical Improvement, of which, in 1828, he was one of the founders. Dr. D. Humphreys Storer was at the time of Dr. Jackson's death the only survivor of the twelve original members.

I often urged Dr. Jackson to embody in a work on pathological anatomy the results of his observations. I appealed to his pride and ambition, to his exceptional opportunities, and, above all, to the needs and expectations of his profession; but in vain. He was fixed in his purpose—whether from an excess of modesty, inherent diffidence, or distrust of his fine powers, I could never ascertain. He ought to have become the Rokitansky of America. But he died without having produced any worthy literary or scientific work, having contented himself with furnishing a catalogue of each of the museums of which he was so long the presiding genius. These publications contain, it is true, much excellent material; but the material is isolated and unsystematized, and therefore comparatively valueless.

Dr. Jackson was born at Boston in 1806; and after graduating in belles-lettres in Harvard University, he took his degree in 1829, at a time when his uncle, Dr. James Jackson, then in the zenith of his fame, was Professor of Medicine in the medical department of that institution. His natural tastes induced him to devote himself to the study of morbid anatomy; and he had hardly been in the profession eight years when he was appointed Professor of Pathological Anatomy in his Alma Mater, a position which he retained up to the time of his death. As a lecturer, he never attained a high rank. His manners before his class were constrained, and he lacked that grace and animation so necessary to success in teaching. Despite these defects, however, he always commanded the attention of his pupils, all of whom became warmly attached to him on account of his amiable qualities, the accuracy and extent of his knowledge, and the pains which he took to instruct them. To know him was to love him. Early in life Dr. Jackson, like most professional men who have risen to eminence, was poor.

For nearly a third of a century Dr. Bigelow had lived in retirement, and was, consequently, little known to the present generation of medical men. They were of course familiar with his name and with what he had done for his profession and the public. Blessed with wealth, a loving family, warm friends, and high social position, he tore himself away from the drudgery of his profession at a comparatively early period of his life, and spent the remainder of his days in the study of philosophy and in the contemplation of nature. It is said that he had unbounded confidence in, and reverence for, the Deity, as the great architect of the universe; but that he seldom conversed upon religious matters, or engaged in theological researches or discussions. As stated in a previous page, he was totally blind during the last few years of his life, and it is sad to think that during most of this time he was unable, in consequence of an attack of hemiplegia, to leave his bed. To an old friend, Dr. Storer, who visited him only a short time before his death, he jokingly remarked, "To live till one is ninety is not what it is cracked up to be." To the last he retained his intellectual faculties. He conversed slowly, but distinctly and pointedly with his friends upon a great variety of subjects, and his memory was particularly keen in regard to the earlier events of his life. In speaking to Dr. Bowditch, another old and valued friend, respecting the University of Pennsylvania, then the only medical school in Philadelphia, and of its professors, he said, "Rush and Wistar I knew; they were kindly, and the latter, especially, was warm-hearted. They received the students. Physick was a savage, and would have no intercourse with us. We never were allowed to enter his house. Barton was egotistical, a bad reader and speaker. Rush was enthusiastic and eloquent, an earnest believer in medicine and drugs. He was an ultra practitioner. He often said, 'We can have no reliance on nature, gentlemen. We must turn her out-of-doors in our practice, and substitute for her efficient art.' When I was in Philadelphia there was constantly battling going on between the professors belonging to the Faculty. Rush and Physick were on the one side; Wistar and Barton on the other. The Philadelphia school had many students from all quarters of the country, except from New England. Very few went from here." Dr. Bigelow received his degree from the University of Pennsylvania in the twenty-first year of his age; and the strictures passed upon his teachers derive piquancy from the fact that they were strictly true. Physick, it is well known, was always an icicle in the presence of his pupils outside of the amphitheatre.

Whether Bigelow became disgusted with the heroic treatment of disease inculcated by Rush, or with his lack of confidence in the resources of nature, certain it is, as observed by Dr. Bowditch, that in less than twenty-five years after he left Philadelphia he utterly ignored the precepts of his master, and substituted a practice of his own entirely at variance with that which he had been taught in the lecture-room. If he did not discover the philosopher's stone, he taught his professional brethren to think, and gave to the art of medicine a simplicity which it never had before. The leading idea of his doctrine was that many if not most diseases, especially the eruptive, are self-limited; that their natural tendency is to spontaneous cure; and that, while the system is struggling under their effects, very little aid is required from the physician, save what relates to food, drink, and hygienic regulations. While not discarding medicines or drugs altogether, he confined himself to the mildest and most simple remedies, such as are calculated to aid, and not to thwart, nature in her efforts at restoration. Such, in few words, were the views promulgated by the Boston philosopher before he had reached his fiftieth year. These views were afterwards embodied in a short tract, which may be regarded as one of the most valuable contributions ever made to medical science. It need hardly be added that these doctrines were slowly adopted by the profession; but their value is now universally acknowledged and acted upon; and they are the more honorable to American medicine because they antedate by several years similar views expressed by Sir John Forbes in his celebrated paper, originally published in the British and Foreign Medical Review under the novel and attractive title of Young Physic.

The estimate which I have placed upon Bigelow as a medical philosopher and reformer is not, I think, too high. That posterity will confirm it, whatever my contemporaries may think about it, I am quite sure. Had he never written anything else than the brochure which I have mentioned, he would have been regarded as one of the wisest physicians of the nineteenth century; but he produced other works which would have transmitted his name to posterity. His Florula Bostoniensis, published soon after he received his medical degree, is a standard production; while his American Medical Botany, illustrated by splendid engravings, made his name widely known here and in Europe, and conferred honor upon American medical literature. Born at Sudbury, Massachusetts, in 1787, soon after the close of our Revolution, he was at the time of his death the oldest physician in the State, if not in the United States. In 1816, at the age of twenty-nine, he was appointed Rumford Professor, and Lecturer on Materia Medica and Botany in Harvard University, a chair which he occupied for many years. He delivered early in his professional life a series of lectures on the application of science to the useful arts. These had the effect of diffusing among his fellow-citizens a taste for the cultivation of physical science and the fine arts—a taste which finally culminated in the establishment of the Institute of Technology, of which all Bostonians are proud. In private life he was one of the most agreeable of men. Naturally of a jovial temperament, gentle, and light-hearted, he was a delightful companion. During his declining years, usually accompanied by Mrs. Bigelow, he made frequent visits to different parts of the country in search of amusement and change of air and scene. When they came to Philadelphia they never failed to pay their respects to my dear wife and myself.

CHAPTER III.

ON the 10th of April, 1879, my Philadelphia confrères, in commemoration of the fifty-first year of my entrance into the profession, gave me a complimentary dinner at the St. George Hotel. Dr. D. Hayes Agnew, Professor of Surgery in the University of Pennsylvania, the oldest member of the committee, presided. The number of subscribers was limited to one hundred. Among the invited guests were many of the most prominent surgeons and physicians of the United States, not a few of whom had been my pupils or colleagues in different medical schools. Those who could not attend the reunion, either on account of the distance or other causes, sent kind letters or messages. A telegram from Cincinnati afforded me more than ordinary gratification, as it served to connect the past with my present history. It ran thus: "The Medical College of Ohio, whose annual circular forty-six years ago announced Samuel D. Gross Demonstrator of Anatomy, sends its heartiest congratulations to America's great surgeon." Among the invited guests at the dinner were the two Flints, father and son, Benjamin Silliman, David W. Yandell, Nathan Bozeman, Alfred C. Post, James R. Wood, Lewis A. Sayre, Theophilus Parvin, Alan P. Smith, W. C. Van Bibber, Basil Norris and G. A. Otis, U. S. A., Morris J. Asch, Traill Green, and G. F. Shrady,

editor of the New York Medical Record. My younger son
was the only layman present. Professor Yandell came ex-
pressly from Louisville; he arrived early in the afternoon,
and left late the same evening. He had attended my
lectures soon after I became connected with the chair of
Surgery in the University of that city. His speech,
delivered in behalf of the invited guests, is replete with
interest, and I cannot resist the temptation of appending it
in full:

"MR. CHAIRMAN: When the invitation to unite in this
offering came, I was deeply touched. It revived memories of my student life, when, as the pupil of your guest, I
came before him for examination for the doctorate, now
thirty-three years—a generation—ago. The teachings of
that period have remained a part of my life. The method,
the system which the great master observed, as in his earnest way he gradually unfolded to the minds of his hearers
the grand truths which lie in the upper planes of surgery;
the painstaking, conscientious care with which he infused
interest into the dry details of his subject; his fiery zeal, his
never-flagging industry, and better than all this, the solemnity with which he declared that to be a truly great
physician it was essential to be at the same time a truly
good man—all these are as fresh to me this evening as
when I made one of his hearers, now so long ago.

"Mr. Chairman, I obeyed with alacrity the summons
to be here. I came with pleasure. Nay, more, I came
with feelings akin, I fancy, to those which animate the
pilgrim as he turns his footsteps toward the tomb of the
Prophet. With fitting reverence, sir, I stand in this august presence.

"I come, sir, as the humble representative of a great
people, the people of Kentucky, who send you greeting on
this auspicious occasion. I come, empowered by them, to
lay at the feet of your illustrious guest the homage of that
renowned commonwealth. I come to wish him yet many

years upon the earth, and to say that, though his name and fame have become a common heritage, Kentucky still claims them as peculiarly her own, since it was in her borders that he laid the foundation of a reputation which has not only irradiated this continent, but has penetrated wherever civilization is known or surgery is cultivated as a science. I feel, Mr. Chairman, that it is an honor to be called on to speak on such an occasion, and for such a people—a people which has given to statesmanship a Clay, a Lincoln, and a Breckinridge; to arms a Johnston, a Preston, and a Buckner; and to surgery a McDowell and a Dudley. A goodly company! Stately names! Would you think me as exceeding the limits of good taste if I added, and chief among all these is that of him who bears the mark of our guild—Ephraim McDowell? For, sir, will not the labors of the statesman yield to the pitiless logic of events, the voice of the orator grow fainter in the coming ages, and the deeds of the soldier eventually find place but in the libraries of the student of military campaigns, while the achievements of the village surgeon, like the widening waves of the inviolate sea, shall reach the uttermost shores of time, hailed of all civilizations as having lessened the sufferings and lengthened the span of human life?

"Again, would you think me very far wrong were I to couple the victorious issue of the late war and the operation of ovariotomy as in different fields the two most stupendous events of modern times? Sir, both are to be credited to Kentuckians. Mr. Lincoln effected the one. Dr. McDowell accomplished the other. Nor yet, in my opinion, do the two achievements admit of comparison. Powerful cabinets, far-seeing ministers, renowned captains, a daring and multitudinous soldiery, a rich, a steady, a united, and a persistent people contributed to the success of the former. Its glory was won amid the blare of trumpets, the groans of men, the shock of contending armies.

The glory of the other belongs to but one man, is single and indivisible, was born under the eyes of fair women, and by the cunning of a single hand, which, amid supreme peril, plucked victory from an enemy which before McDowell's time had defied all that was subtlest in art, and repulsed every assault of science.

"But, sir, I would fain have done. I feel that it is good to have been here. I shall return to my people and recount to them what I have seen, and what heard, and repeat to them what I now offer in their name:

"To our guest, the illustrious son of Pennsylvania, the foster-son of Kentucky, who, to the nimbus which ever encircles great deeds, has added the milk-white flower of a stainless life."

When Professor Yandell had concluded, I responded as follows:

"May my illustrious pupil carry back the assurance of my deep respect for the people of the State of Kentucky, and my undying attachment for the men, the women, and their happy homes! Though absent nearly a quarter of a century, my heart burns for my early home among them. May God preserve Kentucky and its people!"

Of the many letters sent on this occasion I select the following, not only because of its intrinsic beauty and of many tender expressions it contains, but because Dr. Richardson was my private pupil and long my intimate and much-cherished friend. The master and pupil always vied with each other in performing mutual acts of courtesy and kindness:

NEW ORLEANS, April 2, 1879.

To D. H. AGNEW, THOMAS G. MORTON, R. J. LEVIS, and J. EWING MEARS, *Secretary.*

GENTLEMEN OF THE COMMITTEE: Permit me to thank you sincerely for your polite invitation to attend a complimentary dinner to be given on the 10th inst. to Professor S. D. Gross, commemorative of his fifty-first professional birthday, and at the same time to express my great regret that I shall be unable to take advantage of your distinguished courtesy.

The occasion is one which draws upon the strongest sentiment of my nature, and in contemplating this evidence of the love and veneration with which my noble old master is regarded by those with whom he has been associated for the past twenty-three years, I envy you the privilege of sitting down with him as your guest.

Thirty-four years ago I entered his office as a private pupil, and enjoyed his society almost daily for a period of more than twelve years, during which time and ever since my esteem for him as a man in whom there is no guile, my admiration for him as a true physician, and my love for him as a personal friend have continuously grown and strengthened with increasing years. It is not needful that I should speak to you of his many virtues—of the purity of his life; of his sacred regard for the marital relation; of his tender devotion to his family; of his ready sympathy with the distressed; of his delicate consideration for his juniors; of his unremitting interest in every scheme for the advancement of medical science, the prevention of disease, and the care of the infirm; of the vast benefit which he has conferred upon the profession by his example no less than by his precepts; of his unceasing labors; of his courteous demeanor toward all; of the delightful cheerfulness of his temperament; of the light which he ever carries into the darkened chambers of the sick; or of the innumerable other beautiful traits of character and admirable qualities of mind which combine to make him what he is, a friend of the young, a teacher of teachers, a model physician, an illustrious citizen, a benefactor of his race. These are all as familiar to you as to me, but at the mention of his name they crowd so thickly upon my attention that I cannot wholly repress their expression.

In consideration of the fact that my early professional life was immediately fashioned by his fatherly hand; that his example has ever been to me a pillar of cloud by day, and a pillar of fire by night; and that his personal confidence is treasured in my heart as a jewel of priceless worth, I beg that when you take your seats at table you will allow me, by your hands, to place upon his breast the accompanying simple badge as a token of remembrance from his devoted pupil who on this occasion can only in spirit partake of his joy.

With renewed thanks for the honor you have conferred upon me, I am, very truly, your servant,

T. G. RICHARDSON.

The Committee of Arrangements originally consisted of Drs. D. Hayes Agnew, Richard J. Levis, and Thomas G. Morton, to whom was afterwards added Dr. J. Ewing Mears as Secretary. The following correspondence will serve to show that the undertaking had its origin with the Surgical Club of Philadelphia, a private association which meets once a week during the autumn and winter for mutual improvement and the cultivation of kindly feeling. It had been intended to extend this compliment to me the year before, on the occasion of my semi-centennial professional birthday, but the celebration had to be postponed on account of my domestic bereavement. The proceedings were soon after published in a neat volume of forty-two pages.

The following letter was sent to me by the committee:

PHILADELPHIA, February 18, 1879.

PROFESSOR S. D. GROSS.

DEAR DOCTOR: A number of your friends in Philadelphia, out of love for your many personal virtues, and from a high appreciation of your distinguished professional position as the representative surgeon of America, have expressed a desire to extend to you the compliment of a public dinner; and the undersigned have accordingly been appointed a committee by our Surgical Club, with whom the subject originated, to ascertain your feelings in the matter, and to receive any suggestions which may enable them successfully to carry out the contemplated object.

Very sincerely, your friends,

D. HAYES AGNEW,
THOMAS G. MORTON,
R. J. LEVIS.

I answered as follows:

DRS. AGNEW, MORTON, and LEVIS.

GENTLEMEN: I have the honor to acknowledge the receipt of your letter of the 18th inst., proffering me, in the name of my friends, a public dinner as an appreciation of my private and professional character. Your communication, so expressive of personal kindness, profoundly touches my heart; and, although I cannot see things exactly in the light in which you see them, I cannot forego so pleasant an opportunity of meeting you and those you represent on an occasion which will be likely to be attended with so much enjoyment. I therefore cordially accept your kind invitation, leaving it to you to appoint the time for the entertainment.

I am, my dear friends, with many thanks for your kindness, very truly and affectionately, yours,

S. D. GROSS.

PHILADELPHIA, February 22, 1879.

Justice having been done to the excellent and varied bill of fare provided for the occasion, Professor Agnew announced the first toast of the evening, "Our Guest," and addressing me, indulged in the following eloquent strain, which was repeatedly applauded during its delivery:

"The honor of speaking to this toast devolves upon myself, and I may say that it gives me great pleasure to be the medium of extending to you, on this occasion, the friendly congratulations of your professional brethren here present. Fifty-one years is a long time, my dear sir, for a man to labor in any department of knowledge. Will you recall for a moment just a few of the events which have transpired during this period? Two generations have played their part in the great drama of life, and have left the stage. Dynasties which bid fair to rival in perpetuity that of Rome itself have risen, flourished, and passed into decay. Engineers have struck their levels, and laid down great iron roadways from one end of this continent to the other, uniting together the waters of the Atlantic and the Pacific. The most distant parts of the earth have been reached by

threads of iron over which pass the thoughts of men in
chariots of electric fire. The telephone has made the
world a great whispering gallery; the powder cart and
the subtle arts of diplomacy have reconstructed the entire
map of Europe; and an American medical and surgical
literature has grown up to which you have been one of
the largest contributors—a literature which is not only read
on this side of the Atlantic, but in every civilized country
on the face of the globe. And yet here you still remain,
my good friend, sturdy and strong as a great oak of the
forest; or, like Moses, with eye undimmed and strength
unabated. It is, I fear, too commonly thought, in these
days of mad haste for preferment, place, or power, that
men, when they have passed threescore and ten years,
should gracefully retire to the shades of private and inactive life, leaving the field to younger athletes. This is a
great mistake. Look at old Plato, at eighty-one, delving
away at his studies with all the enthusiasm of youth; at
Isocrates, delivering his great Panathenaic oration at
ninety-six. No, no! There is something in the grace
and dignity of age. Its serene complacency of mind,
when coupled with an affluent wealth of knowledge and
rich stores of observation and experience, renders the
presence of old men in our midst pillars of strength, not
only in a profession like our own, but to the community
at large, indeed to the world. The wisdom of old Fabius
was more than a match for the trained legions of the
youthful and wily Hannibal. It was not for men like
Milo, or Ajax, for which the Captain of all the Greeks
prayed, in order that he might humble the proud battle-
ments of Troy, but for men like Nestor. Long may you
yet live, my dear sir, actively to engage in the duties of
the profession which you have dignified and honored!
and when the inevitable hour comes, as come it must
to each and all of us,—that supreme hour, on which all
the hours of human life concentrate,—may your eyes

close on the scenes of earth calm and quiet as a summer evening!

"It only remains for me, my dear sir, to place on the lapel of your coat this little decoration. It is the gift of the gentlemen who sit around this board. And also this book, which contains the names of those who participate in this interesting ceremonial. These souvenirs may serve, when you shall have laid aside the harness of conflict, to recall some pleasant memories of the past; and they may also tend to fire the ambition of your sons to emulate the ambition of their noble sire."

When Professor Agnew had finished his address, he attached to the lapel of my coat a gold medal, having on one side the monogram "S. D. G." in diamonds and brilliants; and on the other this inscription: "Presented to Dr. S. D. Gross by his medical friends in commemoration of his fifty-first year in the profession, April 10th, 1879." The book consisted of leaves of tinted paper which contained the names, neatly written, of the invited guests and subscribers, and which were placed between covers of Russian leather.

In response to Professor Agnew, I said:

"In rising to respond to the toast offered by the distinguished chairman, I feel deeply oppressed by what Dr. Rush has so well described as 'suffocated excitement.' You need not be assured how much I appreciate the honor conferred upon me by this occasion and by this warm reception. The sentiments embodied in the toast touch my heart, and I should indeed be dead to all the finer feelings of my nature if I did not tender you my most cordial and respectful acknowledgments. It is no light compliment to be in such a presence or to be the guest of such a company. To merit the approbation of my professional brethren and of good men generally has ever been my highest ambition, as it must be of every honest and virtuous citizen. The offer of a public dinner, extended to me a few weeks ago by a committee of my professional friends, took me completely by surprise, and would probably have been promptly declined if it had not been accompanied by such kind and flattering words as at once to satisfy me that they came from the heart. The commendations which you have bestowed upon my private character and public services as a practitioner and teacher of surgery are measured, I am conscious, rather by your own generous feelings than by any deserts of mine. Whatever value these services may possess, it is no ordinary consolation to me to know that they are appreciated by men among whom I have lived for nearly a quarter of a century, with many of whom I have been brought into frequent contact in various relations of life—often, indeed, under circumstances of a most trying kind—with some of whom I have been officially associated, and with none of whom, thanks be to God, have I ever had one word of misunderstanding.

"It is not a pleasant thing to speak of one's self, but there are a few circumstances in the history of my uneventful life to which I may perhaps be pardoned for referring upon this occasion. I have grown old in the profession, for, as pupil and practitioner, I have been in it for fifty-four years, my graduation dating back to March, 1828. A little over one month ago I closed my thirty-ninth course of lectures on surgery. If to these thirty-nine years be added two years spent as Demonstrator of Anatomy in the Medical College of Ohio, and four years passed in the Medical Department of the Cincinnati College as Professor of Pathological Anatomy, it will be perceived that my life as a public teacher extends over a period of forty-five years. During all this time it has been my good fortune to miss few lectures, either from sickness or any other cause.

"Having been thus actively engaged for so many years as a public teacher, it is not surprising that my pupils should be scattered far and wide over the country, while not a few of them are successfully practising in foreign climes. More than five thousand diplomas bear my signature. Of the thirty-seven colleagues with whom I have at various times been associated, twenty-six have fallen by the wayside, for the most part ripe in years and full of honors, leaving eleven survivors, among others Willard Parker, Austin Flint, John W. Draper, Benjamin Silliman, and our distinguished townsman, Joseph Pancoast, five men of whom any profession in any country might be proud.

"Struggles of some kind are the inevitable lot of every man who is not born with a silver spoon in his mouth. I had mine, but they were the struggles of early life, and I thank God for them, for they taught me patience and perseverance and self-reliance, those powerful aids in developing character. But they did not discourage me. On the contrary, I felt as Sheridan felt when he made his maiden speech in the British House of Commons, that it was in me, and would come out of me ; or, as Erskine expressed it on a similar occasion, I felt as if my children were tugging at my coat, and urging me on to industry and perseverance that I might supply their necessities. A brave man never yields to despair. His motto is *Perseverantia omnia vincit!* I have never lost sight of the fact that what a man soweth he shall reap, or that, 'if the spring show no blossoms, autumn will show no fruit.'

"Much has been said about the inspiration of genius. The greatest efforts that have ever been made at the forum, in the pulpit, or in the senate, in ancient or modern times, were the result of hard study and patient labor. Patrick Henry, William Pinkney, Daniel Webster, Rufus Choate, and others like them never made a great argument or a great oratorical display without preparation ; and the same is true of every profession and every pursuit. After fifty years of earnest work I find myself still in the harness ;

but, although I have reached that age when most men, tired of the cares of life, seek repose in retirement, and abandon themselves to the study of religion, the claims of friendship, or the contemplation of philosophy, my conviction has always been that it is far better for a man to wear out than to rust out. Brain work, with constant application, has been a great comfort to me, as well as a great help; it has enhanced the enjoyment of daily life, and added largely to the pleasures of the lecture-room and of authorship; indeed, it will always, I am sure, if wisely regulated, be conducive both to health and longevity. A man who abandons himself to a life of inactivity after having long been accustomed to work is practically dead.

"In taking a retrospect of my life I have no regrets; and although I may not be able to say, *Non omnis moriar*, I trust that I have not lived wholly in vain; for while much remains undone that might and should have been done, it is reasonable to suppose that at least some of the seed which I have sown have produced good fruit. It is not given to every man to be a Harvey, a Hunter, a Jenner, a Bichat, a Morton, a Paget, or a Virchow. 'By the grace of God,' says St. Paul, 'I am what I am.' No man can rise superior to himself.

"What is fame? Is it a phantom, or is it a reality? Alas, too often the former! too seldom the latter! No sooner does an author or a teacher retire from the field of his labor than other gods are worshipped. Happy, thrice happy, is he who in the evening of his life, as he reviews his past conduct, can say to himself, 'I have been true to my profession; I have been ambitious of its glory.'

"As I look back through the dim vista of half a century, what memories crowd upon my mind! Kingdoms have crumbled into dust; new dynasties have sprung up; the world has been drenched in blood by contending armies; millions of human beings have been swept away by pestilence and famine; civilization, commerce, the arts and sciences, religion and education have found new homes ; the uttermost parts of the globe have been explored by intrepid navigators and adventurous travellers; time and space have been annihilated by the telegraph ; and the employment of steam and the application of machinery have changed the occupations of man, and thrown upon us a surplus population which the wisest statesmen know not how to dispose of. The art and the science of medicine have been completely revolutionized and enriched to an extent which fifty years ago would have baffled the wildest conceptions. During these vast changes, so beneficent to mankind, America has not been idle. If she had contributed nothing more to the stock of human happiness than anæsthetics, the world would owe her an everlasting debt of gratitude. The fanciful and mischievous speculations which characterized medicine in the days of my youth have been replaced by sober facts, founded upon more carefully conducted observations and more rational deductions. In preventive medicine a new field has been opened which, if properly cultivated, as it seems destined to be, will add millions of years to the life of a human race. Oh, for a glance at the profession half a century hence, when man, enlightened and refined by education, and redeemed from the thraldom of ignorance and superstition, shall reflect more perfectly than he now does the image of his Maker!

"I thank you, Mr. Chairman, and you, gentlemen, who have honored me with your presence this evening, for the patience and attention with which you have listened to my rambling remarks. Allow me, before I take my seat, to wish you, one and all, prosperity and happiness, and to drink your health with a heart brimful of gratitude for the many favors that have been showered upon me by my professional brethren."

There have been more costly and elaborate dinners than this ; but there never has been one in which there was more rational enjoyment, or in which a more cordial and tender feeling was manifested for the man whom it was designed to honor.

Wednesday, April 30th, 1879.—I left in the 9.45 train this morning for Atlanta, Georgia, as a delegate to a Convention of all American Medical Colleges, the American Medical College Association, and the American Medical Association, all of which will meet in that city—the first on Friday, May 2d; the second on Monday, May 5th; and the last on Tuesday, May 6th. I reached the city at 11.45 on the following night, much fatigued by a dreary, monotonous ride through the States of Virginia, North Carolina and South Carolina, and a part of Georgia. No journey could have been more devoid of interest.

The Convention of the Colleges of the country was, as will be perceived by the following preambles and resolutions, called at my instance. These had been prepared with great care, and were unanimously adopted by the Medical College Association at its meeting at Buffalo in June, 1878. Two previous conventions having been fruitlessly held for a similar purpose, the one at Cincinnati in 1867, and the other at Washington City in 1869, I was determined to bring the subject of medical education by our colleges once more fully before the profession and the public in order that it might be thoroughly discussed, and finally acted upon. Alas, two entire days were spent in idle, vapid talk! and when the meeting broke up there was not a man who had at heart the interests of the profession and the honor of our medical schools that was not bitterly disappointed. Of the twenty-nine schools represented on the floor of the Convention hardly half a dozen had come with authority to adopt the reform contemplated by the resolutions. The Jefferson Medical College, whose delegate I was on the occasion, remained—to her shame be it said—in the background. This meeting, from which I had originally expected so much, adjourned *sine die* at the close of the second day's proceedings, thus ending, like its two predecessors, in smoke.

The subjoined document shows the deep interest I feel in the progress of medical education, and how useless it is to expect substantial aid from our schools as at present constituted:

" *Call for a Convention of all American Medical Colleges, to be held in the city of Atlanta, Georgia, beginning at 10 a. m., Friday, May 2d, 1879.*

"DEAR SIR: At the meeting of the American Medical College Association, held in Buffalo, N. Y., June, 1878, Professor S. D. Gross, a delegate from Jefferson Medical College, of Philadelphia, offered the following preambles and resolutions:

" *Whereas*, It is eminently desirable that the medical schools of this country should adopt a uniform system of instruction of a grade fully in accord with the requirements of the age in other branches of study, and with the practice of the medical institutions of Europe; and

" *Whereas*, All the efforts to bring about such a change on the part of the American Medical Association, of the Association of Medical Teachers assembled at Cincinnati in 1867 and at Washington in 1869, and of different State medical societies, have signally failed; and

" *Whereas*, The present time seems to be peculiarly favorable for taking strong ground upon the subject, inasmuch as it is now attracting general attention throughout the United States: therefore

" *Resolved*, That this Association respectfully and earnestly request that the regularly organized and accredited medical schools of the United States hold at their earliest convenience a meeting for the purpose of adopting some definite and final action upon a subject of such vital importance to the dignity, character, and usefulness of the profession and the welfare of the American people.

"*Resolved*, That in order to impart proper efficiency to this plan each and every college be requested to send two delegates, consisting of one member of each Board of Trustees, and of one member of each Faculty, with full power to act for their respective institutions.

"*Resolved*, That the medical and secular press throughout the United States be respectfully requested to lend their aid in the dissemination and discussion of these preambles and resolutions in order to place the whole matter of medical education prominently before the profession and the people.

"*Resolved*, That a copy of these preambles and resolutions, signed by the President and Secretary of the Association, be transmitted to the officers of every regularly constituted medical college in the United States, with a request to hold the contemplated meeting at Washington City, or at some other central point, on the first Wednesday in September next, or as soon thereafter as possible.

"Professor N. S. Davis seconded these resolutions, and heartily indorsed them.

"Professor T. G. Richardson moved that the time of the proposed meeting be the Friday preceding the meeting of the American Medical Association, and that the place be designated by the president of this Association. This amendment was adopted, and the preambles and resolutions as amended were agreed upon.

"In compliance with this action of the American Medical College Association, its acting president, Professor N. S. Davis, of Chicago, has designated Atlanta, Georgia, as the place of the proposed Convention, while the aforementioned action of the Association has appointed the time at 10 A. M. Friday, May 2d, 1879. It is earnestly hoped that delegates from all 'regularly organized and accredited medical schools' in the United States will promptly meet at the above designated time and place. That the action of the Convention may be definite, it is desired that each college send two delegates, with full power to act for their respective institutions—one of these delegates to be selected from the Board of Trustees and one from the Faculty.

"In general terms, the object of the Convention is to adopt some 'uniform system of instruction more in harmony with the requirements of the age.' Among the questions appropriate for discussion and decision may be mentioned, 'Shall all the colleges require attendance upon three regular courses of lectures during three separate years ere admitting students to become candidates for the degree of M. D.?'

"Is any uniform system possible in this or other things? If so, to what extent is it possible or even desirable at the present time? Each doctor in the land doubtless has in mind an ideal medical college system. But this Convention cannot act upon idealities; it can only act upon that which is practicable to all honest and efficient medical schools.

"It is hoped that the medical press and teaching fraternity will freely and exhaustively discuss the subject-matter of this Convention. The doing of this at once will enable it to enter upon its labors with a complete knowledge of the facts in the case.

"To avoid misconception, let it be distinctly noticed that, although this Convention is called by the 'American Medical College Association,' it is entirely distinct from that body. When assembled, the Convention will elect its own officers and adopt its own methods for transacting its business in pursuance with the object of the call.

"Signed, NATHAN S. DAVIS, M. D.,
"*Acting President of the American Medical College Association.*

"LEARTUS CONNOR, M. D.,
"*Secretary, Detroit, Michigan.*
"*February 6th, 1879.*

"P. S.—It is desired that those colleges which decide to attend the aforesaid Convention by delegates will send

2—10

notice to that effect to the Secretary at any time previous
to April 25th.''

May 5th.—The College Association labored hard, and,
like the Convention above referred to, accomplished nothing.   There was a good deal of angry discussion, many
motions were made, and a number of alterations of the by-
laws were proposed, to be acted upon at New York in May
next.   Before the meeting adjourned I was elected president.

May 6th.—The meeting of the American Medical Association took place this morning, and although the attendance was not large, it was highly respectable.   Several
Southern States—hitherto, since the war, absent from the
meeting—sent delegates.   The utmost harmony prevailed.
A number of interesting and instructive papers were read,
and the address of Dr. Parvin, the president, was a chaste
and scholarly production, delivered in a masterly manner.
Dr. Lewis A. Sayre was elected president, and I acted as
chairman of the Committee on Nominations.   The citizens
of Atlanta entertained the Association most hospitably.
Governor Colquitt gave a reception at the State mansion,
and the medical fraternity spared no efforts to make the
time of the members of the Association pass pleasantly.
Atlanta is not an attractive town, but it has a number of
elegant residences, and is the centre of a considerable
number of railways, which impart to it an appearance of
more than ordinary activity.   It has two medical schools—
neither of them, as might be supposed, in a flourishing
condition.   It also boasts of two medical journals.

Wednesday, May 14th.—Early in February, 1879, I received an urgent invitation to deliver, on the 14th of the
ensuing May, the public address at the dedication of the
monument erected at Danville, Kentucky, by the Kentucky State Medical Society in honor of Dr. Ephraim
McDowell.   As I had been mainly instrumental in placing
McDowell's claims upon a fixed and permanent basis, as

has been stated, I considered it my duty to accept the offer, and at the appointed time discharged what to me had become a pleasant task. The address, which has been published in pamphlet form, was delivered in the large Presbyterian church at Danville, in presence of the Governor, Lieutenant-Governor, Governor-elect, and of other distinguished men, and a large and select audience composed of the citizens of Danville and of the neighboring country. A number of McDowell's descendants were present, and added to the interest of the occasion. One lady, a grand niece, came upon the stage after the exercises were over, and evinced her gratification by giving me a kiss! Immediately after the close of the address my former pupil, Dr. Richard O. Cowling, presented to me, on behalf of the Kentucky State Medical Society, in the most eloquent terms, the knocker which had so long hung upon McDowell's door, and which had so often summoned him by day and by night to deeds of mercy. This gift is now in my possession, and I intend to give it ere long to the Philadelphia Academy of Surgery. I enjoyed my visit to Danville very much, and my address was, I have reason to believe, well received. After the meeting was dismissed, there were a number of public receptions by the more prominent and wealthy citizens of the place. Dr. McMurtry, a promising young physician, and chairman of the Committee of Arrangements, was very kind and attentive to me during my sojourn.

The day after the celebration I paid my respects to Mrs. Young, widow of the late President of Centre College, and daughter of my late friend, Mr. John J. Crittenden, who with her daughters occupies a pleasant house in the suburbs of the city, and who entertained me with some agreeable reminiscences of departed Kentuckians. I also called upon another old friend, Mrs. Dudley, the excellent matron of the Kentucky Deaf and Dumb Asylum, an institution in which she takes great pride and interest.

During my journey from Atlanta to Louisville I stopped over night and spent part of a day at Nashville, where I met my old friend, Dr. W. T. Briggs, the Professor of Surgery in the University of that city, who showed me many objects of interest, among others the Capitol and the College buildings of the Medical Department of the University. I was presented to A. S. Marks, the Governor, a handsome, intelligent, and popular man, who lost a leg in our civil war. The Capitol, situated on an eminence, is built of Tennessee granite, and is one of the finest edifices in the United States. Its dome affords a beautiful view of the city and the surrounding country. The architect, Mr. Strickland, sleeps, tightly incased, in one of its walls. The library-room is studded with tolerably fair portraits of the principal worthies of the State, especially its former governors and chief-justices, prominent among which is the full-length portrait of Andrew Jackson.

The Medical College had large classes before the war. Its prospects are improving, although several years must elapse before it can attain its former prosperity. Its principal pillar is Briggs, who enjoys a wide reputation as a teacher, as a lithotomist, and as a general surgeon. He is assisted by a respectable corps of colleagues, who do good work in their respective departments. The College building is commodious without elegance, and the Museum contains some valuable preparations for illustrating the different courses of lectures. A second medical school was opened a few years ago under the auspices of the late Professor Paul F. Eve, whose son now occupies the chair of Surgery.

As we drove through this beautiful city we stopped at the fine mansion of Mrs. Polk, widow of the late President, whose remains are interred in the garden in front of the house, under a monument erected, if I mistake not, by the lady herself. The door was opened by a colored servant, who ushered us into a large, well-furnished parlor, where we were soon greeted by the hostess with a cordial welcome. I said, "I hope you will excuse me for troubling you this warm morning; but I could not think of passing through Nashville without paying my respects to a lady so much beloved and so widely known;" adding, "I have not had the pleasure of seeing you since I met you at Cincinnati in the autumn of 1836 at the reception given by General Lytle to General Jackson on his way from Washington City to the Hermitage." "Ah!" said she, "that was a long time ago, and I dare say you would like to know how old I am." I replied, "I have no special curiosity on that subject, for, as I have just stated, I called simply to pay you my respects." "Well," she remarked, "I am in my seventy-sixth year, and enjoy excellent health." "You certainly look well," was my answer; "and there is nothing in your appearance to indicate that you have attained that age." She is a well-preserved woman, and very lady-like in her appearance, rather tall, sprightly, and animated in conversation, and loves to talk of her late husband, who, although not a man of the highest grade of intellect, was well acquainted with the duties of government, and made a pure and dignified magistrate. After having passed an agreeable half hour with Mrs. Polk, we took our departure with our best wishes for her happiness.

In the afternoon I took the train for Louisville, where I spent the next two days in the midst of some of my old friends, comparatively few of whom now survive. General and Mrs. Preston with their daughters were especially kind to me, and I received much attention from my professional brethren, several of whom lost no time in pressing me into their service. Great changes and improvements are everywhere visible since my removal in 1856.

September 17th.—My friend, Dr. Henry Wentworth Acland, Regius Professor of Medicine in the University of Oxford, arrived this afternoon with his son Theodore to pay me a visit which he had promised me several years ago. He had just visited Saratoga and Lake Champlain in quest of health and recreation, and was anxious before looking at Baltimore and Washington City to see something of Philadelphia. Before he came to me he had intended to spend a few days with General and Mrs. McClellan, at Orange, New Jersey, where I was to meet him, but owing to the General's sudden indisposition the arrangement, much to our mutual regret, fell to the ground. At a formal dinner which I gave him, among the guests were Mr. Henry C. Carey, Mr. George H. Boker, General Robert Patterson, Professor Alfred Stillé of the University of Pennsylvania, Professor Roberts Bartholow of the Jefferson Medical College, Professor Austin Flint, Sr., and Professor Fordyce Barker of New York. The evening passed in agreeable and edifying conversation. Mr. Carey and Mrs. Orville Horwitz, the only lady present, were especially animated, and added not a little to the life and enjoyment of the occasion. The day after the dinner I drove Professor Acland to the Woman's College, with whose workings he was anxious to familiarize himself, the more especially as no institution of the kind exists in Great Britain, and as he is one of the most influential members of the Medical Council, whose duty it is, under a government appointment, to superintend medical schools and medical education. At half past twelve o'clock he accompanied me to the amphitheatre of the Jefferson Medical College, where he addressed the class in some appropriate remarks, and witnessed an amputation of the hip-joint which I performed upon a Methodist clergyman who had come all the way from Texas for relief. Late in the afternoon he left for Baltimore, but before taking leave of us he ran rapidly to have a final look at my patient, in whom he took the deepest interest, and who, thanks to good luck and kind and unwearied care and attention, made an excellent recovery, surviving the operation two years and a half, living most of the time in perfect health, and always standing up in the pulpit during his clerical exercises.

It would be hard to find in all England a more active man, mentally and physically, than Acland. He is constantly prying into nooks and corners of whatever interests him, or even of what does not specially interest him. He is a rapid writer and a fluent speaker, with a slight lisp that serves to give an edge to whatever he says. He abounds in knowledge, general and medical, which is ever at his tongue's end. There is hardly an American of note who visits Oxford that is not entertained at his table, and shown whatever is of interest in that old, weird city. He takes especial pleasure in pointing out the almost invisible path leading to the narrow creek from which are derived the name of Oxford and that of the great University Museum of which he is one of the founders, and which already contains one of the choicest collections of objects in anthropology, archæology, and natural history in the kingdom. His writings are characterized by strong sense and scholarly taste. He has taken an active part in the famous Contagious Diseases Acts, in hygiene, and in medical and general education. One of his earliest publications was his Plains of Troy. In 1854 he published a valuable memoir on the Visitation of Cholera in Oxford. His memoir of Dr. William Stokes, of Dublin, prepared for the New Sydenham Society, is worthy alike of the subject and of the author.

January 16th, 1880.—I went to New York this afternoon to dine with my friend, Professor Austin Flint, Sr., at the Manhattan Club. The invitations had been issued one week previously, and the day set apart for the dinner was Friday, the only day of the week on which I could leave home for such a purpose. The entertainment, which was given in my honor, took place at seven o'clock, and was in every respect worthy of the host and of the

Club. We sat down at a large round table decorated with choice flowers, and so arranged as to place us within easy view of one another. Smoking began at ten o'clock, followed by the recital of numerous anecdotes, many of which elicited rounds of applause. The occasion was one not soon to be forgotten. The company consisted, besides the host, of Dr. Isaac E. Taylor, President of the Faculty of the Bellevue Hospital Medical College ; Dr. James R. Wood; Dr. Lewis A. Sayre, President-elect of the American Medical Association; Dr. Fordyce Barker; Dr. Detmold, the orthopædic surgeon, and a pupil of Stromeyer of Hanover; Dr. John Gray, Superintendent of the Lunatic Asylum at Utica; Dr. Peters; Dr. D. B. St. John Roosa; Dr. Lusk ; Professor Doremus, the chemist; Dr. Alexander H. Mott; Dr. Austin Flint, Jr.; Dr. "Charley" Smith, the anecdotist; Dr. Draper; Dr. S. W. Gross ; and myself, who occupied the seat of honor between the host and Dr. Peters. With all of these New Yorkers I was more or less intimately acquainted—a circumstance which contributed greatly to my enjoyment. A number of prominent physicians and surgeons who had been invited declined on account of other engagements. The party broke up at fifteen minutes of twelve o'clock, when we drove to Professor Flint's residence, under whose hospitable roof I remained until the next afternoon. Then I left for my home, where I arrived at half past six, having left Jersey City two hours and a half previously.

The journey from Philadelphia to New York is one of remarkable ease and speed compared with what it was fifty years ago. In December, 1828, it took Mr. John Grigg, the publisher, and myself nearly an entire day to reach the latter city. Leaving Philadelphia on a steamboat at eight o'clock in the morning, we landed at Bristol about ten o'clock. Then we took seats in a stage-coach, in which, along with sixteen similar vehicles, we rode to New Brunswick, where we embarked on another boat, which landed us at New York about seven o'clock in the evening. This was considered at that time good speed; and it must be added that the journey was a very merry one, performed as it was in so many coaches, each drawn by four fine horses, and crowded with passengers, the whole forming a line nearly one mile in length. What a contrast between the past and the present! If to-day a man were compelled to move in that comparatively tortoise-like manner, would he not groan aloud? An hour and fifty-five minutes now—ere long to be reduced to one hour and a half! Surely the railroad and telegraph have annihilated space and time.

2—II

CHAPTER IV.

FEBRUARY 20th.—I lunched to-day with Mrs. George W.
Biddle, wife of the eminent lawyer, to meet Mrs. Newman
of Elizabeth, New Jersey, and Mrs. George Biddle, two
daughters of my old friend J. Kearney Rodgers of New
York, whose acquaintance I made during my connection
with the New York University in 1850. Dr. Rodgers was
married twice—first to Miss Nicholson of Baltimore ; and
afterwards to Miss Hosack, daughter of the eminent Dr.
David Hosack, of New York, who still survives. Mrs.
Newman, who is a daughter of the first wife, received me
with cordiality, and I was soon engaged in conversation
with her. She was quite agreeable, and I could not help
telling her how much she looked like an English woman.
She is intelligent, self-possessed, and lady-like. She is
married to a merchant, who is somewhat her senior in
age, very modest, and rather retiring in his habits. Mrs.
Newman spends much of her time in charitable works,
and she is deeply interested in the Sunday-schools of her
parish. Mrs. Biddle is the younger sister, or rather step-
sister, married to a highly promising son of Mr. George
W. Biddle. Like Mrs. Newman, she is intelligent, and
possesses an active and inquisitive mind. The party at

Mrs. Biddle's, though small, was very pleasant, and at the end of two hours I left the table with reluctance.

Mrs. Newman and Mrs. Biddle met me at dinner at my house the following Sunday, when the conversation, although of a more mixed character than at the luncheon on the previous Friday, turned upon their father and Dr. Hosack. The husband of Mrs. Biddle was also present.

February 24th.—The Board of Trustees of the Pennsylvania College of Dental Surgery, at their meeting to-day, unanimously elected me their president, an office filled by the late Henry C. Carey from the foundation of the institution to the time of his death last October. Three members of the board had previously called upon me to ask my consent to be put in nomination, as I had not before been connected with the school.

February 28th.—The College had its twenty-fourth Commencement at twelve o'clock to-day, and it devolved upon me as its chief officer to confer the degrees upon fifty-seven candidates, including two women. In congratulating the graduates upon the completion of their studies and upon their entrance into professional life, I extended my special sympathies to the young women. I spoke to them words of encouragement, telling them that they could not fail to do well if they were true to themselves and to their profession, and that the dentist of the Empress of Germany was a woman, and a graduate of the Pennsylvania College of Dental Surgery. One of them, a native of Germany, took a prize for proficiency in her dental studies, and she is said to possess marked ability, having made herself fairly acquainted with the English language, of which she hardly knew anything on her arrival in this country two years ago.

One Sunday in March I had the pleasure of entertaining at dinner Mrs. O'Sullivan, the eldest daughter of Dr. Rodgers, and Miss Hosack, a daughter of Dr. David Hosack, both of New York. Mrs. O'Sullivan is the wife of our former Minister at the Court of Portugal, well known at home and abroad. She informed me that she had lived twenty-two years in Europe, during which time she was brought into contact with many persons of distinction. She bears a close resemblance to her father, is cultured and refined, talks well, and has a pleasing voice and manner. Miss Hosack is a woman of fine type. She is now seventy-two years of age, and is not ashamed to confess the fact. She told me that the statement circulated by the medical press of this and other countries soon after the death of her father, that he had sustained heavy losses during the great fire in New York, was without the shadow of truth. These losses—it was, I well remember, currently reported—had caused such deep chagrin as to bring on the attack of apoplexy of which he died within a few days. Hosack was an earnest advocate of bleeding, and immediately after this attack came on, although he was partially unconscious and unable to speak, he held out his arm. A vein was speedily opened by his son, Dr. Alexander Eddy Hosack, who happened to be near him at the moment.

These little incidents—two family Sunday dinners and Mrs. Biddle's luncheon—have served to remind me forcibly of some features in the life of Dr. John Kearney Rodgers, which I will briefly refer to. I do this the more willingly because Rodgers was not only well read and versed in his profession, but he was a great operator and an amiable gentleman, a kind husband, a devoted father, and a staunch friend. I recollect him as a stout man, more than six feet in height, well built, with a large head, light eyes, small, slightly sandy whiskers, and an expressive countenance. He was a good talker and loved to converse on professional topics. He was quite free from jealousy, so common in our ranks, and was full of simplicity, the characteristic of a great mind. Born in the city of New York in 1793, he was of Scotch descent, and the eldest son of a physician, his paternal grandfather having been a Presbyterian clergyman of note. He obtained his classical education at Princeton College under the presidency of Dr. Samuel Stanhope Smith, with whom, however, he was not a favorite. As the story goes, the master one day in a fit of anger told his pupil that if he did not mend his ways he might as well shut up his books, for he never could become useful or distinguished as he was then going on. To this taunting remark the future surgeon promptly replied, "The world shall see, sir!" And indeed the world did see! This occurrence was the turning-point in his life. The unfeeling remark stimulated his ambition and roused his dormant energies into full activity. His early medical studies were conducted in the office of Dr. Wright Post, Professor of Anatomy in the College of Physicians and Surgeons of New York, a surgeon famous in his day, rendered so mainly by the fact that he was the first to ligate successfully the subclavian artery, a feat worthy of American surgery. In 1816 he received his degree in that institution—a school which has long ranked among the foremost of the country. Even before his graduation he acted as Demonstrator of Anatomy to his master, served for a time as House Surgeon to the New York Hospital, and then, armed with letters of introduction, went to London to pursue his studies at the hospitals of that city under the famous masters of the metropolis. While abroad he became much interested in the study of ophthalmic surgery, and soon after his return established, along with his friend Dr. Edward Delafield and others, the New York Eye Infirmary. In 1818 he was appointed Demonstrator of Anatomy in the College of Physicians and Surgeons of New York, and four years afterwards Surgeon to the New York Hospital—an office which he had much coveted, and which he retained up to the time of his death in 1851, a period of nearly thirty years.

As an operator, Dr. Rodgers possessed high merit, and

it is certain that he had for a long time no superior in this country, except perhaps Valentine Mott, who so long wielded the surgical sceptre on the American continent. His crowning triumph was the ligation in 1845 of the left subclavian artery on the inside of the scalene muscle on account of a huge aneurism of that vessel, a feat which, up to that time, was universally regarded as impracticable. Those who are acquainted with the anatomy of this vessel, in this portion of its extent, will fully appreciate the difficulties of placing a ligature around it—difficulties vastly increased by the overlapping tumor and the morbid adhesions formed by its pressure. In the skill displayed in its performance this achievement yields in no respect to Mott's celebrated case of ligation of the innominate artery, or even to that of the aorta by Sir Astley Cooper, and placed Rodgers at once in the first rank of the surgeons of the world. The operation, it is true, did not save the patient's life, but all who witnessed it agreed that it was performed in a masterly manner, and that nothing was left undone to insure a favorable result.

Operative skill is not the highest attribute of surgery; it is a great thing in its way, and entitled to all praise. But therapeutic surgery and surgical pathology stand far above it. Rodgers was not only an expert operator and a sound practical surgeon, but thoroughly versed in the principles of the healing art, and keen in the discrimination of diseases and accidents. He had made himself early in life an excellent anatomist, and lost no opportunity of studying morbid structure. Conscientious in dealing with his patients, he never operated merely for the sake of operating, or sought that notoriety in the use of the knife, even when not skilfully wielded, which so often wins the admiration of the vulgar. In consultations he was the wise counsellor, and under all circumstances, in health and in sickness, he was the sympathizing and trusted friend and physician. Surely the career of such a man, so full of philanthropy and genuine manliness, is one worthy of imitation alike of the student and the physician. His death was caused by a rare disease,—phlebitis of the liver, followed by peritonitis. It is to be regretted that Dr. Rodgers left no record of his vast experience. With the exception of the publication of a few brief papers in the medical journals of the day, nothing appeared from his pen.

Dr. David Hosack was a physician worthy to be named with Rush, Physick, Wistar, Chapman, and other savans. He was born in New York in August, 1769. He was of Scotch descent, and early in life evinced strong literary and scientific tastes, which he cultivated with diligence and success, so much so that he enjoyed a high reputation as a scholar, as a writer, as an accomplished teacher, and as a scientist. His classical education was received at Princeton, and his medical education in New York, Philadelphia, and Edinburgh. In Edinburgh he remained several years. His dissertation upon Vision made his name widely known on both sides of the Atlantic. Shortly after his return to his native city he was elected Professor of Botany in Columbia College; and he taught successively in different schools materia medica, midwifery, and practical medicine, the last in Rutgers Medical College. Soon after the college was closed, and thus ended the professional career of the great physician and the eloquent and enthusiastic teacher. I heard him discourse on fevers. He sat in an arm-chair and read from his manuscript; but he frequently indulged in extemporaneous flights, accompanied by flashes of his black eyes, and by graceful gesticulations, which enchained the attention of his pupils. His manner was delightful; his voice commanding. If, as a teacher, he had any fault, it was his dogmatism; and yet it is proper that a man of his talents, experience, and position should not only have decided views upon professional matters but that he should fearlessly express them.

It was by the merest accident that I heard Hosack lecture. Early in November, 1828, I had occasion, as I have elsewhere said, to visit New York to place in the hands of Mr. Bliss, a prominent publisher of that city, a translation of Hildenbrand's monograph on contagious typhus fever. My old friend, Professor John Eberle, had given me a flattering letter to him, which I delivered early in the morning after my arrival; and I need hardly add that it secured for me a kind reception. As I rose to take leave, Hosack said to me, "Perhaps you would like to see our College, and hear some of us lecture;" adding, "my own hour is twelve." I said, "Thank you; I will be with you at the appointed time." He presented me to the class, and after making some complimentary remarks, in which he referred to the object of my visit, proceeded with his lecture. After it was over, he said, "The New York Philosophical Society will meet at my house this evening, and you must not fail to come." On my arrival at his house in Chambers Street, opposite the City Park, I was surprised to find a large assembly of gentlemen and ladies, the former including eminent artists, scientists, and authors, to many of whom I was presented by the host. Supper was served in a spacious dining-room at fifteen minutes of eleven o'clock, when I was kindly placed at the seat of honor on his right. The *menu* embraced every available delicacy, and the wines were of the best quality. The conversation was animated, but philosophy was forgotten in the convivialities of the occasion. One man at least was sick, although I can testify to the fact that he ate and drank in the most temperate manner. It was considerably after midnight when the company separated. I saw Dr. Hosack only once after this pleasant event—namely, in 1832, during the visitation of the Asiatic cholera, when the whole city of New York was wrapped in gloom, and when he himself spent most of his time at his country residence on the Hudson.

Dr. Hosack was an excellent botanist and mineralogist, and the author of three volumes of medical essays, of numerous articles in the medical journals, and of a Life of De Witt Clinton, and of Dr. Hugh Williams. After his death a volume on the Practice of Medicine, edited by his friend and former pupil, Rev. Dr. Ducachet, of Philadelphia, was published, but it failed to attract favorable notice, and may indeed be said to have fallen stillborn from the press. The matter had grown obsolete, and should have been consigned to the flames. The days of nosology had departed, and a new era had been inaugurated. Fortunately the editor had the good sense to suppress a vast amount of the material which Dr. Hosack's will had intrusted to his charge.

Dr. Hosack was a public-spirited man, and took a lively interest in whatever appertained to the welfare of the city and State of New York. Many of his discourses relate to agricultural affairs. He watched with pride the progress of the Erie Canal, and established at Hyde Park, on the banks of the Hudson, a fine botanical garden, rich in exotic plants and flowers. He was elected early in life a member of the Royal Society of London and of that of Edinburgh, and was created LL. D. by Princeton College. He was married three times, twice to ladies of wealth and high social rank. He was of medium height, well built, with a dark complexion, black eyes, heavy brows, and fine features. He was one of the originators of the New York Historical Society, of the Horticultural Society, of the New York Literary and Philosophical Society, and in conjunction with his friend and former pupil, Dr. John W. Francis, of the American Medical and Philosophical Register. He carried on a large correspondence with many prominent literary and scientific men at home and abroad ; and along with De Witt Clinton and Bishop Hobart he was engaged for many years in enterprises designed to promote the arts and sciences, the literary

taste of the community, and the establishment of charitable institutions.   As a connoisseur of the fine arts, none
of his contemporaries excelled him.   His death occurred
in December, 1835.

Among the medical men present at Dr. Hosack's party
there were two to whom I was especially attracted: Dr.
George Bushe and John W. Francis—the one destined to a
premature grave, the other to a brilliant career as a physician and to literary and social eminence.   Bushe was an
Irishman, who had been brought here at the instance of
Mr. William Lawrence, of St. Bartholomew's Hospital,
London, to fill the chair of Anatomy in Rutgers Medical
College made vacant by the retirement of Godman.   He
was more than six feet and three inches in height, with
light blue eyes, delicate features, and sandy whiskers.
There was a hectic flush upon his cheeks.   I heard him
deliver, on the previous morning, an excellent discourse
on the anatomy of the hip-joint, in which he referred, in
glowing terms, to the labors of Bonnetus, Morgagni, and
other pathological authorities, with which he seemed to be
familiar.   The hours passed rapidly and pleasantly, the
attention of every student being rivetted to the subject.
The lecture was able and animated, abounding in flights
of genuine eloquence.

Many anecdotes are told of Bushe, and none with greater
zest and emphasis than those that were related of him by
his former associate, Dr. John W. Francis.   That he was
a man of talent and of not a little genius is certain; but it
is also certain that he was unscrupulous, on all occasions
taking advantage of his fellow-practitioners, so that at
length hardly any one would meet him in consultation.
When Rutgers College was broken up, as it was in less
than three years after he entered it, he was thrown upon
his own resources as a surgeon for the support of his
family; and the consequence was, if report be true, that
he often used the knife where a conscientious surgeon

would not have interfered. He was very poor when he reached this country; and any fee, however small, must therefore have been of importance to him. He possessed much operative skill, combined with an amount of dash that did not fail to take with all classes of people. Some of his operations, such, for example, as the ligation of the common iliac artery in a child only six weeks old for a nævus of the vagina, perineum, and anus, were meritorious achievements. Mott, who could brook no rival, disliked him; and the hatred soon became mutual. Bushe contributed numerous articles to the medical press; and in 1831 he founded the New York Medico-Chirurgical Bulletin, which, however, was suspended at the close of the second volume. The work by which he is chiefly remembered is his treatise on the Malformations, Injuries, and Diseases of the Rectum and Anus, issued in 1837, only a short time before his death. It is a creditable production, and may be consulted with advantage on account of its admirable delineations of the various surgical affections incident to these regions of the body. It is accompanied by a volume of beautiful plates. Dr. Bushe died of consumption in 1837, at the age, if I mistake not, of thirty-seven.

Dr. John W. Francis was the prince of good fellows, the soul of wit and humor, a man of great learning, an excellent talker, a facile writer, a capital speaker—in short, a man whose like we shall not soon see again. Such a face; such a head, with its long curly hair; such a voice; such a pleasant manner; such warmth of expression; such a cordial shake of the hand; such good nature, are things which can never be forgotten. They were peculiarly his own. I wish it were in my power to convey to my readers an idea of his genius, of his flow of spirits, of his intelligence, of his learning, of his conversational powers, and of the fund of anecdotes at his command. Nature had endowed him with rare gifts. He was of German descent by the father's side, and of Swiss by the mother's, and he was born in the city of New York in 1789. In his youth he worked for a time in a printing-office. His classical education was obtained in Columbia College, and his medical education in the College of Physicians and Surgeons of his native city. Dr. Hosack, his preceptor, seeing his professional promise, took him into partnership, and for a time the tutor and the disciple worked shoulder to shoulder in furtherance of their common interests and the common weal. How long this connection lasted I am unable to say; but there is no doubt that it was mutually advantageous, and it is certain that the friendship which grew out of it continued warm and fresh during the remainder of their lives. When the medical department of Rutgers College was organized Hosack and Francis became colleagues, and, along with Mott and other distinguished associates, exerted their utmost powers, although in vain, to build up a great and permanent seminary of medical science. They founded, and for four years edited, The American Medical and Philosophical Register, a periodical which, short-lived as it was, was well received in Europe and America. Francis, as was then the custom with the wealthier and more ambitious American students, spent some time in Europe, passing most of it in London, Edinburgh, and Paris, where he attended the great hospitals and the lectures of Abernethy, Cline, Haighton, Cooper, Bell, Gregory, Duncan, Dupuytren, Roux, and other masters in medicine, surgery, and obstetrics. While abroad he made the acquaintance of a number of eminent literary and scientific men, such as Brewster, Jameson, Walter Scott, Playfair, Gall, and Cuvier. He was successively Professor of Materia Medica, of the Institutes of Medicine, of Medical Jurisprudence, and of Obstetrics—the last in Rutgers Medical College. When this institution was disbanded he retired to private life and devoted himself exclusively to professional and charitable work. He contributed many valuable papers to the periodical press; became again for a short time an editor of a medical journal; brought out an edition of Denman's Midwifery, illustrated by copious notes and additions; wrote numerous biographical sketches, among others one of Dr. Samuel Latham Mitchill for my American Medical Biography; and late in life published his Historical Reminiscences of New York, a work which was most favorably received. He was, in fact, a prolific author, although he never published a systematic treatise on any branch of professional knowledge. He wielded a facile pen, and writing was evidently a source of great pleasure to him. In 1848, soon after the organization of that now flourishing institution, the New York Academy of Medicine, he was elected its President; and in 1850 Trinity College, Hartford, Connecticut, conferred upon him the degree of LL.D. He was a member of many American and foreign societies. He died in February, 1861, in the seventy-second year of his age, ripe in honor and universally regretted.

In summing up the character of Dr. Francis it is apparent from this brief sketch of his life that its salient traits were industry, versatility, benevolence, culture, probity, intelligence, and genius, all developed in a high degree. He had a warm sympathy for his fellow-beings, and a deep sense of the dignity and usefulness of his profession, of which he was so long one of the main pillars in his native city and State. He was eminently speculative, thoroughly orderly and systematic, and he was capable of taking a comprehensive view of everything upon which he was engaged. He took a deep interest in the establishment of the Woman's Hospital in New York, originated by Dr. J. Marion Sims. His interest in the Typographical Association of New York never flagged. Having himself been a printer in early life, he never lost an opportunity to promote the welfare and the respectability of that honored craft. He was a great lover of the fine arts, and of whatever was calculated to refine man's taste. The death of a young and promising son bearing his name was a great shock to him, from the effects of which he was long in recovering. His wife survived him several years. My friendship for Francis was warm, and the pleasantest relations existed between us.

March 14th.—The subjoined letter explains itself. So many aspersions have been cast upon the medical profession, even by some of its members, that I considered it my duty to enter the field and fire a shot at the enemy. A man who will not stand up for his guild when assailed by prejudice and malevolence is unworthy of his vocation. I desire to make a permanent record of this letter that it may be known that I have ever been ready to defend our honor and our rights:

From THE MEDICAL RECORD, *New York, March 13th, 1880.*

THE SOCIAL POSITION OF THE DOCTOR.

TO THE EDITOR OF THE MEDICAL RECORD.

DEAR SIR: In your issue of February 14th occurs the following sentence: "The social position of the doctor in this country is not, on the whole, a very high one; because the individual doctor has not the means, and often, it must be confessed, not the education or taste, to make it such." These remarks, it seems, were elicited by some strictures made by Dr. J. Milner Fothergill, of London, in a letter in a recent number of the Philadelphia Medical Times, respecting the social position of medical men and their wives in Great Britain, the latter of whom he declares to be mere pariahs or social outcasts without any position whatever. With this statement of Dr. Fothergill I have no concern, although I take leave to express my conviction that it is entirely erroneous.

To the assertion of the *Record* I am obliged to take exception, for I am sure it is not true. I have lived a good while in the world, and having seen a great deal of society I am safe in asserting that there is no profession, vocation, or pursuit which, on this side of the Atlantic, enjoys a higher social status than the medical, the clerical not excepted. The refined and educated American physician is a prince among men, and his wife is ever his equal in the social circle. Indeed, she is often a leader in, and a queen of, society. Who has not heard of the late Mrs. Octavia Walton Le Vert, the wife of the distinguished Dr. Henry S. Le Vert, of Mobile, Alabama? This lady, so accomplished as a linguist, as a writer, and as a conversationalist, was everywhere honored and caressed by the good and the great at home and abroad. No American woman ever received more homage or consideration at foreign courts than she. For many years she was a leader of fashion in her own city, rendering her house one of the most attractive in the country, and adding greatly to the reputation of her husband. Many similar instances might be cited of the wives of medical men, who, by their manners, culture, intelligence, and refinement, have attained to the highest social rank. In my own city the educated physician is, and always has been, the peer of the best man in the community, whatever may be his calling. There is never any large dinner-party, an evening gathering, or a club-meeting, at which there is not always a full representation of medical men, who never fail to hold their own by their good breeding, their general intelligence, or the elegance of their manners. The Wistar parties, so called in honor of Dr. Caspar Wistar, the celebrated Professor of Anatomy in the University of Pennsylvania, which, for nearly half a century, were the acknowledged centres of the refinement and intellectual culture of Philadelphia, were largely composed of medical men, among others, of Chapman, James, Dewees, Hays, Bache, René La Roche, Robley Dunglison, and George B. Wood, men who in a social point of view were the peers of the Binneys, the Sergeants, the Ingersolls, the Whartons, the Cadwaladers, and other distinguished laymen. The wives of these men were all on an equal footing. Where their husbands went they went; they were not pariahs or social outcasts. On the contrary, they were refined and cultured, the peers of any similar number of women in the country. What woman in America ever occupied a higher social position than the wife of Dr. James Rush, the author of The Philosophy of the Human Voice? The Morgans, Shippens, Rushes, Wistars, Bartons, and Dorseys of former days held, along with their wives, an equally commanding Social status.

During my residence at Cincinnati and at Louisville I never failed, in attending an evening party, a dinner, or a social entertainment of any kind, to meet with some of my professional friends and their wives, sons, or daughters; and I speak advisedly when I declare, although it may be at the expense of repeating myself, that there is not a city or town of any considerable size in the Union in which the same state of things does not obtain. If you look at the medical profession in your own city, you will find a further illustration of the truth of my statements. In 1828 I was at a Thursday evening reception given by the late Professor David Hosack, one of the medical luminaries of his day, to the New York Philosophical Society, which was graced by a large number of distinguished jurists, divines, artists, and literary gentlemen, including, as I well remember, such men as Francis, Macneven, Mott, J. Kearney Rodgers, and the great and good but eccentric Samuel Latham Mitchill, and their wives. It was one of the most brilliant assemblies I have ever witnessed. It is not necessary to ask what was the social status of such men as Bailey, Bard, Jones, Miller, Wright Post, and others, physicians whose names and fame are indissolubly associated with the glory of New York. It is folly to suppose that these men were deprived of the *entrée* of the best society of your city.

The refined and cultivated society of Boston has always had a large share of the medical element. Its doors have always been open to the Warrens, the Haywards, the Channings, the Bigelows, the Jacksons, the Shattucks, the Bowditches, the Storers, the Reynoldses, and others, as they still are to their descendants. Charleston, South Carolina, at one time contained the most brilliant and aristocratic society in this country. Nowhere has there been on this continent a higher type of civilization, or a greater amount of elegant and refined breeding, than in this once famous city—famous for its pretty and accomplished women, and its noble, chivalric, and intelligent men. Its social entertainments were of the most *recherché* and costly character. More old Madeira and sherry, Burgundy, and champagne were consumed, and a greater number of terrapins annually slaughtered at these reunions than in any other city of its size in America; and who that is familiar with the inner life of Charleston, as it existed only a short time ago, does not know that its society was largely indebted for the *éclat* which it so long enjoyed to its medical men and their wives? The refined Samuel Henry Dickson was a host in himself—a type of the true gentleman who would, in any land, have graced the society of princes. Who is not familiar with the high social position of the Ramsays, the Porchers, the Ravenels, the Holbrooks, the Geddingses, the Prioleaus, the Frosts, and other men whose names adorn the medical history of the United States?

What is true of our larger cities in this respect is emphatically true of every town, village, and hamlet of the Union. Go where we may, the refined and cultured physician is a man of mark, not a whit inferior in his social position to the clergyman, the lawyer, the scientist, or the merchant prince. A great deal is said at the present day of the want of refinement and of the defective education of the medical student, as if he were the veriest boor in Christendom, hardly half-civilized, unwashed, unkempt, and dressed in the shabbiest garb. We are all agreed that our systems of instruction are sadly out of joint; that they are not what they should be, or what, by-and-by, they must and will be; but I am quite sure that if you were some day to drop into my lecture-room, while I am engaged in addressing nearly six hundred students, assembled from all parts of the country, including representatives from different foreign lands, you would be surprised at their orderly conduct, their gentlemanly appearance, and their intelligent countenances. Not only are many of these youths well educated, but they have been reared under the best influences, and are destined to make their mark in the profession as well as in the social circle. Our army and naval surgeons are, as everybody knows, admitted into the best society, both at home and abroad. Again, not a few of our young physicians marry into our most distinguished families, which would assuredly not be the case if they were not well-bred, cultured, and meritorious men.

It might seem invidious in me, if not in bad taste, to institute a comparison between my own and the other learned professions; but I think you will bear me out in the assertion that if we take one hundred medical men, as we meet with them in our towns and cities, and place them side by side with an equal number of clergymen and lawyers, they will lose nothing by the comparison either in mental culture, high refinement, or social position.

I am not sufficiently familiar with the social status of medical men in Great Britain, but, unless I greatly err, Dr. Fothergill has been inadvertently betrayed into an unfortunate slander upon his professional brethren, which no one will probably regret more, or be more anxious to correct, than himself. My two visits abroad brought me into contact with a large number of medical men in England, Ireland, and Scotland, and I can conscientiously declare that I did not meet with one who was not entitled to be called a "gentleman." There are, of course, different grades of society, and it cannot be expected that every medical man should be received into the highest circles. There are comparatively few in any profession who are thus honored.

Every man holds his social position in his own hand. If it be not his birthright, he can, if he choose, or is worth anything at all, gradually attain it, despite untoward circumstances. The requirement for admission into society in Philadelphia is said to be family, or blue blood; in New York, wealth or money; and in Boston, literature or mental culture. This may be so, but it is so only in a certain degree, and these landmarks are rapidly becoming merged into one another. Character alone should be the test of social distinction in a truly civilized country.

I cannot agree with you when you say that social position is not a thing for which men should struggle. I cannot see how this can interfere with a physician's usefulness. On the contrary, I regard it as one of the highest and most sacred duties of the medical man to cultivate the graces and amenities of social life. The absence of this quality lowers any profession in public estimation, and reduces it to the level of the ordinary pursuits of life. Let the medical man aspire to be a refined and cultured gentleman, and do all he can to adorn the higher walks of life, for just in proportion as he does this will he be respected by the community, and add to the dignity of his profession.

> Very respectfully your obedient servant,
>
> S. D. GROSS.

PHILADELPHIA, February 25th, 1880.

[We are glad to hear from Professor Gross on this topic. Except in a few unimportant particulars, to which it is unnecessary now to refer, we entirely agree with him in the position he has taken. But we consider it quite fortunate for the readers of the *Record* that the points of difference were considered by him of sufficient importance to provoke the writing of his very interesting epistle.—Ed.]

At our fifty-fifth Commencement, which was held yesterday, March 13th, one hundred and ninety-six candidates received the degree, among whom were a number of bright, well-educated, genteel young men. The class numbered five hundred and seventy-two. The audience filled every nook and corner of the Academy of Music. The valedictory of Professor Rogers was eloquent and scholarly, and abounded in good advice.

March 15th.—I dined at half past five in the afternoon at the St. George Hotel with members of the American Philosophical Society, which celebrated its one hundredth anniversary. The Society was founded on the 25th of May, 1743, but was not incorporated until March 15th, 1780. The celebration, which was a private one, was under the supervision of William A. Ingham, J. Sergeant Price, and Henry Phillips, Jr. Nearly one hundred gentlemen sat down. The chair at the head of the table was occupied by the venerable President, Frederick Fraley, supported on his right by President Gilman of Johns Hopkins University, and on the left by Professor E. Otis Kendall of the University of Pennsylvania. Among other noted guests were Dr. Green and Professor Guyot of Princeton, Professor Henry Morton of the Stevens Institute, and Professor Gray of Boston. The *menu* was excellent; but, much to my regret, I was obliged to leave at eight o'clock, having previously engaged passage on the nine o'clock train for New Orleans. I therefore heard none of the speeches made during the evening. Among the members of the Society are some men of marked ability. Benjamin Franklin and Thomas Jefferson were its principal originators, and were for many years two of the most frequent contributors to its Proceedings. The Society has a respectable library, and publishes quarterly a small volume of

Transactions. Its foreign membership is very large, and embraces many illustrious savans of Europe.

In the evening at nine o'clock, accompanied by my younger son, Haller, I took my seat in the Pennsylvania railroad train for New Orleans, having previously engaged a section in the Pullman car. I had long ago contemplated performing this journey to gratify a desire to see more of the Southern States than I had yet seen, and to become better acquainted with their people, resources, and institutions. Then, again, Dr. T. G. Richardson and his excellent wife had repeatedly solicited me to pay them a visit, and to make their house my home during my sojourn in New Orleans. Moreover, my health was not very good, and I needed change of air, food, and scene after my hard winter's work. The distance of the Crescent City from the City of Brotherly Love is fifteen hundred and twenty-four miles by way of Louisville, Milan in Tennessee, and Jackson in Mississippi, and was made in two days and a half. The journey did not seriously fatigue me, although I spent three entire nights in the car. On our arrival at New Orleans, Dr. Richardson was in waiting, and drove us at once to his residence, where a cordial reception and a warm breakfast greeted us. The day was chiefly spent in rest. The following day I attended at the Grand Opera House the Commencement of the Medical Department of the University of Louisiana. The venerable Randall Hunt, the President of the Board of Trustees, conferred the degree upon forty-nine graduates, to whom at the close of the exercises, at the instance of Professor Richardson, I addressed a few words of advice and encouragement, in which I laid stress upon the importance of high mental culture, high social position, hard and persistent work, and the cultivation of the finer feelings of our nature. In commenting upon the last subject I referred in strong and affectionate terms to the late Dr. Warren Stone, and I closed by saying that he had been in medicine what Henry Clay had been in politics and statesmanship; and that his name would be handed down to posterity as the great Commoner of his profession. My remarks evidently struck a sympathetic chord, for they were received with applause by the large audience.

The medical department of this school is again in a flourishing condition, although it has not attained the standard it had before the war, when its classes were for several years, with one single exception, the largest in the Union. The school has three lecture-rooms, a large and valuable museum, and an able Faculty. Much attention is paid to the study of practical anatomy, and unusual advantages are afforded for clinical instruction by the Charity Hospital with seven hundred beds, generally well filled.

The general Commencement address, on the Relation of Communities and States during Epidemics, was delivered by Mr. James B. Eustis, formerly a United States Senator, in which he justly condemned the practice of isolating the affected districts by stopping navigation and railway facilities without the sanction of law, as was done during the prevalence of yellow fever in the South in 1878.

Judge Hunt is an aged man, in ill health, although his mind is still vigorous. On the Saturday before my departure from New Orleans I called at his office, and found him busily engaged in writing a lecture, which he intended to deliver during the afternoon to the law class in the University, in which he holds a professorship. He lamented the decline of learning and refinement of the bar, and highly praised the erudition, acumen, and intellectual powers of Marshall, Story, Pinkney, Chase, and other American lawyers. He has himself long been one of the lights of the Louisiana bar, formerly represented the State in Congress, and has been engaged all his life in useful and disinterested work. New Orleans is proud of him.

Two days after my arrival Dr. and Mrs. Richardson gave
me a reception at their residence, which was attended by
more than one hundred prominent medical gentlemen of
New Orleans, as well as by a number of laymen, among
others by the Rev. Dr. Leacock, Rev. Dr. Palmer, and
Mr. Eustis. This reception was as unexpected as it
was gratifying to me, and it brought me in contact with
a number of physicians and surgeons with whose names
I had long been familiar, but of whom personally I had
no knowledge. An equally gratifying surprise was the
banquet given to me by the physicians of New Orleans
on the following Wednesday, March 24th, at the old Spanish Fort on Lake Pontchartrain, fourteen miles from the
city. I subjoin the invitation:

New Orleans, March 23d, 1880.
Professor S. D. Gross, M. D., LL. D.

Dear Sir: In behalf of the physicians of New Orleans I beg
leave respectfully to request you to accept from them a reception
in your honor, to take place to-morrow, Wednesday, March 24th,
at the Spanish Fort, Lake Pontchartrain. A special train will leave
the depot on Canal Street at one o'clock P. M.

I beg leave also to extend an invitation to your son for the same
occasion.

Very respectfully, your obedient servant,
J. P. Davidson, M. D.,
*Chairman Joint Committee of New Orleans Parish Medical Society
and New Orleans Medical and Surgical Association.*

The day was pleasant, and the atmosphere balmy. The
dinner was served at three o'clock. The chairman, Dr.
J. P. Davidson, on taking his seat, extended to me a cordial welcome in the name of the medical societies of New
Orleans, and indulged in some flattering remarks, in which
he referred to my labors as an author, and to my protracted and faithful services as a public teacher of surgery.
On my left sat the Rev. Dr. Watkins, a well-known divine
of Natchez, the father of two promising young physicians

present on the occasion; and on my right sat Dr. Stern-
berger, U. S. A., a member of the National Board of
Health. Directly opposite to me sat Dr. Davidson. The
New Orleans press was represented. A number of toasts
were drunk, in which kind references were made to me.
When the viands were pretty well disposed of, Dr. W. H.
Watkins presented me with a book containing the auto-
graphs of the gentlemen who attended the banquet, accompanied with some felicitous remarks, to which of course I
was compelled to reply. My son said I acquitted myself
with credit, but this I much doubt, as my embarrassment
on such occasions is always great. The most happy effort
was that of my friend, Professor Stanford E. Chaillé, a man
of brains and high culture, always ready on a prandial
emergency. Professor Richardson was kept unexpectedly
away by an obstetric case, and Bemiss was off on an
aquatic excursion in the interests of the National Board
of Health, of which he is a prominent member. After
having sat for two hours and a half at table in animated
conversation, during which the wine was freely circulated,
the whistle gave warning of the time for our departure.
Thus, save the ride to the city, ended a day of which I
shall always cherish pleasant recollections.

During my sojourn in New Orleans, a period of ten days,
I dined with Professor Chaillé and Professor Logan of the
University of Louisiana, and I also breakfasted with Captain and Mrs. Jesse Bell, two old friends, Mrs. Bell being
a sister of the late Dr. Enders, of Baton Rouge, one of my
earliest and most cherished pupils. The pleasure of the occasion was enhanced by the presence of the great preacher,
the Rev. Dr. Palmer, and of Dr. Enders's daughter, Lina,
an adopted child of Mrs. Bell. I had one or two other
invitations to dine which want of time compelled me to
decline.

I could not think of leaving New Orleans without visiting Mrs. Stone, the widow of Dr. Warren Stone; and the

widow of my early friend, Dr. Charles A. Luzenberg. Accompanied by Mrs. Richardson, who is thoroughly familiar with the city, I called upon these two good women, and received from each of them a cordial welcome. Mrs. Stone, with her son Dr. Warren Stone and his children, lives in the house in which her husband died. She is a good-looking, well-preserved woman, now bordering on seventy years. She spoke in the most affectionate manner of her late husband, and a few days after our interview sent me his photograph, with other mementos of him. An excellent full-length portrait of him, painted by a prominent New Orleans artist, hangs in her parlor, and there is another in the parlor of the Charity Hospital, but the latter is on a small scale, and is indifferent both as a likeness and as a work of art.

I did not know Dr. Stone intimately, but we often met, and I had therefore excellent opportunities of forming a proper estimate of his character as a man, as a physician, and as a surgeon. Born at St. Albans, Vermont, in 1808, he entered with a limited education as a private pupil the office of Dr. Twitchell, of Keene, New Hampshire, who long stood at the head of his profession as a surgeon in that part of New England. His degree was obtained in 1831 from the medical school at Pittsfield, Massachusetts, among whose professors were Elisha Bartlett, Alonzo Clark, Willard Parker, and other great teachers. Aware of what little account a prophet is in his own country, he boldly made his way to New Orleans with hardly a cent in his pocket. Though a stranger among a new people, he soon became domesticated, made friends, and found himself usefully, if not profitably, occupied. His first public office was the Demonstratorship of Anatomy in the University of Louisiana. In a few years he was translated to the chair of Anatomy, and, on the resignation of Dr. Luzenberg, to that of Surgery, which he held until 1872, when ill health compelled him to retire from the school. He was for many years one of the surgeons of the Charity Hospital, and in 1839 he opened a commodious private infirmary, in which he treated a great number of patients and performed many of the more important operations. From this infirmary he received no substantial addition to his fortune, and soon after the close of the war its doors were permanently closed for the want of patronage. It will thus be perceived that Dr. Stone worked his way up from an humble to an exalted position, and it will not detract from the merits of his contemporaries to say that long before his death he was the acknowledged head of his profession in the Southern States. His practice was extensive ; his experience vast, both as a surgeon and as a physician. He was a skilful diagnostician. As to his merits as an operator or mechanical surgeon various opinions have been expressed ; and as I never saw him use any instrument, I am not in a position to form a judgment upon the subject. His boldness and decision no one will doubt; and if he was deficient in the finer manipulations of his art, he ably performed all the more common operations. He was of lofty stature, with a noble forehead and expressive features. He was rather slow of speech, and as a lecturer deficient in animation, although he never failed to express himself with force and clearness. No one could listen to him either in the amphitheatre or in private conversation without being convinced that he was a man of great intelligence. He had a vast and most retentive memory. His influence in New Orleans, and, indeed, in the Southern States generally, was great. He had a hand and a heart for every one. During the prevalence of the epidemics which so frequently desolated New Orleans and other Southern towns and cities, the terror-stricken people trusted in him as if he had been a god. Unselfishness was one of the attributes of his nature. Whatever he did or said was without fear or malice.

Dr. Stone left behind him no written monument. He

possessed no facility as a writer, and although he was for a short time the editor of a medical journal, he seldom contributed anything to its pages. It is much to be regretted that his experience was buried with him. One would suppose that a man, absorbed for so many years in practice in the largest and most wealthy city in the South, would have left a considerable estate at the time of his death; but this was not the case. When the war was over he found himself in straitened circumstances, with no prospect of improving his condition. Doubtless his condition was principally due to the misfortunes growing out of the war; but it was also due to sheer mismanagement of his private business, such as the collection of bills, for which he had no taste or qualifications. He could make money, but could not keep it. Dr. Stone died in December, 1872, at the age of sixty-five, deeply regretted by his fellow-citizens, by the Southern people, and by the American medical profession. It is said that, although his manners were blunt, he never had an enemy, and that he was idolized by his patients and friends.

I called on Mrs. Luzenberg a few days after my visit to Mrs. Stone. Mrs. Richardson and I entered a horse-car, or rather a mule-car, and after passing through a number of narrow, crooked streets in the old parts of the city near the river, reached the humble dwelling of this lady, now eighty years of age. For nearly thirty-two years she has been a widow. She was married to Dr. Luzenberg in 1832, when she was a young and wealthy widow of the name of Fort, the daughter of a New York banker. What a contrast between then and now! Her last husband left her a handsome fortune, much of it the accumulations from his own extensive and lucrative practice. The war swept nearly all away. Notwithstanding that she is advanced in years, and withal partially blind, she seemed to be in good spirits, and conversed with animation and directness upon various topics. She frequently mentioned

her husband, whom she idolized. She has only one surviving child, a son, who was educated at Princeton, and
who has for several years been city attorney. A young
granddaughter, Miss Lizzie McCay, shares her solitude,
and contributes to her happiness. I reminded Mrs. Luzenberg of the pleasant breakfast which I took with her
and her husband, in company with Dr. Harlan, the naturalist, at their beautiful residence in 1842, when her husband occupied so conspicuous a place in the profession of
his adopted city, while she was one of the leading women
in fashionable society.

When I entered the Jefferson Medical College in 1826
Charles Aloysius Luzenberg served as Demonstrator of
Anatomy under Professor N. R. Smith. Young as he
was, he was a good talker, and an excellent anatomist and
demonstrator. He took his degree the ensuing spring,
passing a brilliant examination. He settled in Burlington, New Jersey, which place, however, he soon left, in
consequence of some difficulty, the precise nature of which
I never learned. It was thus that I lost sight of him until
some years afterwards, when I was told that he had settled in New Orleans, and was rapidly attaining distinction as a surgeon and general practitioner. I had been
but a short time in Cincinnati when I received a letter
from him urging me to accept the chair of Anatomy in
the Medical College of Louisiana, at that time recently
organized and now known as the University of Louisiana.
My connection with the Medical College of Ohio induced me to decline the offer, and it was not until
1842 that I had the pleasure of meeting him again
during a brief visit which I made to New Orleans.
He occupied for a time the chairs of Anatomy and Surgery in his new school; but meeting with much opposition, he abandoned his cherished object of building up a
great institution, and forswore teaching, which had so
long been the desire of his life. Dr. Luzenberg had a

warm, positive, and impulsive temperament, and it is not improbable that he occasionally gave vent to expressions for which in his cooler moments he was sorry. However this may be, a hostile clique gathered around him, which disgusted him with his associates and induced him to devote himself exclusively to the practical duties of his calling.

Luzenberg was a man of fine intellect and high culture. He had the advantages of a good classical education, of foreign travel, of extensive reading, and of large intercourse with the world. He was born in Verona, in Italy, July, 1805. He removed to the borders of France and Germany, and made himself master of the languages of these three countries—an accomplishment which was of vast use to him in New Orleans, whose population is made up of immigrants from all parts of the world. He was well versed in the Latin language, which he is said to have spoken with fluency. His library was large, and included the choicest editions of the works of the fathers of the profession. His collection of modern works was rich in the departments of natural history, zoology, and comparative anatomy. Most of his leisure hours were spent among his books; and it is due to him to say that he was probably the most cultivated and learned physician whom the South has ever had. He wrote with grace and elegance. A few fugitive pieces in the medical periodicals of the day are all that remain of his pen. His vast experience, like that of Stone, is forever lost.

Dr. Luzenberg was of medium height, well proportioned, with light-blue eyes, fine head and face, and delicate hands. As a husband and a father no one was ever more beloved. His death, in July, 1848, at the early age of forty-three, was caused by disease of the heart, and was deeply lamented.

Luzenberg was an expert operator, and his feats with the knife have associated his name with the history of surgery in this country. Among his greatest triumphs may

be mentioned extirpation of the parotid gland for sarcoma-
tous degeneration; ligation of the primitive iliac artery for
the cure of aneurism of the external iliac; and the excision
of six inches of the ileum in a case of strangulated hernia,
the ends of the bowel being stitched together according to
the principles laid down in my monograph on Wounds of
the Intestines. In all these cases the patients made rapid
and permanent recoveries. He treated numerous cases of
cataract, his favorite operation being couching, then and
for a long time afterwards a common but objectionable
procedure; for the immediate effects, though flattering,
were followed by the ultimate destruction, complete and
irremediable, of the eye as an organ of vision. Dr. Luzenberg was the founder of the Society of Natural History and
the Sciences of New Orleans, and of the Louisiana Medico-
Chirurgical Society, of both of which he was the first president. Of the latter I was elected a member early in my
professional life.

Dr. Luzenberg had a large collection of books on yellow
fever, with whose history, symptomatology, diagnosis, and
treatment he had unbounded opportunities of making himself familiar, both in hospital and private practice. There
was hardly a monograph on the subject in any language
which was not to be found in his library; and it was his
intention to publish an exhaustive treatise upon that horrible disease, illustrated by numerous drawings representing the varied expressions of the patient's countenance
and the pathological changes revealed by the knife after
death. The manuscript was composed in the Latin language. Alas, he did not survive to complete his self-
imposed task! and it remained for my learned friend René
La Roche, of Philadelphia, to fill this gap in our literature.

Dr. T. G. Richardson came of an excellent family, distinguished for its piety, enterprise, and correct citizenship.
He has long been a member of the Presbyterian Church,

and is an admirer of Dr. Palmer, of whose church he is an elder. He has been twice married. His first wife was a daughter of the late Professor Charles W. Short, the Kentucky botanist, by whom he had four children, one of which died of scarlet fever; while the other three perished with their mother on the Mississippi River, the steamer on which they had been passengers having taken fire a short distance below Natchez. Whether they were burned or drowned I believe could never be determined. The maid of the party was alone saved. My poor friend had been expecting his family every hour, and was reading the morning papers in the St. Charles Hotel when the frightful news met his eye. This melancholy occurrence happened soon after the close of the war, and produced an effect from which it is doubtful whether he has entirely recovered. His present wife was a Miss Slocum, a woman of refinement, well known for her lovely character and her charitable deeds. Dr. Richardson lives in a pleasant part of the city, in a handsome house, adorned by a beautiful garden and a conservatory abounding in ferns. His library is not large, but rich in standard authors. His excellent work on Anatomy has reached a second edition. He was for a time one of the editors of the New Orleans Medical Journal, and has contributed a number of valuable papers to the periodical press. His style as a writer is clear and graphic. Having for a number of years occupied the chair of Anatomy in the University of Louisiana, he was, on the death of Dr. Stone, transferred to the chair of Surgery, which he has ever since most ably filled. As an operator, as a general practitioner, and as a didactic and clinical teacher he enjoys a wide reputation. During the war he espoused the cause of the Confederacy; and, like all who were on that side, suffered in his private fortune. A friendly correspondence has long existed between us, and there is no man in the profession for whom I cherish a warmer regard.

Having long been anxious to see Mobile, I availed myself of the opportunity afforded by my New Orleans visit to gratify my wishes. The journey, occupying about six hours, was anything but pleasant, and we were glad when we were set down at our hotel, which, though at one time the best in the city, was now old, shaky, and uninviting. I soon found myself in the hands—I had almost said the arms—of my friend, Dr. Mastin, the accomplished gentleman and able surgeon, who showed my son and myself every attention, driving us through the most pleasant parts of the city and pointing out to us every object of interest. The next day we were presented to the ladies of his family; and at one o'clock we sat down to an elaborate luncheon, at which we met several distinguished physicians, besides members of the Mobile bar. Mobile has many capabilities, but is still laboring under the depressing effects of our late war. It has a medical college, but few students and no great professors.

Augusta, Georgia, was our next objective point. Here we fared well under the guidance of two of its most prominent medical men, my kind friends, Dr. Henry F. Campbell, and Dr. Dugas, the veteran surgeon. The latter, now an octogenarian, crippled in health but still active in mind, was as much interested in the progress of medicine as in his earlier days. He was one of the founders of the Augusta Medical College, and was for many years the leading surgeon of his State. We were indebted to him for a charming drive through the suburbs of the city as far as the Sand Hills, well known for its handsome residences and as a winter resort for invalids. In the evening we were entertained by Dr. Campbell and his family with genuine Southern hospitality.

A journey of eight hours brought us to Savannah, a beautiful city, literally built upon sand, distinguished for its residences, for its square or park, and for the intelligence and hospitality of its citizens. The spring roses, which form so conspicuous a feature in the scenery of the city, had already, early as it was in the season, in great measure ceased to bloom; but there was an abundance of other flowers to atone for their absence. Bonaventure, which is distant four miles from Savannah, is an object of much interest to the visitor. Originally the seat of a wealthy English family, it passed in 1849 from its control into that of the Evergreen Cemetery Company; and although its gates stand wide open, so as to afford the public free entrance, it is essentially a private burying-ground. Its charm lies in its majestic live oaks, so draped in funereal moss as to form archways in every direction, the whole imparting a weird appearance to the place, the home of many of Savannah's dead. Our drive, which lay over a sandy road, afforded much enjoyment, enlivened as it was by our chatty and intelligent cicerone. In the afternoon we lunched with my friend Dr. Thomas and his agreeable family. An hour later we were on our way to Charleston, which we reached the same evening at eleven o'clock.

Of Charleston I have little to say. My visit was too brief to do justice to a city once the residence of Calhoun, Hayne, Langdon Cheves, Dickson, Geddings, and other prominent men—a city so well known for its accomplished men, its refined women, and its cultured society, in which everybody was so much at ease and felt so little concern for the morrow. I wish her every prosperity and a speedy reinstatement in her ancient glory. I knew many of her older medical men, men who were a power in their day and generation; and I loved and respected them, as I love and respect those who have come into prominence since the close of the war.

The morning after our arrival we drove through the city to inspect the various objects of interest; visited the beautiful cemetery several miles beyond, a fit resting-place for Charleston's great citizens; spent the afternoon on Sullivan Island; and in the evening attended the Commencement exercises of Charleston College. The next day we sailed up the Ashley River to Drayton Hall, stuck fast on a sandbar for nearly two hours, and arrived just in time to see nothing, our stay being hardly twenty minutes. The azaleas, so abundant in the proper season, were not in flower. A number of physicians paid their respects to me, among others Drs. Porcher and Kinloch, members of the Faculty of the Medical College of South Carolina. To the younger Dr. Porcher my son and I were indebted for much kindness.

One of the most interesting persons whom I met at Charleston was the Rev. Mr. Yates. In 1828, Dr. Valentine Mott excised his left collar bone on account of a large tumor, the operation occupying nearly four hours. More than forty ligatures were required to control the hemorrhage. When I saw Mr. Yates in 1880 he was seventy-two years of age, and in enjoyment of excellent health, with a good use of the corresponding limb. Mott styled this his Waterloo operation, as it was performed in June, the month in which was fought the great battle.

2—15

CHAPTER V.

MAY 17th.—The following letters were received by me this morning:

CORPUS CHRISTI COLLEGE, CAMBRIDGE, May 4th, 1880.

SIR: It is the intention of the University to confer honorary degrees on certain persons of eminence at the meeting of the British Medical Association in Cambridge in August next.

I am requested by the Council of the Senate to ask whether you will be able to attend on the occasion, and whether you will allow yourself to be nominated to the Senate for the honorary degree of LL.D., the highest honorary degree which it is in the power of the Senate to confer.

I have the honor to be, sir, your faithful servant,

H. Y. PEROWNE, *Vice-Chancellor*.

CAMBRIDGE, May 5th, 1880.

DEAR PROFESSOR GROSS: I sincerely hope the offer of the honorary degree of our University which you will have received through the Vice-Chancellor will tempt you to come among us again, and I write to say that we will receive you heartily, and will provide accommodations for you during the meeting, whether you come alone or bring all your family with you. Kindly let me know as soon as you can whether you will be able to come.

My family unite in very warm regards.

Yours truly,   GEORGE M. HUMPHRY.

This compliment was altogether unexpected by me, and is therefore highly gratifying, because it serves to show that I have warm friends in England unwilling to forget me. Dr. Humphry, of whom I have spoken elsewhere, is a Fellow of the Royal Society of London, an accomplished scholar, and an author of note. His treatise on the Human Skeleton and various other productions have made his name widely known on both sides of the Atlantic. He is an excellent physiologist and comparative anatomist, an original investigator, an able teacher, and a philosophical thinker. He is now the President-elect of the British Medical Association, which meets at Cambridge on the 10th of August next.

Sunday, May 30th, 1880.—I went to New York this afternoon in order to attend to-morrow the meeting of the Medical College Association, of which I was elected president at Atlanta last May. In the car I met Generals Hancock and Augur, the former of whom made himself especially agreeable by the recital of some interesting anecdotes concerning his military life in Mexico. At parting he gave me a pressing invitation to visit him and Mrs. Hancock at their residence on Staten Island.

The Association unanimously adopted the amendment to its by-laws, offered a year ago by Professor Menees, of Nashville, which makes an attendance of three courses of lectures obligatory upon the student before he can become a candidate for graduation. This important regulation is to go into operation in 1882–'83, and there is little doubt in my mind that it will be generally adopted by the schools of the country by that time. When this object, so long prayed for by the leading physicians of the country, as well as by many of our more intelligent laymen, shall be attained, the nation will have cause to congratulate itself upon an event which cannot fail to be of vast benefit to it.

The meeting of the American Medical Association, the

thirty-first, was largely attended, more than a thousand delegates being present. Dr. Sayre, the President, delivered a good address. He dwelt principally upon the brilliant progress of medicine and surgery in this country during the last half century, upon the importance of the adoption of the metric system by the profession, and upon the growing necessity of establishing a medical journal, similar to that of the British Medical Association Journal, so ably conducted by Mr. Ernest Hart, of London, for the publication of our Transactions, thus doing away with the large volumes which are seldom ready until six or eight months after the adjournment of the meetings, and which hardly any one ever consults or even reads. I advocated the adoption of this plan years ago, and the subject was at the time referred to a committee of prominent members, who never reported. What the fate of the present recommendation may be remains to be seen.

The entertainments given to the Association by the medical men and the citizens of New York were on a costly scale, and added much to the enjoyment of the meeting. The Academy of Music, where the principal reception took place, was floored over, and was crowded to excess. The fare was, I am told, very good, and the Committee of Arrangements had wisely excluded wine from the bill. A theatrical entertainment was given on the second night of the meeting, at which Booth, the eminent actor, appeared, with his usual ability, in the character of Iago; Othello was assigned to Mr. Robinson. The crowd was great, a large number of the members being present, many accompanied by their wives and daughters. The receptions given by Mr. August Belmont, by Mayor Cooper, and by Drs. Barker and Thomas at the New York Academy of Medicine were elaborate and well attended. My host, Mr. Samuel Smith, gave me a handsome dinner; and I breakfasted with my old pupil, Dr. Bozeman. I dined with the elder Flint at the Manhattan Club, and

with the gynæcologists at the residence of Dr. Emmet.
Before I left home Dr. Barker had sent me an invitation to
dine with him, but it failed to reach me. I was unable to
accompany the steamboat excursion given by the Messrs.
Wood, the eminent New York publishers. The meeting
of the Association was, on the whole, a success, although
a considerable number of the more prominent New York
physicians failed to participate in it.

One of the objects of my visit to New York was to assist
in permanently organizing the American Surgical Association, initiated by me at Atlanta in 1879. For reasons
which need not now be stated, the effort was postponed
until Monday, May 31st, 1880; and in the mean time a
circular setting forth the objects of the proposed Society,
signed by Professors Dugas of Augusta, Georgia, Briggs
of Nashville, Dawson of Cincinnati, Gunn of Chicago, and
myself, was sent to the principal surgeons of the United
States, soliciting their coöperation, and requesting them to
meet us on the day above named at the hall of the College
of Physicians and Surgeons of New York immediately
after the adjournment of the Medical College Association.
The meeting was organized by calling Professor Lewis A.
Sayre to the chair, and appointing Professor W. W. Dawson secretary. Afterwards Dr. J. R. Weist of Richmond,
Indiana, was made secretary. The constitution and by-
laws, prepared by myself, were temporarily adopted. The
next morning a permanent organization was effected by
appointing me, by a unanimous vote, President; Professor
Dugas of Georgia, and James R. Wood of New York,
Vice-Presidents; J. R. Weist, Secretary; and John H.
Packard, of Philadelphia, Treasurer. The attendance was
slim, not one of the prominent surgeons of the city of
New York being present. The next meeting will take
place at Richmond, Virginia, during the session of the
American Medical Association, at five o'clock in the afternoon on Thursday, terminating on Saturday. I expect

much from this Association, and it is proper here to add that it is an independent organization, having no connection whatever with the American Medical Association. Its object is to foster surgical art, science, education, and literature, to cultivate good feeling in the profession, and to unite the prominent surgeons of the country in one harmonious body.

After consultation with my children I determined to visit Europe, and to avail myself of the honor so graciously proffered by my English friends. I accordingly engaged a room for myself and my son Haller on the steamer Abyssinia for the 23d of June. As the time approached for her departure, the fear of seasickness overcame me and I gave it up. Subsequently, however, I yielded to the importunities of my family and embarked on the steamer Indiana, Captain Sargent, which left Philadelphia on the 7th of July for Liverpool, where, after a very smooth passage, unattended by seasickness on my part, we arrived on Sunday evening, July 18th. The day after we started was my seventy-fifth birthday.

My son and I stopped at the Adelphi Hotel, Liverpool, until Tuesday morning, when we visited Chester to inspect its famous Cathedral and the Roman walls, of which there are some fine specimens in different parts of this ancient town. In the afternoon we left for Bowness, which we reached in the evening. The next day, a charming one, we rode on the top of a tally-ho coach through the Lake region, as it is termed, as far as Keswick on Derwentwater, returning in the afternoon, scarcely at all fatigued by our ride of forty-six miles. The scenery, made up of lofty hills a great part of the way, is beautiful, in many places even grand; but the lakes themselves are insignificant compared with many of those of our own country. In the little churchyard at Grasmere we stopped to see the grave of Wordsworth, and were struck with the simplicity of the tombstone which marks the spot. The grave of his

young and gifted friend, Hartley Coleridge, who died at
an early age from the effects of dissipation, is close by.
In the church itself, where Wordsworth was a frequent
attendant, is a tablet erected to his memory, with an elaborate inscription commemorative of his life and labors.
All the villages and towns through which our road lay
presented a neat appearance, with no marks of poverty.
Many of the dwellings were handsome. Before leaving
the district we spent a day in visiting Coniston Lake and
Furness Abbey, about twenty miles from Windermere.
The ride extended through a lovely stretch of country,
and the lake was in view for several miles. The abbey
is situated in a retired valley, on a lawn embellished with
shrubbery, and it must have been a noble structure in its
day. It is composed of red sandstone from neighboring
quarries. Many of the walls are in excellent preservation.
On our return the train stopped at the foot of Lake Windermere, which we ascended as far as Bowness, a distance
of about six miles, in a small steamer crowded with passengers.

From Bowness, after a sojourn of two pleasant days,
we went to the newly-opened Grand Hotel at Trafalgar
Square, London, where we remained sixteen days, spending much of our time in sight-seeing, the most fatiguing
of all occupations in which a man can be engaged. Although most of the places we visited we had seen in 1872,
yet there was much to interest me, especially in Westminster Abbey, the Houses of Parliament, and the Tower. At
the British Museum I had the pleasure of again meeting
Mr. Richard Owen, the naturalist, whom I saw here in
1872, and soon afterwards at a large dinner party at the
house of Dr., now Sir George, Burrows. The grand old
man, now seventy-five years of age, was descending the
stairway as we were going up. He was on his way to
fill an engagement, and had only time to shake hands
with my son and myself and to express the wish that we

would call upon him the next day, when he should be at
leisure to see us.   Unfortunately our arrangements rendered it impossible to comply with his request.   It was
gratifying to find him in excellent health.   The reputation of Professor Owen as a scientist, naturalist, palæontologist, and comparative anatomist is world-wide ; and
few living men have done more for the advancement of
natural science than he.   He has led a life of incessant
labor, and is still full of ardor and enthusiasm in the pursuit of knowledge.   He is the author of numerous works,
mainly founded upon original observations.   He studied
medicine in Edinburgh and London, and was for a short
time Hunterian Professor at the Royal College of Surgeons.   Notwithstanding his occupations as a naturalist
and scientist, he has devoted much attention, especially
of late years, to sanitary science.   He has been the recipient of many honors, is a member of numerous learned
societies both at home and abroad, and in 1873 was made
a Companion of the Bath.

In London a dinner was given to me by Mr. William
Adams, the distinguished orthopædic surgeon, at which
were present among others Mr. John Wood, the surgeon of
King's College Hospital ; Ernest Hart, editor of the British
Medical Journal ; Dr. Hare, a London physician, and Mr.
Trübner, the publisher.   Several of these gentlemen were
accompanied by their wives.   The *menu* was an elaborate
one, and the conversation animated.   Mr. Erichsen also
gave us a dinner, at which I made the acquaintance of
Dr. Garrod, the author of the famous treatise on Gout and
Rheumatism, and had the pleasure of again meeting Mr.
Christopher Heath, successor to Mr. Erichsen in the London University and University College Hospital, and the
author of several valuable works on Surgery.   Before I
left London I spent an agreeable evening with Sir James
and Lady Paget at their residence.   Many of my friends
were out of town, and hence I failed to see them.   I had

the gratification, however, of shaking hands with Dr. Peacock, Mr. John Gay, and several others whose friendship I greatly value.

I spent a day and a night at Oxford with my old friend, Professor Acland. Although I was quite unwell, I went with him in the afternoon to a regatta, in which his University always takes so deep an interest. The professor was soon in his private boat rowing with his coat off; and he insisted that I should accompany him some distance up the river in order that I might obtain a better view of the races. Since my last visit he had lost his wife, and I was glad to find that a memorial, entitled the "Sarah Acland Memorial and Home for Nurses," had been erected in her honor in Wellington Square, in the city which she so long adorned by her many virtues and her charitable deeds.

While in London I had the pleasure of meeting at St. Thomas's Hospital Mr. John Croft, who performed several operations in my presence under what is called the Lister spray; and at St. Bartholomew's I met Mr. Luther Holden and Mr. Savory. Mr. Savory excised several tumors, operations easy of performance and of no special interest. Most of the London hospitals at this season of the year are slimly attended by patients and students, while some are entirely closed to undergo the necessary cleansing and repairs. One of them, around which many historic memories cluster, is St. George's, the scene for so many years of the labors and triumphs of John Hunter, the founder of modern surgery. The story of his death is a sad one. He had long labored under disease of the heart, attended with occasional paroxysms of suffering. One morning while visiting the hospital he got into a dispute with one of the managers; angry words ensued, and he was immediately seized with an attack of cardiac distress, from the effects of which he died almost instantaneously. He was sixty-five years old, and was buried in the church of St. Martin-

2—16

in-the-Fields, from which his remains were removed in 1859 to the north aisle of Westminster Abbey.

The Hospital, which is situated at Hyde Park, is a large building and contains three hundred and fifty-three beds. At the time of my visit few patients were in it, as the annual renovation was going on, and the surgeons were absent. A new museum and lecture-room had been added— the latter, although small, being very fine, well lighted, and convenient, and the former well stored with rare pathological specimens and a valuable collection of urinary and other calculi. In the passage leading to the museum hangs an interesting relic—the hide of Jenner's famous cow, a short-horn with spotted skin; this furnished the original vaccine matter which has rendered man in all civilized countries invulnerable to smallpox infection. The celebrated preparation of aneurism of the popliteal artery, for which Hunter originally ligated the femoral, is, if I mistake not, in the Hunterian Museum. The library attached to the hospital comprises more than five thousand volumes, most of them being old books. It was in this hospital that Physick, a favorite pupil of John Hunter, served his apprenticeship, extending over a period of four years, and laid the foundation of his immense reputation.

The Hunterian Museum, situated in Lincoln's Inn Fields, in the grand edifice owned by the Royal College of Surgeons of England, comprises a world of objects of interest in human, comparative, and morbid anatomy. The original collection, although large as the result of the labors of one man, was a mite in comparison with the present gigantic accumulation made by many hundred contributors and admirers of the founder. The department of comparative anatomy in particular has been greatly extended during the last twenty-five years, chiefly by the dissections of Professor Owen; while that of pathological anatomy has been enriched by the labors and exertions of its able curator, Mr. Flower. The collection of urinary calculi is by far the finest in the world. There is also a magnificent set of preparations illustrative of diseased bones, joints, and arteries, including a large number of cases of aneurism in all its varieties and forms. The library comprises nearly forty thousand volumes, and is receiving constant accessions from all parts of the world. The Museum is divided into numerous compartments, one of which, the examination-room as it is called, is ornamented with portraits of Harvey, Cowper, Sheldon, Pott, and other illustrious men. In the vestibule, at the top of the stairs, are busts of Cheselden, J. Hunter, Cline, Sir Astley Cooper, Guthrie, Home, Sir Charles Bell, Grainger, and several others. A marble statue of Hunter graces the first room on the lower floor. It is the work of Wilkes, and represents the great interpreter of nature in the sitting posture, in an attitude of contemplation.

We left London for Cambridge, a distance of fifty-one miles, on Monday, August 9th, to attend the forty-eighth session of the British Medical Association. Rooms had been engaged for us by my young friend, Mr. Humphry, son of the President-elect of the Association. About eight hundred physicians from all parts of Great Britain, as well as several distinguished foreigners, were present. Among the latter were Dr. Brown-Séquard, of Paris, and Professor Donders, of Utrecht. There were also several delegates from the American Medical Association. The session was opened without prayer by the President, Dr. O'Connor, of Cork, where the meeting had been held the previous year. After some well-chosen and complimentary remarks the chair was assigned to Dr. Humphry, who presided during the remainder of the session with dignity and ability. The address in surgery was delivered by Mr. Timothy Holmes, the well-known author, Surgeon to St. George's Hospital, and consisted principally of an account of excisions of the hip- and knee-joints, in which he attempted to show that the profession was mainly indebted

to the late Sir William Fergusson for the revival of these
operations.   He did not allude to the labors of the late Mr.
Syme of Edinburgh.   The address was well written and
well delivered, and was warmly applauded by the Association.   On the second day of the meeting—August 11th—at
noon, in the Senate House of the University of Cambridge,
in the presence of an immense audience, the degree of
Doctor of Laws was conferred upon twelve gentlemen,
previously selected for the purpose as representing the
interests and the status of the medical profession of their
respective countries.   The candidates, arranged in pairs,
and arrayed in red gowns furnished by the University,
marched in procession down the aisle and took their seats
on the platform.   After writing their full names in a
register, they were called out one after another by the
beadle and presented to the orator.   In a Latin address
the orator recounted the merits and standing of the candidate and presented him to the Vice-Chancellor, who,
seated in his chair and grasping the candidate's right
hand, closed the ceremony by conferring the degree upon
him in a brief Latin speech, spoken in a gentle tone.
The foreigners headed the list, Brown-Séquard and Donders leading; then I and Sir William Jenner followed.
When the name of Sir William Gull was called there was
a general uproar and hissing, lasting five minutes, and interrupting the ceremonies.   This conduct, in which many
of the members of the Association participated, is said to
have been due to the fact that, a few weeks previously, Sir
William Gull disparaged, in a harsh and disloyal manner,
the skill of Dr. Pavy, a member of the medical staff of
Guy's Hospital, in treating a case of disease in that institution.   The incident, into the particulars of which I shall
not enter, produced much indignation among the physicians of London, heightened, it should seem, by the fact
that Sir William had been equally culpable on several former occasions.   During this interruption he maintained

dignified silence, looking more like a statue than a human being. Of course he must have felt deeply mortified. I will only add that Sir William has, much to his credit, risen from humble life to an exalted rank in his profession, that he enjoys a large and lucrative practice as a physician, and that his ability, experience, skill, and learning are remarkable. His manners are, however, unpopular; and, whether deservedly so or not, he has many enemies.

Two of the gentlemen upon whom the degree was intended to be conferred were absent, namely, Dr. Paul Broca of Paris and Dr. Chauveau of Lyons. By a curious coincidence poor Broca, a month before the meeting, suddenly died from the rupture of an aneurism of the aorta, having only a few hours previously attended a meeting of the Senate, of which he had lately been elected a member. He was a native of St. Foy, in the Gironde, and was only fifty-six years of age at the time of his death. I met him in 1868, first at La Charité, Paris, and a short time after at Dr. Bateman's, of Norwich, during the meeting in that city of the British Association for the Advancement of Science. He was of medium height, had a fine face and commanding presence, and was highly cultured and full of intelligence and good nature. He studied medicine in Paris, soon acquired a high reputation as an original investigator, and was appointed at a comparatively early age Professor of Surgical Pathology in the College of France. He was an able clinical teacher and an expert operator, and thoroughly devoted to his hospital work. His pupils were warmly attached to him, and loved to follow him through the surgical wards and thence to the amphitheatre, where he never failed to delight and instruct them. For many years past nearly all the time he could snatch from his professional labors he gave to the science of anthropology, of which he may be said to have been the founder in France. He wrote numerous papers upon the subject, and established a periodical for the purpose of disseminating correct and useful information among the people as well as among scientists. His death has left a void in this branch of knowledge; but it is gratifying to know that the work which he has left unfinished will be carried forward by his many intelligent pupils.

Dr. Brown-Séquard I had seen many years before, but I had not met him for a long time, and was sorry to find that he looked much older than is usual with one of his age. He is of medium stature, and of rather slight frame, with a white beard and moustache. Although he has been a great deal in my own country, as well as in England, he speaks English indifferently. He was born in 1818 in the Island of Mauritius. His father, Edward Brown, was a Philadelphian, and his mother, named Séquard, was a French lady. He took his degree of M. D. in Paris in 1840, and early distinguished himself as an experimental physiologist. The results of his researches are embodied in numerous papers and brochures, which are universally regarded as among the most valuable ever contributed to the elucidation of the functions and diseases of the nervous system. He was connected with several medical colleges in the United States. A few years ago he was appointed Professor of Physiology in the School of Medicine in Paris, where he will no doubt, despite his restless disposition, reside during the remainder of his life.

It was pleasant to me to meet, as a recipient of the honors of the occasion, my old friend Sir George Burrows. I have spoken of him elsewhere, but it may not be amiss here to say that he is a graduate of Cambridge, both in art and medicine, and that he is Physician in Ordinary to the Queen. He is a Consulting Physician to St. Bartholomew's Hospital, and the author of a monograph on Disorders of the Cerebral Circulation, as well as of a number of valuable contributions to the periodical press.

Dr. Andrew Wood, of Edinburgh, is a member of the General Medical Council, and has for many years been interested in the progress of medical education. He is an elegant scholar, and has acquired reputation by his excellent translations of Horace and of several of Schiller's poems.

After the exercises were concluded the men who had been honored walked in procession to Corpus Christi College, where they lunched with the Vice-Chancellor, the Rev. Dr. Perowne, and the Fellows of the College. On the evening of the same day I dined with the Irish graduates of the University of Cambridge. Dr. George E. Paget, Regius Professor of Medicine, had kindly sent my invitation to Philadelphia before I left home. The company, including many ladies, numbered about seventy. The occasion was a very pleasant one, and it was late before we left the table. Many little speeches were made, among others one by me in response to "Our Foreign Guests"—words which I found on the card on my plate when I took my seat at the table, and which of course spoiled my appetite for the viands spread before me. Among the most witty and humorous of these Irish graduates was the Rev. Dr. Haughton, a Fellow of Trinity College, Dublin, a learned divine, a progressive scientist, and of much repute as a ready and facetious speaker.

On Thursday, August 12th, I met the British Medical Association at dinner, for which every member who occupies a seat at the table pays a guinea. This festival forms one of the chief features of the meeting. Nearly four hundred gentlemen sat down in the hall of Trinity College. The President, Professor Humphry, was supported on his right by the Vice-Chancellor of the University, and on his left by his grace, the Lord Bishop of Ely. My seat was next to that of the Vice-Chancellor, while just below sat Sir James Paget. Immediately below Sir James was Professor Donders, a tall, noble-looking man, grappling with the English language, warm-hearted, and abounding in scientific knowledge. A short distance farther on, on the same side of the table, was Professor Acland of Oxford. At the end of the table, to my left, sat Brown-Séquard; and Dr. Alfred Carpenter, President of the Medical Council of the Association. Directly opposite to me was Mr. Lister, the famous reformer of the surgical treatment of wounds and other injuries. Scattered through the room were many other physicians from different parts of Great Britain, renowned as practitioners, authors, or teachers. I venture to say that the large hall, ornamented with the portraits of illustrious men, never exhibited a finer or nobler display than it did upon this occasion. As I looked across the sea of well-dressed men, many of them with large, striking heads, I thought that I had never witnessed a grander array of humanity. After the grosser viands were disposed of, the president called out the toasts with the names of the speakers, and the toast-master, who took his stand behind him, commanded silence. "Gentlemen," he would say—"Gentlemen, Sir James Paget is about to address you; preserve silence." The toasts were numerous, and it was not until a late hour that the repast terminated. The ominous card, "Our Foreign Guests," was again on my plate, with a request to respond; but this time I was not deprived of my appetite. When my turn came I referred to the fact that this was my third attendance upon the meeting of the Association, the first having been at Oxford in 1868, and the second at Birmingham in 1872. I then dwelt briefly upon the importance of an exchange of friendly feelings at these meetings, and expressed the conviction that this international intercourse would do more to preserve and increase the good understanding between England and the United States than all other things put together. I mentioned an incident which had recently occurred during a visit which I had made to the Tower of London. "When," said I, "the guide had shown us all that was of special interest in the interior of that edifice, he took us down into the yard, and pointing to some huge cannon that lay close by, he said, 'This was taken from the Russians; that from the French; that from the Spanish; this from the Dutch.' And thus he went on, giving the history of one piece after another. When he had finished I asked, 'Are there not any that you have taken from my country, the United States?' 'Not one,' was the reply; adding, 'God forbid we ever should take any! The two nations have too much good sense ever to go to war with each other.'" Such were the noble sentiments of a superannuated soldier who had served a long apprenticeship in the wars of India, who was thoroughly acquainted with the horrors of bloodshed, and who was now eking out the remnant of his life in a place which was once a prison, and is now filled with one hundred thousand muskets, ready at a day's notice to engage in the work of destruction. "Every man present will, I am sure," I said, "indorse these generous sentiments. Let us cultivate social intercourse; we cannot come together too often; we cannot too often shake hands or too often look one another in the face. Let us feel and act as though we are brothers, united by the ties of a common interest, speaking as we do the same language, governed by the same religion, and descended from the same ancestry."

Before the company dispersed the Vice-Chancellor invited my son and myself to breakfast with him in his private room in Corpus Christi College at nine o'clock the next morning; and his grace, the Lord Bishop of Ely, courteously asked us to meet him at luncheon on the same day at his palace at Ely. Both invitations were cordially accepted. Dr. Perowne, the head of Corpus Christi College, and Vice-Chancellor of the University, is refined and affable, of small stature, probably sixty-two or sixty-four years of age, and withal a bachelor. He did the honors of the table with much dignity and suavity, pouring out the

coffee and tea with his own hands, at the same time carrying on an interesting and animated conversation. The only
guests besides ourselves were Dr. and Mrs. Andrew Wood,
of Edinburgh. Mrs. Wood is a sister of the host. At
one o'clock we took the train for Ely, a distance of about
sixteen miles from Cambridge, to fulfil our engagement
with his grace, the Lord Bishop, who had provided an
elaborate luncheon, at which we had the pleasure of meeting again Dr. Acland and Sir James Paget, the latter
having come out to see his daughter. After luncheon
we spent an hour in looking through the cathedral, nearly
five hundred feet in length, and celebrated for the grandeur of its Norman architecture. The Lord Bishop of
Ely is probably sixty-five years of age, very intelligent,
popular, and benevolent, and much beloved by his people.
The palace is an old, unsightly building, the dining-room
of which is adorned with a number of excellent portraits
of his lordship's predecessors, some of them dating back
to a remote period.

In taking leave of Cambridge I must not forget the hospitality and courtesy extended to us by Dr. Humphry and
his family and by Dr. George E. Paget. During my visit
to Cambridge in 1868 the Humphrys were especially kind
to my dear wife, myself, and my son, sparing no pains to
contribute to our happiness. I was particularly sorry to
part with them during my recent visit, for I felt assured
that I should never see any of the family again. To Dr.
Paget, an elder brother of Sir James, I am also under deep
obligations for agreeable attentions. Returning after a
lapse of five days by the way we had come we passed directly to the Isle of Wight without stopping in London
except for an hour to take luncheon. There, at the Royal
Pier Hotel, at the very edge of the ocean, in the small
bathing-town of Sandown, we spent the remaining nine
days of our sojourn in England. I had intended to bathe
here, but after one trial I found the water so cold that I

did not venture into it again. The pleasure of our visit to this charming spot was much enhanced by the presence of our old friends, Mr. and Mrs. Erichsen, who spared no effort to contribute to our happiness. Here we again met Dr. Garrod, who, with his little family, was occupying a beautiful villa at Shanklin, two miles from Sandown. With him and with Mr. Erichsen we made an interesting excursion through some of the neighboring towns along the seaside, as well as passed two very pleasant afternoons. While at Sandown we received a visit from Professor Acland and from the Rev. Dr. Liddell, Dean of Christ Church, Oxford, who was Vice-Chancellor of the University of Oxford in 1872, when I received the degree of D. C. L., and who was now staying with his family at his summer residence at Cowes. This visit we returned on the Saturday before we left for London; and our gratification was greatly increased by the presence of my friend Acland, who, with his son and daughter, came in a carriage from Yarmouth, a distance of thirteen miles, to bid us a final adieu. An anecdote, illustrative of his remarkable industry and love of labor, is told of Liddell in connection with his Greek Dictionary. He had just read one evening the last proofs of a new edition, and was warmly congratulated by a friend on the completion of his task. When his friend called at his house the next morning the Dean was seen to be much occupied, and it was found upon inquiry that he was already engaged in revising the work for another edition.

During my sojourn I obtained a much better idea of England than during my two previous visits. In passing through the country one is struck with its remarkable beauty and fertility, its high cultivation, and the absence of everything like slovenliness. There is not much woodland to be seen anywhere, the whole country presenting the appearance of a garden. In fact, every inch of ground seems to be utilized to the best advantage. Nothing can be imagined more beautiful than the fields of wheat, oats, and barley, in many places ripe for the sickle, which everywhere met the eye, and which formed a striking contrast to the adjoining green grass-fields. Cattle and sheep, of the sleekest kind, greeted the sight in every direction. The horses were less numerous and not in such fine condition. During the middle of August many persons, both women and men, were engaged in harvesting, especially in the southern parts of England. The old sickle seems to be still much in use. In some of the larger fields the cutting was performed with machinery. The crops were very promising, and the fine weather gladdened the heart of the husbandman. The hedges, which are used everywhere, instead of fences as with us, form a striking feature in the landscape, as they do in many districts on the continent of Europe. The roads are in superb condition, without a rut or loose stone anywhere—in other words, singularly smooth and comfortable. MacAdam, who was, I believe, an American citizen, conferred vast benefits upon England in teaching her how to build her public roads and how to keep them in order. In comparison with our country England has few forests, but it is wonderful how carefully every man guards his trees, which preserve everywhere until late in the autumn their remarkable verdure. The number of her native forest trees is, as I am informed by Sir James Paget, only six, among which the elm and the oak are the most conspicuous. In the houses in the rural districts, in the villages, and in the larger towns there is a remarkable likeness, the same yellow brick and the same style of architecture everywhere fatiguing the eye of the traveller. In making long journeys the fields and forest trees seem to have a monotonous aspect. Many of the rural houses are built of stone, and are almost completely covered with ivy. In many places the ivy is also seen creeping in luxuriance over the elm and other trees. The English people are very fond of flowers, which are found at almost every house and cottage, either in front of the building or in the back or side yard. In the larger towns, such, for instance, as Oxford and Cambridge, the flowers are occasionally grown in boxes or baskets in the windows or suspended from the walls, the scarlet geranium and a pretty little blue flower, the name of which has escaped me, being the most common.

I must not omit to mention the gratification with which, in common with a densely crowded audience, I listened, for more than one hour, to the address of Sir James Paget in the Section of Pathology, of which he was president, on the Relations of Vegetable Pathology to Animal Pathology. The subject, which was a novel one to a British audience, was handled in the graceful and masterly manner for which Sir James is so distinguished. He spoke without a single note. It is strange that this subject has never been brought to the attention of any scientific body in this country, inasmuch as numerous treatises have already been published upon it, especially in Germany. The example of the great savans of England will no doubt soon be followed on this side of the Atlantic.

Sir James Paget is a tall, slender man, upon whose quiet, thoughtful brow intellectuality is stamped in a marked degree. The son of a merchant, he was born at Great Yarmouth in 1814. He was Hunterian Professor of Surgery at the Royal College of Surgeons, and subsequently Lecturer on General Anatomy and Physiology at St. Bartholomew's Hospital. As a lecturer and as a writer he is equally distinguished. His large experience as an original investigator united to a mind saturated with varied knowledge enables him to present to the student the latest and most accurate information on the subject of his discourse. His language is at once vigorous and graceful, and he has a ready command of illustrations drawn from the domain of science and of art. His contributions to the department which he has made his own constitute a new era in surgical pathology with which his name will ever be indissolubly connected ; indeed, they are more valuable than those of any man in Great Britain of his day. He stands at the head of his profession in a country which boasts among its members so many gifted men. Of his Lectures on Surgical Pathology, which appeared in 1853, and has passed through several editions, it has been said by an able critic that it is " one of the most valuable contributions" to this subject "since the days of John Hunter."

The popularity of Sir James Paget is unbounded. When it is known that he is to address a meeting the hall in which he is announced to appear is crowded with an earnest, intelligent audience, which realizes that it has come to be instructed and pleased, and that its expectations will not be disappointed. His manner of speaking is entirely free from that drawl and hesitation which are so common to many of his countrymen, and which are nowhere more apparent than in the debates of the Houses of Parliament, or in the addresses of eminent lawyers in jury trials. So great is his reputation for versatility and for the rapid acquisition of knowledge, that it has been said of him, "Give him six weeks and he will lecture on Oriental languages!" He is Sergeant-Surgeon Extraordinary to the Queen, Surgeon to the Prince of Wales, and Consulting Surgeon to St. Bartholomew's Hospital. He is a member of many learned societies at home and abroad, and has been the recipient of the highest honorary degrees of the Universities of Oxford, Cambridge, and Edinburgh.

Sir James is singularly neat in his dress, and writes a hand almost as faultless as copperplate. It is pleasant to witness his unaffected simplicity in the domestic circle and the zeal with which, when surrounded by the members of his devoted family, he unites with them in the relaxation of music and other home pleasures. The enjoyment of my visits to England has been much increased by the hospitality and the courtesies which I have received at his hands.

Professor Humphry, in his presidential address before the British Medical Association, stated that while in a city like Cambridge, with so sparse a population, the establishment of a great practical school of medicine and surgery was impracticable, the foundation had been laid, upon a broad and enduring basis, of a school of biology, or physiology, the beneficent results of which were already apparent in much able, novel, and useful work performed by Dr. Michael Foster and his assistants in the Physiological Laboratory of the University, instituted a few years ago; and he appealed to the Association to sustain and foster the enterprise, by sending their students to a place wherein they might be taught, in a suitable and proper manner, the rudiments of their medical education. The address was received with great applause, and it is evident that the cherished purpose of the professor is an assured fact. What Humphry is trying to do for Cambridge Acland has for years been engaged in doing for Oxford, which, although it has a considerably larger population than her rival, cannot any more than she compete with the London schools in clinical facilities. The Oxford Museum, to which I have already referred, is, in the opulence of its various collections, second only to the Hunterian Museum in London, and is gradually assuming, under the supervision of Professor Rolleston and his associates, the characteristics of a great school of biology, in which young men destined for the medical profession may receive, during the first two years of their novitiate, thorough instruction in chemistry, pharmacy, anatomy, physiology, and microscopy, so that they may devote without any material interruption the remainder of their pupilage to the study of the practical branches.

Since the above was written—in 1880—a fine laboratory has been erected and placed in charge of Dr. Burdon-Sanderson, the eminent physiologist, under whose direction Oxford will soon rival Cambridge in scientific enterprise and experimental research.

Everybody who visits London stops of course to see St. Paul's Cathedral, built by Sir Christopher Wren in the seventeenth century. Thirty-five years elapsed before it was completed. It is one of the noblest structures in the world. To me its crypts in the basement story were of especial interest, containing as they do gorgeous monuments of deceased naval and military heroes, illustrious statesmen, and distinguished physicians. The monuments erected in honor of Nelson and Wellington are grand; but what interested me more than anything else in this vast chamber of the dead was the statue of Sir Astley Cooper, who, after a brilliant career of more than forty years, died in February, 1841, in the seventy-third year of his age. The work is a fine specimen of sculpture, and was erected at heavy cost. Near by is another statue, also a noble work of art, erected in honor of Dr. Babington, a contemporary of Cooper, who was for many years the great London physician, and a most learned, popular, and charitable man.

There was no one to dispute with Sir Astley Cooper the surgical sceptre of London. Soon after his famous operation upon George IV., referred to elsewhere, his practice lay almost exclusively among the nobility and people in the higher walks of life. His first year yielded him only five guineas; and it was not until the ninth year, when he secured a hospital appointment, that he vaulted from the hundreds into the thousands, and finally received unexampled remuneration. One gentleman alone for a long time paid him six hundred pounds a year. Some of his fees were very large. A retired and eccentric West India merchant on whom he had operated for hydrocele threw one thousand guineas at him in a nightcap as he was leaving the room.

Cooper was a native of Brooke, a small town in Norfolk, where he was born in 1768. He received his early education chiefly under his father, and at the age of fifteen was apprenticed to a surgeon and apothecary at Great Yarmouth. In a short time he exchanged him for a paternal uncle, a surgeon of Guy's Hospital, and the latter in turn for Mr. Cline, the eminent surgeon of St. Thomas's Hospital. As an instance of his courage and presence of mind it is related that when a boy he saw a lad fall from a cart and tear open his thigh in such a manner as to wound the femoral artery. He immediately took his handkerchief from his pocket, and tying it tightly round the limb kept the bleeding in check until proper assistance was procured. His progress as a student was rapid, and at the expiration of his apprenticeship he entered upon that career as a teacher, practitioner, hospital surgeon, investigator, and author which made him so illustrious among his contemporaries, and which has immortalized his name. He published great works, all founded upon original observations, and performed many important operations, among others that of ligating the aorta, a feat never accomplished before. He was an incessant worker, an excellent lecturer, and a good writer, without any pretension to elegance of style, the thoughts being conveyed in plain, clear language. I learned my first lessons in surgery from his Lectures, reprinted in Philadelphia soon after I began the study of medicine. Every student should read them, for they abound in good sense and in sound practical knowledge.

Tall and of magnificent proportions, Cooper was one of the handsomest men of his day, noted for the elegance of his manners and his manly bearing. In Paris, at the Hôtel Dieu, as he walked round the wards with Dupuytren, he attracted general attention, and the students exclaimed, "*C'est un bel homme!*" He was genial, but dignified in his demeanor, neat in dress, and very popular as a man, as a lecturer, and as a practitioner. His style of living was expensive, but he was temperate in his habits, and contributed large sums annually to his poor relatives, to indigent members of the profession, and to various objects of charity. He was created a baronet in 1821, was Sergeant-Surgeon to George IV., attended William, afterwards William IV., when he was Lord High Admiral, and received through the Duke of Wellington the Grand Cross of the Guelphic Order. He was a member of the French Institute, and Louis Philippe sent him the insignia of the Legion of Honor. Oxford conferred upon him the degree of D. C. L. in 1834. He retained his office of surgeon to and lecturer at Guy's and St. Thomas's Hospitals, where he laid the foundation of his reputation, until ill health compelled him to relinquish it. Cooper's private character was lofty. A biography of him in two volumes, by his nephew, Mr. Bransby B. Cooper, was published soon after his death. It is far from being a model of what such a work should be. By his will Sir Astley established a triennial prize of three hundred pounds for the best original essay on some professional subject, open to all members of the profession, native and foreign. "My success," says Cooper, "depended upon my zeal and industry"—memorable words, full of encouragement to young men.

We took leave of our friends, Mr. and Mrs. Erichsen, on Monday, August 23d, and spent the night in London. We reached Liverpool by the beautiful and interesting Midland route the following afternoon, preparatory to our embarkation the next day on the steamer Illinois, Captain Shackford. Soon after leaving Queenstown it began to rain and blow, and I was obliged to remain in my berth for six days. I subsisted all this time mainly on milk punch, and I took my meals at table only the last two days of the trip. Even in clear weather the vessel rocked like a cradle, and made me very uncomfortable. We arrived at the dock on Sunday, September 5th, where the kind faces of my children were in waiting to welcome us.

CHAPTER VI.

APRIL 3d, 1881.—I have just received a letter from Mr. William MacCormac, Honorary Secretary, inviting me to deliver one of the five general addresses at the Interna- tional Medical Congress which is to meet in London early in August of the present year. My regret that I cannot ac- cept this invitation is very keen, as the meeting, with Sir James Paget at the head of it, will be by far the most illustrious of its kind ever held. The best men in the profession of Great Britain are vying with one another to insure its success. I have crossed the Atlantic Ocean six times, and my suffering from seasickness has usually been so severe that I am forced to decline an honor which, under other circumstances, it would have given me un- feigned pleasure to accept. Of the five American gentle- men whose names I suggested for the office, the choice fell upon Dr. Billings, of the army, and I am sure it could not have been intrusted to abler hands. Dr. Billings is a high- toned and thoroughly cultured medical man, and therefore eminently worthy to represent us at this gathering.

August 8th.—Oceanic House, Isles of Shoals.—The morning papers bring me the sad news of the death of my friend, General Robert Patterson, last evening at half past eight o'clock at his residence in Philadelphia, at the uncommon age of eighty-nine. Like the sturdy oak which has nobly resisted many a storm, the good old man has at last yielded to the inevitable and gone to his long home, the contemporary of three generations of human beings, and the active participant in the deeds of one of the most remarkable epochs in the world's history. The hero of three wars, General Robert Patterson was for a third of a century one of the most prominent citizens of Philadelphia, with an enviable national reputation, founded upon distinguished services in the field, commercial and manufacturing enterprise, urbanity, integrity of character, and unbounded hospitality. No man in Philadelphia in his day ate so many good dinners or gave so many symposial entertainments as Robert Patterson. Few strangers of note ever passed through our city without having received attentions from him. Talking to a friend some years before his death, he made the following statement, illustrative at once of the force of his character and the esteem in which he was held by his more conspicuous contemporaries: "When I left my father's house, about seventy years ago, I determined not to take an office of profit, but to rely on my own energy and industry to support myself and my family, if I ever had one. I have adhered to this purpose, and have not allowed either of my sons to take an office of profit. I have voted at every Presidential election since the war of 1812, was on intimate terms with Monroe, Adams, Jackson, Van Buren, Harrison, Polk, Taylor, Pierce, Buchanan, Lincoln, and Grant. I have dined with nearly all of them at the White House, and most of them have dined at my house. I had the honor of intimate and friendly relations with Henry Clay, Webster, Calhoun, Benton, Hugh L. White, Tazewell, Grundy, Dallas, Poindexter, Lincoln of Massachusetts, Silas Wright, Marcy, Bayard, Reverdy Johnson, and most of the intellectual giants of the Senate and House of Representatives in bygone days."

Robert Patterson was born at Tyrone, Ireland, in 1792. His father was a farmer, who, in consequence of the active part which he took in the Rebellion of '98, was obliged to flee to this country, where he engaged in agricultural pursuits, and became eventually a prosperous citizen. From him the son doubtless inherited his active disposition and those manly qualities which were of such benefit to him in forming his business habits and in influencing the minds of his fellow-citizens in times of public alarm and impending danger. A Democrat of the Jefferson school, he was ever loyal to his adopted country, and considered no sacrifice too great to subserve its interests. The stain which some of his jealous military contemporaries attempted to put upon him for his conduct in the Shenandoah Valley at the commencement of the war of the Rebellion was triumphantly effaced by a pamphlet which he published soon after the declaration of peace, and which satisfied every impartial person that he had been shamefully maligned and misrepresented. He was proud of his military career.

General Patterson was nearly six feet in height, with a stout, commanding figure, broad shoulders, and a countenance which to the last was strikingly handsome. He had about him an air such as is seldom witnessed even in the professional soldier. He rarely appeared at his own table in the presence of his guests, at an evening party, or at a public entertainment without his buff-colored vest and his blue coat ornamented with gilt buttons and a velvet collar. He was in fact a marked specimen of the gentlemanly, civilian soldier. He was an excellent diner-out, and it was well known that he could drink with impunity more champagne, his favorite wine, than any other guest. He possessed much knowledge of the world, was a good conversationalist, and happy as an after-dinner speaker. He had a large fund of anecdotes derived from his intercourse with distinguished men of all classes of society, and he cordially coöperated in all measures tending to promote the public good. The architect of his own fortune, he lived to win the respect of his fellow-citizens and to see his adopted country rapidly rise in national greatness. He hated England with a cordial hatred; but he fully appreciated her position as a mighty power upon the earth, and he never failed, when occasion offered, to extend courtesy and hospitality to Englishmen. My acquaintance with General Patterson commenced in 1849 during a visit he made to Louisville, when I resided in that city, and our friendship continued without interruption up to the time of his death.

March 28th, 1882.—This day will ever be deeply impressed on my recollection as the one on which I resigned the chair of Surgery in the Jefferson Medical College. The reasons which prompted me to take this step are fully expressed in the subjoined letter, a copy of which was sent to the Board of Trustees at its meeting two days before the Commencement. While I might readily have retained my chair two years longer, and thus completed my fifty years as a public teacher, I deemed it best to retire at a time when I was in the full possession of my intellectual and physical powers, instead of waiting until it should become apparent that I was no longer fit to perform my duties. I always loved teaching and the excitement of lecturing to large classes; and I believe that I am quite justified in saying that I never failed, even in my earliest efforts in this direction, to command the respect, if not also the love and admiration, of my pupils. I was always a strict disciplinarian, but in chiding was never harsh, rude, or sarcastic in my ways or methods. The great majority of young men in every class are well-behaved and ambitious to acquire knowledge. One motive which influenced me in offering my resignation, apart from the motives stated in my letter to the Board, was the assurance that if my chair were divided, as had long been intended, my son, Dr.

S. W. Gross, would be one of my successors; and in the keeping of this pledge I was not disappointed. This was a great solace to me; and doubly gratifying because, in the first place, the change highly promoted my son's welfare; and because, in the second place, I knew perfectly well that in his hands the interests of the chair would be entirely safe. Of all men in the country I felt assured that no one was better qualified than he to teach the principles of surgery. The Board, in accepting my resignation, unanimously adopted resolutions of regret and elected me Emeritus Professor of Surgery. The letter is as follows:

Advancing age and a desire, after a laborious professional life of fifty-four years, to spend the remainder of my days in comparative repose induce me to ask your Board to accept my resignation of the chair of Surgery which, by a unanimous vote, you did me the honor to confer upon me twenty-six years ago. During this long period it was my good fortune to be associated with learned, distinguished, and honorable colleagues, who always received my earnest support in every measure designed to advance the best interests of the school, and to maintain it in that lofty position which it is universally acknowledged to occupy. In severing my relations with you and with my associates, I desire to assure you that I shall ever feel a deep interest in my Alma Mater, and pray that she may continually advance in prosperity and influence, and be in all time to come an honor to her founders, to the various faculties that have ministered at her shrine, and to the trustees who have in successive stages of her career so wisely shaped and controlled her destinies. I lay down the robes of office not without regret, but with clean hands and with the consciousness that in all my teachings, extending in different schools over a period of forty-eight years, I was governed by an eye single to the welfare of my pupils and the honor and dignity of my profession.

May 11th.—A cablegram brings us this morning the sad news of the death of the author of Rab and his Friends. No one who has read this charming tale will fail to heave a deep sigh at the news. The London Spectator, in commenting upon it, has this striking passage: "Early in the morning of Thursday, May 11th, Edinburgh lost its best-known and best-loved citizen, Scotland her son of finest genius, and thousands, wherever the English language is spoken, one toward whom, though they had never seen his face, they felt as to a friend." John Brown was truly the friend of the humble and the lowly. He was not satisfied with merely examining the sick and prescribing for their ailments; he identified himself with their interests, worldly as well as religious. When he went hence to return to them no more the people felt that they had parted with their best and dearest friend on earth.

The author of Rab and his Friends had reached the allotted age of the psalmist. His death, after an illness of only five days, was caused by an attack of pleuro-pneumonia. When the cog-wheels of our machinery are worn roughly by the ravages of time, a slight blow is sufficient to knock it into pieces. The strong religious element in his character was inherited from four generations of sturdy Seceding ministers, men of a rare stamp in any church, and diminishing in number year by year. His early days were passed among the hills and moorlands of Scotland; and it was not until after his father was put in charge of an influential congregation in Edinburgh that he began to enjoy the advantages of society and of a classical education. His professional studies were conducted, as stated in a previous page, under the charge of Mr. Syme. Brown was forty-eight years old before he tried his powers at authorship. He wrote by snatches, and in the midst of interruptions, and, what is remarkable, his medical productions were limited to an occasional paper for the periodical press. He was fond of philosophical contemplations, and was a warm lover of the wild and romantic scenery of his own Scotland, of art in all its varied forms, of music, of children, and of animals, especially dogs. Without being a poet, he had a poetical mind, and but for the want of early training he might have outstripped some of the bards of his own day. His sketches of Sydenham and Locke are masterpieces. It is sad to think that his intellect was occasionally clouded by insanity, for the cure of which his friends were obliged to confine him temporarily in an asylum.

August 24th.—It is now eleven o'clock in the morning, and I have just finished reading the last proof of the sixth edition of my Surgery. Early in February my publishers informed me that they would be ready within the next two months to go to press. For the last few years I had been at work upon the revision, and I now taxed myself to the utmost to meet the requirements of the occasion. Ten years had elapsed since the last edition was issued, and much of the work had to be rewritten. Conscious that I could not perform this gigantic labor alone, I intrusted the revision of the chapters on the Eye, Ear, and Throat to three of my young friends; while my son, Dr. S. W. Gross, and I took charge of the main body of the work. Never did two men work more earnestly or zealously to acquit themselves properly of their task. The work, as it now stands, may, I think, without the imputation of vanity, be regarded as presenting a correct reflection of the existing state of surgery in all its parts; at all events, this is the general opinion of the medical press. I was glad when the hour came for my release from the heat, noise, and dust of the city. The same afternoon I left for Long Branch in search of fresh air and sea-bathing, which had always been of signal benefit to me.

The reason why this work, originally issued in 1859, was so slow in reaching its sixth edition is that the market had been glutted with similar productions, most of them foreign reprints. Erichsen's Surgery was always very popular; and Druitt's, Miller's, Bryant's, Holmes's, and Ashhurst's works were more within the student's means than my two ponderous and much more costly volumes. The Surgery, too, of Agnew, although still incomplete, was well received, and, as a matter of course, was sought in preference to mine by the graduates of the University of Pennsylvania, in which he is a professor.

November 2d.—I went to New York this afternoon to attend the reception of Dr. J. Marion Sims and of his son, Harry Marion Sims, kindly tendered to me a fortnight ago during a visit made to me by the father. At first I rebelled; but, finding that the matter had been thoroughly matured, I yielded my assent as gracefully as I could. Cards were sent to most of the prominent medical men within a reasonable distance, and nearly four hundred responded to the invitation. Philadelphia sent thirty of her best men; Baltimore, Washington, Boston, Pittsburgh, Chicago, Buffalo, Albany, Troy, and a number of other towns and cities sent delegates; and New York and Brooklyn were present in full force. The reception took place in the large ball-room of the Hotel Brunswick, which was brilliantly lighted up for the occasion, and adorned with a profusion of the choicest flowers. The supper was spread upon a long side-table, and was served in excellent style. Champagne corks popped in every direction, and a band of music stationed in the gallery discoursed delightful music. The guests began to arrive soon after eight o'clock, and it was midnight before the last disappeared. The entertainment was a charming one; some lay gentlemen, mainly lawyers, were also of the company. But what, more than anything else, served to enhance the pleasure of the evening was the presence, in an adjoining room, of Dr. Sims's family and of my own. Dr. Sims received numerous letters as well as telegrams from friends who on account of distance found it impossible to attend. Dr. Baldwin, of Montgomery, Alabama, the early professional home of Dr. Sims, and a well-tried friend of both of us, sent a despatch containing nearly two hundred words. To single out the names of gentlemen who graced the occasion with their presence might seem invidious, and I therefore forbear.

When the history of American medicine shall be written, one of its brightest pages will be an account of the services of Dr. Sims, a name as enduring as the hills and valleys of South Carolina, his native State. Born in January, 1813, he received his English and classical education in the South Carolina College at Charleston, and then studied medicine, graduating in the Medical College of the Palmetto State in 1832, and in the Jefferson Medical College in 1835. Thus equipped with more than an ordinary amount of knowledge, and impelled by a lofty ambition to excel in his profession, he selected Montgomery, Alabama, as his future home ; and it was there, in the midst of genial and appreciative friends, in a delightful cotton region, blessed with a charming climate, that he laid the foundation of his fame and usefulness. Meeting with several cases of vesico-vaginal fistule which had repeatedly failed to obtain relief from other practitioners, it occurred to Dr. Sims that an operation might be devised by which a permanent cure of this distressing affection might be effected. For this purpose he opened a private hospital with a capacity for sixteen beds, conducted solely at his own expense. His patients were young slaves, all primiparæ, who, as they were of no use to their owners, willingly placed themselves under his charge. He had, as he told me, originally no taste for obstetrics or gynæcology. His practice was largely given up to surgery. The first two cases of vesico-vaginal fistule that came under his observation were summarily dismissed, because, from all that he had seen and read upon the subject, he considered the affection to be utterly incurable. A third case, brought to him soon after the last, would have shared a similar fate had it not been for an accident. This accident changed the whole course of his life by suggesting the thought which enabled him to lay the foundation of gynæcology, of which he will in all time be regarded as the scientific father. A lady fell from her pony, and, striking on the sacrum, dislocated her uterus, causing intense agony. Called to her almost immediately after the accident, he placed her upon her knees, so as to elevate the pelvis and depress the uterus, and he found to his surprise as well as joy that the organ at once resumed its natural position. New light burst upon his vision; atmospheric pressure, with the slight aid of his fingers, had done the work, and he was not slow in taking advantage of what proved to be a most important discovery. Does not this fact forcibly remind one of the discovery of the law of gravitation by Newton from having witnessed the fall of an apple, and of the construction by Galileo of a clock, in which the pendulum was used, from having observed the swinging of the lamp suspended from the roof of the cathedral at Pisa? Both occurrences had been noticed thousands of times before; but it remained for the fertile minds of these great men to utilize them, and to render them subservient to the interpretation of nature's laws. Sims now set about inventing new instruments, new needles, and new sutures for the more secure closure of these horrid fissures. His speculum is used in every part of the civilized world, and silver sutures have an equal popularity, although they are not indispensable to the success of such operations. He now often had half a dozen cases of vesico-vaginal fistulæ under treatment in his little hospital at one time. In a letter to me he says: "When I began this work I was thirty-three years old, full of life, energy, endurance, and enthusiasm. I was so sure that I could cure any case in a few months that I proposed to the masters of these unfortunate young women to keep them at my own expense if they would clothe them and pay their taxes, and promised not to do anything that would endanger their lives or render their condition worse. As they were entirely profitless to their owners, I easily got control of them, and they were only too happy to come with the hope of getting rid of their disgusting infirmities. Keeping so many patients at my own expense for four years impoverished me, and, what rendered matters worse, my own health gave way. Convinced that I could not obtain relief in the South, I was compelled, in 1850, to go North. When I reached New York I weighed only ninety pounds, and my disease harassed me until 1856. I may mention the fact that when I began my experiments my professional brethren in Montgomery were all ready to come and help me, for they thought with me that I was on the eve of a great discovery; but when they saw only failure after failure they became tired of it, and in the third and fourth years I could get hardly any one to help me. During the last year my principal assistants were the patients; and they always eagerly looked forward to the time of having their operations repeated, often contending with one another who should be the next. All the operations were performed without an anæsthetic. Indeed, I had been at work a year before the introduction of ether.'' Thus, at length, in 1849, after many trials and failures, Sims triumphed over all obstacles, and placed his methods upon a scientific and enduring basis. Upon one of his patients he performed not fewer than thirty operations before he succeeded in effecting complete riddance of her loathsome infirmity. It is difficult to say which to admire most in this case—the fortitude of the poor sufferer, or the patience, perseverance, and skill of the great surgeon. Dr. Sims published the first account of his operation in the American Journal of the Medical Sciences for January, 1852. It was prepared while he was confined to his bed, and was considered hopelessly ill. It speedily attracted general attention.

In 1853 Sims removed to New York, where, in the

following year, he founded the Woman's Hospital, the first
institution on this continent exclusively devoted to the
treatment of the diseases of women.   In this undertaking
he was aided by the influence of such men as Mott, Stevens, Francis, Green, and Griscom, as well as of a number
of prominent women of New York.   If Sims had done
nothing else, the energy and determination displayed in
placing this institution in a proper working condition
would be sufficient to entitle him to the gratitude of the
public, and to establish his claims as a philanthropist.
His early connection with it afforded him an opportunity
of introducing his peculiar operative procedures, and enabled the profession and the public to form a true estimate
of their value.

   In 1861 Dr. Sims visited Europe, and during his sojourn
in Paris was invited to perform his operations in the principal hospitals of that city, men of world-wide renown
sitting at the feet of the American Gamaliel to be enlightened respecting a procedure which was to revolutionize
the treatment of the surgical diseases of women.   The
following year he took his family abroad with a view of
educating his children ; and, availing himself of the reputation which he achieved in his previous visit, he soon obtained a large and lucrative practice, patients flocking to
him from all parts of the Continent, Great Britain, and
even the United States.   He remained abroad until 1868.
He was made a Knight of the Legion of Honor by Napoleon III. ; and the French, Spanish, Portuguese, Italian, and
Belgian governments vied with one another in investing
him with their decorations ; while many of the prominent medical societies enrolled him among their members.
During the Franco-Prussian war he rendered important
services at the head of the Anglo-American Ambulance
Corps, for which he and his assistants received the thanks
of the French government.   At Louisville, in 1875, he
was elected President of the American Medical Associa-

tion; and he delivered his inaugural address the following year—the Centennial Year of American independence—at a meeting of the Association at Philadelphia. Although not a voluminous writer, Dr. Sims has found time to contribute articles to the periodical press, and to publish monographs on Silver Sutures in Surgery, Uterine Surgery, Ovariotomy, Intra-Uterine Fibroid Tumors, and the Microscope in the Sterile Condition. Of late years, owing chiefly to ill health, most of his time has been spent in Europe, where he is always sure to receive a warm welcome and to be greeted by crowds of wealthy patients, including not a few of the nobility. In 1880 he had a violent attack of pneumonia, from the effects of which he was long in recovering. He is one of the most generous and hospitable of men, of winsome manners, with keen perceptions and a mind well stored with varied information. He is of medium stature, well proportioned, with a noble forehead, large blue eyes, and of modest demeanor. That he possesses genius of a high order is abundantly attested by his works. He has acquired an insight into human nature by his constant intercourse with the best society at home and abroad. He esteems money only for the good he can do with it, without perhaps a due regard to the future. The mantle which he has so long and so gracefully worn is destined soon to fall upon the shoulders of his son Harry, a young man rapidly rising into notice. My friend has lately attained his seventieth year, but he is still hale and able to do much work.

Dr. Sims ought to be rich and independent. Some idea may be formed of the proceeds of his surgical work from the following extract from a letter which he wrote to me during his residence in Paris: "No man in our country, 'solitary and alone,' ever made as much money as I have by my profession, except, perhaps, Dr. H., and yet I am comparatively poor and must work for my daily bread. I am not extravagant and never gambled. I have lived well and have educated a large family of children, and I have only found out lately that my agent who managed my business for the last fourteen years stole from me not less than one hundred thousand dollars. To justify myself for remaining abroad let me show you what I have done since I saw you. I went to Rome January 1st, and remained there until April 1st. Of course people could not find out I was there until about the middle of February. From that time until the close of March, a period of six weeks, I made fifty-two thousand francs. Since coming to Paris the following items show the work done and soon to be done: April 22d, operation, 25,000 francs; April 28th, operation, 1,500 francs; April 29th, operation, 15,000 francs; April 30th, operation, 20,000 francs; May 3d, operation, 5,000 francs. Total, 66,500 francs.

"In addition to these I am to operate in the next ten days as follows: 1st case, 10,000 francs; 2d case, 10,000 francs; 3d case, 5,000 francs; 4th case, 15,000 francs. Total, 40,000 francs.

"This makes the incredible sum of nearly twenty-two thousand dollars, all compressed within about one month; but many of these cases followed me from Italy, and you must not think this an average showing. It is an accidental *blocking*. But if I were to settle down here anywhere in a great, ample centre, I am sure I could make with ease fifty thousand dollars a year; so you will see that my self-expatriation for health is justifiable."

In speaking of patients who came to him during his European residence, Dr. Sims states that they invariably expect to pay well for his services, but adds that it had been the rule of his life never to take money from any who cannot easily afford to part with it. The climate of New York is prejudicial to his health, and for this reason, as well as because he can make more money abroad with much less labor, he prefers to exile himself from his native country, revisiting it generally once a year to see his children and to attend to such business as chance may throw in his way. I imagine that the real cause of Dr. Sims's poverty is his inability to husband his means—"easy come, easy go."

Dr. Sims is a man of decided views. His opinions are formed with caution and not easily abandoned, unless when he finds them to be erroneous. His good nature occasionally leads him astray by inducing him to place too much confidence in the unsupported assertions of others. If he is at times aggressive, he is always ready to extend the hand of good-fellowship. As an operator he is bold, sometimes almost to recklessness, but he thoroughly understands the nature of his cases, and carefully weighs the consequences of the employment of the knife, which he wields with consummate ability. The after-treatment never fails to receive due attention. His manners in the sick-room are pleasant; hence it is no wonder that his patients love him. If he had devoted himself to the practice of general surgery, his inventive genius, his fertility of resources in emergencies, and his dexterity as an operator would have placed him in the highest rank of his contemporaries. One almost regrets that he confines himself to the limited field of gynæcology.

Sims has never worn a professor's gown. One of the chief objects of his ambition, as he has often told me, has been to be a teacher of gynæcology in some great school, if possible in his Alma Mater; and last summer, when the failing health of Professor Wallace rendered it only too probable that some of the duties of his chair must soon be resigned to another, I opened a correspondence with Sims upon the subject, at the request of some of the members of the Faculty of our college; but the answer came, "My health will not permit my acceptance of so onerous a chair." He would, I am sure, have made a most popular teacher and have brought influence and reputation to the school. He is an excellent speaker, clear and distinct, with a well-trained, sonorous voice and an earnest and impressive manner, denotive of a full appreciation of what he is saying. I have witnessed bursts of eloquence from him that would have done honor to a born orator.

November 26th.—I am indebted to my friend Professor Flint for this anecdote of Thurlow Weed. Professor Flint attended him during his last illness as one of the consulting physicians. The health of the great journalist had been gradually failing for several months. The immediate cause of his death was starvation, produced by his obstinate refusal to take nourishment in any form whatever. Even water he would not swallow, although when put into his mouth he said it was "so delicious." There was no mechanical obstruction in his gullet. He was simply laboring under the delusion that food and drink would injure him; in other words, he was insane on the subject. The physicians had the greatest difficulty in persuading him to take nourishment by the rectum, given in small quantity several times a day. All medicine was withheld.

January 26th, 1883.—The meeting of the National Association for the Protection of the Insane and the Prevention of Insanity, founded two years ago by a number of philanthropic men and women, took place day before yesterday at the hall of the College of Physicians of Philadelphia. Dr. Joseph Parrish, in the absence of the president and vice-president, was called to the chair. Upon me devolved the delivery of the address of welcome. I took the ground that most of our insane asylums are simply so many boarding-houses under the supervision of incompetent medical men, who, without proper training, are utterly unfit for the discharge of their sacred duties, as is proved by the fact that very few cases are cured under their treatment, and by the fact that no well-considered works on insanity have issued from any of these institutions, with the exception of the work of the late Dr. Isaac Ray, for many years Superintendent of the Rhode Island Hospital. On the same day I offered a resolution, which, with slight modification, was unanimously adopted, namely, that it was the sense of the meeting that every institution for the treatment of the insane should have upon its medical staff an educated and experienced gynæcologist, in view of the fact that many cases of insanity of a curable nature are caused by disorders of the sexual organs. If this plan were generally adopted, immense good would result from it. Another plan, equally useful, would be to subject all applicants for a medical office to a rigid examination by a competent board. Full notes should be kept of each case, and every opportunity embraced to make by dissection thorough investigation of the causes of death. In this manner a flood of light, of the greatest benefit to the human race, could soon be made to issue from every institution of the kind. Apathy would give place to industry, and stupidity and indifference to scientific progress. In the United States, with a population of fifty millions, there are nearly one hundred thousand insane persons, with fewer than one hundred asylums for their accommodation and treatment. One of the anomalies of the age in regard to this matter is that hardly any of our schools have hitherto recognized the importance of giving instruction, either didactic or clinical, on mental diseases. Dr. Charles K. Mills, a young and highly promising Philadelphia physician, read an able and elaborate paper upon this subject, from which I anticipate much good.

The meeting of the Association lasted more than two days, was well attended, and excited much interest. Several of the addresses were excellent, and elicited considerable discussion. The Proceedings and Transactions have since been embodied in The American Psychological Journal, the first number of which appeared in April under the supervision of the president, Dr. Joseph Parrish, of New Jersey, an able writer and efficient worker. On the evening of the first day of the meeting the members of the Association were entertained at my house.

February 19th.—To-day we had at dinner Dr. James E. Reeves, an old friend and an eminent physician of Wheeling. He is enthusiastic, intelligent, and thoroughly in love with his profession. He deserves great credit for the part he took in the establishment of a State Board of Health, and for his efforts to drive charlatans out of West Virginia.

February 21st.—This evening, at the dinner given in honor of Mr. William G. Malin, for fifty-nine years steward of the Pennsylvania Hospital, an old member of the profession, who was for many years one of the physicians of this institution, told me a curious anecdote respecting Physick, with whom he was long and even intimately acquainted: A woman fifty years of age, under my informant's care, was desirous of consulting the "Father of American Surgery" on account of cancer of the breast. An operation was agreed upon, but was deferred for six weeks in order, by a process of rigid dieting, as was then the custom, to put the system in a proper condition. The only food allowed by Physick during this period was a piece of dry bread with a little salt and a glass of cold water three times a day. This, as her appetite was excellent, reduced the poor woman to the verge of starvation. She grew thin, pale, and exceedingly feeble, and, as she expressed it, often felt as if she could bite a piece out of one of my informant's children, such was her craving for nourishment. One day she asked Physick if she might not eat an ear of green corn, then in season. "What fattens hogs?" asked Physick. "Corn," answered the patient. "Then don't eat corn; I don't want to fatten you." The operation was performed in due time, but no change was made in the diet. A few days after this, however, my informant asked whether a little animal food would not be permissible. "Yes; go and see the cook; tell her to give you the leg and thigh of a chicken ; strip off every bit of skin, and then, holding them upright at the foot end, pour over them a pint of boiling water, and give the woman occasionally a tablespoonful of the broth seasoned with a little salt.'' The poor creature recovered from the effects of the operation, but died some months after from a general carcinomatous cachexia. Dudley, the Kentucky lithotomist, used to feed his patients on bran gruel, seasoned with tartar emetic, and, what is worthy of note, many of his pupils imitated his practice. The lancet and starvation were in those days the most approved means of treating diseases, both chronic and acute. Cold water was generally withheld in the treatment of fevers. In the larger towns, when a physician was sent for to visit a sick person, it was the custom among some practitioners to request the messenger to bring at the same time the bleeder along.

It is a source of great pleasure to me, as I think it must be to all American physicians, to learn that the friends of Mr. John Eric Erichsen have just placed his bust, as a testimonial of his great services as a practitioner, as a teacher, and as an author, in the University Medical College. The sum raised for the purpose reached nearly four hundred pounds, leaving, after paying the artist, a considerable surplus, which was presented to Mr. Erichsen, who established with it in perpetuity an annual prize to be awarded for the greatest proficiency in operative surgery. It is creditable to us on this side of the water that a small amount of this money was contributed by American surgeons. Mr. Erichsen was elected for three years President of the Royal College of Surgeons, and the testimonial with which he has just been honored must have been so much the more gratifying to him because it was, in some sense, of an international character. Considering his immense services to the profession, one is surprised that her Majesty has not conferred upon him the honor of knighthood. The friends of T. Spencer Wells, who has been instrumental in saving many hundred lives by his ovariotomies, have as much cause of complaint. Such an honor is trifling in itself, but as showing the appreciation of a great government it is not to be contemned, especially in a country where rewards are habitually bestowed for meritorious services.

March 14th.—I went to New York to-day in obedience to an invitation extended to me two months ago to deliver the valedictory address to the graduating class of Bellevue Hospital Medical College, one hundred and sixty-one in number. The Commencement was held at Chickering Hall. The audience was large, and composed, as is mostly the case on such occasions, largely of women. The candidates were presented by the Secretary of the Faculty, Professor Austin Flint, Jr., and the degrees conferred by Dr. Taylor, the President. My address, which occupied about twenty-five minutes in its delivery, consisted mainly of earnest advice to the young men about to launch out into practice, and was frequently interrupted by applause, especially when I referred to the time so often misspent in idle dalliance, in parting one's hair in the middle, in fashionable society, and in frivolous amusements. My defence of the Code of Ethics, lately attacked by some of the New York physicians, chiefly specialists, elicited marked attention. I said: "Study and observe the requirements of the Code of Ethics of the American Medical Association. Nowhere will you find so trustworthy a guide in all professional conduct as in this chart. The men who framed it were men honored throughout the length and breadth of this continent for their wisdom, intelligence, and integrity. It is the palladium of our rights, the ark of our safety; and the man who wilfully dishonors it dishonors his profession, and is a disturber of the public peace." No prizes are given in this school. Another noteworthy peculiarity is the abolishment of what is called the inaugural dissertation, which, while it consumes much valuable time, is no adequate test of scholarship or of professional attainment.

I had not been in Chickering Hall since the winter of 1850, when I attended a sacred concert given on a Sunday evening by Jenny Lind. I sat in the middle aisle, about three-fifths of the way from the stage, and her voice floated by me as if it had been conveyed on a silver cord. It was the sweetest music that ever greeted my ears, the song of a veritable nightingale.

The evening after the Commencement the two Flints, father and son, gave my son, Dr. S. W. Gross, and myself a dinner at the Manhattan Club, of which both are members. We sat down at a quarter past seven o'clock, and rose at eleven. The guests numbered twenty-five, among whom were Taylor, the President of the Bellevue Hospital Medical College, and Emeritus Professor of Obstetrics; Detmold, who was the first in this country to perform the operation for club-foot; Thomas, the gynæcologist; Vanderpoel, formerly Port Physician of New York; Markoe, Mott, and Hutchison, the eminent surgeons; Otis and Gouley, the surgical specialists; Lusk, Professor of Obstetrics in the Bellevue Hospital Medical College; Dennis, a rising young surgeon of Brooklyn; and Varick, a distinguished surgeon of Jersey City. "Charley" Smith, John G. Adams, and Jared Linsly, with myself, represented the old fogy element. Sayre, always a host in himself, was detained at home by a painful knee.

After the viands were disposed of, the host rose, and in feeling words referred to the time when, as colleagues in the University of Louisville, we became acquainted with each other. He then mentioned as a rare occurrence the fact that a son of each of us was a professor in the school in which we ourselves held chairs. He closed with a toast, the only one drunk on the occasion, expressive of his best wishes for my health, happiness, and long life.

Warmly tendering my thanks, and cordially reciprocating the good wishes of the host, I embraced the opportunity to say that only a few hours before we took our seats at the table the idea had occurred to me that this would be an appropriate occasion to form a club, with alternate meetings once a year in Philadelphia and New York, for the purpose of establishing a closer bond of connection between the medical men of the two cities than had hitherto existed. The suggestion was warmly approved without a dissenting voice, and a committee was at once appointed to carry it into effect. I anticipate much good from this little impromptu speech.

Each of the Flints stands at the head of his respective department as a writer and as a teacher—the father as professor of medicine for nearly half a century and as a voluminous writer on medicine; and the son as a teacher of, and writer on, physiology. Both have distinguished themselves as original investigators. The son is a graduate of the Jefferson Medical College, in which he received his degree, with my son, in 1857, after both had attended our lectures for two years in the University of Louisville. After leaving Philadelphia young Flint went to Paris, where he became a pupil of Bernard and Robin, and fitted himself by hard work for teaching with eminent success that branch of science to which he has devoted his life. The Flints are descended from a family of physicians as far back as four generations, the great-great-grandfather having emigrated from England to this country early in the last century, and settled in Massachusetts, where, at Petersham, on the 20th of October, 1812, my former colleague was born. He is consequently now in the seventy-first year of his age. He is still full of vigor, intellectual and physical, such as few men of his years can boast of. His elementary education was obtained partly at academies and partly at Harvard University, where, in 1832, he took his degree in medicine at a time when John C. Warren, Jacob Bigelow, John C. Ware, and James Jackson, whose private pupil he was, were prominent members of the medical Faculty. The estimation in which he has been held as a public teacher is attested by the fact that he has been connected at various times with not fewer than six medical schools. The Bellevue Hospital Medical College, in which he is still laboring, owes much of its well-merited reputation to him and to his son. Tall, handsome, and of manly form, with a well-modulated voice of great compass, he is as a lecturer at once clear, distinct, and inspiring. During his hour in the class-room no student ever falls asleep. He ranks especially high as a clinical instructor. As a diagnostician in diseases of the chest he has few equals. Nor is this fact at all surprising when we bear in mind the time and the immense labor which, from an early period of his professional life, he has devoted to their investigation. I know of no one who is so well entitled as Austin Flint, Sr., to be regarded as the American Laennec.

Soon after he took his degree Dr. Flint became connected with the Buffalo Medical Journal, to which for ten years he devoted his best energies, and which he edited with great ability. He has contributed many papers to the periodical press, especially The American Journal of the Medical Sciences; and he has published, besides his great work on the Principles and Practice of Medicine, now in its fifth edition, a number of exhaustive monographs on diseases of the heart and respiratory organs, works which have given him a wide reputation at home and abroad. He is a member of many medical societies, domestic and foreign, was President of the New York Academy of Medicine in 1872, and delivered the address in Medicine at the International Medical Congress held in Philadelphia in 1876. He was one of the vice-presidents of the International Medical Congress held in London in 1881. His writings are everywhere received as authority; and it is safe to say that there is no man in this country who has done more than he to advance the interests of medicine. In the early part of the present winter, at the instance of the Philadelphia County Medical Society, the largest organization of the kind in the country, he delivered to crowded houses three discourses on auscultation and percussion in connection with the diseases of the respiratory organs. On the evening prior to the last lecture the physicians of Philadelphia gave him a magnificent dinner at the Hotel Bellevue, at which Professor Alfred Stillé presided, in recognition of his many valuable services and of their appreciation of his lofty character. It will be a long time, I hope, before this noble man's life will be rounded off by a full stop.

Sunday, March 25th.—This ought to be a sad day to the profession; it is certainly so to me, for one of our most distinguished men has dropped out of our ranks. Dr. William H. Van Buren died this morning at his residence in New York after a protracted illness, in which he endured much suffering, from softening of the brain, attended with paralysis and albuminuria. His mind had been clouded for several months, and death was therefore rather a blessing. Born in New York, in 1819, of poor but highly respectable parents, he was, as his name implies, of Dutch descent, his great-grandfather having come from Holland to this country in 1700. His early education was obtained in his native city. He then entered Yale College, which, however, he left in his junior year. He soon began the study of medicine, and for a time attended the lectures in the University of Pennsylvania; but before taking his degree he went to Paris, where, at La Charité, he served as an externe under Velpeau. On his return he wrote his thesis on the Use of the Immovable Dressing in the Treatment of Fractures, and the paper was found to be so meritorious that it was soon after published in the American Journal of the Medical Sciences. His was the first attempt to introduce this practice, now so fashionable, into this country. I recollect with what interest I read his paper, and the strong impression it made upon the profession. The first five years of his post-graduate life were spent in the army, chiefly upon the staff of General Winfield Scott. In 1845 he resigned his commission, opened an office in New York, and acted for some time as prosector to his father-in-law, Dr. Valentine Mott. In 1852, on the death of Granville Sharp Pattison, he was appointed Professor of Anatomy in the University of New York, a position which he held for fourteen years. From 1868 to the time of his death he was Professor of the Principles of Surgery in the Bellevue Hospital Medical College, and he lectured also on Clinical Surgery, especially in connection with the affections of the genito-urinary organs. He was connected with numerous hospitals, either as attending or consulting surgeon, and enjoyed at one time a large, influential, and lucrative practice. His contributions to the medical press were numerous and important. Early in his professional life he translated Bernard and Huette's Operative Surgery and Morel's Histology; in 1870 he published Lectures on Diseases of the Rectum; and in 1874, along with his friend and assistant, Dr. Keyes, an exhaustive treatise on the Diseases of the Genito-Urinary Organs. At the International Medical Congress in this city, in 1876, he read an elaborate and valuable paper on Aneurism—a paper which deservedly attracted much attention. Perhaps his ablest production in a scientific and literary point of view is the chapter on Inflammation which he wrote for Ashhurst's International Encyclopædia of Surgery.

In all the relations of life Van Buren bore himself with the dignity of true manhood. He was of lofty stature, well proportioned, gentle in his voice, bland and courtly in his manners, and scrupulously neat in his dress. As a lecturer he generally was clear, distinct, and instructive, but at times rather prosy. His utterance was slow and deliberate. He operated well but not brilliantly, having an eye to the safety of his patient rather than to effect. He leaned to conservatism, and used the knife only when it was impossible to avoid it. He had no fancy for the sight of blood, or for what we call desperate cases, differing in this respect from many of the great surgeons of the day, whose chief glory it is to perform operations. This brief notice of a great and good man would be incomplete if I were to omit mention of the active part which he took in the organization and management of the United States Sanitary Commission, which rendered valuable services during our late war. Van Buren spared neither time nor money to increase its efficiency; and the sacrifices which he incurred from the loss of practice during the five years of his connection with it must for a while have seriously crippled him.

Van Buren was the recipient of many testimonials of esteem and affection. In 1867 he was elected a member of the Society of Surgery of Paris; and in 1878 Yale College conferred upon him the degree of LL.D. He was for two years President of the New York Pathological Society, and for a short time one of the Vice-Presidents of the New York Academy of Medicine. During the last fifteen years he had a residence at Shrewsbury, New Jersey, where he usually spent three days of the week in elegant leisure, generally from Friday until Monday, when he would return to the city and attend to business. He was married in 1842 to the eldest daughter of Valentine Mott.

April 2d.—I attended at the Academy of Music the Fifty-sixth Commencement of the Jefferson Medical College. The day was beautiful and the attendance immense. The degree of doctor of medicine was conferred upon two hundred and twenty-seven young men by Judge Ludlow, the acting president; and it was remarked that the exercises had seldom been conducted with a grace and dignity so befitting the occasion. The learned Judge was evidently impressed with the importance of his functions.

An able valedictory, in which he eloquently depicted the
trials, hardships, and responsibilities of the professional
life, was delivered by Professor Da Costa. A marble
bust, by Ewing, of the late Professor Joseph Pancoast
was then feelingly presented to the College on the part
of the Alumni Association by Dr. Addinell Hewson, one
of the early pupils of the Professor; and it was received
on the part of the trustees in eloquent terms by Judge
Ludlow.

The annual meeting of the Alumni Association was held
on the 30th of March, when an interesting and philosophical address on the Evolution of a Doctor was
delivered by Dr. J. R. Weist, of Richmond, Indiana, a
graduate of 1861. The next day it devolved upon me, as
its President, to receive the bust of Professor Pancoast, presented to the Association in the name of his family by
Professor William H. Pancoast. The occasion deeply
affected me, and indeed almost unnerved me for the performance of this sad duty. Pancoast and I had been colleagues for nearly twenty years, during which we were on
the most intimate terms, and now the only thing, besides
his towering reputation, that was left of him was his image
reflected from the cold marble before me.

April 5th.—Close upon the announcement of the death
of Van Buren comes that of the loss of another member of
our profession, Dr. Joseph K. Barnes, late Surgeon-General
of the United States Army from August, 1864, until within
a short period. He inaugurated the Medical History of
the War, founded the Medical Museum and Medical Library, and raised the department to the highest standard
of efficiency. He played a conspicuous part in professional
attendance upon Secretary Seward after he was murder-
ously assaulted on the night of Lincoln's assassination,
and upon President Garfield after the attempt by Guiteau
to assassinate him. There is reason to believe that his own
death was hastened by the hardships encountered during

these trials.   He was born at Philadelphia in 1817, graduated in medicine in the University of Pennsylvania, and
passed through various grades as an army officer.   His
career was one of honor to himself and of service to
his country.   In 1873 he was elected a member of the
Academy of France, in acknowledgment of his public services.   Many kind and courteous letters passed between
General Barnes and myself, and I have reason to believe
that he entertained as warm a friendship for me as I certainly entertained for him.

The last volume of the Surgical Series of the Medical
and Surgical History of the War, prepared under the direction of Dr. Barnes, Dr. George A. Otis, and D. L. Hunting-
ton, of the United States Army, has just been kindly sent
to me by Surgeon-General Crane.   It forms, with the
other two volumes previously issued, a monument of military surgery.   Poor Otis has gone to his long home, having
died at a comparatively early age of softening of the brain
from overwork in the office of his chief.   His death has
been widely regretted by the medical profession.

April 13th.—The dinner given yesterday by the New
York medical profession to Dr. Oliver Wendell Holmes in
honor of his long career as a teacher of anatomy in the
medical department of Harvard University and of his
services to literature must have been a grand ovation,
thoroughly worthy of the occasion and one long to be
remembered.   An invitation had been sent to me a fortnight ago, but I was unable to be present.   About two hundred and twenty-five persons were in attendance, including
twenty specially invited guests, representative men of the
profession; and responses to toasts selected from Shakespeare were made by William M. Evarts, George W. Curtis,
Bishop Clark of Rhode Island, Dr. T. Gaillard Thomas, and
Whitelaw Reid of the New York Tribune.   Professor Fordyce Barker, who originated the tribute to Holmes, presided.
The dinner was given at Delmonico's.   After a few words

of greeting by the chairman, Dr. A. H. Smith read a poem of welcome, which was happily responded to by the guest of the evening.

Dr. Holmes will always be better remembered as a literary man than as a physician. Although he has been a teacher of anatomy for more than forty years, he has made no additions to anatomical science. In his daily lectures he infused life into the dry bones and into the dead muscles, vessels, nerves, and viscera, and he must have been an agreeable instructor; but of histology his knowledge was superficial and in no wise abreast of the times. No lecturer, if we may trust report, ever abounded more in entertaining anecdotes, or was more successful in keeping alive the attention of his class. Considering the character of his mind, one is surprised to find that he should have exchanged law for medicine. Early in life he annotated Marshall Hall's Practice of Medicine, wrote several papers for the medical journals, and published a lecture on Puerperal Fever, in which he strenuously and successfully advocated the contagious character of that disease in opposition to the teachings of Meigs, Hodge, and other distinguished writers. At a later period he published tracts on Homœopathy, Currents and Counter-Currents in Medicine, and various other ephemeral articles. He never was a clinical teacher, and his medical practice was sadly limited and uninfluential. If he had remained faithful to his early love, he would, there is no doubt, have gained great distinction at the bar. His forte was literature, and as the author of The Autocrat of the Breakfast Table, Elsie Venner, Songs in Many Keys, of many charming magazine articles, and of many delightful poems, his name is indelibly impressed upon our age and country. In the following lines, read in response to the address of welcome, Dr. Holmes tenderly refers to his early medical friends, and expresses a warm desire to be considered as still belonging to our brotherhood:

" I, who your labors for a while have shared,
   New tasks have sought, with new companions fared,
   For Nature's servant far too often seen
   A loiterer by the waves of Hippocrene ;
   Yet round the earlier friendship twines the new :
   My footsteps wander, but my heart is true,
   Nor e'er forgets the living or the dead
   Who trod with me the paths where science led.

" How can I tell you, O my loving friends,
   What light, what warmth your joyous welcome lends
   To life's late hour ?   Alas ! my song is sung ;
   Its fading accents falter on my tongue.
   Sweet friends, if shrinking in the banquet's blaze,
   Your blushing guest must face the breath of praise,
   Speak not too well of one who scarce will know
   Himself transfigured in its roseate glow ;
   Say kindly of him what is, chiefly, true,
   Remembering always he belongs to you ;
   Deal with him as a truant, if you will,
   But claim him, keep him, call him brother still !''

The American medical profession has produced few poets. Among the most conspicuous of these, besides Holmes, are the two Mitchells—John K., the father, and S. Weir, the son—who have written very fine verses; a colleague of mine, the late Dr. Elisha Bartlett, and James G. Percival, an able scholar and a charming poet. England can claim Erasmus Darwin, author of The Botanic Garden; John Keats, author of Endymion, Lamia, Isabella, and other pieces; Mark Akenside, author of The Pleasures of the Imagination; John Armstrong, author of The Art of Preserving Health ; John Wolcott, celebrated as "Peter Pindar"; Sir Richard Blackmore, physician to William III. and Queen Anne, author of Prince Arthur, The Creation, and other poems; and last, but not least, Albert von Haller, a poet of no mean order, an old copy of whose poems in German has long been one of the most valued occupants of my library.

CHAPTER VII.

APRIL 26th.—I dined with Mr. George W. Biddle this
evening at Augustin's. About thirty, chiefly judges and
members of the Pennsylvania bar, sat down at the broad
table, decorated with flowers. Among the prominent men
present were ex-Judge Sharswood, Chief-Justice Mercur,
Judge Gordon, Judge Sterrett, Judge McKennan, Judge
Butler, Judge Ludlow, and Judge Allison, Attorney-General Cassidy, George Biddle, Jr., George W. Childs, and
Mr. J. L. Claghorn. Chief-Justice Mercur occupied the
seat of honor, and as I was placed next to him I had a
good opportunity of enjoying his society. He impressed
me very pleasantly. We discussed, among other matters,
the education of children, and I found that our views coin-
cided. We agreed that the proper way to bring up children was to treat them as our equals, with confidence and
affection, and to grant them all reasonable enjoyments—
not to regard them as if they were aliens in the family,
and to deny them every privilege in the way of amusement, as is done by austere people, who frequently have
the worst children in the community. Judge Mercur is
evidently an amiable man, a pattern of a good husband

and father. The conversation around the table was of a general character, and became quite animated after the wine had freely circulated. The host, who is celebrated for his hospitality and who is one of the leading members of our bar, made himself especially agreeable by his genial manners and courtesy. Before we sat down at table ex-Judge Sharswood and I had a chat about our early Philadelphia reminiscences. Among other things he asked, "Do you recollect a trial which took place in 1828, in which Dr. George McClellan was defendant in a suit for malpractice on account of alleged want of skill in a case of cataract?" "Certainly," I said; "for I was one of the witnesses." "Did you hear Dr. Physick's testimony?" "I did not." "Well, it was curious. A cranky old judge by the name of Barnes presided, and when Physick was called the judge insisted that he should take a seat with him on the bench, which accordingly he did. 'Dr. Physick,' he asked, 'you must have a large experience in diseases of the eye?' 'I have,' was the answer. 'Will you be kind enough to state what your experience is in operations for cataract?' 'I have performed many operations of this kind, and have occasionally lost an eye; but I have not been quite so unlucky as Baron Wenzel, a German oculist, who declared that he had lost a hatful of eyes before he became an expert.' 'Sit down, great man, sit down! that will do, great man,' added the judge." Dr. Joseph Parrish was another witness in this famous trial, but he showed little familiarity with ophthalmic surgery. He wore, I recollect, his Quaker costume, with his legs incased in high boots with buff-colored tops. One of McClellan's counsel, a young man of great promise as a lawyer, afterwards became a forger and fled to Europe, whence he never returned. A verdict of five hundred dollars was rendered in favor of the plaintiff. The suit, as most frequently happens, had been instigated by professional enemies of McClellan.

Within but one month after this very pleasant reunion of eminent lawyers, poor Sharswood slept, like Asa of old, with his fathers. Seized with apoplexy on the street, he was carried to his bed in a state of unconsciousness, in which he expired in less than a week. He was a great jurist. He was well trained in the depths and subtleties of the law from an early period of his life. His editions of Blackstone's Commentaries, Byles on Bills of Exchange, Smith on Contracts, and of other legal works, are everywhere regarded with high favor by the profession. He is also the author of a small volume on Ethics and Legal Studies, intended as a guide for the student. For many years he held a chair in the Law School of the University of Pennsylvania. He sat on the bench when he was hardly thirty years of age. A year before his death he retired, at the expiration of his term of office, from the chief-justiceship of the State. When a man so ripe in scholarship and in knowledge of legal science closes his mortal career, humanity cannot resist the melancholy satisfaction of dropping a tear on his grave. Sharswood was as good a man as he was a great one.

April 28th.—I received an invitation from the president-elect and the local committee of the British Medical Association to be their guest at the meeting in Liverpool on the 31st of July and the following three days in August, and also a request to send any specimens that might be of interest on the occasion. The fear of seasickness alone deters me from accepting it. This invitation is particularly grateful to me, as it shows the friendly feeling which exists on the part of our foreign brethren, not only toward me personally, but toward the medical profession of the United States. No one perhaps on this continent can bear warmer testimony than I to the courtesy and kindness of our English kinsmen, who on the three occasions on which I was among them made me feel perfectly at home. The British Medical Association, like its younger sister

in this country, is peripatetic, meeting at a different point
of the Island every year; and it makes heavy drafts upon
the hospitality of the place, the president rarely escaping
an expenditure of several thousand dollars for his short-
lived honors.

May 30th.—To-day I leave for Cincinnati, my early
home in the West, accompanied by my two daughters and
by S. W. Gross and his wife—all but the last natives of
the "Queen City"—father and son to attend the meeting
of the American Surgical Association which meets there
to-morrow, and the women to see their friends. The reunion of the Association was a marked success. Some
excellent papers were read and discussed; among others
one by Dr. Senn, a young Swiss physician of Milwaukee,
detailing a large number of experiments on dogs illustrative of intracapsular fracture of the thigh-bone. The Association was strengthened by the election of a number of
prominent surgeons as Fellows. On the second evening
of the meeting it was entertained at the Gibson House by
the Committee of Arrangements, Drs. Conner, Dawson,
and Bramble, assisted by the secretary, Dr. Weist of Richmond. Among the Fellows who took an active part in
its proceedings were Kinloch of Charleston; Campbell of
Augusta, Georgia; Richardson of New Orleans; Briggs of
Nashville; Mastin of Mobile; Gregory of St. Louis; Gunn
of Chicago; Moore of Rochester; Post of New York;
Fifield of Boston; Johnston, Alan P. Smith, and Tiffany
of Baltimore; and Mears, Packard, and S. W. Gross of
Philadelphia. The Association has now nearly one hundred members, the number originally provided for by the
constitution. An amendment, offered a year ago, to increase the membership to one hundred and fifty, failed to
pass, on the ground that the Association would thereby
be rendered unwieldy. The next meeting takes place at
Washington City in May, 1884. As I had occupied the
office of president for four years, and expressed my deter-

mination not to accept it again, Dr. Moore was unanimously elected, and no better Fellow, or one who takes a deeper interest in the Association, could have been selected. I may add that I showed my willingness to contribute my mite to the Transactions, of which a volume is to be published this summer, by reading a short paper on the Value of Early Operations in Malignant Tumors. Our meeting was held on the very site where, more than forty years ago, while a professor in the Medical Department of the Cincinnati College, I delivered four courses of lectures on pathological anatomy.

It was sad for me to see that nearly all the great landmarks of Cincinnati forty-three years ago, when I left it, were so completely obliterated that, if I had been dropped down in the heart of the city, or in any one of its principal streets, I should not have known where I was. All things were changed; nearly all my old friends had long been dead; the few who survived were tottering on the brink of the grave. My children failed to find a trace of the house in which they were born. Houses as well as people have their graves. Cincinnati is a compactly built city. It has many fine houses and public edifices; but its glory consists in its fine suburban residences and grounds at Clifton, Mount Auburn, and Walnut Hills, which for style and elegance are not exceeded anywhere in this country. It is proud of its observatory, opera-house, art gallery, public schools, and public-spirited citizens. Mr. Cist predicted in 1840 that Cincinnati in one hundred years would have as large a population as London. He forgot that it was hemmed in on all sides by hills and water, which must inevitably interfere with its growth. It is surpassed already by St. Louis and Chicago. In an article in a recent number of Harper's Magazine on the growth of Cincinnati, written by a lady, no mention whatever is made of Dr. Daniel Drake, whose Picture of Cincinnati, published in 1812, was largely instrumental in directing the attention of Eastern immigrants to what was then emphatically the Queen City of the West. Many, if indeed not most, of its early settlers were New England people. In 1833 it took me thirteen days and a half to make the journey from Easton, Pennsylvania, to Cincinnati. Now twenty-three hours only are requisite to make the journey from Philadelphia, with scarcely any fatigue. Such is progress.

June 4th.—I left Cincinnati this morning with my two daughters to attend the meeting, the next day, of the American Medical Association at Cleveland. We reached our destination at half past three o'clock in the afternoon, and drove at once to the sumptuous residence of Mr. Henry B. Payne, whose guests, as arranged by previous invitation, we remained until the following Thursday afternoon, when we took our departure for Philadelphia. The Paynes are refined, cultured people, and very wealthy. Their house is large, and it is situated in a beautiful part of Euclid Avenue. In front it has a broad, beautiful lawn covered with rare trees, native and exotic, and enlivened by birds, among which the robin appears conspicuous. Mr. Payne is a lawyer by profession. He represented Ohio in Congress, and was put in nomination for President by the Democratic party at its Convention in Cincinnati in 1880, General Hancock beating him as candidate only by a few votes. Mrs. Payne, a lady of intelligence and much activity, would have discharged the duties of the White House with womanly dignity, and in this office she would have been ably assisted by her two accomplished daughters, Mrs. Gordon of Cleveland, and Mrs. Whitney of New York. Two evenings after our arrival a cablegram from Paris announced the death of one of Mrs. Whitney's children, a girl of loveliness and promise, who was a victim of diphtheria, doubtless contracted on the steamer, for the attack made its appearance almost as soon as the family reached the French metropolis. Notwithstanding the profound grief which this announcement produced, we were treated with great courtesy and attention by our host and hostess, as well as by every member of the family. Private grief is sacred, and we did all we could to assuage its poignancy.

June 5th.—The meeting of the American Medical Association was a success. Dr. John L. Atlee, of Lancaster, Pennsylvania, presided with dignity and self-possession; and his inaugural, devoted to reminiscences of his teachers in the University of Pennsylvania, was a scholarly production, well received by the crowded audience. The addresses were for the most part satisfactory, and much interest was evinced in the work of the different Sections. The plan of journalizing the Transactions, originally suggested by me in 1868, was carried into effect. Dr. N. S. Davis, the founder of the Association, was appointed editor of the new journal; and I had the great pleasure of seeing Dr. Austin Flint, Sr., elected president on my nomination. No man better entitled to the office by his professional merits could have been selected for this position. In choosing him the Association honored itself more than it honored the New York veteran physician.

But for his modesty and his inland residence John L. Atlee would long ago have been elected to the office which he now fills. Born at the close of the last century, he is now nearly eighty-three years of age, with a mind well poised and a body as erect as it was in early youth. It is refreshing to see a man who has led so laborious a life so well preserved. Dr. Atlee belongs to that class of men known as general practitioners, in contradistinction to the specialists who have sprung up during the last twenty years, and whose numbers have become legion. Skilled alike in medicine, surgery, and obstetrics, he has earned an enviable reputation as a diagnostician, as a therapeutist, and as a successful operator. To him much credit is due for his efforts in reviving ovariotomy, in which he had the powerful coöperation of his celebrated brother, Washington L. Atlee. Dr. John L. Atlee was the first who excised both ovaries in the same woman. The patient was unmarried, twenty-five years of age. The operation was performed in 1843, and the subject was alive in 1878. He has contributed numerous papers to the medical press ; and by a singular coincidence one number of the American Journal of the Medical Sciences contained articles from the pen of himself, of his son, and of his grandson, a concurrence rarely witnessed in the scientific or literary world. A good talker, fond of anecdotes, and abounding in knowledge, Dr. Atlee is much beloved and is one of the most popular of physicians. He graduated from the University of Pennsylvania in 1820, and he can congratulate himself upon having devoted sixty-three years of his life to the service of humanity.

Wednesday, June 21st.—The death of Archbishop Wood, so long expected, has at length taken place. I paid him a visit last evening at half past seven o'clock with his faithful medical attendant, Dr. Joseph Lopez, and he expired the same evening at fifteen minutes past eleven o'clock, having been for several days in a state of unconsciousness. The immediate cause of his death was uræmia—the remote cause albuminuria, under which he had been laboring, in a marked degree, for the last six months. His health had been gradually declining for several years, and still it was hard to persuade him that he was sick. He had a powerful will and a remarkable vitality. An ordinary man would long ago have given up in despair. But the Archbishop held on to life and to duty in a manner which reminded one of the Athenian who held on to the ship with his hands, and when they were lopped off seized it with his teeth. On more occasions than one, when in the morning I left him, as I supposed, desperately ill, and did not know whether he would be alive at my next visit, I found him sitting in his big arm-chair busily engaged in writing letters or in arranging papers, shaved, handsomely dressed, and greeting me with his benignant and courtly smile. One of his greatest physical inconveniences was the swollen condition of his lower extremities, which were very hard, and at least twice their ordinary bulk and weight; at times, indeed, they were erysipelatous, very painful, and almost immovable. On looking at them one day, I told him that his limbs reminded me of the anecdote, elsewhere related, of William III., who was similarly affected. The Archbishop laughed heartily at the recital of this incident. I do not think anybody ever enjoyed an anecdote more than his grace. He had himself a large fund of them, drawn chiefly from his own experience. I shall never forget the glee with which he told me that when a little boy he had in climbing a fence irreparably torn a pair of new trousers and slightly scratched his leg. He was, naturally enough, afraid to return home in this condition lest his parents should punish him. It happened that on the same day a sister had been bitten by a dog that was supposed to be mad. Her wound was promptly cauterized; and when the little brother, who had just come in, said that the same dog which had bitten her had torn his trousers and injured him, his leg was subjected to a severe cauterization with the hot iron by Dr. Physick, the pain of which he bore with the fortitude of a Spartan. He said that this lesson caused him afterwards strictly to adhere to the truth. On another occasion my elder son, who had been sitting in a Pullman car in a seat adjoining his, went into the smoking compartment to enjoy a cigar. During his absence a stranger, impressed by the distinguished appearance of the Archbishop, took the vacated seat and entered into conversation. On my son's return the stranger went to his own seat, and the Archbishop, with a bland smile, said, "Do you see that man over there?" "Yes," was the reply. "Well, he must think me a very untruthful man; for he asked me if I was married, and I told him yes, and the father of nearly eight hundred children! You know, doctor, I am wedded to the church, and have nearly that many orphan children in my diocese to look after.''

I attended the Archbishop professionally for more than twelve years—for about half this period alone, and for the remaining half with Dr. Lopez; and during all this time, in the vicissitudes of his ailments, often of a very trying nature, I never heard a murmur of complaint escape his lips. I never saw him ruffled in temper or exhibit the slightest impatience. If he was not always cheerful, his face bore a sweet, benignant expression, indicative of kindness of heart, and of perfect resignation to his situation and to the will of God. His household were devoted to him. The Rev. Father Elcock, the rector of the Cathedral, and the Rev. Father Brennan, his secretary, were in constant attendance on him, and with his faithful body-servant, Tom Bryant, did all they could to aid him in the discharge of his Episcopal duties and to contribute to his personal and spiritual comfort.

There was nothing ostentatious in Archbishop Wood; nothing that denoted luxury or pride of office. His study was devoid of everything but the plainest articles, and his chamber did not contain one elegant piece of furniture. Such a man ought to have had a palatial residence, furnished in the best style, with choice paintings and objects of virtu, to lighten the cares and toils of office; but to all such things he seemed to be indifferent. He lived only for the good of his church and of his people. While he knew as well as any one how to enjoy the pleasures of the table, his habits were temperate. The first time he took a meal at my house was in 1871, when I gave a breakfast to Archbishop Spalding. He subsequently repeatedly dined with me on the Sabbath; and I always felt better for my association with him, because I was conscious that I had been in the society of a good man and a noble Christian. On such occasions his grace was always accompanied by his private secretary—an invariable custom, I believe, with the dignitaries of the Catholic Church.

The Archbishop was an exceedingly kind man. The orphan children of his diocese claimed his special care and tenderness. During the last years of his life from six to eight hundred boys and girls were constantly fed, clothed, and educated by his bounty. He built churches, founded hospitals and asylums, established seminaries and colleges, and worked unceasingly in the interests of morality and religion. While he loved his own church above all others, he was tolerant of many other denominations of Christians, believing there was more or less good in all. He despised cant, deceit, and hypocrisy. He owed much of his popularity and success in building up the church in his diocese to his strong common-sense and to his executive ability. He was educated at Gloucester, England. After his return to his native country he was for a number of years a clerk in two of the Cincinnati banks; and so well did he discharge the duties of his office that much regret was expressed when he announced his determination to abandon his secular work for the ministry. Archbishop Wood's family were Protestants; and it was not without much sorrow and earnest remonstrance that they saw him give up the religion of his forefathers for a religion for which none of them had respect. The father was dead at the time; and the mother, if I mistake not, never afterwards looked kindly at the conduct of her son. But what was their loss proved, ere long, to be the gain of the Catholic Church. After having completed his studies at Rome, his rise was rapid. An assistant of Archbishop Purcell of Cincinnati, he became at no distant day Bishop of Philadelphia. In 1875 he was elevated to the archbishopric, an office which he filled with marked dignity and usefulness to the time of his lamented death, at the age of seventy-one years. I was present when, through a messenger of the Pope, the pallium was conferred upon him. He was at the time in poor health. As his medical adviser, I was kindly invited to a seat in the sanctuary, which was crowded with more than two hundred and fifty priests, including the papal nuncio and a number of the prominent bishops and archbishops of the country. Among the illustrious prelates on this grand occasion was the venerable Archbishop Purcell, an octogenarian, whom in my young days I knew at Cincinnati, a truly good man, but devoid, as was shown soon after this event, of knowledge of finance. No one lamented his downfall more sincerely than Archbishop Wood, whose appeals in behalf of his friend created a widespread sympathy, and exercised a powerful influence, not only in raising substantial aid, but in shaping public opinion. The only error of which Archbishop Purcell was guilty was his faith in the competency of his brother, Father Purcell, to superintend the secular affairs of his diocese. I never knew Father Purcell personally; but I have had reliable information that he was a frolicsome youth, fond of gayety, and not over-exact in his methods of doing business. After he entered the priesthood he no doubt became a pious man; but his career shows that he utterly lacked financial and executive ability.

Archbishop Wood, as I have already stated, was a liberal-minded man, with none of the prejudices which have been so often alleged against the priests and members of the Catholic Church. As an instance I may mention the manner in which he regarded the proper observance of the Sabbath during the Centennial Exhibition in this city. While Protestant clergymen and laymen loudly denounced all attempts to keep the Exhibition open on Sunday, Archbishop Wood expressed himself strongly in favor of the project, and his high position enabled him to exert a powerful influence upon the mind of the public. His views are so rational that I cannot forbear inserting them here in full: "I only state my conviction, derived from the perpetual practice and teaching of the Church of Christ, that any innocent recreation is quite compatible with the holiness and repose of the Lord's day, after one has discharged his religious duty to his Maker. Among the means of innocent relaxation of soul and body, I can see none more harmless than an afternoon visit to the Exposition, where the poor and laboring classes—and they are most numerous among us—may enjoy a few hours of rational pleasure in examining the products of genius and the specimens of art and mechanical skill which have been gathered together in the Centennial Buildings. Such a visit will improve and elevate their minds. Indeed, I believe that it will have a most beneficial effect; that it will tend to prevent many disorders, and check to a great extent that desecration of the Lord's day which is unhappily a growing evil in the community."

He was an enemy to all secret societies, denounced miracle-working among the people of his diocese, and exerted his influence in putting down the misrule and spirit of insubordination among the Irish Catholics in the mining regions of Pennsylvania. He looked with horror upon the conduct of the "Molly Maguires," whose crimes cried aloud to heaven for vengeance. A heavy load was lifted off his mind as one after another, to the number of twenty-three, was led to the scaffold through the agency mainly of one man, Mr. Franklin B. Gowen, President of the Philadelphia and Reading Railroad.

The Archbishop's funeral, as solemn as it was imposing, took place six days after his death. After the body was embalmed and lay in state, it was viewed by thousands of people, among whom were many sincere mourners. The Cathedral, one of the darling objects of his affection, was crowded by a select audience, including many members of other churches, clergymen, physicians, lawyers, and prominent citizens; while thousands were assembled outside its walls anxious to catch a parting glimpse of their venerated friend and beloved pastor. After High Mass was said, and a beautiful and appropriate discourse commemorative of his life and services was pronounced by Archbishop Gibbons of Baltimore, the occupant of the oldest Catholic church in the United States, the remains, arrayed in full canonicals, were carried in procession in a magnificent hearse drawn by six horses around the four squares of the Cathedral, and finally laid at rest in the crypt near the high altar, there to abide until the day of the resurrection. A few days after this event the Archbishop's will was admitted to probate. It was compressed into a few short paragraphs, in which all his personal property, consisting of an insurance policy on his life for ten thousand dollars, was bequeathed to the church which he had served so long and so faithfully. Two aged sisters, the one a widow and the other a single woman, were the chief mourners at the funeral, which was attended by more than four hundred priests, including sixteen bishops and four archbishops. Thus lived and thus died a good and noble man, an honor to his age, to his church, and to his country. Greater men have lived, but the world has seldom, if ever, seen a better man than James Frederic Wood.

July 8th.—My good mother used to insist upon it that I was born on the 8th of July, 1805. If this be so—and none could have known better than she—I must now be seventy-eight years old. And yet I do not feel old; my friends say I look well, and I have no reason to contradict them. My health is excellent. I sleep well, enjoy my three meals a day, and am able to do a good deal of work. For all this I am thankful to God. My children congratulate me, and make me little presents betokening their love for me. I am happy; but would be more so if my dear wife were here to keep me company and share my joys.

July 15th.—The late Rev. Dr. Malcolm, formerly a missionary in Burmah, related to me several years ago a good story about a native doctor, a pompous fellow, who was in the habit of parading the city with his attendants, proclaiming that he had never lost a patient. He had reduced, he said, the whole catalogue of maladies to sixty, for each of which he pretended to have an infallible remedy. "It is true," he added, "I am sometimes baffled, but only for a short time, for if I find after three or four trials that the remedy is not adapted to the cure of the disease I use my universal pill for the cure of the co-diseases, and I have never yet failed of success." Shortly after this conversation Dr. Malcolm was roused in the night by the terrible wailings and lamentations of his neighbors—noises such as are always made when a noted person dies. Meeting the doctor the next morning Dr. Malcolm observed, "What a pity it is you were not here last night. A man died only a few doors from here, and as you have never lost a case he could not have been your patient." "Yes, but he was," was the reply; "he was my patient; but how could he help dying when death killed him? I can cure every disease; but there is no remedy for death." And the doctor went his way.

Medical boasters are, unfortunately, not confined to the Burmese. I have met many such fellows in our own ranks, and they generally take better with the common herd of mankind than does the modest and retiring physician. People like to be humbugged. Many years ago I visited a patient suffering from typhoid fever in consultation with a middle-aged practitioner noted for his bragging proclivities, who declared that he had treated that winter more than eighty cases of that malady and had not lost a single case. Our patient died the same night; and his mother-in-law, sick with the same disease, followed him a few days afterwards! Death, according to the Frenchman of 1793, is an eternal sleep. Lying never dies; it is a principle of our nature, and I have known many cases in which it was hereditary. War is the natural condition of mankind. Children love to strike and scratch one another; chickens fight before the shell is fairly off their backs; and puppies seem never happier than when they are engaged in an angry romp. What insect fights more determinedly than the ant when annoyed or ill treated by its fellow-worker? Truth is the antithesis of lies, and yet how rarely is it told! Cardinal Hildebrand acted a lie when, pretending to be bowed down by the infirmities of age, he assumed a vacillating gait and the appearance of a humpback to deceive the electoral college into the belief that a year or two would put an end to him. The morning after he was elected pope he walked erect, with a firm step, and a face no longer expressive of suffering. For years he had been stooping because, he said, he had all the while been looking for the keys of St. Peter, and having found them, he had no longer any need of doubling himself up.

July 17th.—The subject of Evolution has engaged much, if not universal, attention among scientific and educated men during the last twenty-five years, chiefly through the researches and writings of Charles Darwin, who spent most of his life in its investigation. Devoting his early years to natural history, he proceeded steadily until he reached a height in this branch of knowledge which no one had attained before. He was one of those who work for eternity—one of those who, in England, are sure when they die to find a tablet, if not also a grave, in Westminster Abbey, amidst the tombs of kings and princes, and statesmen, and warriors, and scientists, and discoverers, and inventors, and philanthropists, and literary geniuses. Charles Darwin must be regarded as the founder of the science of evolution; for, although glimpses of it may be traced in the writings of some of the ancient philosophers, and although the doctrine is distinctly shadowed forth in the works of Erasmus Darwin, his grandfather, Charles is unquestionably entitled to the credit of having given form to the material which lay scattered like so much gold in the sands of time. The following sentence, composed nearly one hundred years ago by the author of The Botanic Garden and The Loves of the Plants, embodies the germ of the theory. Like the electric spark elicited by Franklin's kite, it was long hidden in darkness. "Would it be too bold to imagine," says Erasmus Darwin, "that, in the great length of time since the earth began to exist, perhaps millions of ages before the commencement of the history of mankind—would it be too bold to imagine that all warm-blooded animals have arisen from one living filament which THE GREAT FIRST CAUSE endued with animality, with the power of acquiring new parts, attended with new propensities, directed by irritations, sensations, volitions, and associations, and thus possessing the faculty of continuing to improve by its own inherent activity, and of delivering down those improvements by generation to its posterity, world without end?"

If we accept the doctrine of evolution, we must take for granted that creation has been an extremely slow process, and that evolution is still going on and will continue to go on in all time to come. If this be so, how long would it take to evolve a human being from an orang-outang, the highest type of the monkey tribe, or a horse from the animal immediately below it in affinity of form and structure? We have an authentic record of the history of the human race for at least six thousand years, and yet during all this period no such organic modification has been witnessed. Perhaps it may be said that the necessity for such a development ceased with the creation of man and woman. There is plausibility in the assumption. Many of the varieties of form and color observable in man and animals may readily be explained by the changes induced by miscegenation, climate, modes of living, and other interdependent and extraneous causes. If we believe in a great First Cause, as all rational men must, why not assume that all things, visible and invisible, were the product of a special creation instead of a gradual evolution, as asserted by Darwin and his followers? If God could create the earth, the stars, and the mighty planets, of which our world forms only an insignificant part, could He not also, by a special act, have created all the dwellers therein, from the most minute microcosm up to the most complicated form of animal life? I agree with Professor Tyndall that the whole subject of evolution belongs to the dim twilight of conjecture.

Henry Ward Beecher teaches that, while the animal part of man is evolved from beings below him, the spiritual part is derived directly from God; or, not to misrepresent him, "man is the son of God in spiritual value." There is evidently a cunning mental reservation here. The great preacher evidently means that man in his whole being is an emanation from inferior organisms. When he declares that man is not sinful by nature, but voluntarily, and that Adam, poor fellow, is not the father of all the wickedness of this world, I give him credit for his candor and good sense. Adam had enough trouble of his own without being saddled with the sins of the whole human family. If Eve did not worry him, Cain certainly did.

July 18th.—Much diversity of opinion has been expressed of late years in regard to the advantage of the study of the classics as an exercise of the mind, some contending that they are essential to the full development of the intellectual faculties, while others of equal prominence maintain that they possess no advantage whatever as a mental discipline over the study of the modern languages, especially the French and German. Professor Seelye, one of our ablest and most experienced educators, asserts as the result of his observation that the young men who take the Latin and Greek courses in our colleges are better able to grasp the mysteries of science, and that they will eventually reach a higher standard of excellence, than those who do not take them. Hence he is in favor of a given amount of Greek as a requisite for admission into our literary institutions; and in this opinion he is warmly seconded by other teachers both in this country and in Europe. I doubt very much whether the acquisition of a science has much to do with a knowledge of Greek and Latin. Assuredly, many of the ablest and most distinguished scientists of the age have been men of limited classical education—self-made men, as they are called, who have risen to prominence by their own talent, by their industry, and by their will. That a moderate acquaintance with the classical languages is an aid to the comprehension of the technicalities of the law and of medicine every one will admit; but a profound knowledge of Greek and Latin is rarely needed except by the professed teacher and by the student of theology, who is obliged to study the Scriptures in the original tongue, and to make himself acquainted with the writings of the Fathers of the Church. Professor Seelye and his school should not confound a knowledge of these languages with genius and industry, without which a man will never attain usefulness or distinction as a scientist. Any study that exercises the mind tends to strengthen the brain and to evolve a higher nerve-power. The study of mathematics is generally regarded as a powerful means of improving the intellect, and yet I have known several profound mathematicians who, except in their special pursuits, manifested but little intellectual power.

A blow at Greek and Latin was recently struck by the younger Charles Francis Adams in the address delivered by him at the Commencement of Harvard University. He does not believe that, as usually taught in our schools and colleges, they are of much use in the ordinary pursuits of life. He thinks that their value has been much overrated, and to this opinion he has already made a number of prominent converts.

July 30th.—The publication, a few days ago, of Mr. George Ticknor Curtis's Biography of James Buchanan, fifteenth President, recalls a pleasant interview which I had with him in September, 1858. My two daughters and I were on our return trip from the White Sulphur Springs of Virginia, and were desirous of paying our respects to the Chief Magistrate of the nation; and so, having previously ascertained at what hour it would suit him to see us, we drove to the White House. It was the hour of twelve, and the day, I recollect, was very warm. A servant showed us into the large parlor, and presently Mr. Buchanan appeared, welcoming us with that cordiality for which he was noted. After a few inquiries about some of his Philadelphia friends, the conversation took a general turn, and in less than half an hour we left, delighted with our visit. His agreeable manners and the ease of his conversation impressed us most favorably. He was of stalwart frame, more than six feet in height, broad-shouldered, with a remarkably pale face, the pallor of which was heightened by a large white cravat. He stooped somewhat, and, owing to a stiffness in his neck, his head inclined habitually towards the right side, a peculiarity which imparted somewhat of a sinister expression to his countenance. Mr. Buchanan was a bachelor. The history of his courtship is well known, and is invested with an air of romance. The object of his affection was a Miss Coleman, of Lancaster, a beautiful and accomplished woman, the daughter of one of the first families of that city. From some trivial cause the engagement was broken, but it would probably have been renewed if death had not overtaken her soon after. The future President long grieved for the loss of his *fiancée*, and he never afterwards, it is said, addressed any woman with matrimonial intent. The letter which he wrote to her

father after her death, and which is published in Mr.
Curtis's admirable Biography, is full of pathos, and well
calculated, even at this distant day, to excite our sympathy.   Mr. Buchanan was wild in his youth, and Carlisle
College not only refused to give him its degree at the
close of his academic studies, but came very near expel-
ling him.   Whatever we may think of him as a statesman, we cannot deny him strong intellect and scholarly
accomplishments, and the suavity and refinement so necessary in a man of high social and official position.   Mr.
Curtis's Biography, written as it is in excellent style, with
a superabundance of material at his command, and published at an opportune period in our history, will serve as
a scale in which the American people may weigh at their
leisure the claims of Mr. Buchanan to their admiration or
condemnation for the part played by him as Chief Executive of the nation at a time when its life was in peril.
"For my name and memory, I leave it to men's charitable
speeches, to foreign nations, and to the next ages."   Such
was the language of Francis Bacon, the greatest intellect
of his age, and, as has been said, one of the meanest of
men.   James Buchanan was not a mean man, but a man
lamentably deficient in decision of character.

Long Branch, July 31st.—To escape from the heat of
Philadelphia I came here three weeks ago.   This place has
been for a long time regarded as one of our most charming
and salubrious summer resorts, and according to my experience it deserves its reputation.   The bathing, however,
is not good ; the surf is usually high, and the undertow so
strong as to render great caution necessary to prevent accidents.   In this respect Cape May and Atlantic City are far
superior to it.   Long Branch, on the other hand, has com-
pensating advantages.   For instance, it has no mosquitoes,
which abound at the other towns, and all its drives are
excellent.   Ocean Avenue in front of my hotel is crowded
on every pleasant afternoon with stylish equipages, the

majority of them coming from New York. At the How-
land, where I am sojourning, many of the residents are
habitués, some of whom have been here every summer
for twenty years. The guests are composed largely of
ladies with their children, who once a week are visited by
their husbands and fathers, most of whom transact business in New York and Philadelphia, and spend Sunday
with their families. Among the prominent guests are
George H. Boker, Philadelphia's poet and late minister at
Constantinople and St. Petersburg; and Attorney-General
Brewster, a gentleman of intelligence, culture, and courtesy. The most remarkable man, however, in the house
is the Rev. Dr. Weston, one of the rectors of St. John's
Parish, New York. He is a bachelor, somewhat aged, but
full of vigor and good nature, fond of chess, which he
plays every day, and the owner of three fast horses, which
he likes to drive on the avenue. Like myself, he loves
children, as well as everything that is beautiful in nature
and in art, and is a man of advanced views in religious
matters. He is a type of the Christian gentleman. He
is an incessant talker. There is no subject that can be
broached on which he is not at home. He abounds in
anecdote, and quotes poetry with the facility of a Macaulay. In fact, he is a walking encyclopædia. Connected
with one of the richest parishes in the world, his salary is
eight thousand dollars a year. Such an income is princely
compared with that of the poor country clergy, whose annual stipend in many instances does not reach five hundred
dollars. Dr. Weston is said to be very charitable.

This afternoon, in company with my daughter, Mrs. Orville Horwitz, I visited Mr. Hoey's Park, a mile back of
the ocean, laid out in beautiful drives, studded with fine
forest trees, and ornamented with conservatories and
flower-beds. The flower-beds are composed of coleuses
and of echeverias, introduced from Mexico, California,
South America, and Siberia, and planted in such a manner

as to present the appearance of rich Persian carpets; while the conservatories are filled with magnificent palms, ferns, orchids, and roses. Mr. Hoey explained to us everything that could conduce to make our visit agreeable and instructive. I said to him, "It is very kind of you to keep your grounds open six days in the week for the inspection of the public." His answer was: "I do it to improve the taste of my visitors, and to afford them pleasure, as the sight of flowers always does." The expense of supporting such an establishment must be immense, as thirty-five men are continually employed from one year's end to the other. Part of the expense was formerly defrayed, I am told, by the sale of roses in the winter and spring. Such a man is a benefactor. Mr. Hoey made his fortune in the express business. Many years ago he married Miss Russell, the actress. He is highly respected as a gentleman and liberal-minded citizen.

Among the cottages that adorn Ocean Avenue are three belonging to Mrs. Winslow, the inventor and proprietor of a nostrum known as Winslow's Soothing Syrup. Charlatans fare well in this country. Swaim made more than a million dollars by the sale of his Panacea, which at one time had a world-wide celebrity, owing mainly to its alleged anti-strumous and anti-syphilitic virtues. Jayne, Schenck, Ayer, Brandreth, Townsend, and many other vendors of patent medicines have also accumulated large fortunes. Lydia E. Pinkham, who died a year ago at Lynn, Massachusetts, left nearly half a million from the sale of her Vegetable Compound and Liver Pills. Her likeness still graces many of the principal newspapers of the day! It is said that she spent annually more than two hundred thousand dollars in advertising; and this was doubtless the secret of her success. James Morrison, the celebrated London charlatan, amassed two million dollars by the sale of his vegetable pills—composed chiefly of oatmeal and aloes. The duty on his pills for ten years yielded a revenue of sixty thousand pounds to the British Government. Morrison was originally an army officer, and knew nothing whatever of medicine. The government tax on the will of Holloway, the English patent medicine man, was three hundred and twenty-five thousand dollars. Japan has a celebrated secret remedy known as the Dosia Powder, which is so highly esteemed for its curative powers that the people have, it is said, for a thousand years, paid divine honors to Kobodaisa, its reputed discoverer.

Notwithstanding that many of these nostrum-mongers have become opulent, few have ever succeeded in getting into fashionable society. Ingram, the founder and late proprietor of the London Illustrated News, who accumulated wealth by the sale of what he called Dr. Tarr's Life Pills, in which he used the name of the distinguished physician, secured a place in Parliament, but he never attained to high social position.

August 5th.—Yesterday Mr. John Welsh, our late Minister to the Court of St. James, the Rev. Dr. Morton, Mr. Joseph Patterson, and Mr. George W. Childs called upon me at my lodgings, and in my absence left their cards. To-day Mr. Childs repeated his visit with a letter from Mrs. Childs, inviting my daughter, Mrs. B. F. Horwitz, and myself to high tea. The evening was passed very pleasantly—Mr. Childs's guests, the gentlemen I have named, the Rev. Dr. Weston, and a few ladies composing the party. About half past eight o'clock we were joined by General Grant, who deeply interested us by his remarks on Mexico, her political and financial condition, her agricultural and mineral resources, her railways, and various other matters of more or less interest in an international point of view. He talked fluently, and expressed himself in excellent English, and in a terse, forcible manner, completely dispelling the idea hitherto entertained by some of us that he is a "silent man."

Mr. Childs is no ordinary man. Springing from humble

life, he has acquired great wealth and social prominence, and no one knows better than he how to entertain his friends. Few men of distinction or of great worth pass through Philadelphia without sharing his hospitality. He is a noble citizen. No man in Philadelphia contributes more liberally to public or private charity than he, or fulfils more frequently the Scriptural injunction not to let the left hand know what the right hand doeth. The money which he annually distributes in small sums among needy women, men, and children amounts to many thousands of dollars. The world at large is ignorant of these acts. His employés are devoted to him, and well they may be, for no man has ever treated his employés better. His annual dinner to the newsboys of Philadelphia is a striking exemplification of his goodness of heart. The entertainment comes off on every Fourth of July, and is looked forward to by these children with keen anticipation. Several years ago Mr. Childs invited me to be present at one given at the Main Centennial Building in the Park. The day was beautiful. The boys, more than five hundred in number, wore their best "bib and tucker;" and I never witnessed a happier set of fellows. Their ages ranged from nine to eighteen. At the ringing of the bell they all rushed to their seats, and in the twinkling of an eye there was such a clangor of knives and forks and spoons as to drown every other sound. Meats, and vegetables, and cakes, and fruits, and ices were all gulped indiscriminately, with copious draughts of lemonade. After an hour and a half thus spent, each, as he arose, crammed his pockets with cakes, oranges, apples, and other portables. How the poor boys passed the night or felt the next morning may well be imagined. There is no sight more pitiable than that of these poor boys sitting and lying on the pavement on a warm summer's day round a newspaper office waiting for their daily supply of papers. To improve the morals of these children, to educate and refine them, and to restrain them from bad influences, they should be sent to night-schools. This would be an enterprise worthy of noble philanthropy.

I have been much interested ever since my arrival in watching the movements of the fish-hawk. The bird is common here, and it is so much valued because it keeps away predaceous birds that a State law enforces a fine of fifty dollars for killing it. The consequence is that it is very tame, building its nest along the roadside, near barns and dwellings, and sometimes even on the top of an old, unused chimney. The birds live in pairs, and are apparently very happy. They breed only once a year, the female laying two eggs about the size of those of the domestic hen. The nest is built of large sticks and weeds, arranged in circular form, generally on the top of a low tree, especially the locust or sycamore. The interior is lined with soft material to promote the comfort of the parents and of their offspring during the hatching season. Their only food is fish, caught by a sudden plunge into the water. Occasionally the bird seizes a fish too large for its strength, and, unable to disengage its talons, it is drawn under the water and drowned, as happened here a few days ago. Sometimes, again, it is attacked by an eagle, which seizes and carries away its prey. It is interesting to witness the apparent disappointment of the male hawk as he goes homeward on his late afternoon excursion without his prey, leaving his wife and children supperless. The fish-hawk comes punctually about the middle of March and retires about the middle of September, and always, year after year, goes to its old roost.

CHAPTER VIII.

AUGUST 10th.—One does not like to speak ill of one's
brethren; but there are politicians and tricksters in the
medical as there are in every other profession—men who,
from interested or dishonorable motives, do not hesitate
to slander, or undermine the standing of, their superiors.
What makes the matter worse is that the injury is usually
performed in so sly and underhand a manner as to render
it difficult, if not impossible, to counteract its effects. A
humiliating illustration of this fact was afforded by two
"most honorable gentlemen" in a neighboring city. The
patient, an eminent merchant, and his friends were anxious
to have the benefit of my advice, and accordingly requested
a consultation. Instead of promptly acceding to the request,
the attending physicians offered every possible obstacle to
the interview. "We don't know Dr. Gross," said one of
them; and when it was found that this excuse was too
flimsy, they said, "Dr. Gross is old, and no longer practises. It is impossible to obtain a visit from him." And
finally, to crown the whole, they added that "Dr. Gross's
practice of bloodletting had exploded years ago"—as if I
made it an invariable rule to bleed my patients. "From

the first," writes my informant, "they did all they could to prevent my brother from seeing you." Such conduct is, I am sorry to say, only too common in our profession.

The recital of this case induces me to make a few remarks upon what is known as the New Code of Ethics, the offspring, mainly, of three New York specialists, in contradistinction to the Code adopted for its government by the American Medical Association soon after its organization in 1847. The object which this trio had in view in proposing this Code, and by a *coup de main* in securing its adoption by the New York State Medical Society at its meeting at Albany in January, 1882, was to authorize the members of the regular profession to meet in consultation all legally constituted practitioners, of whatever school, sect, or character, thus throwing wide open the doors to all kinds of degrading associations, and thereby humiliating us in the eyes not only of one another, but of the public, and at the same time making us the laughing-stock of eclectics, homœopathists, and others who have drawn an impregnable wall around Hippocratic medicine by their peculiar dogmas and practices. How any respectable and honorable members of the profession could persuade themselves to meet these men in this manner is an enigma which it would be difficult to solve. Selfishness was evidently at the bottom of the movement—a desire to enlarge their practice and to increase their emoluments ; this, and nothing else. Because the Legislature of New York or the Legislature of any other State chooses to place all practitioners of whatever school or grade on a legal footing with us, there is no excuse for us to meet them in consultation or to put ourselves on the same professional level with them. As well might we attempt to mix oil and water. The old Code, which originated three-quarters of a century ago with Dr. Percival of England, and which was extensively modified by a committee of the American Medical Association, consisting of the late Dr.

Isaac Hays, Dr. John Bell, and Dr. Gouverneur Emerson of Philadelphia, is perhaps as perfect a code of ethics as it is in the power of man to frame, and it should therefore be maintained inviolate by every honorable and loyal member of the profession. It is to our profession what the Decalogue is to the religionist, with the addition of Christ's injunction—"Whatsoever ye would that men should do to you, do ye even so to them." This schism has produced a degree of ill feeling which a quarter of a century can scarcely overcome. There can be no compromise where there is so wide a divergence.

August 12th.—The hypodermic syringe, in its varied uses in the treatment of diseases and accidents, affords a singular instance of a lack of application of the inductive philosophy to the purposes of our profession. Hardly twenty years have elapsed since this invaluable instrument, now so extensively employed by every practitioner, was introduced to the notice of medical men by Dr. Alexander Wood of Edinburgh ; and yet it has been known from time immemorial that every venomous reptile and many insects are each provided with such an appliance, either as a means of defence or as a means of livelihood. Had this knowledge been utilized we should have had such an instrument as the hypodermic syringe ages ago, and we should consequently have been spared a vast amount of human suffering. The woodpecker was an auscultator long before Laennec.

August 13th.—I received a few days ago a letter from J. Allen Jack, Esq., Corresponding Secretary of the Managing Committee of the Mechanics' Institute of St. John, New Brunswick, asking me to deliver during the coming winter before the Mechanics' Institute of that city a lecture on the Physicians and Surgeons One Hundred Years Ago and To-day. He informed me that the Institute is not what its name strictly implies, but that it includes the liberal professions, and that its object at present is to impart a specific character to the series of addresses which are to be delivered in the centennial year of the city of St. John and of the province of New Brunswick. Owing to the distance from my home and to the wintry season appointed for the lecture, I have been reluctantly compelled to decline the invitation. The subject would have been an easy one for me to handle, as I am somewhat familiar with the history of medicine and surgery of the period named.

August 15th.—What is marriage? It is a civil contract entered into between a man and a woman to procreate, or, in other words, to beget children. This is undoubtedly a wise provision of nature, for, if it were not for the observance of this law, the world would soon be comparatively depopulated and in a state of chaos. The ancient Israelites practised polygamy, and the Mormons practise it in our own country to-day. Monogamy is undoubtedly more in harmony with God's laws and with our domestic peace and happiness.

Marriage, apart from procreation, is too seldom regarded by those who enter into it as a sacred institution, designed to guard morals, to promote happiness, to prolong life, and to bless the household. Too often it is founded upon base and selfish considerations, and hence it is not surprising that there should be so many cases of divorce, amounting in some of the New England States, such as Massachusetts, Connecticut, and Rhode Island, to nearly ten per cent. of the population. This fact is simply appalling, and goes far to disprove the truth of the old saying that matches are made in heaven. Greed, lust, folly, revenge, haste, ill-temper are the factors which lie at the foundation of most of these unhappy unions, which entail so much misery and disgrace, and make the marriage vow a mockery and a fraud. To render married life truly happy, to enable it to retain the character of a divine institution, to keep it free from reproach, and to make it honorable alike to the parties immediately interested in it and to the public, it is indispensable that everything relating to it should be well considered beforehand, and that nothing should be done in haste, so as to avoid crimination and recrimination. Married life should be a life of mutual dependence, mutual concessions, mutual love, mutual confidence, and mutual good deeds. It should be free from selfishness, reproach, jealousy, and fault-finding. When this is the case it must increase in joy and happiness with advancing age.

I believe in early marriages. I married the woman of my choice when she and I were young. We lived most happily together for forty-seven years and a half. My secrets were hers, and hers mine. She knew my business as well as I. We did nothing of importance without consulting each other. I never did a good day's work or received a good fee without informing her of the fact. During my most arduous struggles for support and reputation I was conscious of my wife's love, esteem, and tender sympathy.

A perfect wife should be neat in her person and her dress, of sweet temper, cheerful even in adversity, choice in her language, loyal and devoted to her husband. A slattern can never command the respect, much less the love, of her spouse. The world will not sympathize with such a wife if her domestic relations are unhappy. All women are fond of admiration; and when it is properly manifested it is a blessing rather than an evil.

Matrimony, according to my observation, seldom turns out well when there is great disparity in age, as when the husband is twenty or thirty years the senior. Jealousy and want of confidence, superadded perhaps to a sense of superiority, rarely fail, under such circumstances, to render life miserable and the marriage vow a delusion. Well has it been said that jealousy is a green-eyed monster which ever lies in wait for something real or imaginary to seize

upon.   Men and women who marry for wealth or position
seldom fare well ; and it is wrong for people of bad temper
to make themselves mutually wretched, for, sooner or later,
the devil will be likely to enter their household.

A want of offspring is often a source of domestic dis-
sension.   On the other hand, a large family is frequently
a misfortune, especially when poverty and sickness keep
the parents in a state of constant anxiety to furnish the
necessary supply of food and clothing.   In such an event
they are sure, unless very lucky, to remain slaves, often
of the most abject kind, all their lives.   If the number
of births could be regulated by law, I should say that
three, or at most four, children should be the limit in a
family.   As it is, population increases at a fearful rate,
particularly among the lower and unrefined classes.

One of the most frequent causes of discontent, if not of
wretchedness, in married life is the lack of means to defray
the necessary household expenses.   It is a sad thing for a
wife to be obliged to ask her husband half a dozen times a
day for money to buy this thing or that.   This practice is
sure to produce trouble—trouble which can be avoided only
by making the wife, where it is possible to do so, a quarterly allowance to meet her personal wants, and a weekly
one to do the marketing and to meet incidental family
expenses.   If a man is determined to make himself and
his wife and children unhappy, all that he has to do is to
play the miser, or to worship his money, and he will be
sure to succeed to the utmost extent of his wishes.   A sensible woman always practises economy.   I adopted at an
early period of my married life the plan I have suggested,
and found it to work so well that I can strongly recommend it.   If there be any strife between husband and wife,
the children should not be permitted to witness it, much
less to become partisans in it.   It is the duty of parents to
make their children happy, to keep them pure before the
world, and to bring them up in "the fear and admonition

of the Lord.'' Alienation of each from the other is a crime. A happy and contented household is one of God's greatest blessings—a crown of glory ennobling the married state.

The Catholic Church prohibits divorce. This prohibition, as a rule, is salutary; but there are instances in which the marital union is accompanied with associations of so degrading a character as to render a separation highly proper. I can see no reason why two persons, wholly offensive to each other, should be forever debarred from contracting a new matrimonial alliance. A second marriage under such circumstances is often very happy and prosperous. Silence and lack of united effort on the part of the Protestant churches with respect to the frequent divorces among their people do the cause of morality infinite harm. The laws in relation to this subject are disgracefully lax and inoperative.

August 17th.—The crimes and misdemeanors which are daily and hourly imputed to God, the great Author of the universe, are shocking to a gentle mind. The sinner and the saint, the ignorant and the learned, the foolish and the wise misrepresent Him and charge Him indirectly with all kinds of misdeeds. If all that is affirmed of Him by a wicked and thoughtless world were true, He would be unworthy of our love and esteem. The wretch who curses God as he is led to the scaffold imagines in the fulness of his depravity that the author of his being is also the author of his crimes. Steeped in iniquity, perhaps from his cradle, he is incapable of realizing the fact that he has brought all this disgrace and misery upon himself by his thoughtlessness and evil conduct. God never did an unkind or unfeeling act. He never injured or destroyed any human being, brute, or insect, tree, flower, vegetable, or blade of grass. When a prominent citizen dies, it is customary for his friends to meet and pass resolutions complimentary of his virtues and public services, generally preceded by a preamble declaring that "Whereas it has pleased Almighty God to remove from our midst our distinguished fellow-citizen, General or Mr. So and So, therefore be it resolved, that we will go into mourning for thirty days," etc. Now all this seems plausible at first sight, but when we come to analyze the preamble we find an implied accusation in it that God was the cause of the man's death; whereas the death was only the natural consequence of the wear and tear of mind and body. God governs the world by immutable laws—laws which have existed from the beginning, and which will, as far as we know and have reason to believe, continue forever; and whenever these laws are violated given effects will be sure to follow. It is appointed unto all men, and I may add unto all living matter, animal and vegetable, once to die. It is rare for a man to reach the age of seventy, seventy-five, or eighty. As a rule, long before this age is attained the machinery of life, as represented by the tissues and organs, is worn out, and "man goeth to his long home." The result is simply due to the laws of nature. We live to-day and are gone to-morrow. Life succumbs to disease, which is dependent upon a bad constitution, upon an inherited taint, upon exposure, upon intemperance in eating or drinking, and upon a thousand other agencies of destruction. It is an appalling fact that two-fifths of the children in this country die under five years of age—many of them from causes over which, because of our ignorance, we have no control. These innocent creatures die because we cannot prevent or cure their diseases. God takes no delight, says the Bible, in the death of a sinner; and I think it may be safely said that He takes none in the death of a saint. In this respect the good and the bad fare alike. All die by and through natural laws, none by and through God's interposition or direct agency; and the same is true whether life is destroyed by disease or by accident, by the upsetting of a carriage, by the pistol's bullet, by a railway collision, by a boiler explosion, by a tidal wave, by a cyclone, or by an earthquake. The machinery of a man who dies from the effects of an accident is just as much deranged as that of the man who perishes by disease, however rapid or protracted.

Many events are inconsiderately ascribed to God's agency. If, for instance, a woman has many children, and if she is obliged to work day and night for their support, it is assumed that it was God's will that they should come into the world; and if her husband becomes a sot, or if her house burns down, she receives the affliction with calm submission, and looks upon it as a punishment which enables her the better to prepare herself for heaven, ignorant that either event is simply the effect of the operation of God's laws.

In these sentiments there is nothing which is irreligious, or to which the most scrupulous moralist or religionist should take exception. Fanaticism, which is a passion deeply implanted in our nature, is gradually passing away. The human mind is becoming more and more enlightened. Superstition and bigotry, those terrible nightmares that have so long weighed down our intellectual faculties, are slowly disappearing; and the conviction is becoming as widespread as it is profound that all things human and divine, visible and invisible, are governed by immutable laws which are made by the great and good God of heaven and of earth.

This radical misconception in regard to the immutability of the laws of nature is well illustrated in the letter of condolence which Martin Luther addressed to Maria, Queen of Hungary, on the death of her husband, Louis II., in 1526: ". . . In this great and sudden misfortune and anguish," says the great reformer, "wherewith the Almighty God at this time visits your Majesty, not in anger or displeasure, but to chasten and to try; that your Majesty may learn to trust alone in the true Father who is in heaven;

and to comfort yourself in the true Bridegroom Jesus Christ, who is also Brother to each one of us; yea, our flesh and blood; and to rejoice in those true friends and faithful companions the dear angels, who are around us, and who are ministering to us." The poor king was slain in battle against the Turks, no doubt fighting valiantly in the cause of his country; and Luther evidently wished to convey to the unhappy queen the idea that he lost his life through God's agency in order that her thoughts might be constantly and piously directed to heaven.

At the risk of the imputation of repetition, I have felt it my duty to express somewhat in detail thoughts which have been briefly stated elsewhere.

August 20th.—The death yesterday of ex-Judge Black recalls an evening which that eminent jurist and statesman spent at my house during the sitting in Philadelphia in 1873 of the Convention to amend the Constitution of the State of Pennsylvania. The occasion was an entertainment which I gave to a Mr. Bellew, a Catholic priest, who had brought me a letter of introduction from my friend, Lady Wilde of Dublin. Among the gentlemen present were Henry C. Carey, ex-Governor Curtin, Morton McMichael, and other members of the Convention. Bellew, who had given a lecture at the Academy of Music, came late. Judge Black was the life of the little group. Anecdote after anecdote, told in the most graphic manner, and interspersed with frequent pinches of snuff, caused roars of merriment. Among other incidents he related was the following, which occurred in a railway car between Philadelphia and Harrisburg. When the Judge entered, all the seats, save one in which sat a shrewd-looking Yankee, were occupied. "Pleasant weather, sir! pleasant weather, sir!" "Very pleasant," said the Judge. "From Philadelphia, I suppose?" said the Yankee. "No." "Been buying goods, eh?" "I am not a merchant." "A drover, eh?" "No." "A dealer in horses, eh?'' ''I am fond of horses, but don't deal in them,'' was the answer. The Yankee then drifted into politics, which at that time—shortly after the war—were at a red-hot point, and he soon began to denounce Judge Black, heaping upon him all manner of abuse, and making him responsible for nearly all the misdeeds of the Democratic party, of which he had long been a conspicuous member. ''You are rather severe on Judge Black. Are you acquainted with him?'' ''Acquainted with him! Of course I am; I have seen him often, and know him only too well.'' The train by this time had reached Harrisburg, when the door of the car suddenly opened and an old friend of the Judge came in. ''Judge Black, how delighted I am to see. you! I hope you have not suffered from the heat this warm morning.'' ''Not a bit. My friend here has entertained me most charmingly.'' It is needless to add that the Yankee asked the Judge no more questions.

I saw Judge Black for the last time a few years ago. We met at Cape May, where we had gone in search of fresh air and change of scene. He was a profound lawyer, a shrewd and far-seeing statesman, a deep thinker, an able scholar, expressing his thoughts in pure and forcible English, and a keen critic, abounding in withering sarcasm. He never consciously abandoned the right for the wrong or allowed mere policy to influence his actions. A disciple of the Jefferson school of politics, he became from conviction early in life a Democrat, and remained true to his convictions. Struggling with poverty for an education, he followed the plough in the day and spent the evening in studying, with the aid of a tallow candle, the classics and the English language. Never happier than when busy, he had no idle moments, and the habit of industry accompanied him to the grave. Work of the brain was as much a necessity to him as work of the body. There were many striking traits in his character. When he was admitted to the bar his father's property, never large, was hopelessly encumbered with mortgages; these, noble son that he was, he lifted one after another, and thus by degrees restored the homestead to its original owner. He loved his father with undying love; and we may well imagine how proud the father must have felt as the son, by his talents and industry, ascended from one eminence to another. Black was a true Christian. At an early age he was baptized by Dr. Alexander Campbell, a noted Baptist minister; and he was steadfast in his religious professions during the remainder of his life. He was a member of Mr. Buchanan's cabinet, first as Attorney-General and afterwards as Secretary of State, in both of which positions he proved himself to be a statesman and a patriot. His chief possessed scarcely a tithe of his judgment and decision of character. His appointment as Attorney-General had been urged by many political friends, but it was secured by the efforts of ex-Judge William A. Porter, of Philadelphia. Judge Porter, as he informs us in an interesting article which appeared in the Philadelphia Press, went to Wheatland a short time before the inauguration. He found Mr. Buchanan inexorable, assigning as his reason for refusing the appointment that he was quite sure that Black was not adapted to the atmosphere of Washington. "At a dinner given to me," said Buchanan, "this winter in Philadelphia, Governor Bigler and Judge Black were also invited. The Governor and I were punctual to the minute. Half an hour had passed, and Judge Black had not come. Seeing that the hostess was nervous, I requested her to order the dinner to be served, saying I will settle it with the Judge. When the dinner was half over, the Judge arrived and made some excuse, which, I told him, we should not accept. Do you think," said Mr. Buchanan, "such a man would make a fit cabinet officer? He would make engagements, forget all about them, and keep me constantly in hot water by his irregularities." And it was not until the 3d of March, the day before the inauguration, that he agreed to make Black his Attorney-General.

I have related this anecdote—substantially in the words of Judge Porter—to show what an apparently trifling thing may influence a man's destiny. Truly was it said by Louis XIV., "Punctuality is the politeness of kings." Judge Black was an absent-minded man. Once absorbed in business, conversation, or in building castles in the air, he was oblivious of everything around him.

When such a man dies, his profession and his country may well mourn their loss. Judge Black was of Scotch-Irish descent. At the time of his death he was seventy-three years of age. He was more than six feet in height and well proportioned, but not handsome. He was a warm friend, but a bitter, uncompromising foe.

September 15th.—The Medical News of to-day contains a brief paper entitled Remarks on the Importance of Having Trained Nurses for the Smaller Towns and Rural Districts and the Proper Method of Securing Them, which I prepared during my sojourn at Long Branch this summer, and from the dissemination of which I anticipate much benefit. A good nurse is indispensable to every sick-room, for she is the right hand of the physician, and often has more to do than the medical attendant himself with restoring the patient to health. If, prostrate with sickness, I were compelled to make choice of my attendant between an indifferent doctor and a well-trained nurse, I should certainly select the latter as the more likely to carry me safely through. In 1868, during my visit to Europe, I took much pains to inquire into the history and management of training-schools for nurses; and on my return wrote an elaborate report on the subject, which, as stated in a previous chapter, was presented to the American Medical Association at its meeting in New Orleans the following year and published in its Transactions. The paper bore good fruit in arousing professional and public attention to the matter; but failed of its object in regard to the establishment of training-schools for the smaller towns and rural districts. The article in the News advocated essentially the plan suggested by me in 1868—a plan which, if it had been seasonably carried into effect, would have been instrumental in saving many valuable lives. The method then proposed, which was entirely original with me, was to confide the whole matter to the county medical societies. These societies were to select the instructors from their own ranks, with a central office or bureau in each district. The plan is a feasible one, and having recently brought it again before the American Medical Association, as well as before the Medical Society of the State of Pennsylvania, and having published it in the Philadelphia Medical News, it can scarcely fail to be generally carried out. *Homo sum; humani nihil a me alienum puto.*

September 24th.—The American Gynæcological Society has just had a three days' meeting in this city. As I entered the room where the meeting was held, Dr. Sutton, of Pittsburgh, was earnestly engaged in reading a paper on cleanliness in surgical dressing, in which Listerism, as it is termed, was of course freely discussed. At the close of the address, I was briefly introduced by one of the Fellows as "the Nestor of American Surgery," and was asked to open the discussion, which I respectfully declined. On hearing the word "Nestor," the president, Dr. Kimball, of Lowell, Massachusetts, quickly turned his head, crying out, "Who is he? where is he?" much to the merriment of the assembly. The meeting was largely attended, and some very able papers were read. Dr. Kimball's inaugural was an account of the life and services of Dr. Nathan Smith, of New Haven, a man of much ability, an original observer and thinker, the founder of several medical schools, a successful teacher, an excellent surgeon, and the father of the late Professor N. R. Smith, of Baltimore. Dr. Nathan Smith was the second surgeon in this country who performed ovariotomy. The date of his operation was 1822. An attempt was made by Dr. Kimball to prove that Dr. Smith had at the time no knowledge whatever that he had been anticipated by Ephraim McDowell, although McDowell's first case occurred in 1809, thirteen years before the one at New Haven, and a notice of that and two other cases had been published in the Philadelphia Eclectic Repertory in 1816, six years before Smith's operation. Is it likely that the New England surgeon was so ignorant of the history of his profession as this assertion would seem to imply? Nathan Smith was a highly intelligent man, quite awake in professional and business matters; and there were in the year named at least two other prominent medical journals in the country which no doubt gave a full account of McDowell's paper in the Eclectic Repertory.

This Society has been in existence since 1876, and has done some excellent work. But has it not nearly exhausted the field? Such a body, like all specialistic bodies, must work continually in a circle, and occupy about the same relation to general surgery, of which indeed it forms merely an integral part, that a rich plate of butter occupies upon a well-spread table, provided with numerous dishes.

September 28th.—The subject of the proper disposition of the dead is now attracting much attention, and, in view of the scarcity and expense of suitable cemeteries in the neighborhood of our larger cities it is one worthy of serious thought. In many of the more populous districts of the Old World the dead are now often sent by rail to a distance of many miles for interment. A hundred or even fifty years hence this inconvenience will be greatly increased. Therefore it is not surprising that our attention should be drawn to cremation. For the revival of the subject we are mainly indebted to Professor Brunetti of Italy and to Sir Henry Thompson of London; while Dr. Persifor

Frazer and my son A. Haller Gross of this city directed special attention to the matter in able public addresses, delivered nearly ten years ago. Since then the daily press and scientific periodicals have abounded in more or less elaborate notices and discussions of the matter. That this mode of disposing of the dead, at one time extensively practised in ancient Greece and Rome, if not also in other countries, is becoming daily more and more popular is proved by the fact that crematories, or furnaces for incineration, are being erected in some of the cities of continental Europe, and that cremation in some of those cities is now of daily occurrence. In our own country we have only two or three crematories, the oldest and best known being that at Washington, Pennsylvania, built by the late Dr. Lemoyne of that town. Notwithstanding that the British Medical Association at one of its meetings publicly recommended cremation as the only decent and proper manner of disposing of the dead, no crematory has, I believe, yet been erected in England, Scotland, or Ireland. I am myself warmly in favor of cremation, and as an evidence of my sincerity have in my will made provision for it in my own case. Indeed, several members of my family have also expressed a desire to have their remains thus disposed of. Before cremation can be extensively practised a vast deal of prejudice will have to be overcome—prejudice based upon the fact, first, that burial has been for ages the universal custom in all civilized countries; secondly, that people like to visit the graves of their departed friends; and lastly, that incineration is opposed to the doctrine of a future resurrection, an idea entertained by many Christians. A man who spends much of his time in the dissecting-room, and looks at the horrible features of the putrefying bodies as they lie before him upon the tables, is not likely to hesitate between burial and cremation. As a hygienic measure cremation is a thousand times preferable to underground or any other form of interment; and for this reason the matter should be well considered by every enlightened community.

In countries in which ground in cemeteries is very dear, economy would dictate the importance of burying people in the upright or standing posture instead of in the horizontal posture, as is now the custom. Rare Ben Jonson asked King Charles I. one day to grant him a favor. "What is it?" said the king. "Give me eighteen square inches of ground." "Where?" asked the king. "In Westminster Abbey." This request evidently implied upright or standing burial. Jonson foresaw that space in this celebrated sepulchre would in time become exceedingly contracted.

October 4th.—I paid my respects to-day to the Right Rev. Dr. Benjamin Bosworth Smith, the senior bishop of the Protestant Episcopal Church of the United States, now ninety years of age, having been born in 1794. I found him stretched out upon his bed, very thin, and much exhausted by long-continued suffering, but still earnest in the cause of the church. I had known the Bishop well in Kentucky. In fact, he was one of my earliest acquaintances after I settled in Louisville. I was glad to see the venerable man. In reply to an invitation to dine with me, he said, "I have not been able to accept such a compliment for the last sixteen years. I am obliged to be fed every three hours day and night. I cannot take a particle of solid food without the risk of its choking me;" adding, "I am good for nothing." Bishop Smith is a native of Bristol, Rhode Island. He studied theology at Brown University, and emigrated to Kentucky early in life. He was consecrated Bishop of that State in 1832 in the city of New York, Bishop White officiating on the occasion. In his visits to my house he often entertained Mrs. Gross and myself with accounts of his trials and sufferings in his early ministrations in his adopted State; of the ignorance and rough character of the people, especially in the remote settlements; of the difficulty he often experienced in obtaining food, the bread being not unfrequently prepared in the common washbowl: and he told us how the gnawings of hunger had occasionally compelled him to eat soap to support life.

The Bishop was neither a strong nor a popular man. As a preacher he had few admirers. He was not deficient in zeal or ardor, but there was that about him which made him an unacceptable rector. His voice was harsh and disagreeable, and his manner strained. During his residence at Lexington he was so unpopular that, in order to get rid of him, his unscrupulous vestry preferred against him charges and specifications, amounting altogether to one hundred and thirty-three, nearly all of them of the most trivial and puerile character, the presentment of which was unworthy of a Christian congregation. Among others which I still vividly remember, notwithstanding the lapse of a third of a century, was this: The Bishop, in a visit to one of his parishioners, on reaching the door suddenly looked at the sky and remarked, "I think we shall have rain to-day." It did not rain, and therefore, as the specifications declared, the Bishop was not a truthful man. He was tried on these charges by a court consisting of three of his peers, of whom the good Bishop McIlvaine was one, and was triumphantly acquitted. He soon afterwards removed to the neighborhood of Louisville, where Mrs. Smith, a noble woman, in due time established a flourishing young ladies' seminary, while the Bishop attended to his diocesan duties. For the last eighteen or twenty years he has been a resident of New York City.

October 5th.—I left Easton, my old home, fifty years ago this morning. The changes which have since taken place in government, in politics, in education, in learning, in discovery, in invention, in the arts and sciences, in our industries, in agriculture and horticulture, and in international intercourse pass all understanding, and inspire one with the conviction that this period is by far the most wonderful which the world has ever witnessed. It is gratifying to know that these changes have, on the whole, been salutary. Men have become wiser and happier; space and time have been annihilated; the various peoples of the earth have been brought into more intimate and friendly relations one with another; many of the barriers of bigotry and superstition have been broken down; the standard of Christianity has been planted in many heathen lands; and, finally, the world has been blessed with the means of breathing a more healthy atmosphere. Many of the men who have been instrumental in bringing about these vast changes lie in their graves; but their memory survives, and their descendants, heirs to the grand inheritance, live to bless them and to carry on their work. When one thinks of one's own labors, how utterly insignificant they appear!

October 9th.—I delivered an address this evening at Association Hall before the Association of the Directors of the Poor of the State of Pennsylvania. The audience, owing to the lack of adequate public notice, was slim; and I felt as I proceeded that what I said was falling upon barren soil. Mr. Philip C. Garrett, Chairman of the Committee of One Hundred, a good speaker, and ex-Governor Hoyt, who is evidently a man of force and education, furnished some interesting statistics. I was glad that a majority of the more prominent delegates expressed themselves the next day in favor of placing the children of the poor of the State in private families instead of crowding them into public institutions, which, as a rule, are simply receptacles for breeding vice and immorality. Such children may not always receive proper treatment in private families, but their chances of ultimately making useful citizens are certainly much increased. Pennsylvania has a poor-house system which is conducted on the most beggarly, narrow-minded principles, wholly inconsistent with the spirit of the age and the resources of a great common-wealth.

Sunday, October 14th.—I gave a luncheon at two o'clock to-day to ex-Governor John W. and Mrs. Stevenson, of Covington, Kentucky, in return for courtesy shown by them early last June to my two daughters, Mrs. B. F. and Mrs. Orville Horwitz, and myself during our visit to Cincinnati. The party consisted of sixteen, including, among others, Mr. George W. Biddle, Mrs. Biddle, Sir William and Lady MacCormac, my two sons, my daughter-in-law, and my daughter, Mrs. Orville Horwitz. Every-thing passed off pleasantly. The only drawback was the excessive heat, accompanied by a muggy atmosphere con-sequent upon the last two days' rain. The Governor, with his wife and their daughter, Miss Stevenson, is in attendance at the Triennial Convention of the Episcopal Church of the United States, of which he is a delegate. He is a man of celebrity in his native State, of which he was Governor from 1869 to 1871, and which he repre-sented as United States Senator from 1871 till 1877. He is seventy-two years of age, but hale and vigorous. Mrs. Stevenson and her daughters are charming women. The Governor is a son of the late Andrew Stevenson, who rep-resented our country at the court of St. James from 1836 to 1841, and who, after he retired from public life, served for some years as Proctor of the University of Virginia. A ride which we took from Louisville to Frankfort, Ken-tucky, on the top of a stage-coach, there being then no railway connection between the two cities, was the means of our acquaintance with each other.

Sir William MacCormac is an Irishman by birth, and was knighted two years ago in recognition of his merito-rious services as Secretary of the great International Con-gress which convened in London in 1881. He is Surgeon to St. Thomas's Hospital, and ranks high as an operator. His contributions to surgery, although not numerous, are valuable, and have made his name widely known. During the Franco-Prussian war he rendered important assistance, alike to the French and German soldiers, in connection with the ambulance service. MacCormac is six feet two inches in height, well proportioned, with a handsome face and a good head. His age is about fifty. He is making a brief tour of the country in company with his wife, and is everywhere received with marked attention by the profession.

October 15th.—I went this afternoon to a reception given by Dr. and Mrs. Agnew at their country residence to Sir William and Lady MacCormac. The *menu* was excellent, and everybody was happy. I warmly congratulated Mrs. Agnew upon the completion of Dr. Agnew's great work on Surgery, a work creditable alike to its author, to the profession, and to the country.

October 16th.—To-day takes place the dedication of the college building of the medical department of Harvard University, to which an invitation was sent me a month ago. I was also invited by the Faculty to an evening reception, to a dinner at Dr. Williams's, and to a dinner at Dr. Lyman's. Swollen ankles will deprive me of these enjoyments. There will doubtless be great doings at Boston to-day.

October 17th.—The dinner given last evening to the Right Honorable Baron Coleridge, Lord Chief-Justice of England, by the University of Pennsylvania, in the University Chapel, was a grand, and in every respect a successful, affair. It was appointed for six o'clock, but it was nearly half an hour later before his lordship arrived. He was received by the Provost, Dr. William Pepper, who presented each of the guests, of whom there were about one hundred and forty, individually. The different professions of Philadelphia were pretty fully represented on the occasion, and there were also some strangers of note present. Lord Coleridge is the son of Sir John Taylor

Coleridge, and a nephew of Samuel Taylor Coleridge, the
poet.   He is, I should think, about sixty-five years of age,
tall, prepossessing in appearance, with a large, well-shaven
face, a long chin, and a head not unusually large, bald at
the top.   When animated his countenance beams with
benevolence.   The dinner was excellent.   The Provost, in
a handsome and appropriate address, toasted his lordship,
who responded in a felicitous speech, in which he referred
in terms of high appreciation to the hospitality and kindness everywhere shown him by the people of this country.
The speech was frequently interrupted by hearty applause.
Mr. Coppée, formerly Professor of English literature in the
University of Pennsylvania, now of the Lehigh University, South Bethlehem, responded to "Literature," Professor Leidy to "Science," and Bishop Clark of Rhode Island
to "Religion."   Mr. George W. Biddle spoke on behalf
of the Law School and the Philadelphia Bar.   I sat on
the platform with his lordship, to the left of the Provost,
sandwiched between Professor Coppée and Judge Allison,
and left a few minutes before ten o'clock, pleased, as I am
sure every one else was, with the evening's entertainment.
The hospitality which this distinguished foreigner has received during his two months' sojourn among us cannot
fail to exercise a benign influence; and it was a happy
thought on the part of the Trustees of the University of
Pennsylvania to extend to him this cordial greeting.   It
was a compliment of a high character, not only to Coleridge, but to Great Britain.   As Mr. Coppée happily expressed it, "In his lordship we shall always have a friend
at court."

In the evening I read the Autobiography of Mrs. Delany,
née Mary Granville, a famous woman in her day, and
found on page 24, vol. ii., the following passage, which I
am induced to copy, inasmuch as it is probably the first
account of what is now known as *aphasia*.   The case is
that of a young man who was strongly attached to Miss

Granville. His mother refused her consent to their union, and the result, as supposed, was that he was soon after struck down with a "dead palsy." "He lost," says Mrs. Delany, "the use of his speech, though not of his senses, and when he strove to speak he could not utter above a word or two, but he used to write perpetually, and I was the only subject of his pen. He lived in this wretched state about one year after I was married." This was written more than one hundred and fifty years ago, and it is as graphic as anything to be found on aphasia in Professor Broca, in Dr. Austin Flint, or in Sir Thomas Watson.

October 23d.—Dr. John Lawrence Smith died at his residence in Louisville, October 12th, in the sixty-fifth year of his age. We were colleagues in the University of Louisville from 1852 to 1856. He was not a brilliant teacher, indeed hardly a successful one. He was not an agreeable speaker. He balked and hesitated, and repeated himself, and this bad habit, for such in reality it was, was not confined to the lecture-room, but characterized his private conversation. As a writer his style was clear and vigorous. Smith was not only a great chemist, but a great chemical philosopher, an original observer, and, especially in his earlier career, a great worker. He loved laboratory work. In his elegant house on Broadway, Louisville, he had a room on the third floor fitted up for chemical researches. It was his workshop, and I recollect with what interest he showed it to us after a handsome dinner given to me and to some other friends in 1875 during the meeting of the American Medical Association. Mineralogy, geology, and chemistry were the fields of study in which he found his chief pleasure, and in each of these he rose to eminence. He never published any systematic treatise, but his contributions to scientific literature were numerous, and always attracted well-merited attention. He was a member of numerous societies, domestic and foreign. He was a chevalier of the Legion of Honor, and a member of the Imperial Order of St. Stanislaus, of the Order of the Medjidie, and of the Order of Nichani-Iftihar of Turkey. The Academy of Sciences of Paris elected him to fill the vacancy occasioned by the death of Sir Charles Lyell of London. For one year he served as President of the American Association for the Advancement of Science. Dr. Smith was a native of South Carolina, and a graduate in medicine of the Charleston College. The practice of medicine was distasteful to him, and he soon abandoned it for those more congenial studies in which he was destined to play so conspicuous a part. He was married to a daughter of Mr. James Guthrie, Secretary of the Treasury under Mr. Pierce. He has left no children. He was a gentleman of warm heart and genial manners, and at the time of his death he was one of Kentucky's most eminent citizens.

October 25th.—Dr. Wolff, the well-known apothecary, has just sent me a pamphlet, recently written by him, giving a brief account of nearly four hundred new articles of the materia medica brought to light during the last ten years. Many of these articles have already been puffed into notice by greedy druggists, backed by the certificates of weak, thoughtless physicians, longing for notoriety, without any knowledge whatever of the therapeutic action or clinical value of these so-called new remedies, most of which, when their virtues shall come to be properly tested, will be found to be utterly worthless. I have no patience with such triflers.

October 26th.—I had an interesting visit this morning from Mr. Robert C. Winthrop, at whose lodgings I called a few days ago to pay him my respects. I had not met him since 1868, when we were introduced at the house of ex-Governor Morgan, who entertained the American Medical Association at its meeting in Washington that year. Mr. Winthrop is here as a delegate to the Triennial Convention of the Episcopal Church, of which he has long been an influential member. It is pleasant to see and to talk with such a man—a man of the highest culture, who rounds off his words and sentences in the purest English. As a writer, he has few equals in this country; and I doubt whether Macaulay excels him in the use of correct and elegant English. Some of his public discourses, notably the one which he delivered at the laying of the corner-stone of the Washington Monument in 1848, and his Centennial oration at Yorktown, Virginia, on October 19th, 1881, are models of composition and of good taste. Mr. Winthrop is a descendant in the sixth generation from John Winthrop, first Governor of Massachusetts, and is now in his seventy-fifth year, having been born in 1809. He is a well-preserved man, of much conversational ability, and of pleasant, genial manners. During our interview I asked him why no Bostonian had yet published a life of Edward Everett. His answer was, "The whole matter is in the hands of his son, a learned but eccentric clergyman, who says he has charge of all his father's papers, which, consequently, no one can touch as long as he holds them. I have published," he added, "A Tribute to the Memory of Mr. Everett, a copy of which I will do myself the pleasure to send you."

November 6th.—My daughter, Mrs. Orville Horwitz, with two of her children, left me this morning, after a sojourn of nearly seven weeks during the absence of her husband and daughter Lulu in Europe. These were pleasant weeks, and we shall probably never spend so many together again. My children and grandchildren have loving hearts.

In the evening I dined with Mr. and Mrs. Daniel Dougherty to meet General Sherman, who has just been retired from the army, and who is about to take up his residence in St. Louis. Among the guests were Mr. and Mrs. Thackara, the son-in-law and daughter of the General; Mr. Hazlehurst; Colonel A. K. McClure, the able and eloquent editor of the Philadelphia Times, and Judge Hanna of the Orphans' Court. The time passed rapidly, enlivened as it was by sprightly conversation, interspersed with agreeable anecdotes. General Sherman, who is a tall, slender, well-preserved looking man, and a good talker, gave a graphic account of his march through Georgia and the Carolinas to Richmond, which was so effective in breaking the backbone of the Rebellion. He referred in pleasant terms to the time when he was denounced as a crack-brained fellow because he declared it would require two hundred thousand men to enable him to retain Kentucky and march to Mobile. Events showed he was correct. He spoke kindly of General Hood, whom in his great march he left behind powerless between him and Nashville, and lamented his early death. "Hood," he added, "had been twice married, and each wife had borne him two pairs of twins." I asked General Sherman what he thought of Draper's History of the War of the Rebellion. His answer was, "It is an honest and faithful record of events, perfectly truthful in all its details." Our genial host told us several interesting anecdotes about Forrest and other actors, and, in the main, I have seldom spent a more pleasant evening. The *menu* was such as Lucullus might have envied, the terrapin amply atoning for the absence of peacocks' brains.

November 10th.—This is the four-hundredth anniversary of the birth of Martin Luther, which will be celebrated to-day and to-morrow—Sunday—with all the pomp and ceremonial due to so great an occasion by all the Protestant churches of the civilized world. If I were asked who have been the greatest promoters of true religion the world has ever produced, I should unhesitatingly say, Moses, who gave us the Decalogue ; Jesus Christ, who bequeathed us Christianity ; and Luther, who emancipated the Church from the tyranny of the priesthood. Luther, the son of a poor miner at Eisleben, was

a prodigy of courage and learning, one of the giants of
the earth. What the Decalogue needed was supplied by
the Saviour when he said, "Thou shalt love thy neighbor
as thyself."

November 16th.—Dr. J. Marion Sims died on Tuesday
morning, November 13th, at his residence on Madison
Avenue, New York, at the age of nearly seventy years.
His demise has robbed me of another of my best and
dearest friends. It is only a little over one year since he
gave me at the Hotel Brunswick, New York, the grand
reception mentioned on a previous page, which was attended by nearly four hundred members of the medical
profession, including some of the best men in the country,
along with a number of scientists, clergymen, and prominent members of the New York bar. The immediate cause
of his death was obstruction of the circulation from athero-
matous degeneration of the coronary arteries. The severe
attack of pneumonia which he experienced in the winter
of 1880 left him with adherent pericardium and adherent
pleura everywhere on the left side. Both ventricles
were dilated and the left hypertrophied. There was also
some fibrous myocarditis, with an incipient aneurismal
pouch in the interventricular septum. The funeral, which
took place to-day, was strictly private. If I had been
invited, I should certainly have made an effort to attend
it. As it was, I contented myself with sending a floral
wreath for the coffin of my poor friend, as a memento of
my love for his character. His remains were interred in
Greenwood Cemetery, the repository of many of New
York's great physicians and surgeons, but of none greater
than J. Marion Sims, or who have left a more fragrant and
enduring memory.

The announcement of the death of Dr. Sims, so sudden
and unexpected, greatly shocked me. As soon as I had
recovered from my surprise I had a copy made of a sketch
of his life written by me a few months ago, which, with

some prefatory remarks, was published this week in the Philadelphia Medical News. I promptly sent a letter of condolence to Mrs. Sims; but, alas! what is condolence under such affliction? The loving husband and the adored father is gone, and the mourners alone remain. "The friendship of a great man is a gift of the gods."

> "His life was gentle, and the elements
> So mixed in him that Nature might stand up
> And say to all the world, ' This was a man !' "

November 25th.—Many of the physicians in our larger cities belong to small clubs which meet during a part of the year once a fortnight or once a month at the houses of one another, and regale themselves with oysters and chicken salad, fortified by ale, beer, or whiskey punch, and seasoned with the latest gossip and stale anecdotes, not always of the choicest kind. In England in the seventeenth century many of the most prominent physicians in London, such as Radcliffe, Mead, and Hans Sloane, after getting through with their daily routine duties, used to spend the remainder of the day and evening at a tavern in drinking wine, in conversation, or in discussing the events of the day, and in giving advice and writing prescriptions at a half guinea each for the patients of the apothecaries or general practitioners, who waited upon them for that purpose. As these grandees did not see the patients themselves, the shots thus fired in the dark must often have failed to reach their mark. The Bull's Head Tavern was a favorite resort of Radcliffe, where he met his intimate companions, and often got into broils by his sharp sayings and biting witticisms. From all accounts he must have been a rough, blunt, unfeeling wretch.

This habit of meeting at public houses for social intercourse was not peculiar to physicians. Lawyers, actors, and literary men indulged in it. Rare Ben Jonson, with his huge belly and seamed, rubicund face, was long the presiding genius at the Mermaid Tavern. He was the chief inheritor of the convivial spirit of Greene and Marlowe, as Dryden afterwards was at Wills's Coffee House. At a still later period a small building near the Strand was the resort of Samuel Johnson, the great lexicographer, and his friends Edmund Burke and Oliver Goldsmith. The bones of the last rest in the small churchyard in its immediate vicinity. It is hard to conceive how such men could have contented themselves in so small and meagre an apartment as that in which they drank their ale, wine, and punch, ate their beefsteak and plum-pudding, discussed the events of the day, and indulged their wit; yet such is the fact. The humble little house is still pointed out to visitors as one of the most interesting objects in all London.

December 4th.—I received a note this morning from Provost Pepper, saying that, at a recent meeting of the Board of Trustees of the University of Pennsylvania, a resolution had been unanimously adopted to confer upon me, at the Commencement in May, the honorary degree of Doctor of Laws. Coming from such a source, one of the most prominent literary and scientific institutions in the country, at my own home where I am so well known, I regard this as one of the highest compliments ever conferred upon me, those of Oxford and Cambridge not excepted.

December 6th.—An attempt is now being made to reduce the duty on certain domestic articles, on the ground that there is more money in the Treasury than we need to carry on the government, and that, as we have greatly reduced our war debt, it is but right that our descendants, who will receive so large an inheritance, should bear a part of our burden. Mr. James G. Blaine recently published an elaborate and exhaustive letter upon this subject, in which he advocates the retention of the duty on spirituous and malt liquors. The income from this source during the last fiscal year amounted, in round figures, to eighty-six millions of dollars, which, he thinks, should be distributed *pro rata*, according to their population, among the different States and Territories, to assist them in paying their public taxes. If this plan were adopted, Pennsylvania would receive, as her quota, seven million four hundred and ninety-three thousand dollars, and Wyoming, the most sparsely settled of the Territories, thirty thousand dollars. Every considerate citizen would be glad to see this duty on spirituous liquors retained ; but malt liquors should, for obvious reasons, be free. People will drink ; and they can drink nothing more harmless than ale and beer, especially the latter. A part of the sum proposed to be thus distributed, say one-fourth, should be annually applied to the improvement of education, the advancement of science, and the encouragement of the fine arts, and other useful purposes. The rich always pay the state taxes, and, unless they continue to do this, to a greater or less extent, the poor will derive but little benefit from Mr. Blaine's scheme, should it be carried into effect, as I hope it may be. On the other hand, if my suggestion were adopted, we should soon become the best educated and most enlightened people in the world.

December 7th.—There is no doubt that mental and bodily activity, conjoined with rational temperance and regularity in eating, is greatly conducive to longevity. David set down the average of longevity at three-score years and ten, an age which, unfortunately, few persons attain. Louis Cornaro lived to be nearly one hundred years old ; and there are at this time not fewer than six members of the Institute of France who are from eighty to one hundred years old. Chevreul is ninety-seven ; Mignet eighty-seven ; Dumas and Milne-Edwards each eighty-three ; Dumont eighty-two ; and Charles Lucas eighty. Chevreul, who was elected a member in 1826, still lectures on chemistry, his special study ; and all these men still take an active interest in their respective pursuits. It would be instructive to be informed of the habits of these great men. I dare say that they are good feeders and that most of them do not hesitate to drink wine at least at breakfast and dinner. Gentle exercise of an organ is always conducive to its health. Inactivity leads to atrophy and premature decay.

December 8th.—The meeting of the so-called Saturday Evening Club at the house of Mr. Frederick Fraley this evening brings to my mind pleasant reminiscences of the Wistar Parties, with which I became associated a few years after I moved to this city in 1856. Mr. Fraley, who is now eighty years of age, is the President of the American Philosophical Society, and President of the Philadelphia Chamber of Commerce. The gathering was a very agreeable one, and was especially noticeable on account of the many venerable and distinguished men who graced it with their presence.

The Wistar Parties had their origin in Dr. Caspar Wistar, who was for many years Professor of Anatomy in the University of Pennsylvania, and the author of a work on anatomy long used as a text-book in our schools. Naturally of an inquisitive mind and of a social disposition, it was his habit during many of the later years of his life to gather around him every Saturday evening in the winter season his more intimate friends and such strangers of distinction as might happen to be in the city, who passed the evening in social enjoyment and in agreeable conversation rather than in the formal discussion of scientific or philosophical subjects. In time these meetings became very popular and widely known as charming reunions. The entertainment was of the most simple kind, consisting of coffee, ices, oysters, and occasionally of sandwiches. After the death of Wistar, in 1818, his friends, as a matter of kindly feeling, if not of pride and gratitude, determined to keep up these gatherings by meeting at one another's houses, and in this way arose what were known for more than forty years as the Wistar Parties. It was one of the peculiar features of these parties that their members were obliged to be members of the American Philosophical Society; whereas, the Saturday Evening Club is composed of nearly all classes of men—merchants, bankers, manufacturers, lawyers, physicians, artists, *et id genus omne*. The Wistar Parties consisted of fifty members, one-half of whom entertained every alternate year. The *menu*, originally so simple, became gradually more and more expensive until eventually it became very onerous, costing seldom less than from three hundred and fifty to five hundred dollars; and if the company was large and terrapin was served, the cost greatly exceeded even that amount. The Wistar Parties continued until the commencement of the war of the Rebellion, when, at the instance of several of the members who had sons or intimate friends interested in the Southern cause, they ceased to exist, and no successful attempt has since been made to revive them. By a singular coincidence it happened that I gave the last entertainment. My turn had come in January, but, being obliged to absent myself for a fortnight from the city on account of my daughter's illness, I did not discharge my obligation until late in April, after all my associates had fulfilled their engagements. Nearly all the gentlemen who were members of the party when I joined it have passed away. Mr. Fraley, Mr. Moncure Robinson, and Isaac Lea, the last a nonogenarian, are the oldest of those who survive.

Dr. Wistar was a popular teacher, beloved by his pupils, and widely known for many excellent qualities. He was of German descent, and a graduate in medicine of the University of Edinburgh. He died suddenly of heart disease in January, 1818. The last sentence he was heard to utter was, "I wish well to all mankind." His religious views partook largely of those of the Society of Friends, "modified by his extensive intercourse with the world."

At our Wistar Parties I often met the late Judge Carlton, a warm-hearted, genial, intellectual gentleman, of courtly manners. On one occasion, speaking of medical men, he observed to me, "When I was a young man in this city my family physician was Physick; when he died I employed Hartshorne; and after his death Dr. Pepper became my professional adviser." This incident reminds me of some curious coincidences. During my residence at Louisville three physicians, Gunn, Flint, and Bullitt, lived within less than half a square of one another. Gunn was a native of Virginia, and the author of Gunn's Domestic Medicine, a work which, without any special merit, passed through a number of editions, and was a source of considerable profit to all concerned in its publication. He was a man of insinuating manners, and ignored by the profession as a charlatan. Flint was a native of Massachusetts, a man of attainments, and a tolerably fair surgeon. He settled at Louisville about 1837, and occupied for two years the chair of Surgery in its University. He and Bullitt were partners in the practice of medicine. The Louisville Medical News of March 24th, 1877, contained the gratifying intelligence that George Washington, Thomas Jefferson, and Napoleon Bonaparte are practising medicine in Louisville, just as any other physicians, within a stone's throw of one another.

At one of the Commencements of the Jefferson Medical College some years ago, during the distribution of the bouquets, the names of White and Black, two members of the graduating class, were called out twice simultaneously at an interval of at least fifteen minutes. In commenting upon this occurrence, a gentleman immediately behind me remarked that in the small town in which he resided there were four men named respectively Short, Long, Black, and White living within a short distance of one another.

Many years ago there was in this city, on Front Street, a sign with the mirth-provoking names of "James Schott and Jonathan Fell.'' The firm was a mercantile one, and long enjoyed a high reputation for its integrity and upright character. Mr. Schott, who attained to a very advanced age, was the first president of the Girard Bank, and accumulated a respectable fortune. His partner *Fell* many years before him.

At Seabright, New Jersey, is a firm named Cook & Kettel, fishmongers.

I once had at dinner three young ladies, each of whose Christian name was Grace; and what was still more remarkable, they all hailed from Canton—two from Canton, Massachusetts, and the other from Canton, Ohio.

December 16th.—Mr. John B. McMaster dined with me to-day. He is Professor of American Literature in the University of Pennsylvania, and is engaged in writing an extensive history of the American People. Only the first volume has been issued. Another volume, the manuscript of which, he tells me, was stolen along with his satchel in a railway car this autumn, will be published early next summer. Mr. McMaster is a rather diminutive man; but he has a large head, and his brain is evidently of a high order, capable of doing great work. He is not yet forty years of age. He seldom wears an overcoat, even in the coldest weather.

December 17th.—Death is busying itself with my old friends. Last evening Dr. Thomas S. Kirkbride, after a lingering, though not painful, disease, died at his residence at the Pennsylvania Hospital for the Insane, of which he had been for more than forty years the worthy and honored superintendent and physician-in-chief. In his death humanity has lost one of its truest friends. Kirkbride was an eminently good man, and thoroughly fitted for the arduous duties of the station to which he so zealously devoted his life. Men who love to sneer at their betters tell us that Washington was not a great general, and that if he had lived during the war of the Rebellion he would hardly have attained the rank even of a regimental commander. Such criticism goes for nothing when we look at facts. Washington was great enough to achieve the independence of his country, and to triumph over the generals of the Old World who were sent over to defeat our armies. What more could any one have accomplished? He was equal to the emergency, and no rational man could have asked or desired more. Kirkbride knew better than any American physician who had preceded him how to treat the insane, and how to build and manage asylums for them. He consecrated his whole life to these objects, and exerted an influence which was as salutary as it was widespread. The Pennsylvania Hospital for the Insane under his administration became a model institution. Foreign alienists considered it their duty to visit it; and the people as well as the medical men of the country for more than a quarter of a century knew it by hardly any other name than that of Kirkbride's Hospital. Kirkbride was emphatically a disciple of Pinel, who was the first toward the close of the last century to knock off the shackles which had so long bound the limbs of the insane in all parts of the world, to lift them out of their dark cells into the light of day, and to treat them as human beings, not, as heretofore, as so many wild beasts. His tender, sympathetic nature, his amiable manners, and his uniform courtesy peculiarly fitted him for the work. The tone of his voice, the movements of his lips, the expression of his eye betokened the fitness of the man for the position conferred upon him by the Board of Trustees when he had hardly laid aside the toga of his student life.

Dr. Kirkbride was born in Morrisville, a small town in Bucks County, Pennsylvania, in July, 1809, and was, consequently, in his seventy-fourth year at the time of his death. He was of English descent, with a strong infusion of the Quaker element in his character and habits. His early education was limited to the study of the English language and mathematics. He received his medical degree from the University of Pennsylvania in 1832. Almost immediately after this event he was appointed physician to the Asylum for the Insane at Frankford; the next year he served as interne at the Pennsylvania Hospital; and on the opening in 1840 of the department for the Insane in West Philadelphia, he became its superintendent, an office which he filled up to the time of his death.

Dr. Kirkbride was a member of different societies, domestic and foreign, and contributed a number of articles to the periodical press, besides being the author of an elaborate and able work on the Construction, Organization, and General Arrangements of Hospitals for the Insane. He was one of the founders, and for eight years president, of the Association of Medical Superintendents of American Institutions for the Insane. He was twice married. His second wife was a daughter of Benjamin Butler, Attorney-General of the United States under Mr. Van Buren. In 1848, he came very near losing his life at the hands of an insane inmate of the hospital, who for some fancied wrong concealed himself in a tree, and watching his opportunity discharged his gun at him, the ball striking the head, but fortunately not penetrating the skull.

In his personal appearance Dr. Kirkbride was eminently attractive. He was of medium height, with a fine physique, a well-shaped head, and a countenance highly expressive of benevolence and warmth of heart. His voice was sweet and gentle, and his presence and demeanor were such as to win at once the affection and confidence of his most wayward patients. Blended with these noble qualities, so necessary in one who occupied so responsible a position, were firmness, determination, and promptness of decision equal to any emergency.

December 20th.—Harvard University in the death of Professor Sophocles, a few days ago, lost one of its most valuable men, certainly the ablest Greek scholar it ever

had. Born in Thessaly in 1807, he received his early
education at Mount Sinai under the direction of a relative
who belonged to the monastic order. He came to this
country a poor youth, and supported himself by his own
efforts while engaged in perfecting his studies. In 1842
he was appointed tutor, and later in life Professor, of
Greek in Harvard University. He published numerous
elementary works on the Greek language which have
been extensively employed as text-books in our schools
and colleges. I recollect Sophocles as a short, slender,
singularly weird-looking man, with black eyes, an olive
complexion, and a white beard, the *tout ensemble* giving
him an appearance not unlike that of an Arab sheik. I
saw him for the first time in the library at Cambridge in
1859; and for the last time a few years ago in the same
building, looking of course much older, but being still
busy among books, and manifesting the same shy disposition which he did twenty years before. He lived, it is
said, in the college dormitory, aloof from everybody, preparing his own food, keeping his own secrets, and asking
advice from no one; and yet he was not a miser, for he
gave freely in case of need, if properly approached. Such
men are scarce in any age; and their history, if it could
be unravelled, would usually be found to hinge upon some
deep-rooted sorrow having its origin in early disappointment in love, which unfits them for subsequent companionship with the world. Sophocles used to say that the
whole philosophy of life was embraced in three books, the
Bible, Don Quixote, and the Arabian Nights—a singular
combination, certainly, and yet one not without a show of
reason.

December 28th.—I attended this evening a party given
by Dr. Wolff to prominent Philadelphia apothecaries and
physicians, the latter consisting chiefly of the younger
members of the profession. The object was a laudable
one, and should be encouraged to promote mutual good

feeling. The apothecary in this country is a person different from his English brother.   Here his office is limited to
preparing medicines, and to putting up prescriptions sent
to him by medical men.   In England, on the contrary,
besides being a general practitioner, he not only prescribes
medicines, but compounds them.   A general practitioner
may be a physician or a surgeon ; and, if he also practices
midwifery, he may, according to his taste, assume the title
of physician-accoucheur, or surgeon-accoucheur.   This distinction is, however, gradually disappearing.   In London
the apothecaries were incorporated as a distinct body, under
the name of the Hall or Society of Apothecaries, in the
fifteenth year of the reign of James I.   No general practitioner can establish himself in practice in England and
Wales without a license from this company.   An educated
apothecary is a useful member of society, and one for
whom I have great respect.   Too often, however, he prescribes across the counter, and thus defrauds the physician.
It is his duty to protect the medical man and his patient
by correcting mistakes, and thus preventing harm—in
cases, for instance, when a prescription, written in haste,
calls for an overdose or for some incompatible ingredient.
Most of the apothecaries in the larger cities and towns of
this country are educated men, graduates of colleges of
pharmacy, of which there are now a considerable number,
the oldest being the one in Philadelphia, incorporated in
1822.

February 2d, 1884.—Wendell Phillips is dead, and the
world mourns the loss of the "silver-tongued orator," the
friend of universal freedom, the eloquent advocate of the
rights of man in all climes and in all conditions of society.
During his last brief illness his agony is said to have been
so severe as to require the use of anæsthesia for its miti-
gation.

I heard Mr. Phillips speak in public but once, namely,
at Concert Hall in this city, ten years ago.   He was then

in full vigor, tall, handsome, and well proportioned. His audience was large, and embraced many of our most intelligent and respectable citizens. His subject was The Rights of the Negro under the New Provisions of the Constitution. He spoke with great composure, in a conversational style, in language abounding in well-chosen words; but he never rose to what I have always been led to regard as oratory. His speech embodied much solid sense, but it lacked animation and pathos, two qualities which leave a lasting impression upon an audience. The fire of Demosthenes, of Henry, and of Curran was not there. While I was edified and interested, he failed in my estimation as an orator, properly so called. Mr. Phillips was born in Boston, November 29th, 1811, and was consequently at the time of his death in the seventy-third year of his age. He was a graduate of Harvard University, and commenced life as a lawyer; but, being in easy circumstances, he soon retired from the bar, and thenceforth devoted himself to more congenial pursuits, among which literary culture and the abolition of slavery were predominant.

February 11th.—I attended this evening the first regular meeting of the Philadelphia Medical Jurisprudence Society, of which I was elected the first president. A better title would have been the Medico-Legal Society; but this name was already in possession of another organization, although one with a different object. The new society promises well, as it embraces in its list of membership a number of distinguished physicians and lawyers, stimulated by a desire to work. Dr. John J. Reese, Professor of Medical Jurisprudence in the University of Pennsylvania, delivered an excellent and exhaustive address on the testimony of experts, in which he exposed the partisan character of such witnesses, the inadequacy of their testimony, and the positive injury which they often do to the cause of justice. He recommended the adoption of the Prussian system, which consists in the appointment by the government of thoroughly educated men who sit on the bench with the judges and assist them in trying the case by giving a proper direction to the testimony of the witnesses. In 1868, in an address which I delivered before the American Medical Association as its president, at its meeting at Washington, I recommended a similar plan, without any knowledge that it was in force in Germany.

February 14th.—Dr. S. W. Gross received a few days ago a letter from Mr. Annandale, Professor of Surgery in the University of Edinburgh. After complimenting my son on the excellence of his monograph on Tumors of the Mammary Gland, of which, he said, he had freely availed himself in writing an article on that subject for Ashhurst's International Encyclopædia of Surgery, he asks, "Is there any chance of your father being able to come over to our Tercentenary in April? I have proposed his name for an honorary degree from our University." I wrote promptly to Annandale, thanking him for the intended compliment, and expressing deep regret at my inability to visit the Scotch metropolis at the time in question. Last year the matriculates of this renowned University numbered three thousand three hundred and ninety-six, of whom one thousand seven hundred and eighty-one attended the medical school. Two hundred and sixty-four were from the British colonies and fifty-nine from other countries.

This communication was followed, on the 5th of March, by one to myself. It read as follows:

UNIVERSITY OF EDINBURGH, February, 1884.

The Senatus Academicus of the University of Edinburgh do themselves the honour of inviting Professor Gross, Senior, etc., etc., to receive the Honorary Degree of Doctor of Laws, in Edinburgh, on the 17th of April, 1884, at the Festival of the Tercentenary of the foundation of the University.

In name and by the authority of the Senatus Academicus.

A. GRANT, *Principal.*

To this communication I replied at once that, while I should esteem it a great honor to receive an honorary degree from an institution of such world-wide renown, my advanced age and the inclemency of the season would prevent me from undertaking so serious a journey as was involved in a visit to Scotland.

NOTE.—The Diary of DR. GROSS closes at this point. No entries were made by him in his Autobiography after February 14th, 1884. For an account of his life during the few weeks which intervened until the day of his death, May 6th, 1884, the reader is referred to the Introductory Memoir of him in Volume I. The remainder of Volume II. will consist of such of the sketches of his contemporaries as were written by DR. GROSS, but were not contained in his Diary.—EDITORS.

SKETCHES OF SOME DISTINGUISHED CONTEMPORARIES.

CHAPTER IX.

SAMUEL LATHAM MITCHILL—THOMAS CHALKLEY JAMES—PHILIP SYNG PHYSICK —WILLIAM POTTS DEWEES—GEORGE McCLELLAN—BISHOP BASCOM—J. J. AU-DUBON—GRANVILLE SHARP PATTISON.

SAMUEL LATHAM MITCHILL.

1764–1831.

DR. MITCHILL was widely known at home and in Europe as a scientist and legislator. He was for the time in which he flourished a great naturalist. Botany, geology, mineralogy, and the fauna of North America received much of his attention. He lived in the midst of stirring events. He took an active part in politics, and was a warm advocate of whatever tended to advance the prosperity of New York, his adopted city. He was a contemporary and personal friend of De Witt Clinton, and gave him his cordial support in the construction of the Erie canal—at that time the greatest enterprise of the kind in the world, by which, as was poetically expressed, the waters of Lake Erie and of the Hudson were made to kiss each other. His learning was immense, and diversified in character. He had a capacious memory, which enabled him to bring up, at any moment, any desired treasure from the depths of his knowledge. His life was one of incessant occupation ; indeed, he allowed himself little leisure, especially in his younger days, except for the inexorable claims of duty. He achieved a high reputation as a scientist

236

before he had reached the meridian of life. He was born at Plandome, North Hempstead, New York, and took his medical degree at Edinburgh, in 1786, at the age of twenty-two. Having an unconquerable aversion to the practice of medicine, he studied law soon after his return from abroad. He was appointed a commissioner to treat with the Six Nations, an Indian tribe residing in Western New York, a position conferred upon him more on account of his benevolent character than on account of his skill as a diplomat. Henceforth Dr. Mitchill devoted himself zealously to the study and teaching of the natural sciences. In 1792 Columbia College elected him Professor of Chemistry; and he afterwards served in a similar capacity in the College of Physicians and Surgeons of New York. For sixteen years he was one of the editors of the New York Medical Repository, the first medical periodical published in the United States. In this labor he was associated with Dr. Edward Miller and Dr. Elihu H. Smith, men of distinction, whose memory will long be revered by our profession. The Repository was established in 1797, and after the lapse of twenty years its publication, for lack of adequate support, was suspended. To show the versatility of Mitchill, and the confidence reposed in him by his fellow-citizens, it is only necessary to mention the fact that he represented his district for some time in the House of Representatives, and subsequently in the Senate of the United States. I am not informed whether he originated any measures of importance while a member of Congress. That he was not an inactive member may readily be supposed.

Dr. Mitchill was one of the fathers of natural science in America. He was active in establishing learned societies, and in 1826, late in life, assisted in founding Rutgers Medical College.

I became acquainted with Dr. Mitchill in July, 1826, and saw him under peculiar circumstances. I was on my way home from a visit made on horseback from Easton, Pennsylvania, to the Falls of Niagara. At Buffalo I was introduced to Dr. Stagg, a physician of prominence, and a former pupil of Dr. Mitchill, who, learning that I was interested in the study of mineralogy, kindly gave me a letter to the illustrious scientist. On reaching Albany I was only too glad, worn out as I was with my journey, to take passage on a Hudson River steamer. At Sing Sing, then an insignificant village, the vessel stopped to take on board the Mayor and Council of the city of New York, who had been there on a visit to inspect the penitentiary then in process of erection. Dr. Mitchill was one of the party, and the way I happened, stranger as I was, to find him out was the fact that, soon after the boat got under way, a man fell headlong, with a terrible thud, upon the floor of the deck. Assistance was promptly rendered him; and upon inquiry I ascertained that the tall, massive, and venerable figure that had lain at full length before me only a minute ago was none else than Dr. Samuel Latham Mitchill. The fall of any one, especially of an old person, is not an uncommon occurrence; but when I learned the cause of it my mortification was profound. It seems that the corporation had just risen from a grand dinner, of which brandy and champagne formed prominent ingredients. Libations had been freely indulged in, and it was evident that the Old Sage had partaken too liberally of the stimulants, although he was not, as I was informed by one of his friends, addicted to strong drink. A little wine or spirits was sufficient to overcome him. It was sad to see so venerable a man make such an exhibition of himself.

The next day I delivered Dr. Stagg's letter, and was most kindly received. Dr. Mitchill conversed with great fluency, told me he had visited Sing Sing the previous day as a guest of the city corporation, showed me some interesting specimens of natural history, and invited me to

breakfast the following morning. My engagements, however, took me in another direction, and I never saw him
again. He died in New York in 1831, at the age of sixty-
seven.

Dr. Mitchill had much simplicity of character, and he
was as credulous as a child—a circumstance which often
induced people to impose upon him. Many anecdotes are
related of him. One day as he was riding through the
country on a stage-coach, the driver, at whose side he sat,
propounded to him this important question: "Why is it,
Dr. Mitchill, that black sheep yield so much less wool
than white?" The learned sage rubbed his ears and assigned numerous reasons, when the Jehu, interrupting
him, laughingly remarked, "Is it not because there are
fewer black sheep than white?" A wag once sent him,
done up in the most careful and elaborate manner, an old
brick with a strange inscription, saying that it had been
brought from the ruins of Nineveh. It was not until after
he had written a long and learned dissertation upon it that
the hoax was discovered by the philosopher.

THOMAS CHALKLEY JAMES.

1766–1835.

MY recollections of Dr. James are vivid. At the time
of my pupilage he held the chair of Midwifery in the
University of Pennsylvania, and was highly esteemed
for his many excellent qualities. He was of Quaker descent, and possessed all the characteristics of a fine gentleman. Although he was an elderly man when I first saw
him in the lecture-room in the midst of his pupils, he was
erect and well preserved, looking a good deal younger
than his actual age might have been supposed to indicate.
He was not an impressive lecturer, although he always
commanded the respect and attention of his class. He

was extremely modest. It was seldom that he raised his eyes from his manuscript, or looked squarely at his audience. His cheeks would be mantled with blushes while engaged in demonstrating some pelvic viscus, or discussing topics not mentionable in ordinary conversation. It was often painful to witness his embarrassment. Yet he was a good teacher, and occupied deservedly a respectable position among his Philadelphia contemporaries. I was predisposed to like him from having read, while a student, his edition of Burns's Principles of Midwifery. This he improved with many judicious and learned notes, which greatly enhanced the practical value of the work. He also annotated Merriman's Synopsis. He used both publications as text-books for his course. With the exception of a small number of papers in the medical periodicals of the day, he made no contributions to the literature of his profession; and his reputation will therefore be mainly traditional. It is interesting to know that James was the first professor exclusively of Obstetrics in the United States, having, if I mistake not, been appointed to that position in 1810. Prior to this period it had been associated with the chair either of Anatomy or of Surgery. He was one of the founders and editors of the Philadelphia Medical Repository, a quarterly journal.

PHILIP SYNG PHYSICK.
1768–1837.

THIS man, who even long before his death was styled the Father of American Surgery, was for nearly a third of a century the head and front of the profession; and when he died a general lament came up from every section of the United States. Doggerel rhyme was addressed to him by invalid and nervous women; and the press, medical and lay, awarded to him the highest praise. That he was a man of marked ability no one who knew him, or who is acquainted with his history, will deny ; but that he possessed talents which towered far above those of all his professional contemporaries is not true. Caldwell, Chapman, Drake, and Hosack, not to mention others, were men of vastly greater mental calibre. If he stood for a long period at the head of surgery in this country, as unquestionably he did, it was because he had the field of surgery to himself. He was really its first settler, and it is therefore not surprising that it was for a full quarter of a century almost his exclusive domain. When he returned from London, where he had for four years been a pupil of the celebrated John Hunter, and where he was for a considerable period a resident of St. George's Hospital, America was destitute of great surgeons. When the people of Philadelphia had an unusual surgical case, or were in need of an important surgical operation, they went to New York to consult Dr. Jones, afterwards the physician of Washington and Franklin. Philadelphia had practitioners for ordinary cases, but none for great emergencies. Physick brought home with him eulogistic letters from his British preceptor, and he was no doubt well grounded in the principles of medical art and science as they were taught in the latter part of the last century. His success, nevertheless, was for a time not at all flattering. For several years he trod the alleys and by-ways of his native city before his income was sufficient to pay for his shoe-strings and the powder on his queue. In 1793, almost immediately on his return from Europe, he rendered important service at the yellow fever hospital at Bush Hill—service which brought him daily for several months in contact with many influential citizens, among others Stephen Girard, and thus aided him in getting into practice.

Physick's forte was conservative surgery. He esteemed it, as indeed every honest surgeon does, a far greater merit to save a limb than to cut it off. I recollect the case of a young man, a lodger at my boarding-house in 1827, whose forearm, the seat of a malignant tumor, was kept for six weeks upon a standing frame in the hope of promoting the absorption of the morbid growth with the aid of some slightly stimulating lotion. At the end of this time the limb was, of course, amputated. Such conservation is as irrational as the inordinate use of the knife. I never saw Physick operate, either in private or in public. During my student-life in Philadelphia he was an old man, and operations had no longer any charms for him. His son-in-law, Dr. Jacob Randolph, had become his right-hand man, and he put him forward whenever he properly could. Physick died on the 15th of December, 1837. One of his last operations was a case of lithotomy, the subject being the venerable Chief Justice Marshall of the Supreme Court of the United States, from whom he removed nearly one thousand calculi, varying in size from a partridge shot to a pea. The illustrious patient made an excellent recovery, and lived for several years in comparative comfort. The favorite instrument of Physick for this operation was the gorget, in his time extensively employed in this country and in Europe, but now displaced by the scalpel. For the removal of cataract he wisely preferred extraction to depression. Early in his career he devised an operation for the cure of artificial anus, still occasionally practised. His treatment of coxalgia, or hip-joint disease, is well known. He insisted upon absolute rest of the affected parts, and for this purpose he used with much effect mechanical appliances in the form of curved splints, and other means to render the joint, at the height of the disease, immovable. Most of the contrivances employed at the present day in the treatment of coxalgia are simply adaptations of Physick's apparatus, the claims of which, if not ignored, are seldom mentioned by their inventors.

Physick laid great stress upon the employment of constitutional remedies and perfect rest in the treatment of disease. The lancet, leeching and cupping, tartar emetic, and calomel and jalap were the active agents in vogue in his day, accompanied with a very restricted diet, especially at the height of inflammatory affections. There was then no beef essence, and milk-punch was not often used. Chicken broth, with rice or barley, vegetable soup, arrow-root, and wine-whey, formed the principal diet of the sick-room. Toast water, lemonade, or some mucilaginous fluid, such as linseed tea or gum-arabic water, were the chief drinks. Those were hard times for sick people. Even in my earlier days much prejudice existed against the use of cold water, especially when mercury had been administered. Physick was a great stickler for venesection. He bled often and bled freely. A former colleague of mine, Professor S. H. Dickson, told me this anecdote: A gentleman, a South Carolinian, a high liver, for many years visited Saratoga for the benefit of his health. On his way thither he invariably stopped in Philadelphia to consult Physick on account of chronic inflammation of his eyes, which was always greatly aggravated by the "riotous living" of the previous winter. The first thing that was ordered on such occasions was a copious bleeding at the arm, followed by an active cathartic, the operation being repeated every forty-eight hours. Under this treatment the patient became greatly exhausted; and yet his eyes were as red and as painful as ever. Physick happened to have another patient in the house. As he passed the door of his Southern invalid, the latter asked him what he should do, adding that his eyes had troubled him a great deal during the previous night. Without examining the eyes, the doctor said, "Send for the bleeder, and tell him to take half a pint of blood." "I'll be —— if I do!" said the offended Carolinian. "If you had looked at my eyes, I might do it; but as it is, I shall not." "Good-morning," said Physick, bowing profoundly. "Good-morning," said the patient; and thus ended their intercourse.

The late Dr. Charles D. Meigs records this remarkable story. He had a patient, a Mrs. Smith, who had a violent attack of conjunctivitis, attended with agonizing pain, and threatening destruction of the whole eye. "She was duly bled," says Meigs, "to-day, to-morrow, the next and next morning, and so on until at last she fainted so badly that terror laid hold on us, and we fled for succor to Dr. Physick. Physick came the next day at ten o'clock, looked at the eye, and asked, 'Who is your bleeder? Send for him, and tell him to take twelve ounces of blood from the arm, and request him to meet you in the morning to repeat, if necessary, the operation.'" Although Meigs was horrified, he complied with the request, and the next day on looking into the eye he could discover only the faintest trace of the inflammation. "In fact," he adds, "the woman was virtually cured."

Physick was essentially an empiric, practising altogether by the light of experience. He had no theories of his own, and was intolerant, in his teachings and his practice, of the theories of others. He was in the habit of employing what he had found useful in one case in the treatment of another of a similar nature. He troubled himself little respecting the pathology or intimate nature of disease. In short, he was what is generally known as a routine practitioner. He possessed, however, what many a routine practitioner does not possess, strong common-sense ; and yet that this was not always manifested is sufficiently proved by Dickson's anecdote.

As a writer, Physick has left no record to perpetuate his name except a few articles on practical subjects. Nor was he much of a reader ; and as for books, he had none worth mentioning, either medical or non-professional. Of his merits as a lecturer, as I heard him only on two occasions, I cannot speak adequately from personal observation. In 1827 I was present at his introductory lecture to the course on anatomy in the University of Pennsylvania.

The subject was Respiration; and his discourse greatly disappointed me, as it did many others; it was quite meagre, and not at all up in its details to the existing state of the science. Nor was it well delivered. The other lecture was descriptive of the muscles of the forearm, of which his adjunct, Dr. Horner, had made a beautiful dissection. The account of them by Physick was brief and imperfect, and his assistant, who sat near him, was obliged to prompt him several times as to their names. His memory of the nomenclature of anatomy was evidently bad. His lectures on surgery, delivered annually from 1805 to 1818, when Gibson succeeded him, have always been spoken of with much respect, although they were mostly read. At times, however, he would lay down his manuscript and speak as became a master, often becoming even eloquent, especially when discussing subjects with which he had made himself familiar, or in relation to which he had distinguished himself as a surgical practitioner. He had no special love for anatomy; and I have always been told that he committed a great blunder when he resigned the chair of Surgery in favor of Gibson.

It is said that Physick was fond of money, and that he loved to accumulate it for its own sake. One of his biographers, Dr. John Bell, states that his income sometimes amounted to twenty thousand dollars a year—a very large sum for the period in which he practised—and that he always invested his surplus means in real estate, never spending anything upon professional objects, in entertainments, or in promoting the interests of indigent young students. However this may be, he left no bequests for charitable purposes, or for the advancement of medical science. His estate at the time of his death was valued at nearly half a million of dollars. His fees for professional services were always very reasonable. One day a stranger who had consulted him on account of his wife's health accidentally met him on the street and handed him a hundred-dollar note. When he reached home he looked at the note, and finding it so large he immediately returned all but ten dollars. In his manners Physick was cold and unsociable. He kept himself aloof from the world, apparently to enhance his greatness, and would not be seen even at a theatre. Yet Physick was at heart a kind man, full of sympathy for suffering humanity. His mind in his old age was much exercised upon religion. He read numerous works upon the subject, and sought counsel from some of his clerical friends. What were the conclusions at which he arrived I have never learned. He had a horror of being buried alive, and enjoined his family to wrap his body in flannel after death. He also requested that his grave should be watched for several weeks after his interment to prevent his body from falling into the hands of resurrectionists. In person he was tall and erect, even when an old man. His face, strikingly handsome, but pallid, looked as if it had been chiselled out of marble. His mouth was well formed, the nose aquiline, and the eye black and shaded by a fine brow. His forehead was angular and of good size, but not capacious, and his hair was powdered and arranged in the form of a queue, as used to be the fashion with Bishop White and some of his other contemporaries. Altogether he was a remarkable-looking man, always neatly dressed and very genteel in his appearance. During the latter part of his life he rode in a small carriage drawn by two black horses in simple harness. He despised ostentation.

William Potts Dewees.

1768–1841.

Dewees, for a number of years an adjunct to James, was a less amiable and modest, but a far greater man than his master, to whose chair, in 1834, he succeeded. He was indeed a man of positive temperament, of great talents, remarkably industrious, and in every sense of the word self-made. His early education was extremely limited; and no subsequent training was sufficient to overcome its deficiency. He was an excellent talker, a good lecturer, and a successful teacher, popular with his pupils, and a master of his department. Unlike James, he did not hesitate to call things by their proper names. No blush suffused his cheek in the lecture-room. Both as a writer and as a public teacher he criticized mercilessly the men who differed from him in doctrinal or practical points. He was especially severe upon Baudelocque and some of his English contemporaries. Owing mainly to this cause he soon acquired immense reputation as an independent thinker and as an authority in obstetric medicine. No American writer had, up to the time at which he taught, made so profound an impression as he upon the professional mind. Whatever he wrote, or spoke in the lecture-room, became law and gospel with medical men. His style as a writer is unscholarly, inelegant, and inaccurate; indeed, not unfrequently ungrammatical. And yet most of his published works were universally accepted and studied. They were found upon the table of every respectable physician, passed through numerous editions, and yielded a handsome profit both to the author and the publisher. I refer here particularly to his treatises on Midwifery, on the Diseases of Women, and on the Diseases of Children. His Practice of Medicine met with no success, and deserved none. Like the monkey in the fable, who cast the net in the expectation of making a great haul during the absence of the fisherman, he became entangled, and was fatally submerged. The work, I believe, never reached a second edition. A reviewer in the North American Medical and Surgical Journal, in commenting upon its style, fitly remarks: "Addison and Johnson have been little imitated in its pages. We must take the work as we find it; be thankful; and, with honest Sancho, exclaim, 'God bless the giver!'"

As an obstetric practitioner Dewees was one of the most popular men of his day. No woman of any social position in Philadelphia considered herself safe if she could not have Dewees in her confinement; and yet, notwithstanding this immense practice and the business necessarily growing out of it, the latter years of this petted favorite were clouded by poverty, if, indeed, not by actual want. He is represented as having been a high liver; and what added much to his distress, he was attacked a few years before his death with apoplexy, followed by hemiplegia, which seriously crippled him both in mind and body during the remainder of his life. He went to Mobile, Alabama, in the hope of benefiting his health. In this, however, he was disappointed, and he died in 1841 soon after his return to Philadelphia, worn out by disease and misfortune, at the age of seventy-three.

Dewees made no important contributions to gynæcology, or to the pathology, diagnosis, and treatment of the diseases of women—a department of the healing art which now, thanks to the labors of many of the greatest men of the day, occupies so grand a position. Herculaneum had not yet revealed its speculum; and the instrument devised by Récamier, of Paris, had not found its way into this country. The organic affections of the uterus were everywhere a forbidden territory. Ocular inspection was considered little less than an indictable offence, at which pious mothers threw up their hands in holy horror. I well remember with what feelings such examinations were regarded even so late as thirty years ago, long after the death of Dewees, and the prejudices which existed against their general introduction. Even many highly respectable physicians arrayed themselves against the use of this valuable instrument, contenting themselves, much to the injury of suffering women, with digital explorations and the employment of the pessary. If Dewees projected himself into the future, it was not in this direction. He left the field of organic uterine complaints as he had found it, uncultivated and unimproved. His forte was practical midwifery; and herein he rendered good service, for which the women of his day could not be too grateful. He was a firm believer in the efficacy of bloodletting in parturition accompanied by rigidity of the uterus, with impending convulsions. Under such circumstances he always bled unsparingly, and he followed a similar practice in puerperal fever. It is much to be regretted that the abstraction of blood in these diseases is so seldom resorted to at the present day.

Dewees shared the prejudices of his colleagues in regard to the establishment of a second school in Philadelphia. When the Jefferson Medical College, although entirely officered by graduates of the University of Pennsylvania, went into operation it met with a degree of opposition on the part of the old preceptors of these gentlemen, of which those unacquainted with the history of medical teaching in Philadelphia can hardly form a conception. Every man connected with the College was tabooed. This prejudice was not confined to the Faculty; the pupils of the school came in for their share of it. A lady, a relation of Dewees, one day warmly eulogized one of its recent graduates, speaking of him as a young gentleman of great talents and professional promise, when she was interrupted by the remark: "That may all be true; but it won't do for my colleagues or myself to recognize the graduates of the Jefferson Medical College." I mention this fact, referred to elsewhere, not to reawaken unpleasant feelings, but simply to show that honorable rivalry seldom fails to be productive of good; that the establishment in 1825 of a second school in Philadelphia instead of injuring was of great benefit to the University of Pennsylvania, inasmuch as more pupils and more money were thereby brought to our city; and that the conduct of the University was eminently illiberal, and made her many enemies.

In stature Dewees was tall, erect, and well formed. His head, however, was too small for a man of his proportions. He possessed fine colloquial powers, and gave up much of his leisure to light literature.

GEORGE MCCLELLAN.

1796–1847.

THERE were a number of young men when I was a student in Philadelphia who, setting out upon their professional life about the same time, all became more or less distinguished either as practitioners, teachers, or authors. Among these the most prominent were George McClellan, John K. Mitchell, René La Roche, Jacob Randolph, John Bell, Francis D. Condie, Franklin Bache, Hugh L. Hodge, Charles D. Meigs, Robert M. Huston, Samuel George Morton, George B. Wood, and Isaac Hays. With all of these men I was personally acquainted, indeed with some familiarly. It is not often that a group of such men can be viewed in contrast or comparison. It is to be regretted that their portraits do not grace the Hall of the College of Physicians to be seen and reverenced by posterity.

Of McClellan an account will be found in a previous chapter of this work. It is sufficient here to say that he was one of the most able, talented, and enterprising of the group, with hardly any one of whom he was on good terms either at the outset of his career or afterwards. The line of demarcation between him and them was always distinctly drawn. Whether this arose from the fact that he dared, soon after entering the profession, to become the founder of a new school of medicine; whether it was because he rapidly acquired a commanding practice, for which some of his competitors were long struggling in vain; or, finally, whether there was something repugnant to them in his manners or in his professional acts, certain it is that George McClellan was for many years, if not during his lifetime in Philadelphia, looked down upon by most of the men I have named. All these men were graduates of the University of Pennsylvania; and it was therefore not unnatural that they should take sides with their preceptors in opposition to the new school. Something undoubtedly was due to the manner of McClellan, who was not always wise or discreet. His impulsive disposition often brought him into trouble; he lacked judgment, talked too much, and made everybody his confidant. Of course the betrayal of his confidence made him many enemies, some of them implacable. He was, moreover, a restless man, always pushing ahead. Most of his contemporaries, on the contrary, were men of quiet disposition, slow in their movements, and inclined to bide their time. If they were less brilliant in early life than he, they were in the end not much, if any, behind him in usefulness and enduring reputation. With many faults, McClellan was unquestionably a man of genius, quick to perceive and prompt to execute. With a better regulated mind he would have accomplished much greater ends and achieved a more lasting fame. Probably no man ever handled a scalpel with more dexterity. Full of resources, he allowed no obstacle to impede his progress. One day, as I know myself, he needed a catheter to relieve a woman of retention of urine. Did he send for one to the cutler or apothecary? No. "Sir," addressing the husband, "bring me a quill;" and in a few minutes the suffering creature was in elysium. On another occasion his saw broke in amputating a poor man's arm; in a moment the limb was bent over his knee and the bone snapped asunder. He was, in the main, a tolerably good judge of human nature. His reputation as a surgeon will be in great measure traditional, for he has left no adequate record of his observations and experience. He has, it is true, transmitted to us a small volume on surgery, but it is read by few persons, and it really possesses no conspicuous merit. His fame will rest mainly upon the fact that he was the founder of a school. Nevertheless, after having been connected with it for a number of years, he left it and established another. The new school was short-lived, and ere long he found himself without a professor's chair. His unquiet disposition at length told terribly upon his health and happiness.

McClellan died poor. He bought town lots, built houses, and lost money. He had a passion for fine horses and a fondness for races. He was one of the most reckless drivers I have ever seen. It was as much as one's life was worth to sit with him in his carriage. He was a perfect Jehu, and yet he seldom met with an accident. He talked with extraordinary rapidity, and was in the habit of buttonholing his friends and acquaintances on the street, often at the expense of punctuality. It was not an uncommon thing for him to appear in the amphitheatre from five to ten minutes after the appointed hour.

His death, which occurred on May 9th, 1847, when he was in the fifty-first year of his age, was frightfully sudden. His health had for several years been on the wane. He was nervous, dyspeptic, and subject to distress in the bowels. In the morning before he died he had felt more than usually uncomfortable, and after ten o'clock, soon after having visited a patient in the vicinity of his office, he was seized with violent pain in the abdomen, attended with excessive shock, speedily followed by collapse, under which he sank in less than twenty-four hours. An examination of the body revealed ulcerative perforation of the small intestine. His death caused regret throughout the country.

HENRY B. BASCOM.

1796–1850.

THE first man of note with whom I came in contact after leaving the East was the Rev. Dr. Henry B. Bascom, afterwards a bishop in the Methodist Episcopal Church South, and President successively of Augusta College and of Transylvania University. He was a passenger on the steamer Gazelle, on his way to Kentucky, and left the vessel, if I mistake not, at Augusta, fifty miles above Cincinnati. My wife and I had made his acquaintance at Easton, and were therefore glad to meet him on our boat, which was bound to what was then considered the far West. He had preached there, only a few months before, a most eloquent discourse on the colonization of Africa— a subject which was attracting much attention at the time, and which was freely discussed during our voyage. He had delivered the same discourse repeatedly before; and it was therefore not surprising that it should have made a deep impression upon those who heard it. The sermon exhibited marked ability, and it abounded in flashes of eloquence, as he depicted the cause of the negro and his future destiny. I had heard able speakers before, and I have heard able ones since; but in my opinion no speaker has ever equalled Bascom in the force and pathos of his delivery, or in the electrical effect which he exerted upon his audience.

Dr. Bascom was a self-made man, a native of Hancock, New York. Several of his earlier years were spent at Easton, in the family of a Mr. Bidleman, who took a deep interest in his education. He was licensed to preach at the age of nineteen, and at twenty-seven he was chosen chaplain to Congress. Of commanding presence and graceful person, he was grave and dignified in his manners, with an appearance of hauteur not exactly becoming in one who had worked his way up from a humble position. He was, however, an agreeable conversationalist, and, when unbent, a most genial companion. He was exceedingly neat in his dress, wore gloves while on the boat, and amused himself by constantly twirling his cane. Although such a man could not be popular with the common people, there was no one in the country who had such a hold upon the Methodist Church, or who for a number of years had the reputation of being so able and eloquent an expounder of its doctrines. Bascom, I believe, was never married. He was elected bishop of the Methodist Episcopal Church South in 1850, and died within the same year, leaving behind him a number of manuscripts, since published in a collected form. His writings, though brilliant, have failed to make a permanent impression as theological productions.

J. J. AUDUBON.
1780–1851.

AUDUBON during the latter years of his life made a visit to Louisville, the scene of his early struggles and of his ornithological labors, to spend a short time among his old friends, and to greet once more his brother-in-law, Mr. William Bakewell, and his charming wife. This, as nearly as I recollect, was in 1846, four or five years before his death. His arrival was announced in the city daily papers. Mr. Bakewell gave him a reception, which was attended by all the prominent citizens of the town, and which was an exceedingly merry one. Audubon was one of the gayest of the gay, enjoying the dance with all the glee of a boy of fifteen. It was delightful to see his white locks shaking to and fro in the air responsively to the music. Old age forgot for a time its dignity in the renewal

of its youth. The occasion seemed to recall his fondness
for dancing, one of his earliest and most cherished amusements. Indisposition prevented me from attending the
party ; but I called the next day, and had the gratification
of a cordial handshaking—an honor which I have always
thoroughly appreciated. To stand in the presence of the
most renowned naturalist of his day, and the greatest our
country has produced, was no ordinary occurrence. I felt
all the better for the interview, which stimulated my ambition. I had long been familiar with his fame and writings. I had studied his Biography of the Birds of America,
and had often spent hours in looking over and admiring
the thick folio volumes of his glorious work on Ornithology in the library of the University of Louisville, which
was obtained at a cost of eight hundred dollars. The life-
like illustrations in these volumes are sufficient evidence
that Audubon was an artist of the highest type. He
sketched and painted birds with marvellous rapidity and
elegance, placing them before the reader as one is accustomed to see them in the field and in the forest, on the
ground, in the thicket, and on the loftiest tree. His descriptive powers have never been equalled by any ornithol-
ogist, if we except those of Wilson. His Biography of the
Birds of America abounds in charming reading, and is
worthy of a place in every library. Audubon, at the time
of this visit, was a well-preserved man, erect, with a clear
eye, long, flowing, almost white hair, and all the vivacity
peculiar to his French nature. He was a born naturalist.
A native of Louisiana, he received his education principally in France; and after his return to this country he
lived for a time on his father's farm on the banks of the
Perkiomen Creek in Eastern Pennsylvania. It was here
that he met Lucy Bakewell, a young, lovely girl, whom
he soon afterwards married, and who, notwithstanding his
roving disposition and his long and frequent absences from
home, seems to have been deeply attached to him. Audu-

bon was not fortunate in his business relations. All his mercantile pursuits were failures. His genius soared far above such worldly occupations. He never was so happy as when, with gun on shoulder and his faithful dog by his side, he was buried in the dense forest, within sight of an unknown bird, of a bear, or of a panther, or in the midst of a mighty storm, or on the bosom of a fierce and relentless flood. His solitary and nomadic life seems to have made him indifferent to danger. His earlier married years were attended with great hardships. At one time he was in such straitened circumstances as to be compelled to give lessons in dancing. Having studied design under David, the eminent French painter, he occasionally, to procure bread for his young family, employed his brush upon a portrait. He was fond of music, and played with skill upon the violin, flute, guitar, and flageolet. During his wanderings in the forest, extending over a large part of his married life, the support of his children devolved entirely upon his good Lucy. What business has such a man with a wife? Early love must indeed have been blind in his case. It is sad to think that the few last years of this great and good man's life were overcast by a heavy mental cloud, rendering him completely helpless. In 1851 his friends laid him tenderly in his final resting-place. But love abode in the family; and the birds of the field and the forest will forever warble hymns of gratitude and praise to the memory of him who made them illustrious.

GRANVILLE SHARP PATTISON.

1791–1851.

GRANVILLE SHARP PATTISON died in the city of New York, November 12th, 1851, in the sixtieth year of his age, after having occupied for nearly two-thirds of his life a conspicuous place in the public eye. It is no exaggeration to say that no anatomical teacher of his day, either in Europe or in this country, enjoyed a higher reputation. There were undoubtedly many anatomists far more profoundly versed in the secrets of the human frame, more dexterous, patient, and minute dissectors, and men better acquainted with the use of the microscope, or the study of the tissues, a branch of anatomy now known as histology. Indeed, it is not too much to assert that if he was not ignorant of histology and microscopical anatomy his knowledge was very superficial. It may, however, be said that these studies were, even at the time of his death, in their embryonic condition. Only glimmerings of light had as yet broken in upon the profession. Pattison's forte as a teacher consisted in his knowledge of visceral and surgical anatomy, and in the application of this knowledge to the diagnosis and treatment of diseases and of accidents, and to operations. He had studied surgical anatomy under Allan Burns of Glasgow, its founder in Great Britain, and I may add in this country, where the republication of his work, entitled The Surgical Anatomy of the Head and Neck, awakened unexampled interest and enthusiasm in this department of science. His great charm in the lecture-room was the earnestness of his manner and the clearness of his demonstrations. He would throw his whole soul into his subject, and use every exertion to make himself felt and understood; and his enthusiasm never failed to infuse itself into the dullest pupil. The appointed hour always seemed too short, so rapidly and pleasantly did it pass. What added interest to the speaker was a slight lisp and a Scotch accent, which never entirely forsook him, despite his efforts to overcome them in early life. Pattison never indulged in any of those physical displays occasionally witnessed in our amphitheatres. On the contrary, he was dignified, entertaining, and instructive. He possessed that peculiar kind of eloquence which is so well calculated to enchain the attention and enlighten the mind of the medical student—an eloquence difficult to describe, but without which no teaching can be attractive or make an abiding impression upon one's auditors.

It was my lot to be associated with Granville Sharp Pattison during the session of 1850-51 in the New York University, in which I served as Professor of Surgery as the successor of Valentine Mott. One morning, in the summer previous to the session, during my residence at Louisville, a telegram was handed to me at the breakfast-table, in which I was asked whether I should be at home on a certain day the following week, the writer adding that he desired an interview with me. When the appointed time arrived I was not a little surprised to see before me a small, elderly gentleman, of medium stature, with black eyes and white hair, who introduced himself as Mr. Pattison. Up to this time I had known him only by reputation. He soon explained the object of his visit. He painted the prospects of the University of New York in the most glowing colors, spoke of his colleagues as though they were the greatest and most learned of professors, and peopled the amphitheatre at no distant period with from eight hundred to one thousand students. I shall never forget his enthusiasm. I was then in a halting frame of mind, for the University of Louisville was in danger of passing out of the hands of its trustees into the management of a board to be elected annually by the City Council, by which the school had been largely endowed. The question propounded to me required time for reflection. Pattison left the next morning, depositing with me a guarantee of four thousand dollars for my winter's labors in the event of my acceptance. At the end of a week I sent an affirmative answer. The history of my connection, however, with the University of New York, and of my return to Louisville, is related elsewhere.

I saw much of Pattison during the winter I spent in

New York, and became fond of him on account of his agreeable social qualities and his unceasing attentions to my wife and myself. He was ever ready to do us a kind act, to entertain us at a *petit souper*, or to take us to the opera, theatre, or other place of amusement. As a colleague he was all that could possibly have been wished—affable, courteous, and considerate, with an earnest desire to promote the interests of the school. Mrs. Pattison, a Scotch lady, whose maiden name was Sharp, was exceedingly proud of her husband and devoted to him; and it was pleasant to hear her speak of him invariably as her "dear Granville." They had no offspring.

Pattison was a man of fine taste; a lover of the sublime and beautiful in nature and in art. He was intensely fond of music; and, although he was no performer himself, few persons in New York frequented the opera and the concert hall oftener than he. He took an active interest in the establishment of the Grand Opera House in New York, and I recollect with what enthusiasm he greeted Parodi upon her first appearance in that edifice. No one was more vociferous in his applause; and his attendance during the whole engagement of that celebrated singer was almost constant. At an early period of his professional life he edited an edition of Allan Burns's Surgical Anatomy of the Head and Neck and performed several important surgical operations, tying, it is said, upon one occasion, the omohyoid muscle instead of the common carotid artery. But his surgical tastes, if he ever had any, never grew upon him, and as he advanced in years the sight of blood became distressing to him. Naturally of an indolent disposition, he spent most of his leisure in reading light literature, in attending places of amusement, and in visiting his friends. Like Izaak Walton and Sir Humphry Davy, he was never happier than when he was casting his fly in a pleasant trout stream in May or June. He often indulged in partridge-shooting. But he was never successful in the chase of the deer, for the reason, as he himself told me, that the moment he saw a deer he was always seized with the buck fever.   He could cook a canvas-back duck to perfection.

The career of Pattison was a checkered one.   He was born near Glasgow, where, at the age of seventeen, he began the study of medicine.   At twenty-one he became an assistant of Allan Burns, and devoted himself to the study and teaching of anatomy.   From Glasgow he came in 1818 to Philadelphia, under a promise of the chair of Anatomy in the University of Pennsylvania, then recently vacated by the death of Dr. Dorsey, a nephew of Dr. Physick.   A cloud, however, followed him to this country, and he was accordingly tabooed upon his arrival. He subsequently engaged in a duel, in which he shot his adversary in the hip, laming him for life.   Despite this adventure, he was soon after appointed to the chair of Anatomy in the University of Maryland, which, in consequence of his brilliant teaching, speedily attained a high degree of prosperity.   In 1828, upon the organization of the now celebrated London University, he was called to the chair of Anatomy.   A serious misunderstanding soon arose between him and the Demonstrator of Anatomy, Dr. Bennett, and he left London in disgust.   He returned to Philadelphia, and served as professor of his favorite branch in the Jefferson Medical College from 1831 until 1840, when he assisted in founding the Medical Department of the University of the City of New York.   Like a rolling stone, Pattison gathered no moss, and consequently left no estate, although his "dear Mary," having means of her own, was comparatively comfortable after his death.

CHAPTER X.

DANIEL DRAKE.

1785–1852.

I HAD been a resident of Cincinnati for four months, when one cold and dreary morning in February a gentleman entered the parlor of my lodgings and introduced himself to me as Dr. Drake. Shaking him cordially by the hand, I bade him to be seated, and we were soon in pleasant and earnest conversation. He said, "I would have called to see you sooner, but I did not wish to prejudice against you the Faculty of the Medical College of Ohio, who are my enemies;" jocularly adding, "They think me the worst man in the world." I told him that I was glad to see him, and cared not what his enemies thought of him, and that, although merely an *attaché* of the school, I was my own master. Drake was at this time a handsome man, with fine blue eyes and manly features. He was well dressed, and around his neck he had a long gold watch-chain which rested loosely upon his vest. He had on a suit of black cloth, and wore crape on his hat in mourning for his wife, although she had been dead a number of years. He was twenty years my senior, and in the enjoyment of a national reputation as a physician. Before he rose I sent for Mrs. Gross, who, like myself, was delighted with him. The acquaintance thus begun gradually ripened into a warm friendship, which continued uninterrupted until the time of his death in 1852.

Dr. Drake affords another memorable instance, of which so many are mentioned in these pages, of a man rising from humble birth to deserved renown. He had natural talent and genius of a high order, and would have become eminent in whatever pursuit he might have engaged. He would have made a good pulpit orator, a popular Methodist exhorter, an astute lawyer, an able senator, a shrewd politician, a great statesman, or a creditable cabinet minister. To talent and genius he added vast industry, untiring zeal, and boundless ambition—qualities rarely combined in the same individual, and yet so necessary to attain to distinction and usefulness. For earnestness of purpose I have never seen him excelled.

Drake was born in 1785 at what was then the small hamlet of Plainfield, New Jersey. When he was two and a half years old his father removed to May's Lick, Kentucky, then almost a wilderness, where the son shared with his parents the hardships incident to a new settlement, doing all manner of work, and attending school in a log-cabin without glass windows even in the winter months. The log-cabin was generally built of unhewn timber with a puncheon floor, and consisted of one apartment, which served as sitting-room, kitchen, and dormitory. The schoolmasters were itinerants, generally from the Eastern States, who for the sum of fifteen shillings a quarter taught their pupils spelling, reading, penmanship, and ciphering as far as the Rule of Three. This was the limit of their acquisitions. Drake received no instruction in Greek and Latin until he began the study of medicine, when, by a special agreement with his preceptor, he devoted six months to them.

With this slender stock of knowledge the youth, at the age of sixteen, set out for Cincinnati, then a small frontier town, to see Dr. Goforth, the principal doctor of the place, a kind of high priest in the temple of Æsculapius, and to arrange with him the terms of his apprenticeship. The agreement was that he should remain in the office of his preceptor four years, should live in the house as one of the family, and at the close of his pupilage should receive four hundred dollars. Dr. Goforth was not even a graduate in medicine, and one of his favorite prescriptions was "radix rhei in the root!" In those days in secluded towns and villages there were no drug-stores, and doctors prepared their own medicines and compounded their own prescriptions. The young student had to perform a great deal of drudgery, grind quicksilver into mercurial ointment, and carry medicines to patients' houses. The first intellectual task of young Drake was reading Quincy's Dispensatory, then Cheselden on the Bones, Jones on the Muscles, Van Swieten's Commentaries on Boerhaave, Chaptal's Chemistry, Cullen's Materia Medica, and Haller's Physiology. These works were at that time the recognized text-books of medical students, with many of whom it was the custom to commit to memory a large part of their contents. The principal remedies were calomel, rhubarb, jalap, castor oil, tartar emetic, and bleeding, with low diet. As the youthful student advanced in knowledge he assisted his master in visiting his patients and in prescribing for their ailments. In due time young Drake, without ever having witnessed the dissection of a human body, or a single experiment in chemistry, was dubbed "doctor;" and as he was sprightly, intelligent, and aspiring he was at once taken into partnership with his late preceptor. But he thirsted for more knowledge; and he attended, in 1805, a course of lectures in the University of Pennsylvania under Rush, Wistar, Physick, Barton, and Woodhouse, then in the zenith of their reputation. He travelled to Philadelphia on horseback, the journey occupying three weeks. He then practised medicine for one year near his former home in Kentucky, and settled permanently at Cincinnati. In 1807 he married Harriet Sisson, a lovely and talented woman, by whom he had three children—one son, Charles

Drake, for a short time United States Senator from Missouri, and afterwards Chief-Justice of the Court of Claims at Washington; and two excellent and devoted daughters, long since deceased. Mrs. Drake died in 1825; and no wife was ever more truly mourned by her husband.

In 1815 Drake attended his second course of lectures in Philadelphia, and was now in earnest made a doctor of medicine, amid the congratulations of his teachers, all of whom looked upon him as a man of remarkable promise. Instead, however, of devoting himself to his profession on his return to Cincinnati, he foolishly dabbled in commercial enterprises, all of which failed, as might have been anticipated.. He soon had the good sense to retrace his steps.

Drake soon became prominent in the medical history of the West; and his practice increased to such an extent that patients were attracted to him from a distance. But in less than two years after he received his degree he accepted the chair of Materia Medica in the medical school of Transylvania University, then recently organized, and spent nearly the whole of the winter at Lexington lecturing to twenty students. This was a sad mistake, as his practice at Cincinnati was thereby for a time broken up. Believing that Cincinnati was a more favorable point for a medical school than Lexington, he founded in 1819 the Medical College of Ohio, in which he took the chair of Medicine. His colleagues, however, were weak men; dissensions of an irreconcilable nature soon arose; and finally, to cap the climax, he was expelled from the Faculty, he himself occupying the chair and putting the vote. Only two of his colleagues were present; one of whom, with great dignity, lighted the late president down-stairs with a tallow candle. Drake often in an inimitable manner referred to this occurrence as one of the most humorous incidents in his checkered career.

Drake now reëntered Transylvania University, but

finally left it for Cincinnati in 1827. The school meanwhile greatly increased in prosperity. His most prominent colleague at this time was Dr. Benjamin Winslow Dudley, who afterwards became so famous as a lithotomist. The other members of the Faculty were of moderate intellectual grade. William H. Richardson, the Professor of Obstetrics, used to talk about "post-mortem examinations after death;" and Dr. James Overton, another professor, on one occasion ripped open the abdomen of a pregnant woman under the conviction that she had an ovarian tumor: "A baby, by ——!" said the undaunted operator, and closed the wound.

In 1830 Drake accepted the chair of Medicine in Jefferson Medical College, then in the fifth year of its existence, and laboring under all the difficulties due to jealousy and to inconsiderate competition. He brought students with him from the West. His fame as a teacher had preceded him; and he made a powerful impression both as a lecturer and as a debater in the Philadelphia Medical Society, among the members of which were Samuel Jackson, William Potts Dewees, René La Roche, Benjamin Horner Coates and Reynold Coates, John K. Mitchell, Hugh L. Hodge, and Charles D. Meigs. The discussions in the winter of that year were of unusual earnestness and force. Drake sent in his resignation before the session was fairly closed. In the mean time, through his friends at Cincinnati, he had organized the Medical Department of the Miami University at Oxford, Ohio. He took with him his late colleague Dr. John Eberle, and Dr. Thomas D. Mitchell, of Frankford, Philadelphia. Dr. George McClellan had also promised to accompany him, but yielding to the counsel of his friends he wisely remained at home, the chair of Surgery being afterwards given to Dr. James R. Staughton.

The announcement of the new school had hardly been published when an injunction, issued by the Medical Col-

2—34

lege of Ohio, crushed the enterprise in its bud. Eberle
and Mitchell accepted chairs in the old school. Drake
took a subordinate professorship, which, as he had neither
a desire nor fitness for it, he vacated at the close of the
session, and once more retired to private life.

The Miami scheme having proved a failure, and the
doors of the Medical College of Ohio being barred against
him, Drake founded the Medical Department of the Cincinnati College. After a successful career of four years this
school was permanently suspended—a result due mainly
to the withdrawal of its originator, who, influenced by a
guarantee, accepted a chair in the University of Louisville,
thus leaving in the lurch all his late colleagues. Drake's
career as a teacher had not only been exceedingly brilliant,
but it had exerted a powerful influence upon the prosperity
of the school. Had he been contented to remain in it he
would undoubtedly have been a happier man, and would,
in all human probability, have prolonged his life for many
years. But he was possessed of the demon of restlessness.
His constant dream was to return to his early love, the Medical College of Ohio, and to make it, with the aid of able
colleagues, a flourishing institution—one which should be
an honor to him as its founder and an honor to the country
—in short, a fit receptacle ultimately for his ashes. It is
melancholy to see with what tenacity and infatuation he
clung to this idea. The following extract from a discourse
which he delivered late in life before the students of the
Medical College of Ohio will place this subject in a clearer
light than any words of my own can. After having referred to his connection with various medical institutions,
to the fact that he had been the first medical student in
Cincinnati, and to the circumstance that thirty years before he had founded the school in which they were then
assembled, he feelingly remarked: "My heart still fondly
turned to my first love, your Alma Mater. Her image,
glowing in the warm and radiant tints of earlier life, was

ever in my view. Transylvania had been reorganized in 1819, and included in its Faculty Professor Dudley, whose surgical fame had already spread throughout the West, and that paragon of labor and perseverance, Professor Caldwell, now a veteran octogenarian. In the year after my separation from this school I was recalled to that; but neither the eloquence of my colleagues, nor the greeting of the largest classes which the University ever enjoyed, could drive that beautiful image from my mind. After four sessions I resigned, and was subsequently called to Jefferson Medical College, Philadelphia; but the image mingled with my shadow; and when we reached the summit of the mountain it bade me stop and gaze upon the silvery cloud which hung over the place where you are now assembled. Afterward, in the Medical Department of Cincinnati College, I lectured with men of power, to young men thirsting for knowledge, but the image still hovered around me. I was then invited to Louisville, became a member of one of the ablest Faculties ever embodied in the West, and saw the halls of the University rapidly filled. But when I looked on the faces of four hundred students, behold, the image was in their midst. While there I prosecuted an extensive course of personal inquiry into the causes and cure of the diseases of the interior of the continent; and in journeying by day, and journeying by night—on the water and on the land—while struggling through the matted rushes where the Mississippi mingles with the Gulf—or camping with Indians and Canadian boatmen under the pines and birches of Lake Superior, the image was still my faithful companion, and whispered sweet words of encouragement and hope. I bided my time; and after twice doubling the period through which Jacob waited for his Rachel, the united voice of the Trustees and Professors has recalled me to the chair which I held in the beginning.''

Dissatisfied with the management of the college, Drake sent in his resignation at the close of the session. He was soon recalled to his chair at Louisville. After a service here of two years he once more went back to his "first love"—but this time only to die. The school had been thoroughly reorganized, and he had fondly hoped that, with the aid of his new associates, most of them men of reputation and of proved ability, he would be able to place it upon an enduring foundation as one of the great medical institutions of the country. Alas for human vanity and human expectation! At the first Faculty meeting, held a few days before the opening of the session, a circumstance occurred which occasioned him deep chagrin, and which was the remote cause of his death in less than a week. I need not recall the particulars of this annoyance, or the name of the man who provoked it—a name which has long since ceased to be associated with that of honorable men. Thus, after a career of thirty-five years as a teacher, terminated the life of this extraordinary physician, more diversified by prosperity and adversity than that of any medical man our country has ever produced. He was often heard to say, "Medical schools have consumed me."

Dr. Drake, as I have said, was a great lecturer. His voice was clear and strong, and he had a power of expression which amounted to genuine eloquence. At times his manner was too vehement. He often seemed to labor like one engaged in special pleading, speaking so rapidly that the student could scarcely follow him or retain the thread of his discourse. When under full way every nerve quivered, and his voice could be heard at a great distance. With first-course students he was never popular; not because there was anything disagreeable in his manner, but because few of them had been sufficiently educated to seize the import of his utterances.

His famous Picture of Cincinnati appeared several years before he received his medical degree, and it had a powerful influence in attracting immigration from the Eastern

States. For a long time indeed Cincinnati was essentially a Yankee city, and much of its intelligence and enterprise was due to its early settlers. In 1827 Drake projected the Western Journal of the Medical and Physical Sciences, the first number of which was issued in April of that year. He chose for its motto, engraved upon a flower of the Cornus Florida on the title-page, the appropriate words, *E sylvis, æque atque ad sylvas nuncius*, for the journal was literally a messenger not only from, but also to the woods. Many of his contributions to medical science are contained in this periodical, which, on his removal to Louisville, was transferred to that city and published for many years under the title of the Western Journal of Medicine. Some of these papers were of much value and interest, such as those on Medical Education, Epidemic Cholera, and Northern Lakes as a Summer Resort for Southern Invalids. But the work upon which his fame as a thinker and a medical philosopher will mainly rest is entitled A Systematic Treatise, Historical, Etiological, and Practical, on the Principal Diseases of the Interior Valley of North America, as they Appear in the Caucasian, African, Indian, and Esquimaux Varieties of its Population. This title sufficiently indicates the character of the work. The arrangement of his matter, gathered, in his extensive journeys, from personal observation and from intercourse with physicians in various sections of the United States and Canada, occupied the leisure of his later years. As a monument of learning and patient research the work is unique in our profession. At the time of his death only one volume was completed; but the other was in so forward a state of preparation that, under the editorship of Dr. Hanbury Smith of Ohio and Dr. Francis Gurney Smith of Philadelphia, it appeared within a few years after the sad event. It is mortifying to think that this work fell stillborn from the press. Had its author devoted his time and talents to the composition of a text-book, his reputation would have been sufficient to secure for it an immense and remunerative circulation. As it was, the book had no readers, and the author and publishers received no compensation for it. But, although physicians of the present generation have neglected it, the work will in the future, I have no doubt, shed lustre upon medical literature and confer an enviable immortality upon the name of its author.

Dr. Drake wielded a pen of rare power. Despite the deficiency of his early education, he wrote with facility, and expressed himself in masculine English. His style was robust, often elegant, and sometimes even eloquent ; never weak or without point. He had a strong imagination, and some of his lighter writings exhibit considerable poetical fancy and tasteful imagery. He possessed keen powers of analysis with quick perceptions, and carried on his mental work in the true spirit of the Baconian philosophy, reasoning from facts to theory, and not from theory to facts. His pen sped rapidly over his paper, but it often retraced its steps to correct or interline. His chirography was bold and easily read. In personal appearance he was commanding. Nearly six feet in height, he was well formed, with handsome features, keen blue eyes, a fine but not expansive forehead, a medium-sized mouth, round chin, and a rather prominent nose. The frosts of sixty-seven winters had slightly silvered his temples, but had made no other inroads upon his hair. His step was light and elastic ; he was accustomed to long walks, and had remarkable powers of endurance. His manners were simple and dignified. He was easy of access, kind and social in his disposition, and unostentatious in his dress and style of living. He was a Whig in politics, and an ardent friend of rational liberty throughout the world. He was, moreover, a Christian gentleman, a lover of peace, and an intense hater of vice and immorality. He abhorred everything that was mean and vulgar. His mode of living was extremely simple. Breakfast was his chief meal. He ate little meat, but he was very fond of pie and fruit. He never used alcoholic drinks, hardly ever took even a glass of wine; never chewed, smoked, or snuffed tobacco; knew nothing of cards; never baited a hook or cast a line; never fired off a gun; and never, as far as I know, visited a theatre. He was devotedly attached to his family and friends, and was never happier than when he was in their society. He was a good talker, had a merry laugh, and was fond of anecdotes, of which he had a large stock at his command. For many years his house was the abode of a warm but simple hospitality. His name was a household word; and he was for a long time Cincinnati's most eminent citizen.

The modesty of Drake bordered on affectation. In 1854, at the meeting of the American Medical Association in Cincinnati, he might easily have been elected President for the ensuing year. But he declined to let his name go before the Nominating Committee; and the consequence was, much to the annoyance of his friends, that a man far his inferior in ability and reputation obtained that honorable post. I often asked him why he did not visit Europe, where, such was his fame, he would have been received with respect and deference; and his answer invariably was, "I don't care to be brought into contact with the great physicians on the other side of the Atlantic, men of university education, whose advantages were so much greater than my own. I think too much of my country to place myself in so awkward a position." And he never swerved from his purpose; never saw the Atlantic Ocean.

Despite his many noble qualities of head and heart, Drake had many enemies, especially in his own profession. He was of an aggressive disposition, and he deemed it his duty to resent every insult, real or imaginary, that was offered to him. This disposition often got him into difficulties, sometimes into newspaper controversies, and, on a few occasions, even into street encounters, until at length he earned an unenviable reputation as a quarrelsome man. As he advanced in life the impulsive feelings of early manhood vanished, and he became one of the most quiet and peaceable of men. It was said of him that he occasionally snubbed a friend to oblige an enemy. During the fifteen years of my connection with him as colleague in the Cincinnati College and in the University of Louisville, where I was for many months in daily official and social intercourse with him, no unkind word or look passed between us, nor, as far as I know, between him and any of his colleagues. As a colleague or companion no man could have been more agreeable, more considerate, or more honorable. Most of the difficulties and annoyances which beset him in his younger days are attributable to his connection with the Medical College of Ohio, and to the fact, everywhere patent, that he generally was greatly in advance of his collaborators in his attempts to improve medical education and to build up a successful school, the idol for many years of his professional life. Drake had nothing bad in him; his faults were errors of judgment, not errors of the heart, which was always in the right place. No man had warmer friends; no man had kindlier feelings for human nature in all its manifold phases. He detested slavery; and he never missed a proper occasion to raise his voice, loudly and emphatically, in favor of temperance, education, charitable work, and charitable institutions.

In public debate I never saw his equal. Without claiming that his arguments were always sound, I am safe in asserting that they were always specious, and that they seldom failed to convince his auditors. At such times his whole soul would seem to be on fire. He would froth at the mouth, swing to and fro like a tree in a storm, and raise his voice to the highest possible pitch. In a debate with Dr. Samuel Jackson on Broussaisism, in 1831, before the Philadelphia Medical Society, in the presence of a large assembly of prominent physicians, he stopped suddenly, and in a loud tone asked the presiding officer whether he was not right. He so confused that gentleman that he jumped off his chair, and involuntarily answered, "Yes, yes, sir!" much to the merriment of the auditors. At Cincinnati, in 1834, in a debate with Professor John Eberle on malarial fever, he literally demolished his opponent by quotations from his own work on the practice of medicine, at that time a standard authority.

Drake cherished a deep affection for his children. During his connection with the University of Louisville he generally, in the winter sessions, ran up every month to spend a week with them at Cincinnati. To accomplish this object he lectured the week previous to his departure twice and sometimes even thrice a day. To his friends he was warmly attached, and he was never happier than when in their society. "His heart was not an island cut off from other men, but a continent that joined them."

His last illness was brief and severe. The immediate cause of his death, which cast a deep gloom over the city in which he had lived so long and which was so much indebted to him for its greatness, as well as over the entire American medical profession, was arachnitis, to slight attacks of which he had occasionally been subject. The seizure was preceded by a violent chill, with slight delirium. To relieve the severity of his headache, he bled himself freely at the arm, whether injudiciously or not no one could tell. However this may have been, he sank rapidly. In less than five days, on the 6th of November, 1852, when he had just completed his sixty-seventh year, he ceased to exist. Had he remained at Louisville, in the quiet discharge of the duties of his professorship, conjoined with the pleasure derived from his literary labors, he might readily, with his powerful constitution and temperate habits, have added ten or fifteen years to his life.

Drake left no money or estate. His medical journal brought him in debt; and his great work did not yield him a penny. But his children were well-to-do; and intellectual wealth, of which no American physician ever had a larger stock, was all the wealth he coveted. The name of Daniel Drake is immortal; while all that is mortal of him reposes in Spring Grove Cemetery near Cincinnati.

WILLIAM EDMONDS HORNER.

1790–1853.

HORNER was the most accomplished anatomist that our country has produced. If any proof of this assertion were needed, it would only be necessary to refer to the beautiful preparations, many exclusively the work of his hands, contained in the Horner and Wistar Museum of the University of Pennsylvania. Not a few of these specimens equal in minuteness and elegance the famous preparations of the celebrated Dutch anatomist Ruysch in the last century and of Hyrtl of Vienna, in our own day. Horner's dissections were models of neatness, evincing unusual patience and manual dexterity. He took especial pride in preparing his subjects for the amphitheatre, and in exhibiting to the best advantage the parts designed for demonstration. For many years he performed his own dissections, and when, in consequence of ill-health and increasing infirmities, he was obliged to avail himself of the labor of assistants, he tolerated no slovenliness and overlooked no imperfections. He took great pains in making his demonstrations clear to his pupils. For this purpose he repeated his descriptions of the same object not less than four times, stopping, as he turned around his table, at the four cardinal points of the amphitheatre, in order to impress what he was describing thoroughly upon the eyes and ears of his young auditors. I venture to affirm that no man ever taught anatomy more conscientiously, or was more painstaking, than Horner. If he was not eloquent or enthusiastic, he was honest and instructive, and always commanded the respect of his pupils.

Dr. Horner was a native of Virginia, and a graduate of the University of Pennsylvania. During our war with Great Britain in 1812–'14, he was stationed for a while at our northern frontier, mainly, I believe, at Buffalo, where, in his capacity of assistant surgeon, he witnessed considerable military practice, of which he published an account soon after he left the service. In 1815 he was appointed prosector of anatomy under Wistar. From this position he rose to be demonstrator, adjunct, and finally professor— a position which he held up to the time of his death in 1853. It was at Buffalo, while making his daily rounds in the hospital, that the young surgeon was accosted by a man who was tittering, and who said that he had just lost an arm. "What is the matter? This does not strike me as a subject for laughter." "It is not, doctor; but, excuse me, I lost my arm in so funny a way that I still laugh whenever I look at it." "In what way?" "Our first sergeant wanted to be shaved, and as I am a corporal we walked out together in front of his tent. I had lathered him, taken him by the nose, and was just about applying the razor, when a cannon-ball came, and that was the last I saw of his head and of my arm. Excuse me, doctor, for laughing so. I never saw such a thing before."

Dr. Horner was uninteresting as an author. His style was heavy and inelegant. He evidently wrote with difficulty. His first effort at bookmaking was his so-called American Dissector, which was published soon after he became adjunct professor of Anatomy to Physick. This was followed in 1826 by a work in two volumes entitled Special Anatomy and Histology, a book written with much care, and embracing a considerable amount of original matter—the result of his personal researches, especially in microscopical anatomy. In this work a full description is given of the tensor tarsi muscle, which was supposed by Horner to have been first noticed by himself, but which had been described as early as 1822 by Rosenmüller of Germany. He also published a treatise on Pathological Anatomy, chiefly valuable on account of the elaborate descriptions it contains of the changes which take place in the mucous crypts of the bowels in Asiatic cholera. A short time before his death he published, in conjunction with his son-in-law, Dr. Henry H. Smith, an anatomical atlas, in which are admirably portrayed the various structures of the human body.

Horner was a victim of an unfortunate temperament. From his earliest childhood he was subject to distressing headache and terrible fits of despondency, which marred his happiness, impaired his usefulness, and greatly augmented the burden of his daily labors. His life was an incessant struggle; and he often—a thousand times is his language—wished himself dead, to be rid of his misery. A man who suffered, as he says of himself, from pain in his head during three-fourths of his waking existence could not be expected to perform much work without great discomfort and dissatisfaction. It may well be imagined how racked his nervous system must have been; and how little his mind was fitted for mental or social enjoyment. His sufferings increased as he advanced in years. The smallest quantity of food taken in the evening oppressed his stomach, destroyed his sleep, and rendered him wretched the next morning. "My mental faculties are hebetated, and I am so vertiginous as scarcely to be able to collect my ideas or to go on with a demonstration." While in this condition he often indulged in self-reproach, and sought solace in prayer. "Does this feeling," says he, "depend upon an act of injustice or of turpitude which

I may have committed at a former period of my life, and
which now, preying upon my conscience, destroys its rest?
None such is in my remembrance; but my actions have
not been perfect. I have attempted to walk faithfully
before men; but have I walked faithfully before God?"
One cannot read without intense sympathy the record of
such misery, and one is lost in amazement that this man
accomplished what he did. Horner was a consistent and
devoted Christian, a devout believer in the truth of the
Catholic religion. His domestic life was eminently happy;
his family worshipped him; and he was the centre of
an admiring circle of friends. His last illness was occasioned by disease of the heart, accompanied with great
suffering.

My acquaintance with Horner began in 1832, when I
sent him for his inspection a vial of blood, taken from the
arm of an intemperate man, of a very plethoric habit, the
subject at the time of pleuro-pneumonia. The blood, as
it flowed from the vein in the arm, was as white as milk,
and so continued until I closed the orifice, the amount
taken being nearly one quart. Two days afterwards it
was of similar appearance. Professor Horner examined
it both chemically and microscopically, and reported to
me the result. The remarkable change of color was due
to the absence of hæmatin and to a great increase of
white globules and of albumen. I was then young, and
I considered it no small compliment to receive this courteous attention from a man occupying so prominent a
position. Perhaps this kindness was due in a measure to
the fact that a few years before I had presented the Professor with a copy of my translation of Bayle and Hol-
lard's Manual of General Anatomy, the receipt of which
he promptly acknowledged. In subsequent years I met
Dr. Horner several times, and was always received by
him with much consideration. A more kind-hearted,
conscientious man probably never lived.

NATHANIEL CHAPMAN.

1780–1853.

CHAPMAN was the prince of good fellows, popular alike with the profession and the people of Philadelphia. For nearly half a century he was without a peer among the medical men of his adopted city. He attracted patients from all sections of the country, and for many years enjoyed an immense practice in the upper walks of life. Considering his vast reputation one would naturally think that he must have coined money, and left a large heritage to his family, and yet, if general report is to be trusted, he was often embarrassed, and died comparatively poor. The truth is that Chapman was not an economist, and, what is worse still, that he had no just appreciation of the value of his services. He lived at a period when the fees of the physicians of Philadelphia were very low, an ordinary visit seldom yielding more than two dollars, and one in consultation not more than five. With such charges, few men, however largely engaged in practice, could become rich. But Chapman was a poor collector, entertained company, and spent money liberally. For many years his wife kept his books, besides attending to the details of the household.

Chapman was a native of Virginia. He was a graduate of the University of Pennsylvania, and rapidly rose to distinction. In 1814, when the school enjoyed high renown, he was appointed Professor of Materia Medica in his Alma Mater. This appointment was followed soon after by the publication of his work, in two volumes, on Materia Medica and Therapeutics, a work which passed through numerous editions, and which for a long time was extensively used as a text-book. Up to the period of its issue no other native treatise on these subjects had appeared. Our information in relation to them was almost wholly derived from foreign sources; and it is therefore not surprising that the work of the Philadelphia professor

should have been a success. Edition after edition was
struck off, and the author became famous. In 1816 he
succeeded to the chair of Medicine. He held this chair
until within three years of his death, which occurred on
July 1st, 1853. Late in life he published several monographs—among others, one on Fever, one on Dropsy, and
one on Thoracic Diseases, which, however, made little impression upon the profession and did not add much to his
reputation. In 1820 Chapman established the Philadelphia Journal of the Medical and Physical Sciences, which,
after a brilliant career of eight years, was succeeded by
the American Journal of the Medical Sciences—a journal
which has to-day a world-wide reputation. For these
two periodicals he wrote many papers, often equivalent to
learned essays, usually under the title of Thoughts—a
title often adopted by Dr. Charles Caldwell, and, at a later
day, by such men as John P. Harrison of Cincinnati, and
John Dawson of Columbus, Ohio. The Materia Medica
and Therapeutics was, as the author states in his preface,
hastily written, and made no pretensions to be a comprehensive work. The treatise in its later editions encountered a powerful rival in the work of Eberle.

Chapman occasionally wrote papers upon literary subjects, and he edited, not long after he entered the profession, several volumes on forensic eloquence, consisting
mainly of selections from British orators and statesmen.
He was a man of fine intellectual taste and acquirements,
a learned talker and a sound thinker, though his style was
florid and diffuse. Despite his vocal defects, he was an
eloquent, enthusiastic, and fascinating lecturer. An apt
anecdote, invariably well told, formed a part of nearly
every discourse. He was very popular, and the idol of
his pupils. In person he was above the middle height,
with a commanding appearance, a large head, and a gentle
expression of countenance. In his youthful days he lost
a portion of his palate—a defect which caused him to ar-

ticulate so badly that few students understood him until
they had heard him for a week. He always read his lectures.

The stethoscope, introduced into this country by the
pupils of Laennec, was not for a long time used by Chapman as a means of diagnosis in diseases of the heart and
lungs. He ridiculed the idea that such an instrument was
necessary for this purpose. Later in life, however, he followed the improved method. It is hard for men who
have long been leaders in any particular line of practice
to get out of the grooves to which they have been accustomed. It has been gravely asserted that a man over sixty
is an impediment to progress. The rule may be true, but
the exceptions to it are many.

Many anecdotes are told of Chapman—some real, others
mythical. One day, after having dined with Dr. Dorsey,
he took his host to the window, and pointing across Washington Square, which was once a Potter's field, to the
southeast corner of Sixth and Walnut Streets, then the site
of the Eastern Penitentiary, he said, "Dorsey, you have
a —— poor prospect across the grave." The sad part of
the story is that in a few weeks after this occurrence Dorsey was numbered with the dead. He was taken ill the
very evening after the delivery of his introductory lecture
at the University of Pennsylvania, and never left his room
alive. He had removed only a few weeks before into his
house at the corner of Walnut and Seventh Streets, now
the site of the large granite building of the Philadelphia
Savings Bank. One Sunday, as Chapman was handing
round the plate, an old West India negro in the corner of
the church dropped a guinea into it. "I always knew,"
said the witty professor, "that you were a Guinea negro."
A baker driving in his cart along a narrow street met
the doctor, and promptly turned out of the way of his
carriage. Chapman stopped, and, politely bowing, said,
"Upon my word you are the best bread man in Philadel-

phia." The last time I met him was in the spring of 1845, as I was walking up Chestnut Street, above Seventh, in this city. As he approached me he held out his hand, saying, "I believe I have the pleasure of your acquaintance?" I replied, "I am glad you have not forgotten me. I am Dr. Gross of Kentucky." Then at once began a series of questions: "How are my old friends Caldwell and Drake, two good fellows?" "What is your school doing?" "How long will you be in town?" and so forth. He had on, as usual, a high white cravat, and I was grieved to see him carry in a sling his arm, recently fractured by a fall. He looked pale, and walked feebly. Chapman and Caldwell had been friends early in life, but in after years they became alienated from each other, and I do not think they ever spoke again. Drake spent the winter of 1830–'31 in Philadelphia as Professor of Medicine in the Jefferson Medical College. He had not met Chapman since 1815, when he took his degree in the University of Pennsylvania. His surprise may therefore easily be guessed when, at the first Wistar Party at which they met, Chapman deliberately turned his back upon him. Drake was then the acknowledged head of the medical profession of his adopted State.

Chapman shared in common with his colleagues the prejudices, at one time so great, against the Jefferson Medical College and its pupils; and yet he did not hesitate before the College had attained its fifth year to grant permission to one of its alumni to dedicate to him a work on Dental Surgery. He could not resist adulation, and the dedication of Dr. Fitch tickled his vanity. During my attendance upon the lectures in Philadelphia Chapman's residence was on Walnut Street above Seventh. Here every morning from half past nine to ten o'clock one could see the chaise of the fashionable doctor standing at the door, attached to a bobtail bay, ready for its day's work.

Nathaniel Chapman will ever be remembered as an eloquent and popular teacher, as a facile writer, as a great practitioner, and as a man of versatile mind, full of wit, humor, and *bonhomie*.   His social habits and genial disposition made him a favorite guest at the table of every social gathering of distinguished men in all the walks of life. The Wistar Parties were always enlivened by his presence.

CHARLES CALDWELL.

1772–1853.

IT was on a bright, sunny May day in 1840, while sitting in my study at Cincinnati, that the door opened and a gentleman of majestic mien entered, and with a courtly bow announced himself as Dr. Caldwell.   "I am," said he, "on my way to Boston, and have called for a moment to shake hands with you and to pay you my respects.   Now that we are colleagues"—I had been appointed only a week before Professor of Surgery in the University of Louisville —"we shall," he continued, "soon see more of each other, and become, I trust, more intimately acquainted."   Such was my first interview with a man of whom I had often heard much, but whom I had never seen.   In the following October I took up my residence in Kentucky, and during the nine years in which he was a member of the Faculty we worked faithfully together to promote the interests of the school, of which, although not the main founder, he was virtually the father, for he did more to place it upon a solid and enduring basis than all his colleagues together. Seceding, along with John Esten Cooke, Charles Wilkins Short, and Lunsford Pitts Yandell, from Transylvania University at Lexington, Kentucky, with which he had been connected from its inception, he brought with him a high reputation as a teacher, and soon by his commanding influence succeeded in securing an appropriation from the city of Louisville towards the erection of an admirable edifice and the purchase of a library, a museum, and the necessary apparatus for carrying on a course of instruction in all the branches of a medical education. The school, like every similar enterprise clamoring for recognition, had its troubles and many warm enemies; but, despite these annoyances, it rapidly rose to prominence and soon became one of the great centres of medical instruction. When Caldwell entered it he was already an aged man, but mentally and physically well preserved, and able to perform his day's work as well as any member of its Faculty. He was unmistakably a great lecturer. His language was scholarly and ponderous. He was quite popular, for he added to great personal dignity the charms of a man of the world. Charles Caldwell never had an enemy among his pupils. If they did not love him, they respected and admired him. As a teacher, he was a failure. If a student were asked, when the lecture was over, what he had learned, the answer invariably was, "Nothing." Caldwell was a quarter of a century in arrear of the existing state of the science of physiology. He was a solidist, and a non-believer in the value of chemistry as an aid to the explanation of vital processes. In his opinion the blood was a mere fertilizer of the tissues, and insignificant in its influence on the great functions of the body. A considerable portion of his course was taken up with phrenology, and his mind often wandered off into the regions of spiritism, or purely speculative philosophy; so that in time he came to be regarded as an unprofitable lecturer. Several of his colleagues and certain members of the Board of Trustees came to the conclusion, in 1847, that he ought to retire—a conclusion in which Miller and I did not coincide. But when, two years later, the Board sent a communication to the Faculty, declaring that, if Caldwell did not vacate his chair, they would vacate it for him, there was no use in holding on to him any longer. The long, sad story of this transaction I do not feel inclined to relate. Suffice it to say that he refused to resign, and that the trustees vacated his chair. The dismissal was impolitic and unjust. Caldwell was the father of the school. He had worked hard in founding it; and he had been a tower of strength in defending it in its early struggles. In a few years he would have retired of his own accord, in harmony with his colleagues and with the Board of Trustees, and in warm sympathy with the institution. As it was, he left the school in disgust and with many maledictions. Although Miller and I had warmly befriended him, he regarded us as his bitter enemies. One of the effects of his dismissal was his inauguration of the University of Nashville, which, although he never obtained a chair in it, soon became a powerful rival of the school from which he had been ejected. It is a bad plan to dismiss a professor without just cause. It is better to "bear the ills we have than fly to others that we know not of."

It is worthy of note that Caldwell was a knight of the sword before he became a knight of the lancet. Owing to his handsome form and oratorical powers, he was selected by a military company to accompany a detachment of thirteen men, denotive of the number of States, to escort General Washington on his visit to the South from the confines of the two Carolinas to Charlottesville, where an enthusiastic reception awaited him. He had prepared a grand speech for the occasion, but when his eyes fell upon the Father of his Country his courage forsook him, and the speech was never delivered. During the Whiskey Insurrection in Western Pennsylvania, he accompanied the Eastern troops in the capacity of surgeon.

Caldwell was of Irish descent, and was born of respectable parents in a log-cabin in North Carolina in November, 1772. He died in July, 1853, at the age of eighty-one. Much of his leisure in the latter part of his life was spent upon the composition of his Autobiography, which was written in execrable taste, and in the worst possible style, and which was edited, after his death, by his sister-in-law, Miss Harriot W. Warner. It was the custom of some of the early Greeks, when a greatly deformed child was born, to throw it into a pit prepared for it; and it is a pity that there is not in all civilized countries an appropriate receptacle for worthless literature. Some of the descriptions by Caldwell of men and scenes are quite dramatic. His account of his rencounter with Rush, in defending his thesis for the degree of Doctor of Medicine, is as interesting as that of a bull-fight. The combat took place in the Hall of the University of Pennsylvania in the year 1794, probably in the month of March, in the presence of the Provost, the Trustees, and the Faculty, and of a large audience, drawn out, if one may believe Caldwell, by the interest of the occasion; for, as he asserts, it had become widely circulated that Rush was to be assailed, if not slaughtered, by the great Carolinian. The contest was a long, and in the end a bitter one, resulting of course in the discomfiture of the preceptor and the splendid triumph of the pupil. One can hardly believe that the words said to have been uttered on this occasion were tolerated by the distinguished Provost and his colleagues of the Board, for the impudence they display is as reprehensible as it must have been distasteful. The account of this scene occupies a dozen pages of the Autobiography, and it is one of the curiosities of American medical literature. For assurance and insolence I do not think its equal can be found. It is in every sense a Caldwellian performance—a graphic illustration of the character and idiosyncrasies of the man. "The battle was over," says the boaster; "but, although victory perched on my brow, it cost me the chair of Medicine in the University, which but for this circumstance would have been within my grasp." Surely this was a heavy penalty for a morning's folly! And the moral of it all is that an ounce of modesty is worth a pound of swaggering. I may add that the subject of the thesis which caused this unseemly contest, and the final alienation between the master and his pupil, was The Use of Cold Water in the Treatment of Fever—a publication which antedates by several years the famous treatise of Dr. James Currie of Liverpool.

In his younger days Caldwell might occasionally have had a patient; but after his removal to the West he abandoned himself to teaching and writing, and few persons ever sought him professionally. He was for half a century essentially a closet student. He was a prolific writer, but mostly of essays, reviews, and newspaper and magazine articles. Early in life he translated Blumenbach's Physiology, annotated Cullen's Practice of Medicine, and edited Delaplaine's Portfolio. In my opinion his ablest essay is that on the Original Unity of the Human Race. In the Preliminary Discourse prefixed to his edition of Dr. Cullen he exposed with marvellous skill the fallacy of Dr. Rush's doctrine of the unity of disease—an absurd doctrine which had been gaining ground among his countrymen. In 1819 he published The Life and Campaigns of General Greene, which was much criticized on account of the free use which he made of the writings of others. The work abounds in plagiarisms. It is said that when Haywood published his Life of Henry IV. Queen Elizabeth became much enraged at him, and inquired of Bacon, the Lord Chancellor, if there was not treason in the book. "No, madam," he replied; "but I am certain it contains much felony, for I find many passages which he has stolen from Tacitus." From whom Caldwell pilfered I do not know. He wielded a caustic pen. It is said that his review of the work of the Rev. Samuel Stanhope Smith, President of Princeton College, on the Causes of the Varieties of the Complexion and Figure of the Human Race was of so scathing a character as to occasion that author much chagrin and annoyance. His review of Professor Samuel Jackson's work on Medicine was an equally severe production, and killed the book. Caldwell considered himself the apostle of phrenology in this country—a subject on which he lectured for many years in the principal cities of the Union, and on which he contributed numerous articles to the periodical press. Notwithstanding his unwearied exertions, he outlived the delusion—one not likely to be revived. An overweening vanity was the specific characteristic of this extraordinary man. It jutted out upon all occasions, in season and out of season—in his manners, in his walk, in his conversation, in his writings. In addressing a large and select audience on phrenology at Lexington, Kentucky, he said, "There are only three great heads in the United States: one is that of Daniel Webster; another that of Henry Clay; and the last," pointing to his own, "modesty prevents me from mentioning."

"It requires," says Sydney Smith, "a surgical operation to get a joke into a Scotch understanding;" and Caldwell was, I am sure, equally dull in this respect. He was married twice. His first wife and he early disagreed, and a separation was the consequence. The issue of this union was a son, who, to his shame be it said, forsook his mother in her domestic trouble, although she was not guilty even of a serious fault. The son married a beautiful woman, who proved faithless to him. The consequence was a duel, in which he maimed her paramour for life.

The death of Caldwell was no loss to society or to the profession. If conceit could have made him great, he would assuredly have occupied the loftiest of pedestals. He misapplied talents of a high order, which, if they had been properly directed, might have enshrined his name among the great men in medicine of the nineteenth century; and he wasted his resources upon comparatively trifling matters, and left behind him little that is worthy of permanent record.

CHAPTER XI.

THEODRIC ROMEYN BECK.

1791–1855.

IN a visit made by myself and my son, Samuel W. Gross, to Albany in 1853 I had hoped to see Dr. Theodric Romeyn Beck; and I accordingly called at his house. I was greatly disappointed to find that he was out of town. Before leaving Albany I wrote him a note, expressing my regret at his absence, and wishing him, in true Irish style, health, happiness, and long life. Several weeks afterwards he acknowledged my note in a charming letter. We never met.

Dr. Beck belonged to a remarkable family. There were five brothers. Dr. Lewis C. Beck was an eminent naturalist, chemist, and botanist. One of the brothers, a promising lawyer of St. Louis, I believe died young. John B. Beck was for many years Professor of Materia Medica in the College of Physicians and Surgeons of New York. He was an excellent and amiable man, an accomplished physician, an erudite writer, and a capital teacher; he died in 1851, after a lingering illness. I saw him often during the latter part of his life, and freely conversed with him on many subjects, especially medical themes. He was a man of refinement and much culture, a devoted father, and a loving husband. Theodric Romeyn Beck was the author of Medical Jurisprudence, the first edition of which was issued in 1823; and it is referred to both by lawyers and medical men as a standard authority. The many editions through which it has passed in this country, its reprint in Great Britain, and its translation at Weimar into the German language, show in what estimation it has been held at home and abroad. Like Robley Dunglison, Beck was a capital compiler; and his work, which is a production of surpassing excellence, will always be quoted as reflecting the views of medical jurisprudence of the period in which it flourished. From this work I imbibed my love for the study of juridical medicine. I read it with the pleasure with which a person peruses an interesting novel. The chapters on Criminal Abortion and Infanticide in this work, which are from the pen of Dr. John B. Beck, are conspicuously able.

We left Albany on one of the great steamers plying between that city and New York. A large flock of sheep was on board. We reached the wharf at New York early the next morning. We had hardly landed when a sheep, evidently the bellwether of the flock, jumped high into the air, although the surface was perfectly level, and every sheep that followed did likewise. Philemon, the Greek poet, died of laughter on seeing an ass eat figs; and I laughed most immoderately at witnessing this extraordinary feat of our fleecy companions. It was a long time before I could control my risible faculties. Such a scene reminds one forcibly of the political bellwether, who, when he takes the stump and leaps into the air, is sure to be followed by the rest of the flock. Men are easily led by the nose.

MARSHALL HALL.

1790–1857.

IT was in the spring of 1853 that I had the honor of welcoming this great and good man to Louisville. He had left England on the previous February to make the tour of the United States, Cuba, and Canada—a visit which he had long ago contemplated, but which until then he had not been able to consummate. He was accompanied by Mrs. Hall, a tall, slender lady, and a son, an only child; and he brought me a card of introduction from the late Dr. Lawson, of Cincinnati, Professor of Medicine in the Medical College of Ohio. It is needless to say that we both felt at once at our ease, for I had long been familiar with Dr. Hall's reputation as an author, as a celebrated physician, and as a profound student of the physiology of the nervous system. When quite a youth in the profession I had read his treatise on the Mimoses, or mimicking diseases, and various other productions of his pen. Dr. Hall at the time of this interview was sixty years of age; but, notwithstanding his laborious life, all his faculties, mental and bodily, were unimpaired. He was a rapid, fluent talker, active in his movements, and light of foot. He was about the middle height, well proportioned, with light eyes, and fine, expressive features, indicative of a kind heart. It was hard for him to sit still for any length of time; for he had been all his life accustomed to be "on the go;" and hence the semi-erect posture, except when he was engaged in deep study or in performing some experiment, was evidently irksome to him. He was neat in his person, and economical in the disposition of his time. He had a quick eye, fine powers of observation, and rare facility as a writer. His industry was vast.

Upon inquiring what I could do for him to make his sojourn among us pleasant, he replied, "I wish to remain in your city five or six days to perform some experiments on the spinal cord, with a view of demonstrating to your physicians the functions of the reflex system, to study the condition of your colored people, and to offer some suggestions for the abolition of slavery." The announcement of Dr. Hall's arrival was sufficient to induce the more prominent members of the profession to pay him

their respects and to extend to him every possible courtesy. On the second day after his arrival Mrs. Gross and
I invited a number of prominent ladies and gentlemen
to meet him and Mrs. Hall. The evening passed pleasantly, the company breaking up at a late hour. Young
Hall had brought with him a flute, upon which he
played several pieces, to the delight of my guests. The
evening after this entertainment I met Dr. Hall at Dr.
Samuel B. Richardson's, where a number of medical gentlemen were already assembled to witness some experiments on the reflex action of the spinal cord of frogs, of
which a supply had been furnished the previous morning. The results were eminently satisfactory; and not
the least gratifying circumstance connected with the occasion was the enthusiasm of the experimenter, whose
soul seemed to be absorbed in his subject. His dissections were conducted with great care and delicacy, and
it was evident that he had no idea that he was inflicting
any wrong upon the poor reptiles. Bergh and his fanati-
cal coadjutors had not as yet declared war against vivi-
section, which has thrown so much light upon the physiology of animal life. The labors of Dr. Hall in this
direction have been of immense service to the human
race. They cleared up many subjects that had hitherto
remained unexplained; and their practical bearing can
only be fully appreciated by those who are familiar with
the history of physiology. They have opened a new field
of inquiry, to the elucidation of which this great man devoted a large portion of his life. Although other labors,
even at an early age, had brought him prominently before
the profession and the public, it is mainly to his researches
upon the physiology of the nervous system that he is indebted for his fame as an original thinker and investigator.

During his sojourn at Louisville Marshall Hall wrote
several letters on Self-emancipation, as he styled it, which
were published in the famous Louisville Journal, then

edited by George D. Prentice. The plan proposed was very simple; and although not likely to be adopted, even if the great civil war had never broken out, it was ingenious and worthy of consideration. Dr. Hall detested slavery. He regarded it as an institution irreconcilable with the principles of civilization and the requirements of Christianity. Without an attempt to enlighten the colored man, the abolition of slavery, he declared, could be of no advantage to him. He therefore strongly advocated the propriety of common-school education, of sending the negro to church, and of rendering him familiar with the teachings of the Bible. Dr. Hall's next plan was to let him work so many hours a day for his master, and be paid for any surplus labor that he might be able to perform, the proceeds thus accruing to be placed in a savings bank, so that eventually he might accumulate a sufficient sum to purchase his freedom. All this looked well on paper; but it apparently never occurred to the great philanthropist that task-work was hard work, and that there are few men, certainly very few women, who, after finishing their ordinary day's work, are in a condition to perform an amount of extra labor adequate to secure the desired object. Emancipation at such a price would have been a cheerless and an endless undertaking, which few slaves, whose natural proclivity is to indolence, would have been willing to attempt.

His visit to America extended over a period of fifteen months. Everywhere he was received with the courtesy and hospitality due to so distinguished a personage. Wherever he went his brethren vied with one another to do him honor. On the other hand, he lost no opportunity to enlighten them on the reflex actions of the nervous system, generally illustrating his lectures by some simple experiment upon a frog or snake. In New Orleans, where he was sumptuously entertained at a public dinner tendered him by physicians and prominent citizens, an alligator was placed at his disposal, through the agency of Dr. Bennet Dowler, himself no mean physiologist. This circumstance afforded him much gratification, as he was thus enabled to confirm more effectually some of his previous investigations.

Hall, a native of Basford, a small town near Nottingham, England, was the son of a cotton-spinner and a practical chemist, to whom Great Britain is indebted for her present mode of bleaching. His early education was defective; but he overcame this drawback by hard work, close study, and constant intercourse with intelligent people. He spoke French fluently, wrote his thesis in Latin, and had considerable knowledge of Greek. He took his medical degree in 1812, at the age of twenty-two, in the University of Edinburgh, and was shortly thereafter appointed clinical clerk in the famous Infirmary of that city. While serving in this capacity he delivered courses of lectures on clinical medicine, took extensive notes of cases, and thus laid the foundation of his work on Diagnosis, which was published in 1817. Having spent five years at Edinburgh, he visited the principal medical schools and hospitals on the Continent. He then settled at Nottingham, exhausted in pocket, but rich in knowledge, and determined to succeed in his profession. To give him an outfit, a kind friend advanced him one hundred pounds, which he soon repaid from his earnings. In 1824 appeared his treatise on the Effects of Loss of Blood—a work which revolutionized the practice of medicine, and which has been instrumental in saving many thousands of lives. Up to that time bleeding, or the abstraction of blood in some form or other, was the universal custom, not only in Europe, but in this country, no matter how insignificant the complaint was, or how bloodless the patient. The fashion was inexorable. Dr. Hall had witnessed the evil effects of this indiscriminate practice, and he depicted them in vivid colors. His reputation now rapidly increased, and, although he enjoyed a large and lucrative practice, he panted for a wider and more inviting field than the provincial town of Nottingham. His fame had reached London, and his books were read with profit by the luminaries of the English metropolis. Thither accordingly, in 1826, he sped his way, and he soon bounded into full practice, much of it being in consultation with the leading medical men of the city. In less than three months he had not a moment of leisure at his command, except when he took his summer vacation on the Continent, generally accompanied by his family.

Soon after Dr. Hall took up his residence in London he published his Commentaries on Some of the More Important Diseases of Females. This was followed, in 1830, by Researches on the Morbid and Curative Effects of Loss of Blood. His pen was never idle. He wrote upon a great variety of subjects, and his writings abounded in useful suggestions of a highly practical character. We find him at one time engaged on sewerage; at another on fertilizers; and at another on the "ready method," as it is termed, for the recovery of persons apparently dead from drowning. To the elucidation of the study of the physiology of the nervous system, especially of its reflex functions, he devoted twenty-five years of the ripest period of his life. Numerous societies, domestic and foreign, did themselves honor by enrolling him among their members. In 1832 he was made a member of the Royal Society of London; and in 1855 the Institute of France elected him to fill the vacancy caused by the death of Arago, his competitors being Rokitansky of Vienna, Christison of Edinburgh, Chelius of Heidelberg, and Riberi of Turin. The vote was nearly unanimous.

Marshall Hall died on the 11th of August, 1857, in the sixty-seventh year of his age, after a protracted illness. His disease was a cancerous stricture of the œsophagus, which became so tight as eventually to prevent the passage of food and drink into the stomach, resulting in death from inanition—a sad end of so noble a life. He bore his cruel suffering with Christian fortitude, and his demise caused a profound sensation throughout the medical and scientific world.

I feel that I have done but feeble justice to the character of this great man whose whole life was a continuous labor in the cause of suffering humanity and of scientific truth. Patience, perseverance, honesty of purpose, love of truth, and straightforwardness in all his dealings with his fellow-men were predominant traits of his character. His discoveries are invaluable to science and creditable to the age in which he lived. He rendered the medical profession a vast service by setting it an example of intellectual self-reliance. His name will live in perennial vigor.

My excellent and learned friend, Professor Henry Fraser Campbell, of Augusta, Georgia, has put forth a claim of priority to the discovery of reflex secretion and of the excito-secretory system of nerves. Whether this claim is well founded I must leave to others better acquainted with the subject than I to decide. However, it is but just to Dr. Campbell to say that the value of his labors in this department of physiology is acknowledged in England and America. Marshall Hall himself bore willing testimony to their importance and scientific interest; and in an article in the London Lancet for May, 1857, he awards to the Georgia physiologist at least an equal share of the honor of the discovery.

JOHN K. MITCHELL.

1798–1858.

DR. JOHN K. MITCHELL and I were colleagues for only two sessions. He had had a stroke of apoplexy when I entered the school, and he died in April, 1858, from an attack of pneumonia. He was one of the famous seven

brought together on the reorganization of the Jefferson
Medical College in 1841. As a lecturer on the practice
of medicine he was popular; for he was a ready, fluent
speaker, and had the happy faculty of interspersing his
discourses with interesting and spicy anecdotes. He was
a handsome man, tall and well formed, with agreeable
manners, and a countenance generally lighted up with
a pleasant smile. Such men are not often found in the
lecture-room to beguile the weary hours of the care-worn
student.

Mitchell was an excellent writer. The volume of poems
published by him in the meridian of his life comprised
some charming pieces, which were received with considerable favor. In his earlier years he was much interested in
physiology and chemistry, which he illustrated by various
experiments. His experiments on the absorption of fluids,
based on those of Dutrochet of Paris, were highly appreciated. His treatise on the Cryptogamous Origin of Mala-
rious and Epidemical Fevers attracted much attention, and
measurably anticipated some of the accepted doctrines on
that subject. He also published some important practical
observations in relation to spinal diseases, in which he
laid much stress on the value of absolute rest as a remedial
agent. A small volume of his collected writings was published, soon after his death, by his distinguished son, Dr.
S. Weir Mitchell.

Dr. Mitchell graduated from the University of Pennsylvania in 1819, and soon after made three voyages to China
as ship's surgeon. For a time he lectured on physiology
in what was known as the Philadelphia Medical Institute,
which was organized at the instance of and with the assistance of Professor Chapman; and for several years before he entered the Jefferson Medical College he discharged
the duties of lecturer on Chemistry in the Franklin Institute. With such training and such qualifications it is not
surprising that he should at once have taken a high stand

as a teacher of medicine; and it is questionable whether any member of the Faculty contributed more to the prosperity of the school than he.

───────

ROBERT HARE.

1781–1858.

HARE was the first chemist of his day in this country. His invention of the Oxy-hydrogen Blowpipe at an early period of his career made his name widely known both at home and abroad among scientists, and imparted a new impulse to chemical analysis. For more than a third of a century he was a hard worker in his laboratory; and although he made no such discoveries as those which rewarded the labors of a Gay-Lussac, or a Davy, or a Faraday, he nevertheless achieved an enduring reputation. He occupied for a long time the chair of Chemistry in the University of Pennsylvania, and was known as a brilliant experimenter. But he was a dull and uninteresting lecturer. His class was often uproarious, especially when, as occasionally happens with the most dexterous manipulator, his experiment proved to be a failure. To guard against this unseemly conduct he usually, it is said, had a few ladies upon the stage, knowing that their presence would shield him from insult. His great trouble was a want of power of expression, which increased when he came before his pupils. He certainly did not lack this power in ordinary conversation. In 1828 Hare published a Compendium of Chemistry, which embodied some original observations, and was long used as a text-book in the University of Pennsylvania; and he was a liberal contributor to the periodical press. He was a patient investigator, and a man of capacious intellect. In his old age I used to see him at the

Wistar Parties. He was a grand specimen of the *genus homo*, with broad shoulders and an immense head. If his brain had been examined, its weight would probably not have fallen below that of Cuvier, Humboldt, or Webster. He read much, thought much, talked much. Upon almost every subject he possessed a fund of information. It is strange that a man of an intellect and of culture such as his should in the later years of his life have been led astray by the phantom of Spiritualism. For several years he gave himself up to its study and contemplation. At Albany, at a meeting of the National Academy of Science, he was permitted, after much opposition, in deference solely to his age and to his reputation as a scientist, to read an elaborate article upon the subject, which did not appear in its published Transactions. Dr. Hare was of English descent, and was born in Philadelphia. He died in 1858, in the seventy-eighth year of his age. The immediate cause of his death was, if I remember rightly, softening of the brain.

GEORGE COMBE.

1788–1858.

PHRENOLOGY dates from the early part of the nineteenth century. It was a conceit bred, like homœopathy, in the brain of a German mystic. The name of this mystic was Gall, who, soon after he became profoundly convinced that our mental and moral faculties are craniologically indicated, went to Paris to secure, if possible, the full development of his system. He was ingenious, plausible, and enthusiastic. There soon gathered around him a number of disciples and admirers. Prominent among these was Spurzheim, who afterwards came to this country, and resided mostly in Boston, where, after having delivered several courses of lectures on Dr. Gall's system, and made many converts among the intellectual class of that city, he died. Long before Spurzheim visited us phrenology had a warm and zealous advocate in Dr. Charles Caldwell, of whose annual courses of lectures in Transylvania University, and afterwards in the University of Louisville, it formed a conspicuous feature. In the East the most enthusiastic advocate of the system was Dr. John Bell, of Philadelphia. Lesser lights proclaimed the doctrine in different parts of our country; and for a while it was the custom for almost every person, male and female, to have the head examined phrenologically. The Fowler brothers had for many years rooms in Philadelphia, where doting mothers took their children to ascertain their mental peculiarities and their aptitudes for the different pursuits of life. Similar establishments existed in New York, and in fact in all the principal cities of the Union.

In 1838 George Combe came to the United States as the avowed champion of phrenology. His arrival attracted attention, for he was a gentleman of respectability, culture, and refinement. He was born at Edinburgh in 1788, and practised law for many years in that city. In 1833 he married a daughter of Mrs. Siddons, the actress. His brother, Dr. Andrew Combe, had long been favorably known in this country by his works on physiology and hygiene. I had a charming interview with Mr. and Mrs. Combe. They were both tall, the husband rather slender, and the wife somewhat stout and good-looking. They were seated at a large table covered with books, pamphlets, magazines, and writing materials, and the conversation turned at once on the subject of phrenology, in which the lady took an active part. Her appearance was imposing, and, true to her descent, she talked, as we say, like a book. My object in calling on Mr. Combe was to obtain his consent to come to Cincinnati, then my home, to deliver a course of lectures on his favorite topic. But business recalled him to Scotland, and I never saw him again. His lectures in the Eastern cities were very popular, and he left us much pleased with his visit.   He died in 1858. His essays on phrenology and kindred subjects, embodied in a volume, were issued in 1819; but the work by which he will be principally remembered is The Constitution of Man in Relation to External Objects, which, originally published in 1828, had in 1860 reached its ninth edition. Ninety thousand copies of it were printed in Great Britain. It had a large sale in this country ; and translations of it were made into German, French, and Swedish.

During the last twenty-five years phrenology has been regarded as an exploded science.   It is not likely that it will be revived.   It had no substantial foundation upon which to rest its pretensions.   To map off the cranium into thirty or forty distinct regions, and to assign to each region a corresponding portion of brain indicative of a specific mental or moral characteristic, is a patent absurdity; and this was simply what the advocates of phrenology claimed to do.   The localization of the functions of the brain as a physiological problem of the deepest interest in a scientific as well as in a practical point of view is now engaging the serious attention of the medical profession everywhere; but, with few exceptions, the data thus far collected are of little value in settling the question. Thousands and tens of thousands of brains under every form of disease and accident will have to be dissected before we can hope to shed substantial light upon a subject so intricate as to baffle ordinary methods of inquiry. "The science of nature," says Liebig, "is modest."   To induce her to disclose her secrets, she must be wooed, generally for a long time and in ways much varied.

Of the ardor with which phrenology was cultivated in the first half of the present century some idea may be formed from the collection of crania of man and animals by Mr. Deville, a member of the Institution of Civil Engineers of London. Mr. Deville became interested in the study of the subject as early as 1821, and began his collection of casts and crania almost immediately afterwards. At the time of his death, in 1846, his cabinet contained five thousand four hundred and fifty specimens, of which three thousand were crania of animals, and two thousand four hundred and fifty illustrations of the human cranium. His collection embraced more than one thousand casts of the heads of living persons, more or less remarkable for distinctive mental qualities, such as musicians, composers, poets, authors, clergymen, painters, sculptors, architects, navigators, travellers, pugilists, criminals, and lunatics.

Thomas Dent Mütter.

1811–1859.

The death of Dr. Thomas Dent Mütter in March, 1859, at the age of forty-eight years, was a loss to the profession. The event, which occurred at Charleston, South Carolina, where he had many friends who watched his closing hours with the deepest solicitude and the tenderest devotion, was not unexpected, for he had long been a great sufferer from gout, which had pursued him from a comparatively early period of his life up to that of his death. Although he had long been a resident of Philadelphia, his remains repose in the cemetery at Middletown, Connecticut, where his widow erected to his memory a mausoleum and a memorial church under the control of the Episcopal diocese. Mrs. Mütter, who was considerably younger than he, has since followed him to the grave. No children blessed their union.

Dr. Mütter was born in March, 1811, at Richmond, Virginia. He was of German stock, with an element infused by a Scotch ancestor on the mother's side. His father was "a factor and commission merchant." His elementary education was received at different schools; and it is said that he spent some time at Hampden and Sidney College, an institution at one time of considerable note, but now almost extinct as a seat of learning. While quite young he entered the office of Dr. Simms, an eminent physician of Virginia, and thence he went to the University of Pennsylvania, in which, after having attended two courses of lectures, he took the degree of doctor of medicine. Anxious to extend his knowledge, and to improve his health, he went to Paris to avail himself of the great lights in medicine and surgery in the French metropolis, much more distinguished at the time of his visit than now as a great centre of medical education. Dupuytren, Roux, Lisfranc, Velpeau, Louis, and Chomel were then at the zenith of their renown. In this group of eminent men was Baron Larrey, who was pronounced by Napoleon to be the most honest man he had ever known. After he became a teacher, Mütter loved to refer to these men as his "friends," and to hold them up to the admiration of his pupils. Like most of the young doctors who went abroad in those days, and indeed for a long time afterwards, he considered one Frenchman equal to a dozen Americans, so much does "distance lend enchantment to the view" and exalt the imagination. To be able to speak of my friend Dupuytren, Louis, or Liston is ecstatic, and sounds far better in the ear of one's pupils than the mention of the name of Mott, or McClellan, or Drake, or Jackson. Besides, it discloses the fact that one has had the advantage of foreign travel, no slight passport to practice. Mütter was fond of such references in his lectures, and the effect of them no doubt was of practical advantage to him.

Mütter remained in Europe more than a year, and then began to seek practice, especially surgical, in this city.

The field of surgery in Philadelphia was then occupied by such prominent men as Gibson, McClellan, Barton, and Randolph. Physick and Parrish had nearly finished their course; while a number of younger men, a little older than Mütter, such as Pancoast, Peace, Goddard, and Norris, were gradually making their way to professional distinction. Mütter crept along slowly, notwithstanding that he made himself conspicuous by his tall gray horse, his low carriage, and his servant in livery as he drove through the fashionable streets of our city. His first essay as a public teacher was made in the Philadelphia Institute, a sort of nursery for teachers, as the assistant of Dr. Thomas Harris, who, as a naval surgeon, was often compelled to absent himself from his post. In these intervals Mütter occupied the place of his chief; and he soon won the esteem and affection of his pupils by his fascinating manners and by his efforts to please as well as to instruct. In his dress he was the pink of neatness; and there was that dash, enthusiasm, earnestness, and action about him which never fail to elicit attention and create popularity. He was of medium height, slender and graceful in form, with light eyes and a handsome forehead. His voice, remarkably clear and distinct, had unusual strength and compass. In 1851, during my temporary residence in New York, I made a three days' visit to Philadelphia purposely to hear the more distinguished teachers lecture; and there was not one of them in the two great schools who impressed me more pleasantly as a good speaker than Mütter. He appeared to be thoroughly familiar with the subject of his discourse, and every member of the class was seemingly an attentive listener.

The reputation acquired by Mütter in the Institute was of great use to him; and when in 1841, in consequence of the withdrawal of McClellan, the chair of Surgery became vacant in the Jefferson Medical College, the eyes of the Faculty and of the Board of Trustees were at once directed to the young teacher. At first the chair was divided between him and Jacob Randolph; but the latter soon withdrew, and left Mütter its sole occupant. The school rapidly grew in reputation, and Mütter became one of its most useful, popular, and distinguished teachers. Students were attracted to it from all parts of the continent, and even from foreign countries, and praises of its Faculty were reëchoed far and wide. The seven professors—Dunglison, Pancoast, Meigs, Bache, Huston, Mitchell, and Mütter—stood, like a solid phalanx, from 1841 till 1856, when the first break occurred by the resignation of Mütter, brought about by ill health.

As an operator Mütter attained a high position, although he was said to be deficient in the boldness so characteristic of his friend and colleague, Pancoast. He, however, wielded his knife gracefully, and generally with marked ability and self-possession. He was particularly distinguished in plastic surgery, and in operations performed for the relief of deformities arising from scalds and burns, in which he introduced some important improvements. Orthopædic surgery was another field in which he gained many laurels. Strange to say, he never held any hospital appointment.

Mütter had no fondness for authorship, and did not possess much ability as a writer. Judging from what he has left us, he must have found composition difficult. Apart from several contributions to the periodical press, he left nothing but his edition of Liston's Operative Surgery, and a treatise on Clubfoot, which was published early in his professional life, evidently as a bid for practice. The book was written in a poor style, and it is chiefly remarkable for its numerous notes of exclamation. He had long contemplated writing a work on Surgery; and with the aid of some of his private pupils, of whom he always had a goodly number, he had made some progress in collecting material, which, however, was never moulded into shape.

The fact is, he had slender qualifications for such an undertaking. His library was small, and he did not read much beyond what was necessary to enable him to keep abreast of the knowledge required for his lectures. He lacked two prominent characteristics of the genuine student—patience and endurance.

As a companion, Mütter was one of the best of good fellows. He was fond of anecdotes, and had always a good supply on hand for ready use. He was not over-scrupulous in the recital of his cases in the amphitheatre; and occasionally, it is said, he drew a long bow in the retirement of private life.

It is not too much to say that he was all things to all men, not unfrequently at the expense of other persons' comfort and convenience. His colleague, Robert M. Huston, who was for many years Dean of the Faculty, was often, as he repeatedly told me, annoyed in this manner. Mütter, full of good nature, was ready to promise a student anything; but, instead of doing the favor asked, he always sent him to the Dean with a full knowledge that the granting of it was impossible. Mütter availed himself of the trick of having himself frequently called out of church on Sundays. It was not uncommon for him, as I have been informed by one of his private pupils, to make an appointment for his assistants to meet him at a given house, at a particular hour of the day, to aid him in performing an operation in a case where nothing of the kind was thought of by the ambitious master. Such tricks are not uncommon even at the present day.

His reputation will in time depend probably upon what is known as the Mütter Museum, which is in the possession of the Philadelphia College of Physicians, to whose guardianship it was transferred by his executors soon after his death, with the sum of thirty thousand dollars for its preservation and steady augmentation. In connection with his munificent gift, he made provision for the establishment of a lectureship, to be known by his name—a lectureship which has long been in successful operation—ten lectures on some scientific subject, illustrated by preparations in the museum, being delivered every three years. As a teacher, few men have impressed themselves more deeply on the minds of his pupils than Mütter. His portrait, painted I believe by Allston, adorns the hall of the College of Physicians. I have heard it said that the Jefferson Medical College would have received his museum if its trustees could have been induced to provide for it a fire-proof building.

Franklin Bache.

1792–1864.

If posterity should not regard Franklin Bache as a great man, it will not fail to award to him in a high degree the merit of having been a conscientious teacher and writer. Born in 1792, he was proud that he was, on the mother's side, the great-grandson of Benjamin Franklin. His father was a journalist, the owner and publisher of the General Advertiser, a paper which took delight in abusing George Washington and John Adams, and in opposing their administrations. How the young man spent his early years I do not know; but he contrived to obtain a good education; and in 1810 he received from the University of Pennsylvania the degree of Doctor of Medicine. That he passed an excellent examination I can well imagine; for, judging from his after-life, he must have been a faithful, industrious, capable student. He early evinced a proclivity for the study of chemistry and the physical sciences, which he possibly inherited from his eminent ancestor, for such characteristics often reappear in families at long intervals. Electricity—the original electric kite, no doubt—

had strong attractions for him, which led him to pay more than ordinary attention to the subject. Nine years had hardly elapsed from the date of his graduation when he put forth his System of Chemistry, designed especially for the use of students of medicine. My recollection is that the work made a somewhat favorable impression. Dr. John Gorham of Boston published a similar treatise about the same time. In 1831 he was appointed Professor of Chemistry in the Philadelphia College of Pharmacy, from which he was shortly after transferred to the Jefferson Medical College, with which he remained connected until the time of his death in 1864. For eight years we were colleagues in this school; and although no intimacy ever existed between us, I formed a high estimate of his character. If as a lecturer he was dull, he was earnest and faithful; and the students, if at all intelligent and attentive, could not fail to be instructed by him. But it must be confessed that few of them ever displayed much knowledge of chemistry at their final examination; and the result was that the master usually deposited a negative vote when the final ballot was taken in full Faculty meeting. On one rare occasion, however, his was the only vote cast in favor of the unfortunate candidate, all the other members having rejected him. His delight was so great that he jumped off his chair and laughed heartily for several minutes, much to our amusement. As a colleague Bache was one of the most agreeable of men; always kind, courteous, and considerate. As a writer his name will be indelibly associated with the United States Dispensatory, which was the joint offspring of George B. Wood and himself—one of the most elaborate and erudite works ever published in this country.

VALENTINE MOTT.

1785–1865.

VALENTINE MOTT occupied for nearly half a century a conspicuous position in the history of his profession, and for more than two-thirds of that time he was the acknowledged head of American Surgery.   Physick died in 1837, and up to that period he was the peer of Mott.   Dudley was in the zenith of his renown as a lithotomist; but his reputation as a general surgeon never equalled that of his Eastern contemporaries.   The rise of Mott as a surgeon began with his ligation of the innominate artery, performed in 1819, when he was hardly thirty-three years of age.   It was a bold undertaking, one never attempted before.   The news of the operation soon rendered his name famous. Still greater achievements, at that time comparatively novel in this country, followed apace—such as excision of the jaws and of the clavicle, amputation at the hip-joint, and the ligation of the principal arteries, including the common iliac.   He gave much attention to lithotomy; and many patients were indebted to him for the restoration of sight. Orthopædic surgery received a new impulse at his hands in this country; and when the novel but futile operation for the relief of stammering, originally suggested by Dieffenbach, received favor on this side of the Atlantic he became one of its most enthusiastic advocates.   He was a fearless operator—fearless because he had no dread of the sight of blood, and because he was so thoroughly grounded in a knowledge of topographical anatomy that he experienced no difficulty in discerning the relations which one structure bears to another.   To this knowledge, combined with the coolness due to his organization, he was without doubt mainly indebted for his surgical triumphs.

Mott lived before the microscope had come into general use, and, consequently, like most of his American contemporaries, was ignorant of the nature of minute structure upon which so much stress is justly laid at the present day. His knowledge of pathological anatomy, however, must have been quite extensive, and for all practical purposes he seems to have been as able to diagnosticate a malignant from a benign disease as the most accomplished microscopist of the present day. If a man has not strong common-sense, a delicate touch, and a keen eye, backed by thorough experience, I would not give much for his surgical pretensions, if he were the most scientific microscopist living. Mott had a large collection of morbid specimens, the outgrowth chiefly of his own operations. These specimens, put up and preserved with great care, were all lost in the fire which in 1866 destroyed the edifice erected for the medical department of the University of the City of New York. This accident, which admitted of no repair, rendered him inconsolable.

As a public teacher Mott long occupied a prominent position. His lectures were essentially devoted to operative surgery, and exhibited the results of his rich personal experience, but they were always far in arrear of the existing state of the science. Another feature of them was their egotistical character. He could not help talking about the ligation of the innominate artery, the excision of the clavicle—styled by him his "Waterloo operation"—and other feats, the record of which, however amusing it might have been for a time to young students, could not fail sooner or later to become tiresome, if not offensive. This was Mott's weakness. If he possessed a certain degree of strength as a teacher of operative surgery, he was at fault as a teacher of surgical pathology— a fault shared until recently by most of the professors of this branch of science in our medical schools.

He has left us no great work on surgery; indeed, I may say, no work at all. A record of his important operations is embodied in Dr. Townsend's translation of Velpeau's Operative Surgery, to which the name of Mott is affixed as editor. Excepting the preface, the additions consist mainly of transcripts of his operations from medical periodicals, notably the American Journal of the Medical Sciences, which seems to have been a favorite medium between him and the profession. In 1840, soon after his return from abroad, he published his Travels in Europe and the East. Towards the close of his life Dr. Samuel W. Francis, of New York, published a small volume professing to be an abstract of Mott's lectures. The truth is the great New York surgeon had but moderate scholarly tastes or attainments; he could wield his knife much better than his pen. A surgeon rarely combines in his person all the accomplishments of a successful operator, practitioner, teacher, and author. Such qualities are as uncommon as they are to be envied.

I saw Dr. Mott for the first time in the autumn of 1828. I was on a visit to New York, and while there went to Rutgers College, in which he was at the time Professor of Surgery, to hear him lecture. His subject was Injuries of the Skull, and I was deeply interested in what he said. His language was plain, simple, and apparently well chosen, and he was evidently deeply impressed with the great truths he was uttering. He sat while speaking. I met him again in July, 1832, when, on handing him a letter of introduction, he received me with marked courtesy, extended to me the hospitalities of his table, and did all he could to further the objects of my mission. He had at that time a very high reputation as a surgeon, and his gentle, amiable, and courtly manners made an abiding impression upon me, for I had then been only a few years from the lecture-room of my Alma Mater. I was especially struck by his manly figure. He was fully six feet in height, and well proportioned. He had a handsome face, with a benevolent expression, an aquiline nose, a good but not capacious head, large hazel eyes, and a small mouth with thin lips. In his movements he was deliberate and dignified. He had a light, elastic step, and the bearing of the elegant, well-bred gentleman. Shortly after the commencement of the war of the Rebellion I met Dr. Mott again. He was then far advanced into the seventies, but with few of the accompaniments of old age. His figure was as erect as ever; he walked with a firm step; and his mind showed no signs of decay. After this I saw him occasionally at his mansion in Gramercy Park. Shortly after his death I prepared an elaborate sketch of his life and services, which was published by his widow in an elegant volume, illustrated by an excellent photograph likeness.

Mott was born in August, 1785, at Glen Cove, Long Island. He was of Quaker descent, and was known in early life as "the handsome young Quaker doctor." He pursued his classical studies at a private seminary, and retained his fondness for Greek and Latin up to the time of his death. He received his medical degree in 1807 from Columbia College, New York, then the only medical school in that city. Soon after his graduation he went to Europe, where he availed himself of the instruction of Cooper, Abernethy, Cline, Charles Bell, and others of London, and of that of Gregory, Monro, Hope, Duncan, Horne, and Thompson of Edinburgh. On his return he settled in New York, where his rise was rapid and brilliant. His services were soon sought by various medical schools; and in 1840 he founded, jointly with Draper, Bedford, and Paine, the Medical Department of the University of the City of New York, in which he remained as Professor of Surgery until 1860, when he resigned and went to Europe. Abroad he was everywhere received with the consideration and respect due to a man of high professional and social position. He had years ago been elected a member of the Institute of France; and having travelled extensively in Europe and the East in 1835 and 1836, the way had been thoroughly prepared for a pleasant visit. His numerous foreign friends were glad to greet the veteran surgeon, and vied with one another to do him honor.

Dr. Mott died on the 26th of April, 1865, at the age of eighty years. His illness, caused by spontaneous gangrene of one of his legs, was brief and his death unexpected. To the last he retained his consciousness, and passed away without a struggle. "Order, truth, punctuality" were the last words he uttered as he lay upon his couch—fitting words of a great and upright man. His body reposes in the family vault in Greenwood Cemetery.

Take him all in all, Mott was a great surgeon. Many years ago one of his former colleagues, who was a man of note in his day, said to me, "Mott was an inspired idiot." Alas for human judgment! The man who uttered this disparaging sentiment is already nearly forgotten, although scarcely a dozen years have elapsed since his death; while the fame of the eminent New York surgeon grows greener and brighter with each revolving year.

REUBEN DIMOND MUSSEY.

1780–1866.

THE town of Pelham, Rockingham County, New Hampshire, gave birth to Mussey June 23d, 1780. Dartmouth College educated him in the classics and in belles-lettres; and the University of Pennsylvania, in 1809, conferred upon him the degree of M. D. His father was a respectable physician, but too poor to afford his son substantial aid in the prosecution of his studies. The consequence was that the youth had to struggle on as best he could, teaching school during the winter, and working on a farm during the summer—a practice then, as now, quite common in New England. He received his medical training under

Nathan Smith, who was for many years a professor at New Haven and at Dartmouth College, in the latter of which he taught, for a considerable period, nearly all the branches of the healing art—for a while, indeed, even chemistry. During his residence in Philadelphia Mussey engaged in a series of experiments upon cutaneous absorption, by which he upset the doctrines taught in the University of Pennsylvania, and established for himself a high reputation as an original observer. He now settled at Salem, Massachusetts, where he soon acquired a large and influential practice. After some years he was elected, first, to the chair of Medicine, and then to that of Anatomy and Surgery, in Dartmouth College. In 1818 he lectured on Chemistry in the College at Middlebury, Vermont; and afterwards on Anatomy and Surgery at Bowdoin College, and on Surgery at the Medical College at Fairfield, New York. In 1837 he was called to the chair of Surgery in the Medical College of Ohio, at Cincinnati. In 1852 he united himself with the Miami Medical College, a new school, which has since attained some distinction. As an operator his name was widely known at a comparatively early period of his professional life. Some of his surgical exploits were of a brilliant and fearless character. One of these was a case in which, for the cure of an extensive nævus of the scalp, he tied both the primitive carotid arteries after an interval of only twelve days—followed by the excision of the morbid growth and the recovery of the patient. His operation for the removal of the scapula with a large portion of the clavicle, after previous amputation at the shoulder-joint, is, like the ligation of the carotids, classical. He lithotomized forty-nine times, with only four failures. He was also successful in herniotomy, and in subcutaneous ligations for the cure of varicocele.

As an operator, Mussey was painfully slow. His hand, from some defect of his nervous system, was tremulous. In watching its movements one almost felt inclined to seize the knife, and either run away with it, or do the cutting one's self. I shall never forget how long, on one occasion, when he was tying the femoral artery for the cure of a popliteal aneurism, his scalpel hovered over the site of the artery before it pierced the skin; and yet the operation was finally well performed. I have been told that he frequently spent more than an hour in lithotomizing a patient, and in removing the upper or lower jaw. This must have been a sad experience for the poor patient prior to the use of anæsthetics. Notwithstanding this lack of dexterity, Dr. Mussey's success was far greater than that of many surgeons better skilled in the use of the knife. Much of his success was no doubt due to the care which he took in preparing his patients, of whom he superintended the after-treatment in person. It is reported of him that he often, before an important operation, prayed for his patient, the better to secure his confidence, and to inspire him with hopes of safety. However this may be, there is no question that he was a conscientious surgeon and practitioner.

In 1829 Mussey visited Europe, spending several months in attending the hospitals of Paris and London, and in witnessing the practice of their great surgeons. When, on his return, he reached Dartmouth College the course had considerably advanced, and he was obliged, we are told, to lecture two and three times a day to make up the lost time.

As a lecturer Mussey was dull in the extreme. He was not only slow in his delivery, but deficient in power of expression, in animation, and in grace of manner. His words came forth tardily, as if he were in doubt as to their precise import, or as to the construction that might be put upon them by his hearers; and yet, if we may credit those who professed to be able to judge of them, and who had listened to other teachers on similar topics, his lectures must have been instructive. Learned, profound, or discursive they certainly were not, for Mussey was not a man of reading. His library was small, and few of the books that were in it were of recent selection. His lectures owed their chief value to their practical adaptation to the daily and hourly wants of the practitioner. It is due to their author to say that he always commanded the respect of his pupils.

The chief production of Mussey, apart from his contributions to the periodical press, which consisted mostly of reports of cases and operations, was a small work entitled Health; its Friends and its Foes. His last production, issued in his eighty-fourth year, was a short tract, What Shall I Drink?

Mussey was an avowed enemy of everything in the form of stimulants in the practice of medicine, as well as in private life and in the social circle, and he omitted no opportunity strongly to inveigh against their use. The Counterblast of King James against tobacco was not couched in more denunciatory language than the protest of the distinguished surgeon. Against the use of alcoholic drink he was more severe. To coffee he was so much opposed that, in a description of some experiments which he had performed, he dwelt with emphasis upon the injurious effects of its moderate administration upon sheep! He became at an early age a zealous lecturer upon intemperance, and took an active interest up to the last days of his life in the establishment of temperance societies. In religious matters he was equally zealous. He was all his life a devout and consistent Christian, held morning and evening service in his family, and was a regular attendant upon church on the Sabbath, and also, when practicable, during week-days. His mode of living was peculiar. Having long been a dyspeptic, he was induced to try various kinds of food, and was finally led to conclude that a farinaceous diet was the only diet intended for man by his Creator. For sixteen years he eschewed animal food entirely. At the end of this period, while slowly convalescing from a severe illness, he was after much entreaty induced, as his physicians Drs. Richards and Harrison informed me, to use a mixed diet; but in a few weeks he abandoned it, and never afterwards, I believe, tasted animal food. He was very fond of fruit, especially of the peach, the pear, and the apple, of which he ate large quantities. Milk, water, and lemonade were his common drinks. Tea he seldom drank, believing it to be hurtful. During the illness just referred to his attendants insisted upon the necessity of his taking brandy. He resisted as long as he could, and when at length he yielded, he would take only a few drops. When asked at the morning visit how the brandy had affected him, his reply was, "I have taken altogether about half a teaspoonful since last evening, and I am quite sure that it has increased my fever and made me worse."

Having found that a vegetable diet agreed with him, and that it enabled him to perform his daily labor with more satisfaction than with a mixed diet, he attempted to establish the system upon a scientific basis. "With this view," says his biographer, Dr. Alpheus B. Crosby, "he calls our attention to the fact that the orang-outang, chimpanzee, and gorilla most nearly resemble man both in their organs of mastication and digestion; that these animals are all vegetable eaters, and fall into ill health and frequently die on a mixed diet; that Adam and Eve before the fall were vegetarians, and that afterwards on a mixed diet the duration of human life constantly diminished; and finally, he adduces instances both in ancient and modern times where vegetarians were celebrated not less for their muscular power than for their mental vigor; and shows us that the extreme nervous acuteness of Caspar Hauser was only dimmed and obtused when he had learned to eat meat."

It is related of Mussey that, on passing through a certain village in New England, he was requested to see a little child lying at the point of death, for whom he prescribed

"Graham gruel," telling the mother that the poor sufferer would certainly recover if she would feed him on it. The gruel was tried—but the second meal did the work! When Mussey, on his return the next day, stopped to inquire after the health of the patient, the mother gave him a severe scolding, saying he had killed her child.

Mussey was of low stature, of an attenuated form, with high cheek bones, a prominent chin, a small gray eye, and an ungraceful gait. His head was of medium size, and he possessed none of that personal magnetism which gives a man a commanding influence over his fellow-men. The evening of his life was spent in Boston, where, after having lain for two years in a helpless condition, he passed calmly away at the age of eighty-six, at peace with God and all the world.

My last interview with Dr. Mussey was at my house, a few years before his death, as he was passing through Philadelphia on his way to Boston. He looked thin and haggard, walked feebly, and bore all the marks of one whose sands in the hour-glass of life were gradually but surely running out.

Dr. Mussey left two sons. General Mussey served with distinction in the war of the Rebellion. Dr. William H. Mussey died in August, 1882, at the age of sixty-four years—in the memoir of whose life recently published by his nephew, Mr. Edward Mussey Hartwell, of the Johns Hopkins University, many interesting facts are recorded in illustration of his stern integrity, his deep sense of humanity, and his detestation of everything that is mean and vulgar. He took a lively interest in our struggle for the preservation of the Union; and he was in active service as brigade surgeon or as medical director from the beginning almost to the close of the war. In the latter capacity he was assigned to the Fourth Division in the Department of the Ohio, commanded by General Nelson, who was notorious for his insolence and inconsiderate conduct. Mussey was not the surgeon Nelson had wished or expected, and he was received at headquarters with rudeness and profanity. Not in the least intimidated, Mussey said, "General, I have reported to you under orders. Do you decline to receive me in obedience to those orders?" Nelson's bullying ceased at once, says Mr. Hartwell, and thenceforth Mussey was always treated with due courtesy and respect.

Nelson had been an officer in the navy, and the incident here narrated recalls a circumstance which took place on board the frigate Constitution, at anchor in the Bay of Naples. After breakfast the conversation turned upon the system of education then in vogue at the Naval Academy. "My class," exclaimed Bully Nelson, "was the very first sent to Annapolis. We were called upon in alphabetical order to recite, and Charley Aby was the first man at the blackboard. I remember, the maximum being one, that he attained one-half!"

"Ah!" exclaimed Assistant-Surgeon Horwitz, probably for want of something to say, and confounding in his mind the figure ½ with the decimal .5; "if I had been the first man called up, I would have contrived to obtain a higher decimal than that."

"Do you call a half a decimal?" cried out the bully; "you a member of the learned profession, too! By —— it is my opinion that you don't know the difference between a decimal and a vulgar fraction."

"Oh, I hope I do," modestly responded the doctor.

"Well, I don't believe you do. Give me a definition, showing the difference. You can't do it; I defy you!"

"Nelson," responded the doctor, "I am not good at definitions; I never was; but I can give you an illustration, if that will answer."

"I don't believe you can even do that," said Nelson.

"Well, sir," exclaimed Dr. H., "since you are so anxious, I will try: If I were cut into ten parts, any one would be a decimal of the whole. If you were cut up into any number, any one would be vulgar."

A shout of laughter from the entire mess greeted this retort, amid cries of, "Good, Bully! the doctor's got you!" "Bully William," as he was sometimes called, retired to his state-room, and said nothing further about decimal fractions.

This anecdote, which I have given in the words of my friend Dr. Horwitz, who during the war acted with so much distinction as Chief of Bureau of Medicine and Surgery, is too good to be lost, and I am prompted to assign it a place here as illustrative of Nelson's character. I knew Nelson well. He was more than six feet in height, with broad shoulders and an immense chest, a stentorian voice, and the courage of a lion. His rough manners and supercilious air led him into constant broils. His end was a sad one. In 1862, at the Galt House at Louisville, he had an altercation with General Jefferson C. Davis, of Indiana, whom he struck in the face with his glove, and by whom he was shot dead a few minutes after the insult was offered.

CHAPTER XII.

BENJAMIN FRANKLIN SHUMARD.

1819–1867.

IN 1841, one morning as I was sitting in my office rumi-
nating over the occurrences of the preceding day, I was
timidly saluted by a youth who announced his name as
Shumard, a student of medicine, adding that he had come
to place himself under my instruction, if, as he hoped, I
would receive him. Begging him to be seated, I took a
keen survey of him. In stature he was about the medium height, with blue eyes, of light complexion, and of
decidedly awkward manners. "My family," he said,
"recently moved to Louisville from Cincinnati, and my
father is now engaged in manufacturing blacking. We
are poor but honest people, and my desire is to prose-
cute in your school my medical studies begun in Philadelphia." The youth who thus addressed me was destined,
contrary to my anticipations, to make a figure in the
world, and to leave behind him an enviable, if not an
enduring name. There was nothing in his appearance or
conversation which denoted special talent. When he graduated the following spring he gave no evidence of exceeding
the ordinary standard; and I took for granted that little, if
anything, would be heard of him after he left the halls of
his Alma Mater—in a word, that he would soon be lost in
the mass of general practitioners. In truth, I do not think

that he was ever fond of his profession. Shortly after he received his degree he opened an office in the country, at some distance from Louisville, and whenever he met me his answer to my question, "How are you getting on?" was, "Practice is an up-hill business." He had already turned his attention to the study of palæontology. The hills near his residence abounded in prehistoric remains and deeply interested him. I had made a collection of this kind myself at the Falls of the Ohio, and on certain hills twenty miles back of Louisville, which was especially rich in encrinites and trilobites. In these excursions I was accompanied by Dr. J. Cobb, Dr. Henry Miller, Dr. Lunsford P. Yandell, and by Dr. Clapp, an eminent naturalist of New Albany, Indiana. I have always thought that this collection, which was lost in the fire which in 1856 destroyed the University of Louisville, did much to develope the taste of Shumard for the study of palæontology and geology. However this may be, he found genial spirits in his preceptors, Cobb and Yandell, who were engaged in similar occupations, especially the latter, who had formed a valuable collection of these organic remains. A love for these pursuits of course led Shumard away from his profession. People will not employ a man that prefers his hammer and his bag to his books and his pocket-case; and they are wise in their decision. Franklin used to say, "Keep your shop, and your shop will keep you." It was thus that my young disciple gradually drifted away from his profession, to which necessity alone prompted him to return. It was evident to all around him that his heart was not in his original vocation. His father, disappointed at his want of success, said, "Benjamin had too many rocks in his head to have any room for medicine."

The frequent and prolonged excursions which this enthusiast made around Louisville and into the interior of Kentucky soon resulted in a large and interesting collection of prehistoric remains, which in due time were systematically arranged and described; and as not a few of these specimens were unknown, his fellow-naturalists, as a just tribute to his labors and researches, bestowed upon them the name of their discoverer—a practice usual with scientists. These explorations gradually developed a taste for the kindred science of geology; and we accordingly find that the services of Dr. Shumard were ere long required in a manner highly agreeable to his desires. Dr. David Dale Owen, engaged in the geological survey of the Northwestern Territories, under the direction of Congress, selected as his assistant the young scientist, whose fitness for the position had been shown by his previous labors. Shumard served in this capacity for several years both in the field and in the laboratory; and the value of the scientific documents issued by the government was greatly enhanced by his contributions. Conjointly with his friend, the late Professor Lunsford P. Yandell, he furnished, in 1847, for the Western Journal of Medicine and Surgery an elaborate paper entitled Contributions to the Geology of Kentucky, in which he attempted to show the connection between certain geological formations and particular diseases. The paper attracted much attention, and was widely copied by the medical and secular press.

Other positions of trust and honor awaited Dr. Shumard. In 1850 he assisted in making a geological survey of Oregon; and soon after his return home he was employed on the palæontology of the Red River country, in continuation of the explorations commenced by his brother, Dr. George G. Shumard. In 1853 he was appointed assistant geologist and palæontologist in the Missouri Survey. Five years afterwards he was commissioned as geologist of Texas. He entered upon the duties of his new position with more than ordinary enthusiasm, for he felt that he was now a chief instead of a mere assistant. But, after he had been busy at work for two years, and was almost ready to publish his report, he was suddenly, in consequence of a change in the Governorship of the State, superseded, and of course obliged to retire from the field. This proved to be his last effort as a public geologist. He had long sighed for an independent position; it had come at last, but only to elude his grasp.

Shumard was now poor. What added to his embarrassment was the fact that only a short time before he was thrown out of public employment he had married a young lady, who, although highly respectable, brought him no dowry. Under these circumstances the only thing he could do was to return to his profession. His family was settled in St. Louis, and he forthwith opened an office in that city and became a candidate for practice. For a time business came slowly, but by degrees his patients increased in number and influence, and in consequence he drew daily a longer and freer breath. In 1866 he was elected Professor of Obstetrics in the University of Missouri, thus adding somewhat to his slender income. After some time, however, his health broke down, and he was obliged to abandon, not only his chair, but his practice. A violent cold greatly aggravated his pulmonary trouble; and on the 14th of April, 1867, he breathed his last, in the forty-ninth year of his age, lamented by all who knew him. Many scientific societies, foreign and domestic—among others, the Geological Societies of London, Paris, and Vienna—had enrolled his name among their members, and, when the news of his death reached them, passed resolutions of regret at their loss. At the time of his decease he was President of the St. Louis Academy of Science. All of his contributions to scientific journals, which were numerous and varied, had a bearing more or less direct upon geology and palæontology, with the history of whose progress on this continent his name will live.

In a beautiful and highly appreciative memoir of Shumard which he published in 1870, the late Professor Yandell says, "Among the many good and true men with whom it has been my privilege to be intimately associated in life, no name revives in my mind recollections more agreeable than his; hardly one recalls a disposition so artless, gentle, genial, amiable, or a character so faultless. It is doubtful whether he has left an enemy behind him in the world, or ever made one in his life."

WILLIAM GIBSON.

1788–1868.

IT was on a hot summer morning near the close of our late war that, as I was sitting in my office busily engaged in writing, a sweet, pretty young girl about fifteen years of age, accompanied by her colored maid, gracefully handed me a note, which read as follows:

MY DEAR DOCTOR GROSS: I am confined to my bed by an attack of rheumatism, and desire to consult you, at your earliest convenience, professionally. The bearer, my daughter, will explain to you everything about the trains for Cornwall Station, my present residence.

I am, very truly, yours,   WILLIAM GIBSON.

Being busy at the moment, and finding that the case admitted of delay, I begged Miss Gibson to tell her father that I would visit him the next day. Upon arriving at the house I was shown into a small chamber, with a solitary bed, on which lay the great surgeon extended at full length. I never saw a more venerable figure. The long, white, flowing beard added grandeur and dignity to his pallid features, which were set off by his white head, his ample forehead, and his shaggy brows. His keen blue eyes had apparently lost none of their early lustre. After a cordial greeting and an interchange of civilities, I sat

down at his bedside and began to make some inquiries
about his condition.   But I soon found it to be quite impossible to obtain anything like a connected account of
his case.   After answering a few questions he invariably
broke the thread of my inquiries by making irrelevant
remarks, descanting upon the beauties of an Alderney
cow, or quoting some passages from Ovid, Horace,
or Virgil.   His rheumatism seemed, at all events for a
time, to have vanished, leaving his mind at liberty to
wander whither it listed.   By dint of exertion, however,
I was at length enabled correctly to diagnose the case, and
I suggested a course of treatment, consisting mainly of an
occasional dose of Dover's powder and the proper regulation of the diet.   By this time more than an hour had
elapsed—an hour to me full of interest on account of the
exalted position and the eccentric conduct of my patient.
The servant now called me to tea, and at the table I had
the pleasure of again meeting, along with her elder sister,
the young lady who brought me her father's message on
the previous day.   The meal being over, I returned to my
patient and took my leave of him, wishing him a speedy
restoration to health.   He had been confined to his bed
for some weeks, and spoke discouragingly of his recovery,
as he had long been a victim of rheumatism, which often
rendered his life miserable.   I never met Dr. Gibson again
until I saw him in his coffin, at the house of his son-in-
law, Professor John J. Reese.   He died at Savannah,
Georgia, March 2d, 1868, aged eighty years.   The occasion was rendered doubly solemn for me, as I was one of
the pall-bearers, my colleagues being Isaac Hays, René
La Roche, and George W. Norris.   Only a few of the
professors and not one student of the University of Pennsylvania attended the funeral.

He occupied the chair of Surgery in the University
of Pennsylvania from 1819, when he succeeded Physick,
until 1855, in which year advancing age and increasing

infirmities constrained him to retire to private life. His successor was Henry H. Smith. Gibson was an able and impressive lecturer, and never failed to command the attention of his class. His characteristic qualities were clearness, accuracy, and earnestness. He made no pretensions to eloquence. For illustrating his course he had a large cabinet and numerous diagrams, many of them the work of his own hands. His models of hernia were especially fine. He was the first to tie the internal iliac artery; and, although the case terminated fatally, his example was soon followed by other surgeons, who had hesitated to undertake the operation. He handled his knife with great skill, and was one of the foremost operators of his day. His practice was never large, either as a surgeon or as a physician, owing, it is alleged, to the fact that he was never popular with the profession of Philadelphia. His greatest feat, a feat which has made his name widely known in Europe as well as at home, was the performance of the Cæsarean section twice upon one woman, saving mother and child in both instances.

In 1824 Gibson published The Institutes and Practice of Surgery, which was designed mainly as a text-book for his pupils. The work, however, had a wide circulation, and at the time of the author's death had reached its sixth edition. The later editions were marked improvements upon the earlier, which were inexpressibly meagre. In fact, the work was never up to the existing state of the science. Its great merit was the remarkable clearness of its style. In 1841 appeared his Rambles in Europe, a duodecimo volume, comprising sketches of prominent surgeons, physicians, medical schools, hospitals, and literary personages. The book is written in a pleasant, chatty vein, and attracted considerable attention. In Europe it was severely criticized on account of what, in many instances, the medical press regarded as breaches of confidence and private hospitality.

Gibson was born in Baltimore March 14, 1788. He was an excellent classical scholar; and he always retained his fondness for the Latin poets, of which, so prodigious was his memory, he could recite page after page. Ovid, Horace, and Virgil were his favorites. His medical education was received at the University of Edinburgh. His thesis, descriptive of necrosis, was written in Latin, and was much admired for its classical style and for the accuracy of its delineations. After he left Scotland he continued his studies in London and Paris, where he made the acquaintance of the masters in medicine and surgery. He was a particular admirer of Sir Charles Bell, who afforded him special facilities for the study of military surgery. One of his most celebrated exploits after his return from Europe was the extraction of some wadding and other foreign matter from the shoulder of General Scott, who had been wounded at the battle of Lundy's Lane in Canada, and who had experienced for years much suffering in consequence of the inability of the parts to heal.

It is said that one should not speak ill of the dead. Far be it from me to do so; but I cannot ignore the fact, known to most of his professional contemporaries, that Gibson was not an amiable man. His ill temper often betrayed him into unkind expressions, even in the lecture-room. My acquaintance with him was slight, and I was therefore not a little surprised when I received the message to visit him at his country residence. An old friend, to whom I mentioned this fact, exclaimed, "Don't you know that he has no friends in the medical profession of Philadelphia?" I have reason to believe that Gibson had a warm regard for me, and that this was why he asked for my advice. In 1855, when he resigned his chair in the University of Pennsylvania, he strongly advocated my claims as his successor; and he subsequently told me that he would have been very glad if I had consented to become a candidate for the place.

Gibson often indulged in offensive language against his opponents. McClellan, Mütter, and Pancoast were especially obnoxious to him; and Granville Sharp Pattison also came in for a share of his dislike. Against Dr. Potter, of Baltimore, once a colleague of his, he had a bitter feeling. Potter was the editor of the Maryland Lyceum, a medical journal; and in speaking of him Gibson took delight in emphasizing the syllable *Ly.*, in reference to Potter's well-known infirmity. Gibson was a non-believer in the feasibility of extirpating the parotid gland, and before his own class he openly accused McClellan of falsehood for having asserted that he had repeatedly performed the operation. For a long time there was a warm controversy on this subject between the rival schools, in which Pattison at length took an active part in favor of McClellan. Some ten years afterwards Gibson and McClellan became partially reconciled; and after the latter had withdrawn from the Jefferson Medical College he was invited to witness an extirpation of the parotid, in the University of Pennsylvania, in the presence of the class and of many physicians who had come to see the "fun." The tumor was skilfully removed; and when the operation was over Gibson, turning towards the audience, remarked, "Gentlemen, I have performed what is generally called extirpation of the parotid gland; but it is not an extirpation of that gland. The mass I have removed is only a tumor overlying that gland, not the gland itself." "Gentlemen," said McClellan, "my distinguished friend has extirpated the parotid gland, but, unfortunately, he does not know it"—a remark which caused convulsions of laughter in the large assembly. McClellan is said to have performed this operation altogether eleven times. The friendship thus patched up between the two surgeons did not last long. The pamphlet which Pattison wrote in defence of his colleague was widely circulated, and from its piquancy attracted much attention.

Dr. Gibson had a son, Charles Bell Gibson—named for Charles Bell, the physiologist—who settled in Richmond, Virginia, in the Medical College of which he was for a time Professor of Surgery. At the outbreak of the war he espoused the Southern cause, became dissipated, and soon after the collapse of the Confederacy died in a state of destitution. He had inherited his father's valuable collection of morbid specimens, especially rich in bones, which was sold after his death to the Army Medical Museum at Washington for the small sum of eleven hundred dollars. It had been previously pledged for debt to Dr. Cullen, an old friend.

ROBLEY DUNGLISON.

1798–1869.

OF all the colleagues—nearly forty in number—with whom I have been associated, Robley Dunglison was by far the most learned. His range of knowledge was almost encyclopædic. With his vast acquisitions he combined remarkable clearness of intellect and soundness of judgment. Even at the Green Row Academy, where he received most of his early classical education, he was distinguished for rapid progress in learning, and for systematic habits. Whatever seemed to him to be of special importance he faithfully recorded in his note-books, which were remarkable for their neatness and for the extent and variety of their contents. His after-years were given up to literary toil.

The Human Physiology, originally rejected by our Philadelphia publishers, was issued at Boston in 1832, and at once assumed a high rank as a class-book for students, superseding the work of Bostock and other authors. Robert Walsh, the editor of the Philadelphia Gazette, an influential literary paper, wrote a lengthy and interesting notice of it; and the medical press of the country spoke of it in terms of high praise. At the time of the author's death the work had reached its seventh edition. Its great merit consisted in the fact that it was always abreast of the science of which it treated, while its style was so lucid as to adapt it to the comprehension of the humblest intellect. What Albert von Haller's great work accomplished for physiology in Europe in the eighteenth century Dunglison's accomplished for it in America in the nineteenth. Each affords a complete summary of the literature of the science at the time at which it was written. Each is rich in learning, accurate and logical in its statement of facts, exhaustive in matter, and philosophical in its deductions. Each marked an era in the history of physiology. As works of reference they can never die.

His Medical Dictionary, one of his earliest productions, and a work of marvellous labor and erudition, earned him a world-wide reputation. During his lifetime it passed through numerous editions, each of which was a great improvement upon its predecessor. The last edition issued before his death contained more than six thousand new terms and subjects not included in the previous edition. Under the judicious supervision of his son, Dr. Richard J. Dunglison, the Dictionary, which is without an equal in English medical literature, is destined to live for an indefinite period.

The Physiology and the Dictionary were followed in rapid succession by treatises on Materia Medica and Therapeutics, Hygiene, the Practice of Medicine, and New Remedies, all of which, except that on Hygiene, passed through numerous editions, and were long used as textbooks in our schools. Dunglison seemed to possess the happy faculty of discerning the needs of the profession; hence the unwonted success of his books. Besides the labor involved in the composition of these works and in the preparation of ever-recurring new editions, he was copiously contributing to the periodical press, medical and lay, and editing Forbes's Cyclopædia of Practical Medicine and several other foreign works. He was the founder and publisher for five years of the American Medical Library and Intelligencer, a serial devoted to the reissuing of foreign works and to the dissemination of medical news. This enumeration but faintly indicates the amount of his literary labor. It would take more space than I can afford even to mention the titles of his minor productions. The celebrated Dictionary for the Blind, in raised type, on the basis of Worcester's English Dictionary, was written jointly by him and by William Chapin, Principal of the Pennsylvania Institution for Instruction of the Blind. This was the first work of its kind, on a large scale, published in this country, and it has been an inestimable boon to those for whom it was prepared. He took a deep interest in the insane poor, and wrote several valuable articles on the importance of providing for them suitable asylums. Dunglison never wrote an unkind paragraph against any human being in or out of the profession. He shrank from acrimonious disputation, and he did all he could to discountenance and repress it. He was eminently a man of peace; a gentleman in all the relations of life, with a heart full of the warmest sympathy for all living creatures. His sensitive nature never allowed him to engage in physiological or other experiments involving the infliction of pain or the destruction of life. Like his great prototype, Von Haller, he could not bear the sight of blood.

Dunglison was born in 1798, at Keswick, a small town in Cumberland, England, famous for the beauty of its scenery and as the residence of the Lake poets. He was originally intended for mercantile pursuits, and would probably never have entered the medical profession if it had not been for the unexpected death of his uncle, Joseph Robley, a wealthy West Indian planter, for whom he was named. Having studied the classics and the mathematics, and made himself a master of English composition—a subject too much neglected in our seminaries of learning—he commenced the study of medicine under a village physician in the seventeenth year of his age, and afterwards attended lectures at Edinburgh and Paris, as well as some private courses in London. He passed his final examination in 1819 at the Royal College of Surgeons and at the Society of Apothecaries. His medical degree was obtained, by examination, from the University of Erlangen. His early predilections, probably derived from his intercourse with Mr. Haden, a celebrated London obstetrician, induced him to select midwifery as his future occupation; and in May, 1824, he publicly announced a course of lectures upon that subject. Before, however, he could carry his design into effect, a circumstance occurred which completely changed his plans as well as his future destiny. He accepted an invitation from Mr. Jefferson, the founder of the University of Virginia, to take a seat in the Faculty of its medical school as Professor of Anatomy, Physiology, Surgery, Materia Medica, Pharmacy, and the History of Medicine—a boundless field for a man hardly twenty-six years of age. Surely the great ex-President, with all his philosophy and learning, could not have had a just conception of what he was doing. Fortunately, after the arrival of the young Englishman in this country, several of these branches were lopped off; and Anatomy and Surgery were replaced by Medicine, as better adapted to his taste and ability. Owing to adverse winds, the vessel in which Dr. Dunglison and his little family were passengers did not reach our shores until nearly three months after her departure, a fortunate event, as it enabled him to increase his resources for his appointed work. After a residence of nine years at the University, during which

he enjoyed the highest social position in the charming
society of Charlottesville, and the friendship and confidence of Jefferson and Madison, to the latter of whom he
had dedicated his Physiology, and whom he was called
upon to visit during his last illness, Dunglison accepted
the chair of Materia Medica and Medical Jurisprudence in
the University of Maryland, and thus became a citizen of
Baltimore. The small fees—fifteen hundred dollars a year,
with a dwelling-house—did not enrich him; nor was his
income in his new home such as to induce him to accept
the position as a permanency. The trustees of the Jefferson
Medical College, knowing of what great value he would
be in building up their institution, appointed him to the
chair of the Institutes of Medicine; and the following autumn he removed to Philadelphia, which became his future
home—a change alike beneficial to himself and to the institution which has since played so conspicuous a part in
the public medical teaching of this continent.

Dunglison, on his arrival in Philadelphia, found dissensions in the school, the outgrowth mainly of jealousy and
personal bickering; and he was therefore not sorry when,
in 1841, it was thoroughly reorganized, and thus placed
upon a better footing. With the reconstructed Faculty,
embracing some of the great men in the city, the school
rapidly grew in strength and influence. The retirement
of Mütter, in 1856, caused the first break in the new organization. One after another dropped out of the ranks,
until Dunglison and Pancoast were the sole survivors.

Dunglison died on April 1st, 1869, after six months of
the most cruel suffering. During nearly all of this time he
was confined to his bed, propped up by pillows, with his
feet resting upon the floor. He could not lie down even
for an hour. He had long been the victim of heart disease, and no one could witness his distress without the
deepest sympathy. Yet no murmur escaped his lips. At
times, indeed, he was even cheerful, although he knew

that he was a doomed man. He had always been a great lover of music, and in not a few of his solitary and heavy hours he was cheered by the dulcet strains of his pianoforte. He was always glad to see his friends, and took a lively interest in public affairs and in the school of which he had so long been the pride and the ornament.

As a lecturer, ready, fluent, entertaining, and instructive, Dunglison had few equals. His presence was commanding, his voice mellifluous, his manner graceful. He never was at a loss for a word. If he had any fault, it was that he talked too rapidly and too much in a monotone. Perhaps, too, he did not make points enough. He never, as he repeatedly told me, went into the presence of his class without due preparation, and the consequence was that he was always abreast of his subject. What a pity that all teachers do not pursue a similar course! As a husband, father, brother, neighbor, friend, there never was a kinder or better man. In all the relations of life he was a model. As a profound medical scholar, ages will probably elapse before the profession will have another Dunglison. His executive ability, his industry, and his power of endurance were remarkable. As Dean for many years, he performed his arduous duties with promptness and fidelity. He did not approve of frequent Faculty meetings, believing, from long experience, that they were prejudicial to the interests of the school—an opinion fully concurred in by his colleagues. The fact is, he was in every respect conservative; perhaps at times a little too much so. He thought that seven chairs in any college were quite enough; and he never could see good in an auxiliary summer school. He had a large, well-selected, and costly library. System was the great factor in his success as a writer and as a teacher. Practice he never coveted, and he made no effort to get it. He had little faith in active or heroic medication, and had a firm conviction that Nature, assisted by rest, abstinence, and good nursing, was fully competent in ordinary cases to dislodge disease and restore the sick to health. His mind was one of the best balanced I ever knew. In person he was about the middle height, with a handsome face and a noble head. He was a fluent talker, an insatiable reader, and a rapid writer. Daniel Webster said that the word "would," in Rufus Choate's handwriting, resembled a small gridiron struck by lightning. The chirography of Dunglison was so angular and so crabbed that it was difficult to decipher it. Before I became his colleague I often received letters from him, which, after a cursory perusal, I generally laid aside for a more careful reading the next day. Printers, however, soon became used to his copy.

His literary work was usually finished in the forenoon. He had none of the cares and anxieties of practice, and hence he could give free scope to his pen. Like all men who perform literary labor, he worked systematically and persistently for a number of hours daily, or until the brain became fatigued, when he would quit the table, and seek relaxation in exercise, amusement, or light reading. His books for consultation and reference were arranged on a rotary stand within easy reach, an admirable time-saving plan which cannot be too warmly commended. His income from his works was large; for, as before stated, most of them had a wide circulation. Dunglison was a member of many native and foreign societies, and for a time one of the Vice-Presidents of the American Philosophical Society.

What rare Ben Jonson said of a contemporary may be applied to Dunglison:

"Thou art a monument without a tomb,
    And art alive still, while thy book doth live!"

The great medical lexicographer possessed, but in a vastly higher degree, what the great English lexicographer ascribed to Mark Akenside, the poet-physician—"uncommon amplitude of acquisitions."

ALDEN MARCH.

1795–1869.

IT was late on a Saturday evening, in the latter part of August, 1853, that the Montreal train reached Albany, New York. My son, Samuel W. Gross, and I, after having spent a week at the Falls of Niagara, had gone down Lake Ontario and the river St. Lawrence to Lower Canada as far as Quebec and the Falls of Montmorency, whence in due time we returned to Montreal. The train on which we were passengers was due at Albany in time for the evening boat for New York; but it arrived too late, and we were consequently detained in that city until the next evening. On the whole I did not regret the delay, as it afforded me an opportunity of seeing my old friend, Dr. Alden March, a man very much after my own heart, the more especially as he was a self-made man, a surgeon, practitioner, and teacher of wide reputation, and high in the esteem and affection of his profession and the public. Accordingly, soon after breakfast the next morning, I sent him my card, which brought from him a regret that, inasmuch as his family was out of town, he could not invite us to dinner, but he said that he would be glad to show us the museum of the Albany Medical College and other matters of interest. Although the College had been established only a short time, its museum was rich in elegant preparations in human anatomy, and contained many fine pathological specimens of much interest and value. A number of these specimens were illustrative of the various stages of coxalgia, a subject which had long occupied the attention of this observant surgeon, and which had lately been a subject of controversy between him and Professor Gibson of the University of Pennsylvania. Gibson, in common with other writers, had, in his Institutes of Surgery, asserted that this disease, in its more advanced stages, is generally, if not invariably, attended with dislocation of the hip-joint. March justly contended that the displacement which occurs under such circumstances is not a genuine luxation, but simply a shortening of the thigh-bone dependent upon the absorption or destruction of its head along with a portion of its neck. This opinion, confirmed by my own dissections, was based upon extensive personal experience and a careful examination of some of the principal anatomical museums at home and abroad, the result of which permanently settled this important question. The College collection also contained some valuable specimens in comparative anatomy, many of them the contributions of the distinguished surgeon himself. The fact is, March was a skilful dissector, and taught anatomy in several New England schools during the first ten or twelve years of his professional life. Hence, when he was elected to the chair of Surgery in 1830 in the Albany Medical College, he was thoroughly prepared for the successful discharge of the active and laborious duties of his office. He settled in Albany in 1820, and soon rose to eminence. For more than a third of a century he enjoyed a lucrative practice, and was looked up to as a chief in his department. As an operator, he possessed great coolness and dexterity. He had an ample field for the exercise of his talents. Albany was a growing city; the surrounding country was studded with towns and villages; and he was often summoned to great distances to see patients and to perform operations. He invented several useful surgical instruments, and devised, modified, or improved certain surgical processes. As a teacher, although not brilliant, he was instructive, painstaking, and well grounded in knowledge. His pupils were warmly attached to him; and the Albany Medical College was indebted to him for much of its prosperity.

March was born at Sutton, Massachusetts, in 1795, studied medicine with an elder brother, an army surgeon, and graduated in what was formerly the Medical Department of Brown University. He was a member of many of the more respectable medical societies of the United States, received the degree of LL. D. from Williams College of his native State, and was elected President of the American Medical Association in 1868. He died in 1869, profoundly mourned by his fellow-citizens, and universally regretted by the profession. In person he was tall and well formed, with a fine head, brown eyes, and a handsome face. His early life was passed upon a farm, and he nobly worked his way up to an exalted position. Albany had reason to be proud of one who contributed so much to its reputation. He spent his money liberally upon objects of charity, and was a devout Christian. He had long been a great sufferer from an incurable disease; and his death was hastened by the exposure and fatigue incident to the long journey which he had made a few weeks previously to attend the meeting of the American Medical Association at New Orleans.

I have always held that March was a great surgeon, and such, I think, is the verdict generally accorded him by his surgical compeers on this side of the Atlantic. We are too apt to think that men who live in small towns and cities are not favorably situated for the performance of great deeds. We forget that London, Paris, Berlin, Vienna, New York, and Philadelphia produced, while their population was comparatively sparse, many illustrious men—doctors, lawyers, divines, statesmen, and artists. Dudley achieved his reputation in Lexington, Kentucky; at Heidelberg Chelius became an illustrious surgeon; and in 1812, when Rush died, the population of Philadelphia was hardly one hundred and fifty thousand. There is no doubt that circumstances materially assist in developing or repressing talent and genius; but a man who is a man reacts upon circumstances, and makes them subservient to his own purposes.

CHARLES D. MEIGS.
1792–1869.

OF the great men with whom during a period of half a century I have been brought prominently in contact, I regard Charles D. Meigs, for six years my colleague in the Jefferson Medical College, as one of the most extraordinary, whether we consider his versatility, his learning, his talents, his enthusiasm, his eccentricity, his dramatic power, and his love for his profession, or the reputation which he attained as an obstetric practitioner, as an author, and as a teacher. He was one of those men who excel in whatever situation of life they are placed. In person he was of middle height, slender, and erect, with a thin, sallow visage, slightly reddish whiskers, light eyes, and a large, well-formed head, with but slight tendency to baldness even in advanced life. His manners were warm and genial, and he had a cordial welcome for every one who properly approached him. His voice had little compass, and was attended with a kind of "squeakiness," particularly noticeable in the lecture-room, which rendered it decidedly disagreeable. For this reason it was often difficult for pupils who sat upon the back seats to hear or understand him; and yet, despite this defect, Meigs was an exceedingly interesting lecturer. He abounded in anecdotes and odd sayings, and had a peculiar way of making and stating his points. He never wearied his students; and in only one instance did I hear a pupil say that he had not been instructed or materially benefited by his prelections. His mode of lecturing was conversational, not at all rhetorical. His habit was to walk around the arena of the amphitheatre, when he was not engaged in demonstrating, with one hand in his pocket and the other on the railing, earnestly talking as it were to the group of young men immediately before him, apparently forgetful that he was in the presence of anybody

else.   Like Rufus Choate, who, it is said, seldom lost a
case argued before a jury, Meigs always aimed to make a
strong personal impression; or, in other words, to place
himself in intimate personal relations with his pupils, thus
flattering their vanity by inducing the belief that, if they
were not special favorites, he at all events took a particular
interest in their welfare.   Such a mode of lecturing possesses great advantages, and is sure to be popular, for by
it the whole audience cannot fail to be benefited and
enlightened.   On certain occasions Meigs was eminently
dramatic, and seemed almost to be inspired.   The attention of the students was completely on the stretch, and
loud and repeated applause would break forth to diver-
sify the exercises.   What could have been more graphic
than his account of Adam when he found Eve in labor?
or of Eve herself as she was passing through the pangs
of parturition? or of the dressing of the baby? or of
the first joys of maternal love?   Assuredly these scenes
could not have been more vividly portrayed upon canvas
than by the word-painting of the lecturer!   They never
can be forgotten.   He spoke of the pelvis as a divine
idea.   Meigs possessed all the requisites for success upon
the stage—remarkable powers of mimicry, great enthusiasm, and a strong perception of the ludicrous.   In the
lecture-room he was the best actor I have ever seen; and
it is deeply to be regretted that there are not more of such
teachers in the amphitheatre, especially in the afternoon,
when the student, exhausted by the fatigues of the day,
finds it difficult to keep awake.

The lack of system in his lectures was conspicuous.
Owing to this circumstance he often repeated himself, and
at times wandered sadly away from his theme.   Interesting as these digressions generally were, they did not fail
to detract from his merits as a public teacher, and thus
occasionally to form the subject of severe criticism on the
part of some of his more intelligent pupils.

Prejudice was an element deeply rooted in his character. Thus, for instance, he was a violent opponent of the use of chloroform as an anæsthetic. His opposition to it was founded, not upon personal experience, but upon the reports of medical journalists, who inconsiderately exaggerated its evil effects. Soon after the discovery of this agent by Sir James Y. Simpson, of Edinburgh, Meigs had four sheep brought into the amphitheatre, in order to afford his class, as he alleged, a practical illustration of its dangers. Each animal died—whether by accident or design is not known. But from such an experiment there was of course no appeal; the sheep had perished, and chloroform had done the work. He knew that I much preferred chloroform to ether, and he seldom met me on clinic days without exclaiming, "Well, Gross, are you going to administer chloroform this morning?" "Certainly, my dear friend," was the invariable answer. "Then, by ——, I hope you will kill your patient!" was the invariable rejoinder. On such occasions I often twitted him about his murdered sheep, adding, "You will find it hard when you die to pass the gates of St. Peter, opposed as you will be by vast flocks of sheep, the family, friends, and descendants of those you so unceremoniously and unkindly immolated upon the altar of science by purposely giving each an overdose of chloroform." A hearty laugh always followed this interchange of pleasantry as each turned away to attend to his business.

Meigs was all his life a non-believer in the infectious nature of puerperal fever, notwithstanding that for a time numerous facts demonstrative of the incorrectness of his belief almost daily stared him in the face. One Philadelphia obstetric practitioner alone had during one season in rapid succession nearly thirty cases of this disease, traceable from one house to another, the result beyond question of direct inoculation. Although Meigs saw some of these cases in consultation, he could not perceive the re-

lation of cause and effect between this sequence and infectious communication; but the attending physician did,
and he was obliged to leave the city in search of another
field. Professor Oliver Wendell Holmes's admirable monograph on this disease failed to convince him, and he finally
died a non-contagionist.

Meigs was undoubtedly conscientious in whatever he
did. He was not slow in reaching conclusions, and was
firm in maintaining them. He was of a warm temperament, and was inclined, I have sometimes thought, to
make his wishes bend to his will, his practice to his pre-
conceived notions. He was a strong advocate of the use
of the lancet, and I have it from good authority that he
sometimes carried the abstraction of blood to an irrational
extent.

Meigs was descended from New England stock. His
ancestors, as we are informed by his son, Dr. J. For-
syth Meigs, were people of moderate possessions, who, as
farmers, manufacturers, and hatters, "were well inured
to daily labor, and to habits of simplicity and economy."
Piety was one of their characteristic traits. We find, for
example, such names among them as Silence and Submit,
who were twins of his great-grandfather, born in 1711;
these were given, it is said, because on the arrival of the
first the father said "Silence!" to check any undue re-
joicing of the family; and on that of the second, moved
by his patient spirit, he said "Submit!" The name of
the grandfather of Charles was Return Meigs; and his own
middle name was bestowed upon him in remembrance of
an uncle, who had been called Delucena after a Spanish
gentleman. His father, who seems to have been a man
of considerable scholastic attainments, was for some time
Professor of Mathematics and Natural Philosophy at Yale
College; and subsequently he assisted in founding the University of Georgia at Athens, of which he was the first
president. Charles was born in February, 1792, in the

island of St. Georges, one of the group of the Bermudas. In 1809 Meigs graduated in the University of Georgia. He then studied medicine under Dr. Thomas Hanson Marshall Fendall, with whom he remained three years, serving as apothecary boy as well as apprentice, and performing for his master various kinds of labor, such as bleeding, cupping, blistering, and manufacturing a certain plaster, "of which he used to make, with long-suffering watchfulness and stirrings, great quantities." Afterwards he attended the lectures in the University of Pennsylvania, which in 1817, two years after his last course, conferred upon him the degree of M. D. Selecting Augusta, Georgia, as his place of residence, he soon acquired business; but, owing to the aversion of Mrs. Meigs to the institution of slavery, he remained there only two years, when he settled permanently in Philadelphia. The loss of his first patient, which occurred soon after he began practice, was to him a source of indescribable misery, over which, in after life, he used to be greatly amused. The patient was a person of considerable influence, the subject of an attack of fever, for which the youthful doctor, in conformity with the practice of the day, freely bled and purged him, and thus no doubt helped to ease him of his sufferings! It was the custom in that part of the country, when a person of any note died, for the physician to walk in the funeral procession. Meigs, as I heard him more than once relate the story, would rather have been flogged than have been seen in such a position; but there was no escape for him. He had to go; and as he marched along he thought that all eyes were turned upon him, and that the treatment of his late patient was the subject of general comment and criticism. Of course he considered himself ruined for life, and was accordingly most wretched until he found that the case had not only done him no harm, but had actually been of service to him in introducing him into business. The manner in which he used to describe this scene was most ludicrous, and afforded a happy illustration of his dramatic powers.

During his residence at Augusta a malady, supposed to have been what was then called peripneumonia, prevailed somewhat extensively, with considerable mortality, and caused great alarm among its inhabitants. The father of Dr. Meigs, writing in 1816 to his friend Dr. Drake, of Cincinnati, says, " My son Charles, who is a physician at Augusta, tells me that the diseases there are most exceedingly sthenic, so much so that he has frequently been compelled to bleed four, six, eight, and once thirteen times." Now it is not more than sixty miles direct from Augusta to Columbia, South Carolina, where, the son informs the father, the constitution of the atmosphere is so asthenic that one bleeding is often sufficient to produce death.

Practice came to Dr. Meigs very slowly in Philadelphia, and it was only by the strictest economy that he was able to keep his head above water. His wife's family, although very respectable, was of no service in securing him business, and several years elapsed before he began to float upon the surface. These years were not spent in idleness or in indifference, but in hard professional study, in the acquisition of general literature, and in a review of his classical knowledge. He also busied himself in drawing and in modelling in wax, accomplishments which he found serviceable afterwards in illustrating his lectures. He gave way to no repining, to no misgiving; he knew that it was only necessary for him to wait, to work, and to be patient. He had the future in his grasp. He gradually collected around him a coterie of genial medical friends, who remained true to him during the remainder of his life. He displayed his powers as a debater in the Philadelphia Medical Society and in the College of Physicians of Philadelphia; became one of the editors of the North American Medical and Surgical Journal; delivered for several years lectures on Midwifery in what was known

as the Philadelphia School of Medicine; and in 1831
published a translation of Velpeau's celebrated treatise
on Midwifery. His first original work was Philadelphia
Practice of Midwifery, which appeared in 1838 in a duodecimo volume of less than four hundred pages. Four
years afterwards this work was reproduced, greatly improved, in the form of a large octavo. It was followed in
1847 by Woman, Her Diseases and Remedies, written in
the form of letters addressed to medical students; and in
1849 by Obstetrics, the Science and the Art, a continuation,
with additions and emendations, of his former treatises upon
this subject. In 1850 he published a small volume on Certain Diseases of Children; and in 1854 a treatise on Acute
and Chronic Diseases of the Neck of the Uterus. In the
same year he produced an elaborate work on Childbed
Fever. He contributed to the Transactions of the American Medical Association an able paper on Fibroid Tumors
of the Uterus; and translated a Treatise on the Diseases
and Special Hygiene of Females, by Colombat de l'Isère,
which was a closely-printed octavo volume of more than
seven hundred pages. Many of these works reached a
second, and some a third, if not a fourth, edition. The
question may well be asked, How did this man accomplish
all this vast labor? Our astonishment is increased when
we reflect upon the fact that he had for many years an
immense practice in obstetrics, and that he was for a long
time the acknowledged leader in this branch of the profession, not only in Philadelphia, but in the United States.
Meigs wisely improved his time. He took care of the
minutes, and let the hours take care of themselves. It
was his wont when he was called to a case of labor to
carry his pen and paper with him, and to write in an adjoining room until his services were needed. He rarely
frequented the social circle; and, although he was for a
number of years a member of the Wistar Party and of a
medical club, he was seldom seen at their meetings.

2—44

In 1841 Meigs was appointed Professor of Obstetrics and of the Diseases of Women and Children in the Jefferson Medical College of Philadelphia, a position which he filled until the spring of 1861, when he retired from public life, and in great measure from practice. He had resigned his chair one year previously; but he was induced, at the earnest entreaty of his colleagues, by whom he was greatly beloved, to lecture another session, inasmuch as the person who had been elected as his successor was unable, by reason of ill health, to enter upon his duties. He now, like a wise man, bought for himself a small farm, some twelve miles from the city, which he called Hamanassett, after a little stream in Connecticut, hard by where his forefathers had settled, erected a house and other buildings, and gave himself up to agricultural pursuits, the contemplation of philosophy, and the recreations of literature. For the first few years he occasionally came to town to prescribe for some of his old patients and familiar friends; but even this business became irksome to him, and his visits grew gradually less and less frequent, until at length even his children and grandchildren seldom saw him. It was in this retired and tranquil spot that death overtook him. Only two days before the event he presided at a Sunday dinner with his accustomed grace and vivacity, attended by two of his sons from distant parts of the country. On the morning of the 22d of June, 1869, when all nature was redolent of life, and the air laden with the fragrance of the rose and the honeysuckle, this great and good man was found dead in his bed, having apparently died without a struggle, at the age of seventy-seven years.

Thus, to borrow a felicitous expression, a happy old age concluded his life, at once brilliant and useful. For many years Meigs had suffered severe pain in one of his legs, but, like a Christian gentleman, seldom made known his ailments to excite the sympathy of his family. He was all his life a great reader, and was especially fond of

works which treated of the history of the human race.
His favorite author was Count de Gobineau, with whom
for a long time he carried on a correspondence, and whose
novel, entitled L'Abbaye de Typhaines, he translated only
a short time before his death. Medical works he had come
to regard with positive aversion. He never considered his
education finished. At Hamanassett he kept regularly for
several years a diary of the products of his farm, in which
he noted the proper season for planting seeds, the ripening
of crops, the nature of soils, and other matters of interest.
He would speak with rapture of his little world. When
asked how his new house at Hamanassett was looking,
he would exclaim, "Looking! By George, it looks like
Windsor Castle!" He often invited me to visit him at
this spot, which added so much to the happiness of his
declining years; but as no day was ever set for the visit
I never went—a circumstance which I have always regretted.

Meigs had no doubt a just appreciation of the value of
his professional services, although it must be admitted that
he did not place a sufficient money estimate upon them.
His fees were generally miserably low, not at all in proportion to the time and labor bestowed upon his patients. He
said to me one morning that he had just come from a visit
to a lady from Texas, whom, after she had been in the
hands of a number of prominent physicians, he had cured
in a few weeks of a very troublesome ailment. He asked
me what I thought he ought to charge her. I replied that
such services ought to command at least two hundred and
fifty dollars, if not twice that sum, especially if the lady
was rich. "That will never do," he added. "I cannot
in conscience take more than twenty-five or thirty dollars;"
and off he went. Such a man could not have become rich
if he had practised medicine a hundred years.

BENJAMIN WINSLOW DUDLEY.

1785–1870.

IN January, 1841, in company with my colleague, Professor Daniel Drake, I visited Lexington, Kentucky, to gratify a long-cherished desire to see Dr. Benjamin Winslow Dudley. He had occupied the chair of Anatomy and Surgery ever since the opening, in 1819, of the Medical Department of Transylvania University, and during all that time had very unwisely lectured nine times a week. Whether the motive of this undue labor was vanity, or what is worse, jealousy—to prevent the introduction into the school of an anatomist who might eventually become a rival—I am unable to affirm. Certain it is that it would have been easy to find competent men for this field of labor. But from the beginning of the school Dudley had his own way. His motto was *Cæsar aut nullus;* and it was not until late in life that he permitted Dr. James Bush, his late Demonstrator, to fill the chair.

At the time to which I refer he was at the height of his reputation as a surgeon. He had no rival in the West, and, with the exception of Mott, scarcely any in the East. Physick had been dead for several years. Dudley's lecture on the day of my visit was on the anatomy of the muscles of the forearm, and a more puerile discourse I have never listened to. It would hardly have been creditable to a tyro in anatomy. All that he did was to give the origin and insertion of the muscles. He did not refer to their functions or to their relative position—matters of so great importance in a practical point of view.

Dudley was well skilled in the use of the knife. He was an excellent mechanical surgeon, or, in other words, operator. Of surgical pathology he knew little or nothing; certainly his teaching was far in arrear of the existing state of the science. His lectures on Surgery, however, were always interesting, from the fact that they abounded in practical matter, the result of wide and ripe experience. His forte was lithotomy, in which he was for a long time *facile princeps.* For many years he nearly monopolized this department of practice, attracting from all sections of the Mississippi Valley patients affected with calculous diseases. It is said that he performed lithotomy altogether two hundred and twenty-five times, with a loss of only six or seven cases. I have, however, never given credence to this statement, because it was not verified by statistics. Dudley kept no record of his cases, of their sex, age, residence, or of their condition before or after operation. As most of his patients came from a distance, they were all lodged in one building, which was in charge of an ignorant steward. This man acted as nurse, and when interrogated about the number of cases operated on in any given time he helplessly racked his brain for an answer. Doubtless the success of the surgeon was great; and one cannot help regretting that so much uncertainty hangs over the matter. Dr. Bush, who assisted in many of these operations, might have cleared up the mystery; but he never did. Dudley's favorite method was the lateral, which was performed with the gorget.

Dudley did some good work in the ligation of arteries, chiefly limited, however, to those of the neck; and he may be regarded as the pioneer in this country in the use of the trephine for the cure of epilepsy dependent upon injury of the skull, in which his success was remarkable. He laid great stress upon the preparation of his patients in all operations involving danger—a practice now certainly too much neglected. His after-treatment was equally a matter of solicitude with him. Chicken and bran broths were his favorite articles of diet, and tartar emetic and calomel his favorite remedies for controlling excitement and correcting the secretions. In spinal curvature his practice was to keep the patient

rigidly in the recumbent posture, upon a diet barely sufficient to sustain life.   He was a great stickler for the roller
in the treatment of fractures and external inflammations,
and was an expert in its application; but some of his
pupils who were less dexterous in its employment committed errors which led occasionally to loss of limb, of
reputation, and even of life, followed by vexatious suits
for malpractice.

Dudley was one of those men who never correct the
deficiencies of their early education.   His style as a writer
was execrable, and his thoughts were clothed in ungrammatical English.   Some of his letters would have disgraced
a school-boy.   His contributions to surgical literature were
limited to a few articles, consisting mainly of brief details
of cases, published in the Transylvania Journal of Medicine.   As a teacher he was earnest and attractive.   He had
a clear, sonorous voice, with sufficient compass to be heard
in the most remote parts of the amphitheatre.   He was
of medium height, well built, and had a good head, with
brownish hair.   He had an infusion of French mannerism.
He was always neatly dressed, and never wore an overcoat or a glove, even in the coldest weather.   In 1840
he came very near losing his life from blood-poisoning,
caused by a puncture in his hand while engaged in amputating the arm of an elderly man affected with a malignant tumor.   His sufferings were severe and exhausting,
and a long time elapsed before he regained his health
and strength.   His death occurred in 1870, in the eighty-
fifth year of his age, preceded by a state of mental imbe-
cility bordering on fatuity.   For nearly thirty years he
had been the reigning monarch of the Medical Department of Transylvania University, which, in 1817, along
with Blythe, Brown, Richardson, Short, and Caldwell, he
organized, but which did not go into operation until two
years later.   Notwithstanding the many adverse influences
to which it was exposed, the school was in a very flourish-

ing condition until the secession, in 1837, of Caldwell, Cooke, and Yandell, who thenceforth, with Drake, threw all their strength into the University of Louisville, the increasing prosperity of which finally led to the downfall of the Lexington College. Soon after this, Dudley retired to private life at his country-seat, but not without allowing his name to head the annual announcement of the Kentucky School of Medicine, which was established as a rival of the University of Louisville, with one of his nephews, Dr. Ethelbert Dudley, and Dr. James Bush, his old and fast friend, at the head of the Faculty.

Dr. Dudley was a native of Kentucky, and graduated from the Medical Department of the University of Pennsylvania in 1806. In 1810 he went to Europe, where for four years he availed himself of the instruction of such masters as Abernethy, Cooper, and Cline of London, and Boyer, Larrey, Marjolin, and Dubois of Paris. Soon after his return he rose to eminence and usefulness. He had many private pupils, hardly one of whom became a great surgeon. His teachings, as I have often heard it said, tended rather to repress than to inspire confidence in the use of the knife on the part of his young disciples. He was not a student. Medical books had no charm for him; and his practice was essentially routine.

CHAPTER XIII.

GEORGE D. PRENTICE.

1802–1870.

I WENT to Louisville in the autumn of 1840 as Professor
of Surgery in its medical school, and had been in the
city only a few days when I received a call from this
widely-known journalist, whose acquaintance I was very
desirous of making. The ten minutes he sat with me
passed rapidly and pleasantly. Mr. Prentice was of medium stature, with a round face, dark eyes, and a good
forehead. His gentle voice, genial manners, and sweet
laugh did not correspond with the impression which I had
derived from reading his incisive and often abusive edi-
torials. His quick, abrupt movements denoted a man of
great mental activity, who was not likely to put off until
to-morrow anything that should be done to-day. After
this interview I saw him frequently, indeed often daily,
during the years which I spent in the delightful society
of Louisville. After my removal to Philadelphia he did
not fail to visit my family and to partake of my hospitality whenever he came to the East, whether on pleasure
or on business.

For sixteen years I was a constant reader of Mr. Prentice's paper, the celebrated Louisville Journal; and if I had
not known the editor personally, I should have been led to

suppose from the perusal of his political articles that he was a Mephistopheles, a fiend incarnate. But he had a heart as tender as that of a child. His castigations were a trick of the trade. He never spared his enemies or political opponents. He took delight in unveiling the most secret histories of their lives. No moral anatomist or surgeon ever wielded a sharper knife, or more keenly exposed the vital organs. He often pounced upon his adversary unawares. But there were times when, in apparent simplicity of heart, he forewarned him of his intentions, and thus afforded him an opportunity of retreating or retracting. This asperity, which gave the Louisville Journal a national reputation, often brought upon Prentice the severest denunciations, and involved him in many bitter feuds and personal rencounters, in which, however, strange to say, he never sustained any serious injury. Cutting sarcasm and personal vituperation were his principal weapons of offence and defence. He was utterly fearless, if not reckless. A rival editor, during a popular excitement, sent a belligerent card to his office, and received the following reply: "Tell Mr. Hughes I will be down as soon as I have loaded my pistols." It is hardly necessary to add that the offended gentleman was not there when Mr. Prentice reached the front door. On another occasion Prentice considered himself aggrieved by a paragraph reflecting upon his conduct, and he warned the editor that, if he did not retract the language, he would be held personally responsible. No apology came, and the result was an exchange of two shots, in which each combatant was slightly wounded. The only Kentucky editor who was anything like a match for Mr. Prentice, or who could successfully parry arms with him, was Shadrach Penn. It was not uncommon for them to abuse each other like cutthroats in their respective papers, and then to settle their quarrels over a mint julep or a glass of Bourbon, for which both had, unfortunately, too great a fondness. Prentice could forgive an insult, or even an attempt upon his life, as readily as any one. A man met him on the sidewalk, and deliberately fired at his heart. Prentice knocked him down and placed his foot upon him. "Get up, you rascal!" he said; "I don't care to kill you." Many years afterwards, at a watering-place, the assailant, now a mere spectre, exhausted by consumption, thanked him for his life.

Preston, Connecticut, was his native town. Graduating at Brown University in 1823, he was for a while in charge of a school at Hartford, and then studied law; but, finding the pursuit uncongenial to his tastes, which were strongly literary, he joined, in 1828, Mr. John G. Whittier in the management of the New England Weekly Review. A few years afterwards he went to Kentucky, where he established the Louisville Journal, with which his fame is identified, and which he edited until a short time before his death. He was a brilliant writer, a wit, a humorist, a punster, and a poet. He was the author of a Life of Henry Clay, with whom he was long on intimate personal relations; of many fugitive poems; and of a book of his own witticisms, entitled Prenticiana, issued in 1859. For many years he was identified with the Whig party, of which he was for a long time the great leader in the West. He espoused the Know-Nothing party, and continued, despite the remonstrances of his friends, to support it until its downfall. At the outbreak of the Rebellion he placed himself on the side of the Union, and exerted all his influence to prevent the secession of his adopted State. After the war was over he advocated the unconditional admission of the Southern States.

George D. Prentice became poor. Intemperance deranged the business interests of his Journal, and he had the mortification, late in life, to see it placed in other hands, while he himself received an insignificant salary as associate editor. He died at Louisville in January,

1870. Since that period the paper, under the name of the Courier-Journal, has had different editors, all of more or less ability, but none equal, in point of talent and wit, to Mr. Watterson, who has for some years been in charge of it. Mr. Prentice was married in 1839, if I mistake not, to Miss Benham, a daughter of Judge Benham, of Cincinnati, a warm-hearted, generous, and accomplished woman, by whom he had two sons. A good Life of him has been written by his friend, G. W. Griffin, who was our consul at Copenhagen.

Mr. Prentice, in order to improve his financial condition, became an itinerant lecturer. For this purpose he visited the principal cities of the Eastern and Northern States. But his success was indifferent; his voice was devoid of compass, his style was inanimate, and he seldom drew a full house.

GUNNING S. BEDFORD.

1806–1870.

THE name of Gunning S. Bedford will not soon die, although he was not a popular man with his medical contemporaries, many of whom were in the habit of depreciating his talents and skill. Outside of the profession, however, he had many staunch and devoted friends, and he enjoyed for many years a large and substantial practice. One cause of his unpopularity was doubtless his energetic, enterprising disposition. It was said that he was not always fair in consultations, or overscrupulous in taking patients in charge of other physicians. Of this I know nothing from personal observation. In his manners he reminded me more of Dr. George McClellan than of any other person I ever came in contact with. Like the great Philadelphia surgeon, it was difficult for him to sit still, or remain for any length of time in one place. Like McClellan, too, he was a constant and rapid talker, and had an active brain. Whatever his enemies may say of him, it is certain that he was a man of much ability, and that he achieved, despite the prejudices against him, a high reputation.

A great hue and cry was raised against Bedford on account of his college clinics. He was the first obstetrician on this continent who dared to take a woman into the amphitheatre and employ the speculum before his class. For this practice, which now obtains in our best schools, he was severely taken to task both by the medical and lay press of the country. The exposure was denounced as an outrage upon decency, and some persons went so far as to declare that the author ought to be indicted as a nuisance. A healthful reaction soon took place. The poor women thus treated were the best certificates of the success of the method. The news of their cure spread to their neighbors, who in turn came to swell the clientele, until at no distant day the gynæcological clinic of Bedford became the centre of attraction, not only to the physicians of New York, but to physicians all over the country. Even some of its violent detractors occasionally visited the clinic, and at length, as might have been supposed, all opposition to it ceased. To Bedford, therefore, is due the honor of establishing gynæcological teaching upon a solid basis in the United States. Dr. White, of Buffalo, was one of the first to follow in the footsteps of the New York professor, not, however, without for a time encountering much opposition. There is no doubt that the clinics of Bedford greatly contributed to the general extension of the use of the speculum and to the prosperity of the University of New York, of which he was one of the most brilliant teachers. Before his class he was an enthusiast. His examinations were elaborate, and he took great pains to explain their results; but he never lost or bewildered either himself or his pupils in side issues. So admirable were these lectures that I was often tempted to attend them when I had leisure. The amphitheatre was always crowded, and no one left it without feeling that he had been instructed. If Bedford had any fault as a clinical instructor, it was his mannerism; but this was a part of his nature.

Bedford was born in Baltimore in 1806. He pursued his classical studies at St. Mary's College and graduated in 1825. His medical degree was obtained, I believe, in the University of Maryland. Soon after he left his Alma Mater he was elected a professor in a medical school at Charleston, South Carolina, and afterwards in the Albany Medical College. In 1836 he settled in New York; and in 1840, on the organization of the Medical Department of the University of New York, he was appointed Professor of Midwifery and of the Diseases of Women and Children—a position which he occupied until within a few years of his death, when ill health compelled him to relinquish it.

In 1850, as Mott's successor in the chair of Surgery, I became associated with Bedford. He received me most cordially; and I spent many happy hours with him and with his amiable family during my short residence in New York. He had always agreeable company about him; and his little dinners were of a *recherché* kind, composed of choice viands, well prepared and well served. A lady of Charleston, a grateful patient, had sent him that winter half a dozen mast-fed hams, of delicious flavor and tender fibre, such as might well have provoked the envy of an epicure.

Bedford was the author of two works of note in their day—the one a systematic treatise on Midwifery, and the other Lectures on the Diseases of Women. Even now they are much consulted by the profession. They are the more valuable because they are based upon prolonged personal observation. The ample opportunities afforded by the gynæcological clinics of the University of New York are here appropriately utilized. The style of these works is at once lucid and graphic.

Dr. Bedford was of medium height, with a good head, a handsome countenance, and agreeable manners. He was a gay flatterer, courted popularity, and was a decided favorite with women. He died in 1870, after having suffered for several years from the effects of apoplexy, which caused a halt both in his speech and in one-half of his body a few months before his death. I met him for the last time at Long Branch. He was a wreck. He was restless, sought solitude, and was disinclined to converse. Evidently he was ill at ease with his condition, well knowing what it foreshadowed. He left an estimable wife and several sons. One of his sons was elected, at an early age, to a judgeship in the city of New York; his fearless conduct on the bench displeased the rowdies, and when his term of office expired he was not renominated. Another son is a member of the medical profession.

During the early part of his connection with the University of New York Dr. Bedford delivered an introductory lecture. A few days afterwards this lecture became the subject of severe criticism and animadversion on account of the fact that it had been largely copied, *verbatim et literatim*, without acknowledgment, from a volume on Popular Physiology by Dr. Southwood Smith, a recent English writer, whose book was in the hands of many physicians on this side of the Atlantic. The address and the borrowed matter appeared in full in the New York Herald in double columns; and one may well imagine with what avidity the paper was read by the profession and the public. How the inverted comma happened to be omitted in the printed copy was never explained. Inasmuch as Bedford was an able writer, the plagiarism was inexcusable.

GEORGE C. BLACKMAN.

1819–1871.

IN 1854 Dr. Blackman succeeded Dr. Baxley in the chair of Surgery in the Medical College of Ohio. He was a native of Newtown, Connecticut, and a graduate of the College of Physicians and Surgeons of the City of New York, of the class of 1840. He subsequently pursued his studies in London, working heroically under difficulties. His means were so limited that he was compelled to live on twopenny rolls a day, and, to avoid the expense of fire, to keep himself warm with his bed-clothes. He worked his way back to this country on a Liverpool vessel as assistant surgeon, and soon after settled at Newburg, on the Hudson. There he rapidly obtained practice, wrote essays and reviews for medical journals, and translated Vidal's celebrated work on Venereal Diseases. In 1856 he brought out, with numerous additions and emendations, a new edition of Mott's Velpeau's Operative Surgery, a work in three bulky volumes, the reading of the proof of which alone was an immense labor. At Cincinnati he was an associate editor of a medical journal, and for many years a voluminous contributor to the periodical press. He was a rapid writer, a close thinker, and an acute and bitter critic. Naturally of an irascible, suspicious disposition, he delighted in controversy. His sensitive mind could not brook restraint or contradiction, and hence he often did and said what in his cooler moments he deeply regretted. He frequently brooded over sorrows which had no solid foundation, and at times almost yielded to despair. When his sun was clear and the air genial he could be as cheerful as any one. A man like Blackman could not have been an agreeable colleague, or even always agreeable in his own household. Men of this class, with unbalanced minds, moody, desponding, and variable as the wind, are often said to be men of genius.

Blackman wielded his scalpel with a bold and dashing hand. That he was at times reckless those who knew him best did not hesitate to assert. He served with credit during the late war, rendering important services, both as a surgeon and as a general practitioner, to the sick and wounded alike in the hospital and on the battlefield. His lectures were unequal in merit. He was not unfrequently erratic, he lacked system, and he was seldom punctual with his class. His best lectures were clinical. He was not a surgical pathologist, and I take for granted that a man with such a temperament and such habits could scarcely attain a high standard in his teaching. His fees varied greatly—sometimes inordinately low, and at others exorbitantly high. He enjoyed for years a large practice, but, through mismanagement, if not downright recklessness, he was often obliged to borrow money, and at last died poor, leaving his family destitute. One is sorry to be obliged to speak thus of so gifted a man. With a happily balanced mind, Blackman might have achieved fame. His vagaries were doubtless due to the fact that he was for a long time a martyr to dyspepsia and neuralgia; and there is reason to believe that he was not wholly free from the "opium habit." He died in 1871, at the age of fifty-two years. I have said that I knew him well. I was fond of him, and while I was not blind to his faults I appreciated his merits as a surgeon. When he was offered the vacant chair in the Medical College of Ohio, he came all the way to Louisville to consult me as to the propriety of accepting it; and I promptly advised him to do so. He was by far the ablest surgeon the college had ever had. John D. Godman, who for one session occupied the chair, was no surgeon; and Jesse Smith, a narrow-minded New Englander, was more famous for the manner in which he held his beefsteak in his hand as he rode on horseback through the streets of Cincinnati than for surgical skill or for ability as a teacher. James Staughton, the son of an eminent Philadelphia Baptist clergyman, was a weak man, who was cut off prematurely in 1833 by an attack of Asiatic cholera. He was succeeded by Alban Smith, better known by his changed name of Alban Goldsmith, who was very inefficient as a teacher, although he possessed a moderate degree of skill and boldness as an operator. At the time Goldsmith was brought into notice by Eberle he was living at Louisville, and had acquired some notoriety as a former partner of Ephraim McDowell, the ovariotomist. I saw much of him during my connection with the College as Demonstrator of Anatomy. He was vain, shallow, conceited. His lectures were largely made up of verbatim readings from the works of Cooper and other foreign authors, the needed book often lying open before him during his hour. After a connection with the school for three years, he suddenly disappeared; and every one who knew him was amazed to hear that he had turned up as Professor of Surgery in the College of Physicians and Surgeons of New York. At the end of two sessions he was found to be a failure, and Willard Parker became his successor.

ARCHBISHOP SPALDING.

1810–1872.

I PROFOUNDLY appreciate the charitable deeds of the priests and the sisterhood of the Catholic Church. I have seen enough of both to satisfy me that they are among the most unselfish and the most self-sacrificing of people, never wearying in doing good, always at work in relieving the poor and destitute, in comforting the sick and the dying, in erecting asylums for the orphan and the helpless, and in planting the standard of Christianity wherever there is a ray of hope of doing good. Many priests and several bishops and archbishops of this church have done me the honor to select me as their professional adviser, and I have invariably found them to be considerate and generous, ever ready to do me a favor. I never heard them make an unkind remark about Protestants or the Protestant Churches. During my residence at Louisville I was almost in daily intercourse, as Surgeon to St. Joseph's Hospital, with the Sisters of Charity; and I shall ever feel grateful for their devotion to my patients; for the sacrifices they underwent whenever an important operation or a case of serious illness needed unusual care; and for their kind coöperation whenever I offered suggestions for the improvement of the institution. No murmur ever escaped the lips of these noble women. They were always in good humor, always kind and thoughtful, always intent upon the scrupulous performance of their duties as nurses and as Christian women. It is only of late years that Protestants seem to have become aware of the influence which the Sisters of Charity, as they are called, have exercised in making proselytes for their church. Instead of contenting themselves with distributing tracts, these sisters wait on the sick, feed the hungry, comfort the weary, and watch at the bedside of the dying.

This train of thought was suggested to me by the reception from my good friend Archbishop Wood of a copy of the Life of M. J. Spalding, Archbishop of Baltimore, by his nephew, J. L. Spalding, now Bishop of Springfield, Illinois. Archbishop Spalding was for many years my warm personal friend. During my residence at Louisville I was brought into frequent association with him. I attended him in more than one severe illness, and he was always a welcome, as well as a most agreeable, visitor at my house. After his removal to Baltimore I met him whenever I visited my children in that city; and on several occasions I enjoyed the pleasure of his company at my table during his visits to Philadelphia. On one of these his grace

met me at breakfast with a party of distinguished ladies
and gentlemen, among whom were Mrs. Chapman Coleman and my daughter Mrs. B. F. Horwitz; Bishop, now
Archbishop, Wood; Henry C. Carey; Daniel Dougherty;
and Dr. Foley, now Bishop of Chicago. Mrs. Gross was
absent on account of illness. The Archbishop talked a
great deal, was very facetious, and related excellent anecdotes. Mrs. Coleman and my daughter added much to
the interest of the entertainment. Mr. Carey and Archbishop Wood did not have much to say, and it was only
now and then that Foley took part in the conversation.
Dr. Bittinger, a chaplain in the navy, abounded in anecdote. Mr. Dougherty was, as usual, full of wit and humor.
Among the dishes was one of which Archbishop Spalding was very fond—broiled frogs—which he often ate at
my house in Kentucky, and which, in my opinion, is
always deserving of a special blessing. It was at this
meeting that Archbishop Spalding gave Mrs. Coleman an
account of a speech delivered by her father, Mr. John
J. Crittenden, at the great Southwestern Whig Convention assembled at Nashville in August, 1840. The speech
seems to have been one of the Kentucky statesman's happiest efforts. "Though thirty years have elapsed," said
the narrator, "I have not forgotten the deep impression
made upon my mind by one of the most brilliant and im-
passioned bursts of oratory it has ever been my privilege
to listen to either in Europe or America. The whole scene
is before me now, as fresh and vivid as it was on that
morning when I stood enraptured by your father's eloquence. I still hear his silvery voice. I still hear the
acclamations of thirty thousand people, whose very souls
he commanded and bore along with him throughout his
masterly oration."

The father of Spalding was a farmer, and originally
very poor; but long before he reached his fiftieth year
he had become independent by his thrift and hard work.

His ancestors, partly English, and partly Scotch or Scotch-Irish, had emigrated from Maryland to Kentucky at a time when the latter State formed part of Virginia, and when it was everywhere infested by Indians, who made frequent incursions into the settlements of the whites, killing their inhabitants, burning their cabins, and carrying off their horses and cattle. The future prelate was born in May, 1810, on the banks of a little river known as the Rolling Fork, a short distance from Lebanon. He was one of twenty-one children. His father was married three times. His first wife, a sweet and gentle woman, had the honor of giving birth to Martin, who was so frail, so delicate, and so sickly that it was thought he could not long survive. The mother made a great pet of her son, treated him with much tenderness, and always called him her little bishop, probably never dreaming that he was destined to become a burning and shining light in God's sanctuary. When the boy was hardly six years of age the mother died, leaving him in the care of his eldest sister, herself a mere child, who spared no exertion to develop his constitution and to train him in the knowledge and love of God. Under her guidance he soon became fond of books, learned rapidly, and, in a single day, near the close of his eighth year, made himself master of the multiplication table. At the age of fourteen he was appointed, by Father Byrne, the founder of St. Mary's College, near Lebanon, Professor of Mathematics in that institution; and creditably, it is said, did the youth discharge the duties of his chair. After having been at this college five years, Spalding graduated with distinguished honor, and then entered the Theological Seminary at Bardstown, having long before determined to consecrate his life to the service of the Catholic Church. At the age of twenty he was sent to Rome as a student at the Propaganda, where, by his correct deportment, close attention to his studies, and fervent piety, he soon won the

esteem and affection of his teachers. He had not only
great fondness for the study of languages, but remarkable
aptitude for acquiring a knowledge of them; and he tells
us how delighted he was whenever he caught a glimpse of
the celebrated Mezzofanti, who was a frequent visitor at the
Propaganda, who spoke more than thirty languages with
ease and fluency, and who, it is said, could acquire a new
language in a few days. It was not uncommon, says the
young Kentucky student, to hear him converse in seven
or eight minutes in seven or eight different tongues.
Spalding was an excellent Latin scholar; and he spoke
Italian, French, and Spanish with facility and accuracy.
Of his progress as a student at the Propaganda, we may
form some idea from the fact that he publicly defended for
the doctor's cap two hundred and fifty-six propositions,
which were founded upon certain theological treatises and
upon the canon law. He hurled defiance at his opponents,
all of whom were men of great learning and ability, and
received at the end of the contest the congratulations of
the cardinals, who sat in judgment upon the merits of the
disputation. From the arena he was triumphantly carried
off by his fellow-students.

Such was the student-life of Spalding in Rome. Surely
no man of ordinary capacity could have accomplished so
much in so short a time. His success at the Propaganda
implies not only vast industry, but extensive erudition,
deep thought, a well-disciplined mind, great subtilty in argument, extraordinary courage, and an uncommon amount
of native talent. He left the Eternal City in 1834, at the
age of twenty-four, having been ordained priest a few days
previously to his departure.

His fame as a scholar and as an able and earnest theolo-
gian had preceded his arrival in the United States. His
first charge was the cathedral at Bardstown, from which
he was afterwards transferred to that at Lexington, then
known as the Athens of the West. Upon the removal

of the See of the diocese of Kentucky to Louisville Spalding was recalled to his former charge at Bardstown, where he remained until 1844, when he was appointed Vicar-General of Louisville. Here an ample field was opened to him. Bishop Flaget and his coadjutor, Bishop Chabrat, were bending under the infirmities of old age. Bishop Chabrat, besides, was laboring under partial loss of sight, which in a few years terminated in total blindness. In due time Spalding became the successor of Bishop Flaget; and until his appointment to the Archbishopric of Baltimore, in 1864, his life was one of incessant toil and of arduous devotion to the interests of his people. His popularity was very great, not only among the members of his own church, but among those of other Christian denominations. He had pleasant ways about him, was fond of telling anecdotes, and had a laugh that was almost infectious. Spalding was nearly five feet ten inches in height, with broad shoulders, a fine round face, broad and expansive forehead, a hazel eye, and a slightly olive complexion. His hair was bushy, and in his youth it was raven black. In his later years he was somewhat inclined to corpulency. His hands and feet were small and well-shaped. He was one of the most single-hearted men I have ever known. He had a special sympathy for the colored race, and after the close of the war he took a lively interest in establishing schools for emancipated slaves. His household affairs were conducted in the most orderly manner. System and punctuality were two of his cardinal virtues. He was very fond of children, often corresponded with them, and was never more happy or more animated than when he was in their society. He was fond of a good dinner, and did not always refuse a glass of wine; but no one ever abhorred intemperate eating and drinking more than he. During his residence in Kentucky he established a colony of Trappist monks, an order of priests for which he had great respect, founded an institution for

the deaf and dumb, and advocated the establishment of
parochial schools, his heart's wish being that every child
in his diocese should receive the blessings of a good education.

He was an indefatigable writer. He was the founder,
and for a long time the editor, of the Catholic Guardian,
a magazine devoted to the interests of the Church and to
the dissemination of useful knowledge. With this magazine he retained his connection until 1858. He published
Sketches of Kentucky, and a Life of his venerable friend
and predecessor, Bishop Flaget, who died in 1850. His
most elaborate production was his History of the Protestant Reformation in Germany, Switzerland, and Other
Countries, issued, in 1860, in answer to D'Aubigné's celebrated work. His Evidences of Catholicity has passed
through five editions. Another work which cost him
much labor was an introduction to the translation of Dar-
ras's Church History. He was a copious contributor to
the periodical press. As a lecturer he attracted large and
attentive audiences wherever he went; and there was not
a large city in the Union which in that capacity he did not
visit. He had a remarkable fondness for controversy, and
seldom failed to demolish his antagonist. Few men could
write a more caustic, learned, or critical review.

His health for many years was bad. He suffered much
from disorder of the liver and stomach, which was often
followed by great lassitude, and sometimes by severe suffering. In 1848 I attended him, along with the late Professor Henry Miller, of Louisville, for a violent attack
of dysentery, which brought him almost to death's door.
For many weeks he was confined to his bed, and several
months elapsed before he recovered. His last illness was
a violent attack of bronchitis, which was contracted during
a visit which he made to New York. For six weeks he
struggled with this painful disease, alternately better and
worse, until, on the 7th of February, 1872, he yielded up

his life at the age of sixty-two years. He succeeded Archbishop Kenrick in the See of Baltimore in 1864. In
1865, as apostolic delegate, he convened the second national Plenary Council at Baltimore, presiding, at the request of the Pope, over its deliberations. It was at this
meeting that he presented an elaborate and learned Manual
of the American Catholic Canon Law. Five years afterwards he took a prominent part in the Vatican Council,
"in which he urged immediate action on the subject of
papal infallibility, but contended that it should be indirect
and implied rather than positive and affirmed, but finally,
in union with the other American prelates, yielded in favor
of the latter."

I have thus dwelt at some length upon the life and
character of Archbishop Spalding, because of the warm
friendship that had existed so long between us, and because I knew him to be a most upright man, zealous of
good works.

SAMUEL HENRY DICKSON.

1798–1872.

DR. DICKSON entered the Faculty of the Jefferson Medical College in 1858 as the successor of Dr. John K.
Mitchell, who died the previous April. Austin Flint was
the choice of some of its members; but the wishes of the
Dean, who was all-powerful with the Board of Trustees,
prevailed, and every one acquiesced in the appointment.
Dickson was at the time a resident of Charleston, South
Carolina, where he was remarkably popular; and as nearly
two-fifths of our classes were drawn from beyond Mason
and Dixon's line, his selection was regarded, apart from
his eminent fitness for the position, as a compliment to
our Southern medical friends. But the war of the Rebellion soon followed his appointment. Dickson warmly
sympathized with the people whom he had so recently

left, and who had always so much loved and admired him, and the supply of Southern students was cut off. I have elsewhere stated that nearly two hundred left us in a body soon after the publication of the ordinance of secession. The consequence was that our income was greatly diminished, and Dickson, who was never rich, suffered more than any other member of the Faculty. In consequence of an indiscreet expression in an intercepted letter addressed by him to a friend in Mississippi he came near being shut up in Fort Lafayette. During these trying times he had our warmest sympathy. We all loved him, and did all we could to make him comfortable, if not happy. After the close of the war he accepted the inevitable; but the Southern students were unable to return to our school, and Dickson remained a poor man when, on the 31st of March, 1872, death overtook him. As a practitioner he never took root in the soil of Philadelphia. He had no family practice; and Philadelphia doctors shirk consultations if they can. His funeral was private. The pallbearers were his late colleagues, who laid him with heavy hearts in Woodlands Cemetery.

Dickson was a graduate of Yale College, and was a fine scholar and an excellent writer, with an intense love for the beautiful in nature and in art. In many respects he resembled Elisha Bartlett, so distinguished thirty years ago as a teacher and as a writer on Fever. Both were men of exquisite taste, of extensive literary attainments, classic writers, and easy, fluent, eloquent lecturers, who never failed to command the attention, the love, and the admiration of their pupils. I knew both well. They possessed in an eminent degree what some of the strong men whom I have known were destitute of—native refinement, gentlemanly instincts, winning manners, and high breeding. Dickson was not a clinical teacher; and his colleagues willingly gave him an assistant to assume that portion of the duty of his chair. His work on the Practice of Medicine passed through several editions, and was for a time extensively used as a text-book. He was the author of numerous brochures on medicine and other subjects, and he contributed much to the periodical press. His essay on Life, Sleep, Pain, and Death is a noted specimen of elegant composition. As a colleague and as a companion he was equally charming. He received his medical degree from the University of Pennsylvania in 1819, and a few years after was appointed Professor of Medicine in the Charleston College. For two years he occupied the chair of Medicine in the University of New York. He was of slender form, of medium height, with a good head and light-blue eyes. For many years he was an invalid from nephralgia, for which he was obliged constantly to take large doses of morphia. He was seldom seen on the street without gloves; and in company he was a centre of attraction. He was thrice married, and lost most of his children, I am told, by phthisis.

Dickson, despite his amiability and marked refinement, had a singular fondness for witnessing executions. He said to me, a few years before his death, that he had attended not fewer than thirty-nine of them, and that his desire was to witness more! If Macaulay may be believed, even William Penn was not free from a similar penchant. It is reported of the eccentric Selwyn that he went purposely to Paris to attend the execution of Damiens, who was torn with red-hot pincers, and finally quartered by four horses, for his attempt to assassinate Louis XV. As he was pressing up close to the scene of action, the executioner requested the crowd to make way for him: "*C'est un bourreau Anglais.*" "*Non, Monsieur,*" replied Selwyn; "*je n'ai pas cet honneur; je ne suis qu'un amateur.*" I have seen one man swing on the gibbet, and that sight was enough for me. He had choked his wife to death, and richly deserved his fate, which depended largely on the strength of my testimony.

SAMUEL JACKSON.

1787–1872.

SOON after my removal to Philadelphia I made the acquaintance of Dr. Samuel Jackson, then Professor of the Institutes of Medicine in the University of Pennsylvania. My acquaintance with him was never intimate, but I knew him sufficiently to appreciate his noble qualities and unselfish nature. In his last illness, which for a long time confined him to his chamber, I visited him repeatedly, and was deeply impressed with his *bonhomie*, his intelligence, and his culture. Years before he died he was confined to his room by partial paralysis of lower extremities, but he was in the enjoyment of his unimpaired intellectual faculties. Nothing seemed to disturb his serenity. His condition forcibly reminded me of the lines addressed by Mr. Smith, of London, to Mr. Strahan, the king's printer:

> " Your lower limbs seemed far from stone
>   When last I saw you walk;
>   The cause I presently found out
>   When you began to talk.
>   The power that props the body's length,
>   In due proportion spread,
>   In you mounts upwards; and the strength
>   All settles in the head."

Dr. Jackson was a charming conversationalist. It was always a great pleasure to me to listen to him. His face was one of the most beautiful I ever saw, radiant with gentleness and benevolence; his eyes were of a light blue; and his white hair hung in graceful ringlets over his magnificent head. At the time I became acquainted with him he was more than seventy years of age. His health had been failing for several years; but he was still able, with the help of a seat, to perform his duties as professor in the University. The students were warmly attached to him; and the school never had a more popular teacher, or one who was more beloved by his pupils. The hour occupied in his lecture passed pleasantly and rapidly; there was no yawning, no scratching of the floor, no looking at the watch; every one was deeply interested, and listened to him with profound attention. Though always entertaining and always interesting, it may be said that he was a specious rather than an instructive teacher, a popular rather than a great one. His mind, although well stored with knowledge, lacked profundity. Moreover, there was little in his day in physiology that was permanently settled. Hence it is not surprising that he should sometimes have said to his class, "Do not accept what I tell you this morning as at all established. Everything may be different a month or a year hence. For the present it is the best I can give you."

Dr. Jackson wielded a facile pen, but he has left behind him little that is worthy of his name. Most of his productions are details of cases, with running commentaries, which were published in the American Journal of the Medical Sciences. His Principles of Medicine, issued in 1832, was a failure, founded as it was upon the doctrines of Broussais, which are now regarded by scientific physicians as visionary speculations. The book, of which there are few copies extant, was severely handled by the critics, especially by Dr. Charles Caldwell, of Kentucky, who reviewed it unmercifully. When the edition was exhausted the author wisely allowed the work to perish. The mind of Dr. Jackson was too speculative to enable him to produce a great work on therapeutics or the practice of medicine.

I met Dr. Jackson but in two instances at the bedside. The first was a case of abdominal dropsy, accompanied by erysipelas of the lower extremities. Two other physicians were in attendance, and I was called in, as a last resort, to give my advice as to the treatment of the latter affection. I was then a comparative stranger in Philadelphia, and I shall never forget the cordial manner in which Jackson saluted me. The other case was one of my own—that of an old Kentucky friend, a lawyer, who, after having been for some years in successful practice at San Francisco, came to Philadelphia to consult me on account of a malignant tumor in the abdomen. Before he left the city, I said to him, "You have come a great distance for advice. Let me beg you, before you go, to call in some one to examine your case with me. Even if he should do you no good, the visit will be a source of gratification to your friends." "Whom would you suggest?" was the query. "Professor Jackson," I said "a physician who stands in the front of his profession, and whom everybody knows." We met the next morning, and I need not say that the case received a thorough investigation. As the professor rose to depart, my friend said, "Dr. Jackson, what is my indebtedness to you? I shall leave town to-morrow, and shall probably not see you again." "Five dollars," was the reply. When we reached the adjoining room, I said, "Dr. Jackson, what in the world made you ask so small a fee? The patient is rich, and he expected to pay you well for your services." "Well," was his rejoinder, and vividly do I recall it, "it is the —— Philadelphia custom ; Chapman got me into the habit, and I have never been able to extricate myself from it." Fifty dollars would have been a proper fee, and it would have been cheerfully paid.

Dr. Jackson was a native of Philadelphia, and after taking his degree he carried on for some time the business of an apothecary, attending also to a little practice. In 1827 he was appointed assistant, and in 1828 adjunct to Professor Chapman, performing the duties of lecturer on the Institutes of Medicine. In 1835, on the separation of the two branches taught by his chief, he was appointed Professor of the Institutes, a chair which he occupied until

advancing age and increasing infirmities compelled him to
retire from the school.   Dr. Francis Gurney Smith, who
was eminently worthy of the position, succeeded him.
Late in life Jackson married a pretty and intellectual
Scotch lady by the name of Christie, who, after the death
of her husband, in 1872, returned to her native country.
The marriage was a happy one.   This good man was for
a long time a martyr to neuralgia, and he often told his
class that there was no remedy so efficacious for the relief
of that disease as the soft and gentle touch of a lovely
woman's hand.   Who would not prefer such a prescription to every remedy that has ever been suggested for the
cure of this painful malady?

The funeral of Dr. Jackson was largely attended by his
friends and professional brethren.   An eloquent discourse
was delivered on the occasion by the Rev. Dr. Beadle, and
it made a deep impression upon his hearers.   It was just
such a discourse as a considerate clergyman would preach
at the funeral of a good man, free from cant, and consoling
to one's feelings.   When the eloquent divine descended
from the stairs, I grasped his hand and said, "If I die
before you, I hope you will do for me what you have just
done for our deceased friend."   To this he smilingly replied, "Certainly;" but death soon snatched him away
from us.   Dr. Beadle deservedly occupied a high position
as a pulpit orator and as an expounder of Christian charity
and Christian duty.

RENÉ LA ROCHE.

1795–1872.

RENÉ LA ROCHE was so fragile that it seemed as if a
heavy wind might readily blow him over.   It is said of
Philetas of Cos that he was so thin that leaden weights

were tied to his heels to prevent him from toppling over. My friend was almost as infirm in appearance as he. I knew La Roche personally for more than a third of a century, a part of this time intimately, and during all this period he retained his attenuated form. He had frequent attacks of indisposition, seldom of severe illness, and was often the subject of an annoying cough. To look at him without being acquainted with his habits and natural conformation one would have supposed that he was gradually sinking under the exhausting influences of pulmonary phthisis. Indeed, nearly twenty years before his death, his physician, Dr. Gerhard, an experienced and skilful auscultator, told him that he was laboring under tubercular deposits, which would in all probability gradually soften and destroy his life. La Roche not only long outlived the period assigned for his decease, but died of another disease. He had naturally a feeble constitution, and would never have grown fat if he had daily consumed half a dozen pounds of beef and a gallon of the best milk. Yet he could endure much physical exertion. During the latter years of his life his gait was often unsteady; and it was a beautiful sight to see him, as he slowly moved along, resting upon the arm of his son, Dr. Percy La Roche, who with filial piety was seldom absent from his side when he took his morning promenade on Walnut or Chestnut Street.

Dr. La Roche had an expressive and intellectual countenance, a handsome eye, and a good forehead, although his head was not very large. His highly-organized and well-balanced brain enabled him to perform a vast amount of labor. In his habits he was retiring; and he never seemed so happy as when he was in his library up to his elbow in his manuscripts. He was fond of his friends, and his friends were fond of him; and they can never forget his pleasant social visits, enlivened as they were by agreeable conversation and the recital of pertinent anecdotes, of which he had a supply of rare value. He was a charming conversationalist, always instructive, and free from affectation and pedantry. He was a great reader of light literature, was well informed respecting passing events, and could talk well upon almost any subject.

His style was perhaps at times a little diffuse; but his sentences were well rounded and constructed with classical accuracy. He was never verbose, in the true sense of that term, or given to rhetorical flourish. Simplicity and directness were among his chief excellences. He wrote slowly, took much pains in composition, and often cancelled whole pages if their style did not accord with his fastidious taste. Every important expression or statement was well weighed before it went into the printer's hands. He was one of the most erudite medical writers which our country has produced. His Yellow Fever is a monument of learning and of patient research, a work which has conferred the highest credit upon our profession. In my History of American Medical Literature, published in 1876, I thus spoke of it:

"As a work of profound erudition, at once complete and exhaustive, written in a scholarly style, and evincing the most patient and extraordinary research, the monograph on Yellow Fever, by Dr. La Roche, is without a rival in any language. The author was at great pains and expense in obtaining everything that had been written upon the subject, and, as he himself expresses it, neglected no opportunity of rendering himself practically familiar with the disease of which he thus became the distinguished historian. The facts borrowed from the numerous writers consulted by him seem to have been verified in every instance by personal reference to their works, a task in itself of immense labor—enough, indeed, to cause the eye and brain to ache and the hand to tremble."

This, assuredly, is high praise, but it is deserved. His library on yellow fever embraced the literature of all countries—the United States, Cuba, Mexico, South America, Spain, the East and West Indies, France, Germany, Italy, and Great Britain. One shudders to think that after the death of La Roche nearly the whole of this invaluable collection was put up at auction, and scattered to the winds. The College of Physicians of Philadelphia obtained, it is true, a portion of the books; but the question may well be asked, Why did it not secure all of them, and thus at once raise a monument to the original possessor and to its own sense of liberality? The world is made up of inconsistencies. If the question be asked why La Roche did not give his collection to this Society, the oldest of the kind in the country, the answer is that poverty compelled him to part with it.

La Roche was a liberal contributor to the periodical press, and for a number of years was one of the editors of the North American Medical and Surgical Journal, his associates in this enterprise having been Hugh L. Hodge, Benjamin H. Coates, Charles D. Meigs, and Franklin Bache, all men of renown in their respective pursuits. In 1864 he brought out a treatise on Pneumonia, in its Supposed Connection, Pathological and Etiological, with Autumnal Fevers and Malaria—a learned and elegantly written octavo volume of five hundred and two pages. The work was well received; but it never, I believe, reached a second edition. It was dedicated to his friend, Dr. Charles D. Meigs.

EDWIN FORREST.

1806–1872.

I BECAME acquainted with Mr. Forrest under peculiar circumstances. In the summer of 1828 Professor George McClellan called at my office at Library and Fifth Streets, in this city, to ask me if on the morrow I would accompany Mr. Edwin Forrest to the Pennsylvania Hospital, adding that the young actor was studying the character of Lear and was anxious to see a Mr. Rush, who had long been confined in that institution on account of insanity. My answer was, "Certainly; it will afford me much pleasure to be of service, in any manner possible, to you or to your friend." Punctually at twelve o'clock, the hour appointed for our meeting at McClellan's house, we were presented to each other; and Forrest and I strolled off, talking pretty briskly as we passed along, to the office of the steward, to whom I introduced my companion. In a trice we were at the desired spot. Mr. John Rush was a son of Dr. Benjamin Rush, and had been educated for the Philadelphia bar, then perhaps the most famous bar in the United States, adorned as it was by many of the leading minds of the country. The case of Rush was a singularly melancholy one. In an evil hour the young lawyer quarrelled with his bosom friend, a Mr. Bingham, who occupied a high position in the social circle. A meeting took place soon after—in Canada, I believe—and Rush killed his adversary. Remorse seized him, and in a short time he became a victim of incurable insanity. At the time of our visit the insane were confined in the basement story of the building; and Rush was in the habit of pacing to and fro in the corridor, with his hands behind his back, engaged in incoherent mutterings, in which the word "Bingham" was conspicuously noticeable. He was then an old man, although he was still erect, with a handsome, open, manly countenance. Through the grating in the heavy iron door of the corridor Forrest stealthily studied the conduct of the demented duellist. He visited the hospital a number of times, and finally came away perfectly convinced of the madness of Lear, as graphically portrayed by Shakespeare. Forrest thenceforth made a special study of the character, and how faithfully he delineated it is too well known to require comment.

In 1837, at an advanced age, Rush died in his cell, the light never having reëntered his soul. His illustrious father, who was the author of a work on the Mind, which is still frequently quoted with approbation, was not able to discover among his remedies any balm for his unfortunate son.

Except at an occasional visit to the theatre at Louisville, New York, and Philadelphia, in which I saw Forrest in some of his great characters, such as Hamlet, Lear, Othello, Brutus, Virginius, and Richard III., I did not meet him again until June, 1870, when he came to my office with his sister, Miss Eleanora Forrest, who had a cancer of the mammary gland, for which my advice was sought. We shook hands cordially. I said, "Mr. Forrest, do you remember the summer of 1828, in which, in the company of a young man who had been introduced to you by Dr. George McClellan, you visited the Pennsylvania Hospital to see Mr. Rush, an insane inmate?" "I recollect the circumstance," he replied, "but have forgotten the name of the gentleman." "I am that man," I said, when he again grasped my hands. "Well, I am very glad to see you after so long a separation, during which we have both grown older, and, I hope, a good deal wiser." After this I saw Forrest frequently at his own house, where he received me with the greatest kindness and courtesy. At his funeral, in 1872, I acted as one of his pallbearers, with General Patterson, Mr. Oakes, and Mr. Alger, of Boston, Dr. Jesse Burden, Daniel Dougherty, and two others whose names I have forgotten. At the numerous visits which I made to his sister, Forrest was often absent attending to private business in the city or occasionally making brief journeys to New York and Boston. He evinced the greatest affection for her, and was eager to do all he could to make her comfortable and contented in her trying situation. She cordially reciprocated his love; and it was easy to see that they were warmly attached to each other.

After her death he remarked to me that another link in his checkered life had been severed. During the two operations which I performed for her relief he held her arm out of the way and manifested his tenderness for her in every manner he could. He kissed her and patted her on the cheek when my work was over and when she had recovered her consciousness from the effects of the anæsthetic which had been administered to her. I never witnessed greater devotion and affection between brother and sister. It has been said that Forrest was a cold-blooded creature, without any of the finer sensibilities of our nature. If this was so, I had no evidence of the fact. That he was soured towards the world is no secret. It had treated him harshly, often unjustly, sometimes cruelly. His wife had given him much trouble and vexation; the courts, to which for years he appealed for justice, granted heavy alimony, often divided among greedy lawyers; scandal with her forked tongue was ever pursuing him; many of his brethren of the stage were jealous of him; the newspapers abused him in unmeasured terms; the windows for a time groaned under caricatures of him; in a word, he was subjected to constant annoyance and acrimonious criticism, which well nigh drove him to madness and despair. He could hardly have been more tormented if he had been immersed in an atmosphere of bees and wasps buzzing about his ears, and discharging their venom into his person. Such unfeeling assaults were enough to spoil the temper of any man, and to make him misanthropic. I believe that Nature had made Edwin Forrest a generous, warm-hearted man. His early struggles might have somewhat ruffled his temper, but they could not have left a lasting impression upon his finely constituted mind. Other agencies over which he had no control did the work; and it is well that the public, in forming an estimate of Mr. Forrest's private character, should properly consider this point in the history of his wonderful career. His goodness to his relatives was unbounded; they were all poor, and his greatest happiness was to look after their wants and to contribute to their comfort. The debts left by his father at his death were liquidated by Forrest when he was himself struggling for a livelihood. After much hard work he succeeded in laying by a few thousand dollars, which he at once invested in the purchase of a house for his mother and sisters, depositing the balance in the bank for their support. Meeting a friend, he told him what he had done, and exclaimed, "Thank God! I am not worth a ducat."

Like all men, Forrest was subject to earth's infirmities. It was apparent that he was not always happy, so deeply did his introspection impress itself upon his countenance.

He spent much of his time when at home in his library, a well-selected and splendid collection of books, in rich binding, and embracing the best editions. It was especially opulent in Shakespearian literature, and in history, biography, and poetry. A considerable portion of this collection, the work of a lifetime, was destroyed by fire soon after its owner's death. Mr. Forrest was a great reader, and had fine intellectual tastes. With the history of the stage he was thoroughly familiar. He had a capacious memory, which enabled him, almost at any moment, to call up with ease scenes and events long past, or but dimly remembered by others. He was an admirable talker, and could relate an anecdote with telling effect. The stage had enriched him. He built a palatial residence on the banks of the Hudson, which is now used as a Catholic convent; and his elegant mansion, with its noble galleries, at the southwest corner of Broad and Master Streets in this city, was for a long time an object of much interest to the passer-by. He had many choice pictures and statuary, which it afforded him pleasure to show to his friends. His own bust, in Parian marble, by Rodgers, which graced the main hall, was a good likeness, as well as an exquisite specimen of art.   After he had broken down in health and spirits, he rarely entertained; but in his palmy days his house was the abode of a generous hospitality and the resort of refined people.   He despised pretension without merit, disliked ostentation, hated his enemies, and loved his friends.   For many years Mr. Forrest had suffered from gout, which he inherited from his father, and which, at one of his performances in a poorly heated theatre on a very cold night, developed into full activity.   From that time he frequently had similar attacks, which were occasionally so severe as to prevent him from fulfilling his engagements.   His last illness was frightfully brief.   He had retired to his chamber and was evidently in the act of undressing himself when he was struck down by apoplexy, and, from all appearances, must have almost instantly expired.   When found by his domestics he was lying dead across the bed with his feet upon the floor.   Thus, at the age of sixty-six, on the 12th of December, 1872, died one of the most illustrious tragedians the world has ever produced.   It will be long before the stage will see his like again.

In looking at Forrest as he stood upon the stage one could not fail to feel that he was in the presence of a great actor, in full sympathy with the character he was attempting to personate.   Above the medium height, with broad shoulders, a large head, fine features, a keen, hazel eye, and magnificent muscular development, he looked like a Roman in the best days of the Republic.   His voice was deep, sonorous, sometimes too loud, but marvellously distinct and well intoned.   His gestures were grand and well-timed, while his strut upon the stage was majesty itself.

One of the noblest acts of Mr. Forrest was the endowment of an institution on the banks of the Delaware, nine miles above Philadelphia, for the support of superannuated and disabled actors.   The grounds upon which it is situated are large, well-timbered, adorned with shrubbery, and provided with conservatories, pictures, statuary, and the remnant of his library. Despite its external attractions and intrinsic advantages as a retreat, the people for whom it was designed found its exactions so great as to be unwilling to conform to them. What a pity that so noble a bequest should be hedged in by narrow-minded restrictions! Actors are liberal persons, but ill-disposed to brook restraint. An excellent Life of the great actor was published in 1877 by his friend, Rev. William R. Alger, of Boston.

Forrest was the offspring of mixed parentage. His father was a Scotchman; and his mother, a Miss Lauman, was of German descent on both sides of her house. There were three sisters, all of whom at a ripe age died unmarried. One of his three brothers signally failed upon the stage, and died young. Until the age of thirteen, when he lost his father, Forrest obtained his education at the common school. His subsequent intellectual development was due to his own unaided efforts. Compelled to earn his own bread and to assist in supporting his destitute family, he sought employment in a shipchandlery store. While thus occupied he joined a Thespian club, which gave occasional performances; and in a few years he appeared in a Philadelphia theatre as Rosalie de Borgia. But the clothes he wore were too short for him, and a playmate in the pit, seeing his large feet and ankles exposed, burst into laughter, which not only greatly disconcerted the actor, but provoked him to such a degree that he soon after gave the offender a severe chastisement. Forrest was originally intended for the clerical profession. It would be a nice question for the sophist to determine whether he would have done as much good as a preacher as he did as an actor.

HENRY MILLER.

1800–1874.

DR. HENRY MILLER, for many years Professor of Midwifery in the University of Louisville, was a man whose friendship I enjoyed for more than a third of a century, and one to whom I was warmly attached on account of his great personal and professional worth. A purer and more conscientious man in all the relations of life I never knew. As a lecturer he was prosy and monotonous, expressing his ideas with difficulty, often hesitating for the proper word, and not unfrequently repeating himself; and yet there were few men in the school during my connection with it who were more beloved by their pupils or whose teaching was received with greater favor. He was essentially a strong man, with a well-ordered and philosophical mind. Whatever he knew, he knew well. Like a well-equipped vessel he sailed majestically along, defying wind and breakers, and always freighted with sound knowledge and useful instruction. As a writer, he wielded a sharp and vigorous pen. He was fond of disputation, took delight in criticism, and never missed an opportunity to demolish his adversary, who was generally some English or French author on midwifery or the diseases of women. His contributions to medical journals did much to expose error and to diffuse correct principles at a time when obstetric and gynæcological science was less understood than it is at the present day. He was a pioneer in the West in the use of the speculum. I well remember the opposition which he encountered in the use of that valuable instrument.

Miller's treatise on Obstetrics was written in a clear style, in excellent English, and was well received. The first edition was reissued in London, and the English press generally noticed it with favor. The work served to establish the reputation of the author as an accomplished obstetrician and as a solid writer, fully abreast of his subject. He had a large practice, and attracted many patients from a distance. In his own neighborhood he was consulted in all difficult cases of labor by his younger brethren, many of whom had been his pupils. In his habits, Miller was simple and unostentatious. He was conscientious in all his dealings; an agreeable colleague; a kind father; a faithful husband; an upright citizen; a good Christian. Late in life he committed the error of leaving the University of Louisville, so long the theatre of his ambition, his usefulness, and his renown, and connected himself with the Louisville Medical College—an error which was due to some misunderstanding, but which caused him much annoyance, if it did not embitter his existence. Such a step is nearly always in the wrong direction. After I left Kentucky many letters of the most friendly character passed between us; and the announcement of his death in February, 1874, in the seventy-fourth year of his age, caused me sincere sorrow.

ANDREW JOHNSON.

1808–1875.

IT was my lot in the summer of 1859 to be consulted professionaliy by Andrew Johnson, then a United States Senator, who came from Washington to obtain my advice respecting an injury which he had received in his left elbow eighteen months previously. Finding the joint completely anchylosed, but in all other respects free from disease, I informed him that nothing could be done to restore its functions. After we had chatted a while he rose to take his leave, but not without asking me for my fee. I said, "Senator, I have no charge against you; I am only too glad to be of service to a gentleman of whom I have heard so much, and whom I have been so long desirous of seeing." I saw Mr. Johnson only once afterwards, and that was in Philadelphia, when he was on his way to Chicago after he had become the successor of the lamented Lincoln. It was during that tour, which his enemies designated "Swinging round the circle," that he indulged so freely in abuse of Congress. This abuse was the remote cause of his impeachment by that body for malfeasance of office—one of the most humiliating positions in which a public functionary can be placed. The trial, which was tedious, but which ended in his acquittal, left a sting from the effects of which he never recovered.

The career of Andrew Johnson reads like a fairy tale. He was born at Raleigh, North Carolina, in 1808. He lost his father in childhood, and at the age of eleven years, without any education, was apprenticed to a tailor who was as ignorant of learning as himself. Soon after the expiration of his indenture he settled at Greeneville, Tennessee, where he married and contracted a fancy for study, which until then had been undeveloped. His wife, who had some culture, now became his preceptor, instructing him in the elementary branches of an English education, directing and refining his tastes, exciting his ambition, and fitting him for the enjoyment of a higher life than the one to which he had been accustomed. He was determined, if possible, to throw off his native shyness. Without talent for public speaking, he joined a debating society, composed mainly of the students of Greeneville College. In this exercise he was soon so proficient that he was able to take part in political meetings. The attention of his fellow-citizens being thus directed to him, he was made, first, an alderman, and next mayor of the city on a workingmen's ticket. From these humble beginnings Johnson successively rose to be a member of the Lower, and then of the Upper House of the State, then Governor of Tennessee, then a member of Congress, and finally a mem-

ber of the United States Senate. When the war broke
out he was an uncompromising enemy of secession, and
incurred the odium not only of his adopted State, but
of the entire South. Appointed Military Governor of
Tennessee, he spared no efforts to promote the cause of
the Union, often at the peril of his life. He was Vice-
President of the United States when Abraham Lincoln fell
by the hand of an assassin. On the 15th of April, 1865,
Andrew Johnson woke up and found himself famous as the
Chief Magistrate of a still bleeding nation.

Andrew Johnson made a poor record as a reconstruc-
tionist. The truth is, he lost his head. His own party,
with whom he soon became extremely unpopular, would
gladly have displaced him had it been possible to do so.
The conviction was strongly rooted in the minds of many
good men that his conduct, if not speedily checked, would
undo all the good that had been done by the armies of the
republic. After his term of office had expired he returned
to Tennessee, which he again represented in the Senate
in 1875 during its extra session in March. He died in
July of the same year. Johnson was undoubtedly a great
man, but he lived too long for his own fame. His pas-
sions and intemperate habits ruined him. He was deficient in native dignity, stubborn, and conceited—grave
faults in private life, but unpardonable in a statesman
and in the Chief Magistrate of a great people. He was
about five feet ten inches in height, well built, with light
eyes, a large head, and a handsome, intellectual face, with
none of the characteristics of the plebeian. His quarrel
with John W. Forney will not soon be forgotten. His
public speeches on the stump, in the State Legislature, in
the House of Representatives and Senate of the United
States were often tinged with the most biting sarcasm.
He was an excellent debater, and possessed rare executive
abilities.

MARTYN PAINE.

1794–1877.

DR. PAINE was noted for his thorough acquaintance with modern medical literature and for the wide range of his knowledge of contemporaneous authors. In this respect he was not surpassed by Dr. Charles Caldwell, who, to a familiar knowledge of passing events in and out of the profession, was well read in the old Latin writers on medicine. Neither, however, had the learning of Dr. John Redman Coxe of Philadelphia. The contemporaries of Paine have not done him justice. His voluminous writings, embracing many abstruse topics, few have read, and still fewer have taken the trouble to understand. To many they have been distasteful on account of their controversial character. Their author was a merciless critic, unveiling with an unsparing hand the weak points of his opponents. His exposure of Dr. Carpenter's plagiarisms is one of the finest specimens of scathing criticism in medical literature, if not indeed in the English language. It attracted general attention, silenced the great physiologist, and placed its learned author in the front rank of polemic writers and reviewers. Dr. Paine touched few subjects which he did not exhaust, or which he did not adorn. He was a closet man, a strong thinker, and a bookworm, reading much and digesting well what he read. A man of fortune, he had an abundance of leisure, never allowed himself to be annoyed by the practice of medicine, mixed little in society, and was seldom seen at places of amusement. His life was a life of introspection. It would doubtless have been better for him if he had been less of a recluse; but he had a splendid library, and he made books rather than men his companions. Books do not talk unless they are opened, and when one becomes tired of them they can be laid aside. But a babbling friend or acquaintance it is not easy to get rid of without giving offence. Martyn

Paine loved solitude, and was a miser of time; and once in his chair, he generally sat for hours together, during which he performed a large amount of mental work. He was frugal, avoided the luxuries of the table, and was strictly temperate in all things. For many years, as he feelingly told me in 1850, when we were colleagues in the University of New York, he was a prey to dyspepsia; this occasioned him much suffering, and often cast a shadow over his mind, which he found it sometimes extremely difficult to dispel. Dyspepsia, as is well known, is the bane of a persistent literary life, and it is easy to conceive what must be its influence upon one's health and labors. Many of the most caustic reviews have been penned under the lash of this unrelenting demon; and many a criminal has been sentenced to the penitentiary for ten, fifteen, or even twenty years, when he should scarcely have had five, because a disordered stomach had muddled the brain of the judge. Indigestion has caused many crimes, many harsh expressions, and many bitter denunciations. If these facts were generally known and appreciated, the world would be less censorious than it seems to be in dealing with this class of sufferers.

Dr. Paine composed rapidly, and, for the most part, accurately. If he erred in anything, it was in diffuseness. He contributed frequently to the periodical press. His first published treatise of any note—a book on cholera, which was issued in 1832—was a compilation, intended to meet the existing emergency, not a production founded upon personal observation. His Physiological Commentaries, in three large octavo volumes, a work of vast erudition and of caustic criticism, appeared in 1840. It was followed by a small volume on Materia Medica, a text-book for young students. In 1847 he published a treatise on the Institutes of Medicine, which comprised a comprehensive review of the existing state of the science of physiology, and which was undoubtedly his most original work. It passed through several editions, each enriched by much new matter. His Soul and Instinct, a strictly philosophical treatise, interspersed with much theological matter, appeared in 1849.

Paine was born at Williamstown, Vermont, in 1794. He received his education at Harvard University, studied medicine with Dr. John C. Warren, and took his degree in the medical school of Boston in 1816. In 1841 he assisted in founding the Medical Department of the University of New York, in which he occupied for many years the chair of Materia Medica. He was an unattractive lecturer. Like Dr. John Redman Coxe, of Philadelphia, he drew too heavily upon the materia medica of the past to the detriment of that of the present. Moreover, he read his lectures—a mode of instructing young men fortunately seldom witnessed at the present day.

Paine was of medium height, well built, with a fine head, and an expressive brown eye. He had a thoughtful, pensive mien, and was often buried in fits of abstraction. The loss of his son, an only child, at the age of nearly twenty-one, brought on a profound and lasting depression. A few years later he lost his wife from, if I rightly recollect, cancer of the breast. His son had been for several years a pupil at Harvard University, and it was expected that he would take his degree at the approaching Commencement. He had been known as a devoted and exemplary student, but it had been remarked that he was subject at times to deep melancholy. The sequel is easily told. He was found dead in his room under circumstances that justified the conviction that he had taken his own life. Incessant study, combined with exquisite sensitiveness and dejection of spirits, was supposed to have been the cause of the rash act. His father, to commemorate his virtues, wrote an elaborate biography of him, which was published in a beautiful quarto volume and extensively distributed among his friends. Martyn Paine died November 10th, 1877, at the age of eighty-three.

CHAPTER XIV.

JOSEPH HENRY.

1799–1878.

JOSEPH HENRY, Secretary of the Smithsonian Institution, died on the 13th of May, 1878, at the age of seventy-nine years. His loss caused universal regret. He was born at Albany, New York, December 17th, 1799. After having received a common-school education he followed the occupation of watchmaker. He early showed a marked taste for chemistry and natural philosophy. In time he became Professor of Mathematics in the Albany Academy. In 1832 we find him at Princeton College engaged in teaching natural philosophy and in laying the foundation of his fame as a scientist. In 1846 he was appointed Secretary of the Smithsonian Institution, a position which he retained until his death. He was President of the American Association for the Advancement of Science, of the National Academy of Science, and of the Philosophical Society of Washington. He was the chairman of the Government Lighthouse Board, and was a member of numerous scientific bodies, domestic and foreign. In 1847 he was solicited to take the chair of Chemistry in the University of Pennsylvania, made vacant by the death of Dr. Robert Hare, and afterwards so ably filled

by one of my former colleagues, Dr. James B. Rogers.   It
is to be regretted that he did not accept this position, as it
would have afforded him that leisure for the prosecution
of scientific pursuits which was so long the object of his
ambition, but which the exacting and absorbing cares of
office at Washington rendered impossible.   The claims,
however, of the noble institution over which he had recently been called to preside outweighed all personal considerations, and compelled him to resist the flattering offer.
The laboratory work of Professor Henry at Princeton foreshadowed the invention, if indeed it was not the foundation, of the electric telegraph, afterwards perfected by
Morse and others, as well as many discoveries in magneto-
electricity, which have led to important scientific results.
His services to the Marine Signal Service can scarcely be
overrated.   Union College in 1829, and Harvard in 1851,
conferred upon him the degree of LL. D.

Professor Henry was a man whom to know was to love.
Blessed with a cheerful disposition, "radiant," as one of
his biographers has said, "with a sunny temper," he shed
light and joy upon all who came into contact with him.
He was deeply beloved by his family.   He was one of the
most gentle of human beings.   I saw him for the first time
in 1869, at a Wistar Party at my house, and was at once
irresistibly attracted to him by his charming manners, his
unaffected deportment, and his mild and benignant countenance.   I said to myself, "Here is a great man without
the consciousness of being great, a truly unselfish man, a
man who knows no guile, one of the noblest works of
God."   It is sad to know that he died poor ; but it is refreshing to know that men more blessed in worldly goods
than he have not forgotten the mourners.   A statue of
Professor Henry now adorns the grounds of the Smithsonian Institution.   It was executed by Mr. W. W. Story,
the American sculptor, at a cost of fifteen thousand dollars,
appropriated by Congress.   It is in bronze, of heroic size,

and represents the philosopher in a standing position, in an attitude of studious contemplation, the right arm gathering about him the folds of an academic gown. It was unveiled on the 19th of April, 1883, by Chief Justice Waite, with appropriate ceremonies.

GEORGE BACON WOOD.

1797–1879.

THE name of George Bacon Wood will live in the history of American medical literature. For more than a third of a century he was conspicuous in his profession, and he made a record of which few modern physicians can boast. My acquaintance with him began in 1836, during a tour which he made to the West in company with his wife. He travelled in his private carriage, four-in-hand, with servants in livery, and attracted not a little attention by the elegance of his equipage—a sight which was uncommon in the country through which he was passing. He moved at the rate of twenty-five or thirty miles a day, stopping whenever any object of special interest presented itself, or when he needed repose. His arrival at Cincinnati, where I then resided, was duly announced; and soon after the news had reached me I called at his lodgings to pay him my respects. He was not in. But the next morning he returned my call; and I well recollect the favorable impression he made upon me. I did not see him again until 1852, when, during a brief visit to Philadelphia, I met him in his lecture-room in the University of Pennsylvania, in the presence of five hundred students. When in 1856 I became Professor of Surgery in the Jefferson Medical College, he was one of the first of my professional brethren to welcome me. Subsequently we often

met.   In his journey in 1836 he visited Louisville, Lexington, and the Mammoth Cave; and my impression is
that he went as far south as Nashville, Tennessee.
Wherever they stopped he and Mrs. Wood received courteous attentions from the more prominent citizens.   At
Cincinnati Dr. Drake did in his behalf the honors of
the city.   Though Wood at that time was a rising man,
the splendid superstructure of his fame remained to be
reared.

Wood was born at Greenwich, a small village in New
Jersey, March 12th, 1797.   He was of English descent, of
Quaker proclivities—the founder of the family in this country having emigrated from Bristol in 1682, at the time of
William Penn's second visit to our shores.   His father,
says Dr. John H. Packard, who is married to one of his
nieces, was a well-to-do farmer, and gave his son a liberal
education.   Wood took his degree in arts in 1815, and
his degree in medicine three years after, at the University
of Pennsylvania.   His medical preceptor was the well-
known Dr. Joseph Parrish, with whom he afterwards associated himself in private teaching.   About this time the
Philadelphia College of Pharmacy was established; and
its trustees had the good sense to elect Wood to the chair
of Chemistry, from which, at the end of ten years, he
was transferred to that of Materia Medica and Pharmacy.
On the retirement, in 1835, of John Redman Coxe from
the chair of Materia Medica in the University of Pennsylvania, Wood was appointed to fill the vacancy.   He
occupied the chair until 1850.   He then became the successor of Dr. Nathaniel Chapman in the professorship of
Medicine, an office which he worthily filled until his withdrawal from public teaching in 1860.   He was then sixty-
three years of age, and in the possession of unimpaired
mental and physical powers.   For years he had made up
his mind to retire from office before there should be any
failure of his strength; and in this he acted wisely.   It is

sad to see a teacher hang on to his chair until there is
nothing left of him but shreds—a picture of decay and im-
becility!

Soon after his resignation his friends gave him a public
dinner in appreciation of his manifold services to the profession. The entertainment, which was presided over by
his warm friend Dr. René La Roche, came off in the
foyer of the Academy of Music early in May, and was
largely attended by the representative physicians of Philadelphia. A few days after this event he set sail with Mrs.
Wood for a prolonged tour in Europe, during which he
visited not only Great Britain, but a large portion of the
continent, including Spain and Portugal. Everywhere he
received the attention and courtesy due to a man whose
fame had long preceded him.

As a lecturer, Wood was clear, forcible, direct, instructive, and fully abreast of his subject. He had at hand
ample means for illustrating his courses. As Professor of
Materia Medica it was his duty to teach botany. In order
to do this to the best advantage he built in his garden a
conservatory, which he filled with medicinal plants, native
and exotic; of these he had a good supply upon the stage
conveniently arranged for demonstration. This mode of
teaching has become obsolete; but in those days it was
considered important, and it had a marked influence upon
the popularity of* the teacher. When he accepted the
chair of Medicine he spent twenty thousand dollars upon
diagrams, casts, and models. Such efforts to instruct the
student had never been made in this country; and I know
of no instance in which they have been repeated. In
1852 I happened to be present when he lectured on the
Normal Sounds of the Lungs; and I counted upon his
tray not fewer than seventeen stethoscopes, of all forms
and sizes, including the instrument of Auenbrugger and
that of Laennec. Such teaching I thought not only
finical, and needlessly minute, but calculated to confuse

rather than to enlighten the pupil. But whatever Wood did he did exhaustively and conscientiously.

He was one of the most voluminous writers of the age in our profession. He will be best known by the United States Dispensatory, which was written in conjunction with his lifelong friend, Dr. Franklin Bache. For the production of this work he was eminently fitted by his knowledge of chemistry, botany, and materia medica. The first edition appeared in January, 1833. With the assistance of his nephew Professor Horatio C. Wood, and of Professor Bridges, the author lived to complete the fourteenth edition. The enormous labor implied in this publication and in its repeated revisions can be better imagined than described. Few works of its kind can be compared to it for excellence of style, for accuracy of detail, or for scientific profundity. His Therapeutics and Pharmacology reached the third edition; and his Practice of Medicine the sixth edition. Both were everywhere received as high authority. For several years the Practice of Medicine was largely used as a text-book in some of the schools of England and Scotland. Dr. Wood was also the author of many minor productions, such as addresses and historical monographs, all of which were characterized by his clear and classical style. I doubt whether there is in his writings a badly constructed sentence. The income from his works must have been very large. Of the Dispensatory alone one hundred and fifty thousand copies were distributed during his lifetime. His wealth, however, was principally derived from Mrs. Wood, who inherited much of her father's estate. No offspring blessed their union.

Dr. Wood took an active part in the preparation and revision of the United States Pharmacopœia. He was physician of the Pennsylvania Hospital from 1835 to 1859; President of the College of Physicians of Philadelphia for thirty-four years; President of the American Philosophical

Society; and in 1855 President of the American Medical Association, in whose early struggles he took a deep interest. He had a warm heart, and was in sympathy with human suffering, irrespective of race, color, sex, age, or condition in life. He spent his means with a lavish hand. He gave liberally to the Pennsylvania Hospital. In the University of Pennsylvania he established at an expense of fifty thousand dollars what is known as the Auxiliary Department, for instruction in botany, chemistry, geology, mineralogy, and zoology, under the charge of a distinct corps of instructors. To the College of Physicians he gave his library and fifteen thousand dollars. Numerous other benefactions were provided for in his will.

Dr. Wood never enjoyed a large private practice. He shunned intercourse with the world, such was his fondness for books, science, and literature. His chief field of observation was the medical ward of the Pennsylvania Hospital, where for a third of a century he discharged his duties, both as a physician and as a clinical teacher, with scrupulous fidelity. As far as I am aware, he added nothing original to our knowledge of the nature and treatment of disease. He was, I think, the author of the turpentine treatment in typhoid fever—a treatment of doubtful efficacy.

Wood was about six feet high, with broad shoulders, a fine face, and a good head. His manners were dignified and formal, and, on first acquaintance, cold; but they warmed on closer intimacy. In his latter years he became unwieldy, and for some months before his death he was obliged to keep his bed. He expired at his residence on Arch Street, where he had so long lived, March 30th, 1879, at the age of eighty-two years. His wife had preceded him to the grave by twelve years. His habits were singular. Most of his literary work was performed after ordinary mortals had retired to rest: namely, between ten o'clock in the evening and four in the morning. He was frugal in his meals and economical of his time. All his engagements were performed with precision. For many years his office was filled with private pupils, over whom he exercised scrupulous supervision, compelling them to study diligently, and to recite to him thrice a week. Regularly at a certain hour the colored servant would open the door and announce his master, who examined each student in succession. Any one who failed to answer correctly or intelligently was sure to receive a reprimand, with a more severe one if the offence was repeated. The exercises over, the Professor would stand in the doorway, and as each student approached he would shake him cordially by the hand and wish him good-by.

I attended Wood's funeral, which, if I mistake not, took place on the 3d of April, four days after his death. It was appointed for half past two o'clock. When I reached the house a goodly number of persons had assembled. When the hand of the clock pointed nearly to four, silence was broken by the undertaker screwing the lid on the coffin. Not a word of service had been uttered. Finally one of his old pupils sitting by my side said, in a tone almost loud enough to be heard over the office in which he had been wont to be examined, "Poor Wood must feel as if he could rise in his coffin at this want of punctuality in his friends!"

The funeral of Dr. Wood recalls an incident in which the solemnity of the occasion was similarly disturbed. The anecdote was told me by a lady. She was an eye-witness of the occurrence. The friends of the dead man had been assembled for a long time, during which not a word had been uttered. At length the undertaker was about to close the coffin, when a gentleman rose, and in a squeaking, nasal tone said, "Perhaps the vital spark is not entirely extinct, and it might be well—" "Screw him down!" exclaimed one of the heirs.

ISAAC HAYS.

1796–1879.

THE name of Isaac Hays is indissolubly associated with the progress of American medical journalism. For more than half a century it was a household word with the reading members of the profession. The American Journal of the Medical Sciences was as well known abroad as it has been at home. It was upon the exchange list of every respectable medical periodical in Europe; and its contents were freely read and quoted everywhere. To be its editor demanded talent, industry, and influence of no ordinary kind; and all these qualities Dr. Hays possessed in an eminent degree, as was shown by the success of the enterprise. The Journal was high-toned from the beginning; and nothing of a personal nature sullied its pages. Its reviews were sometimes severe or caustic if they were imperatively demanded by the public interest. It never indulged in unmerited laudation. It aimed to be just and truthful. Its object was, as it still is in the hands of its present able editor, Dr. I. Minis Hays, to be useful; to establish a lofty standard of journalism, one that should be an honor alike to its founders and to American medical literature; to hold out inducements to young men to become finished writers; to encourage scientific investigation; and to winnow with a discriminating judgment the wheat from the chaff of the medical press. In this manner this Journal has become a great library; so much so that, as has often been remarked, if all other American works were blotted out, it would afford an adequate illustration of the state of our medical literature during the last fifty years. Nature had formed Dr. Hays to be an editor. The contributors to his Journal, styled by him collaborators, comprised a long list of prominent writers and teachers in all parts of the country, who received from the publishers what I have always regarded as an inadequate compensation for their labors, especially in view of the amount usually paid for magazine articles. What the hard-working editor himself received has never been made public; but it is safe to affirm that the sum fell short of what so talented a man deserved.

The American Journal of the Medical Sciences is his best monument. When I behold the one hundred portly volumes of this Journal, as they rest upon the shelves of my library, comprising more than fifty thousand pages of closely-printed matter, and representing an abstract of the most important facts accumulated in medicine and the allied sciences during half a century, I am ready to exclaim, in the language of Sir Christopher Wren's epitaph, "*Si monumentum quæris, circumspice!*" His work, like that of the architect of St. Paul's, is immortal.

Dr. Hays never had much practice in the field of general medicine. His tastes early in life led him to the study of ophthalmic surgery, in which he gained his celebrity as a practitioner. He invented an excellent cataract knife, much prized by the surgeons of this country. He was long connected with Wills' Hospital, and gained considerable reputation in bringing out, with important additions, Lawrence's great work on the Diseases of the Eye. This work reached several editions. He edited an American edition of Arnott's Elements of Physics and of Hoblyn's Dictionary of Medical Terms. He translated, jointly with Dr. Robert Egglesfield Griffith, the celebrated treatise on Chronic Phlegmasia, and soon after the Principles of Physiological Medicine, both by Broussais. He also edited an edition of Alexander Wilson's American Ornithology. He projected the American Cyclopædia of Practical Medicine and Surgery, of which, however, only two volumes were published, the country not being sufficiently rich to bear the expense incident to such an enterprise. His contributions to the medical press were numerous and valuable. At the time of his death he was the oldest journalist in America. As a writer his style was free, simple, and scholarly, without any effort at ornament or display. He had a large and well-selected library, rich in works of the fathers of the profession and in periodical literature, much, if not most, of the latter having been sent to him in exchange for the American Journal of the Medical Sciences.

Dr. Hays was a remarkably handsome man, nearly six feet in height, well proportioned, erect even to the last, with blue eyes, a well-formed head, finely chiseled profile, and a countenance beaming with benevolence. In his manners he was emphatically a gentleman of the old school, bland, gentle, and dignified, with a sweet and subdued voice, and a warm, sympathizing heart. His habits were those of the diligent student. Whatever he had to do he did promptly. His daily task as a journalist was usually completed in the early part of the day. His duties as an editor required an immense correspondence. He was an early riser, and punctuality was one of his cardinal virtues. Death overtook him in April, 1879, at the age of eighty-three years, in the enjoyment of vigorous mental faculties. It is hard to imagine a purer life than that which was led by Dr. Hays. An admirable sketch of the life of the great journalist was prepared soon after his death by Professor Alfred Stillé for the College of Physicians of Philadelphia. I wrote a biographical notice of him for the American Journal of the Medical Sciences for July, 1879.

HENRY C. CAREY.

1793–1879.

THE death of Henry C. Carey, on the 13th of September, 1879, deprived Philadelphia of one of its most widely-known literary citizens.

My acquaintance with him commenced in 1828, when I sought a publisher for the translation of a small work on General Anatomy. In 1856 I removed to this city and became his neighbor. Not long after my arrival he did me the kindness to call upon me and my family. Gradually a warm friendship sprang up between us, and for years there was no more welcome visitor at my house than he— no one whom my dear wife, myself, or my children were more glad to see, to converse with, to amuse, or to entertain. The death of Mrs. Gross nearly four years before that of Mr. Carey did not interrupt his visits; and when he himself passed away we missed him as a greatly beloved friend and genial companion.

Mr. Carey was born in Philadelphia in December, 1793, and was consequently nearly eighty-six years old at the time of his death. His father was the celebrated Mathew Carey, an Irish patriot, who, having made himself obnoxious to the English government, was obliged to exile himself from his native country. He sought refuge in France, whence, after a brief sojourn, he came to the United States. On his arrival he settled in Philadelphia, where, by his intelligence and enterprise, he soon attracted general attention, and finally became one of its most useful and conspicuous citizens. Among his earlier undertakings was the issue of a newspaper. This was followed in 1787 by the American Museum, the most costly and important periodical of the kind that had yet been attempted on this side of the Atlantic. It met with a wide circulation, and had a prosperous career of six years, when it ceased to exist. In 1789, to meet a growing want, widely felt, Mr. Carey opened a publishing house for the encouragement of native authors and the reprint of foreign works. His business flourished, and his establishment soon became the most extensive and best known in the country. Combining the labors of a publisher and bookseller with those of a writer, Mr. Carey wrote pamphlet after pamphlet upon politics, statistics, industrial pursuits, religion, medicine, and social science, until the product of his pen reached, it is asserted, many thousands of pages. He retired from business in 1825, but continued his work as an author till within a short time of his death in 1839. His tracts on the Yellow Fever of Philadelphia in 1793 and 1794, in which years he played a prominent part as a philanthropist and nurse, rank among the best works of that period in the history of our profession. Mathew Carey was a man of large heart, with powers of observation which allowed nothing to escape him.

The son, it should seem, became at an early age interested in the business of his father; some of whose biographers make the statement that the lad, at the age of nine years, was sent to New York to attend a Literary Fair, the forerunner of the Trade Sales which he afterwards so successfully inaugurated. The same authorities allege that in his twelfth year he had charge of a branch bookstore in Baltimore. He was known as "the bookseller in miniature." Doubtless he was precocious; but one can hardly believe that so sensible a man as the elder Carey would send a mere child, inexperienced in the ways of the world, at a time when travelling was difficult and tedious, on such important missions. Tales are told of children who at the age of three or four years have read Greek and Latin fluently, and have solved intricate problems in mathematics; but who believes them? Mr. Carey was sent on business to Raleigh, North Carolina, at the age of nineteen. He became associated with his father in the book business in 1814, when he had just attained his majority. On the retirement of his father, seven years afterwards, he formed a partnership with his brother-in-law, Mr. Isaac Lea, who has since become so distinguished as a naturalist. The new firm was for a long time the largest and most influential publishing establishment in America. To its enterprise the country was indebted for the Encyclopædia Americana, in thirteen octavo volumes; for the works of Washington Irving, of J. Fenimore Cooper, and of Sir Walter Scott; and for a large number of medical works, native and foreign. Mr. Carey had charge of the literary department of the firm, conducting a large correspondence, and acting as the censor of its publications. The so-called Trade Sales, which he instituted, have closely cemented the bonds of good-fellowship among publishers. Tired of hard work, and in need of rest, Mr. Carey retired from the firm in 1835. His labors had been rewarded by an ample fortune; and he was satisfied that he had materially assisted in laying the foundation of an independent national literature. The firm of Carey & Lea was among the first, if not the first, to pay foreign authors for the American reprints of their works.

The career of Mr. Carey as an author commenced in the year in which he retired from business. He had for a long time contemplated writing on political economy, and to qualify himself for the task he had read many of the principal treatises upon the subject, especially those of Malthus, Adam Smith, Ricardo, Say, and McCulloch. He had often as a youth discussed political economy with his father, from whom he had no doubt derived important lessons, which, if they did not adequately guide him, served to encourage him in his future studies. Henceforth this branch of science was the chief pursuit of his life. His essay on the Rate of Wages, which appeared in 1835, was rapidly succeeded by the Harmony of Nature, as Exhibited in the Laws which Regulate the Increase of Population and of the Means of Subsistence; by the Principles of Political Economy; and by the Credit System in France, Great Britain, and the United States. In 1851 he issued the Harmony of Interests, Manufacturing and Commercial. In 1853 appeared the Slave Trade, Domestic and Foreign. In this year he also published a series of letters on International Copyright. In 1858 followed his

System of Social Science; and in 1872 the Unity of Law. He also wrote numerous pamphlets on various subjects; and an immense number of articles on political economy and social science for the editorial department of the New York Tribune. He carried on an extensive correspondence with men at home and abroad who were interested in the study of these sciences. Several of his works were translated into the principal languages of Europe, and one of them was honored by a translation into the Japanese tongue. A French writer, Bastiat, was called to account for too free a use of some of Mr. Carey's doctrines. His works were especially well received in Germany and Russia, in which, as well as in other Continental countries, they greatly influenced the controversies between protectionists and free-traders. In Great Britain, where free trade is the belief of almost everybody, his doctrines were regarded with hostility.

Mr. Carey wrote with facility, expressing himself in well-chosen language, free from ambiguity and affectation. He was so thoroughly at home upon political economy and social science, and was so well informed of the views and opinions of previous and contemporary authors, that he was able, at brief notice, to furnish an elaborate article on any topic which had the slightest affinity with these subjects. When absorbed in his studies, he worked hour after hour, unconscious of the lapse of time, until, overcome by mental fatigue, he would leave his seat for a while, pace his room, and then renew his efforts, if possible, with increased energy. The leading object of his writings was the benefit of the working classes and the amelioration of society in its various and complex relations to government. He labored long and hard to convince our people that their real interest lay in a protective tariff; and to accomplish so beneficent a measure he was willing to encounter all the obloquy which he received from the press of his own country and from that of Europe. Despite opposition, misrepresentation, and abuse, he worked on until he succeeded in establishing his doctrines upon an immutable basis. The school of political economy which he founded has many disciples in both hemispheres, and it is destined to grow steadily, like some mighty rock, by accretion. The learned Professor Dühring, of Berlin, did not go too far when he compared the discovery by Mr. Carey of the fundamental principles which underlie economic and social science to that of Copernicus.

Mr. Carey was freely consulted by Mr. Chase, the able Secretary of the Treasury during Mr. Lincoln's administration, and also by various banking houses during and after the war, as to the best method of shaping the financial policy of the country at those critical periods; and his suggestions, although not always adopted, bore good fruit. For Mr. Chase's successors he had little respect. I often heard him denounce them as charlatans and political tricksters, wholly unacquainted with the principles of economic science, finance, or government.

Mr. Carey visited Europe three times. His first voyage was made in 1825, accompanied by his wife, whom he had just married, and who was a sister of Leslie, the artist, and a woman of high culture and refinement. His second visit was made in 1857; and his third in 1859. Each of these visits lasted about six months. He spent much of his time on the Continent in inspecting objects of interest, in studying history and politics, and in forming the acquaintance of eminent statesmen and political economists. With many of these men he afterwards carried on a friendly literary or scientific correspondence. In 1872, in the eightieth year of his age, he took his seat in the Convention assembled in Philadelphia to revise the Constitution of his native State, and took an active and influential part in its deliberations.

Socially Mr. Carey was one of the most charming of men. He had fine conversational powers. His mind was stored with all kinds of knowledge; and he had at command apt illustrations and a large fund of anecdotes. He had seen much of society, and had been brought into contact with celebrated men from all parts of the world—philosophers, littérateurs, travellers, scientists, physicians, lawyers, divines, artists, and inventors. From his youth he had been a great reader of novels and of all kinds of light literature. He read rapidly, and could quickly skim the cream of an ordinary book. His memory was remarkably retentive. He had a large and well-selected library, especially rich in works on political economy and social science, which he bequeathed to the University of Pennsylvania. His collection of pictures, many of them by the best masters of the day, was given to the Philadelphia Academy of Fine Arts. His house was for many years noted for its hospitality. His Sunday Vespers, as they were called, had acquired a national reputation. They were held at from four to six o'clock in the afternoon, and were attended chiefly by his select friends, conspicuous among whom were William D. Lewis, Morton McMichael, General Robert Patterson, ex-Judge William D. Kelley, Joseph R. Chandler, and George H. Boker. Distinguished visitors who happened to be in town were sure to be present. The guests sat around a large table, and discussed in an informal manner such topics of private or public interest as might happen to be introduced. On many occasions the range of discussion assumed a wide latitude. During the war and for some time after its close subjects of grave importance were often brought under consideration. Every man said pretty much what he pleased; there was no restraint; everything was free and easy. A few bottles of wine, of which there was an ample supply in the cellar, served as the only refreshment. As the amiable host was wont to say, in speaking of these agreeable reunions, "We discuss everything, and decide nothing."

From 1833 until 1855 Mr. Carey resided at Burlington,

New Jersey—at first only in the summer, but subsequently throughout the year. After his return to Philadelphia he seldom left it even in the heat of summer, preferring to spend his time in reading and writing. When he retired to private life he made some unlucky investments, and at the time of his death was poor.

Mr. Carey was a very handsome man, nearly six feet in height, well proportioned, with a large, well-shaped head, finely chiseled features, heavy brows, and remarkably black eyes, which retained their beauty and brilliancy to the time of his death. He wore neither moustache nor whiskers. Almost to the last his gait was steady and his form erect. He had a pleasant and contagious laugh, and a way of chatting which denoted a warm heart and a genial disposition. He was fond of the society of his friends, of places of amusement, especially the opera and the theatre, and of the meetings of the various clubs which abound in Philadelphia, of some of which he was an active member. During the latter years of his life many of his evenings were passed at my house, either in conversation or in playing euchre. With my wife he loved to discuss the passing events of society, the drama, the opera, and the latest novel. It was pleasant to listen to them as they talked of the writings of Richardson, especially Pamela, Sir Charles Grandison, and Clarissa Harlowe; Jane and Anna Maria Porter, Sir Walter Scott, Bulwer, Thackeray, Dickens, and a hundred others—their conversation often interspersed with pointed, mirth-provoking anecdote. Euchre was played by him and myself. He was a poor hand at the game, but he always enjoyed it, and laughed heartily when he won the rubber. A glass or two of sherry, with a cordial good-night, would always wind up the evening. When the weather or the walking was bad, either I or one of my sons accompanied him to his own door.

Long after Mr. Carey had reached the age of threescore years and ten he was comparatively vigorous, and able to

perform more or less intellectual labor. But his sight
had become somewhat impaired, his step less elastic,
and his attacks of rheumatism more frequent. Death
had no terrors for him; he often spoke of it as a
thing that was near at hand, and rather to be desired
than to be put off. It came at a time when his friends
were unprepared for it. The previous week he had
attended the annual dinner of the Hibernian Society,
where he contracted a cold which resulted in fatal pneumonia. But little suffering accompanied the attack, and
it is pleasant to know that he was conscious up to the
time of his departure. Four days afterwards we laid him
softly and tenderly in the cemetery at Burlington by the
side of his wife, whom he had loved so dearly and devotedly, and near a cedar-tree, whose evergreen foliage is
an emblem of his undying fame. I had the melancholy
satisfaction of being one of the pallbearers, consisting
solely of his old personal friends and admirers.

Mr. Carey was a man of liberal and enlarged mind. He
belonged to no church or sect. He believed that true
Christianity consists in doing all the good that it is possible to do to others, irrespective of creed or country. Enlightened as he was, he was not free from prejudice. He
was a man of strong feeling, and occasionally indulged in
significant expletives when he wished to express his abhor-
rence or disapproval of unhallowed acts. He detested
slavery, and had no love for England, although he loved
Englishmen. As the son of an Irish patriot he could not
fail to perceive and deprecate the wrongs of Ireland. He
was one of the noblest of men, in warmest sympathy with
all the world—adding dignity to his age, and wealth and
happiness to his country.

James Aitken Meigs.

1829–1879.

In 1868 Dr. James Aitken Meigs entered the Faculty of the Jefferson Medical College, of which he was a graduate, as the successor of Professor Dunglison. At the opening of the session in the autumn of that year he delivered an inaugural dissertation on the Correlation of the Physical and Vital Forces, a subject which he discussed with masterly ability. The discourse was widely disseminated, and had many readers and admirers. He had for a long time made a specialty of the study of physiology and the natural sciences, and was well qualified for his department. He had been a professor in two medical schools—the Philadelphia Medical College and the Pennsylvania Medical College; had edited Carpenter's work on the Microscope and Kirkes's Manual of Physiology; and had furnished a number of valuable papers on various subjects connected with anthropology and natural history. Indeed, no one could have been better prepared by previous study for the work upon which he was about to enter. A ripe scholar, with that command of language which is the offspring of a tenacious memory and a well-disciplined mind, he stood before his class the peer of any member of the Faculty, a man of full stature, capable of doing well and truly all that his chair demanded of him. The title of the chair—the Institutes of Medicine—I never liked. It is an importation from the University of Edinburgh, where it had been in use for several generations. This title still disfigures the annual announcements of the College. Literally interpreted, the Institutes embraces—besides Physiology—pathology and therapeutics, or the general principles of medicine. Meigs wisely confined himself, as Dunglison had in great degree done before him, to Physiology, a field sufficiently extensive for any man.

Meigs was an excellent lecturer. His manner was earnest, even enthusiastic; he never hesitated for a word; and, like one entirely imbued with his work, he carried his class with him. He made frequent use of his blackboard and magic-lantern, and occasionally vivisected a dog, a rabbit, or a frog to impress his matter more deeply upon the minds of his pupils. If he had any fault, it was that he was at times too minute, and overrated the capacity of his auditors. Latterly he got only half through his course; in other words, it took him two sessions to do what should be done in one session. All that any man can do in a five or six months' course of lectures is to give an abstract of the existing state of the science which it is his office to teach. The purpose of teaching is to instruct, and when a lecturer is too profound, or unduly elaborate, he does injustice not only to himself, but to his pupils, very few of whom are able to follow him.

It is much to be regretted that no substantial memorial of the life-work of Meigs remains. I often urged upon him the importance, to himself as well as to the school, of writing an elaborate treatise on philosophy; but, although he always said that he would execute the task, he died without fulfilling his promise. No man in America could better grapple with the great problems of the science of life, or could better appreciate the plan on which such a work should be constructed to answer the requirements of the profession. For some years before his death he had contemplated the publication of a work on the Intellectual and Moral Status of Woman as Compared with that of Man; but it does not appear that he had made any progress in furtherance of his purpose. A collection of his more important papers might form an acceptable memorial volume.

Meigs was of English and Scotch parentage by the father's side, and of Scotch and German by the mother's. He was of humble origin. He held his parents in profound love and reverence. He grieved for a long time for his mother, and after her death he seldom, even in bad weather, appeared in his buggy without having his aged father by his side. The father, as might well be supposed, was proud of his son, whom he often accompanied into the lecture-room that he might listen to the exercises of the hour. Mutual love and devotion could not have been stronger. Meigs's habits were domestic. He had no taste for society, and seldom spent an evening from home, except when he visited the theatre, of which he was very fond. He had, in fact, strong Thespian proclivities, and a rare acquaintance with the elder dramatists. In his younger days he not unfrequently engaged in private theatricals. Much of his leisure was spent among his books, of which he had a very fine collection in different languages, mainly illustrative of the natural sciences, anthropology, travels, and physical geography. His practice was large and laborious, and lay chiefly among the middle and lower classes. I often pleaded with him to make it more select that he might have more leisure for recreation and literary pursuits; but my efforts and those of other friends were unavailing. He seldom absented himself from the city, even during the heat of summer, and then only for a short time. The fact is, he led what might be called a suicidal life. His principal pleasure consisted in the accumulation of money, so that he might ultimately, as he frequently told me, be independent, and thus be able to devote himself to teaching and to authorship. At the time of his demise he was estimated to be worth two hundred thousand dollars, all the result of small fees and of the practice of economy for nearly thirty years. He died without a will, and the only heir is the father.

The death of Meigs, on the 9th of November, 1879, in the fifty-first year of his age, was sudden. He had been for several days missed from his post, but few of his colleagues were aware of his illness. He was confined to his chamber scarcely half a week. He was supposed to be convalescing. Only half an hour before his death he rose, washed himself, and expressed a wish for something to eat. He had been in his bed only a short time when his father noticed that he had great difficulty of breathing, with lividity of the face, and in less than fifteen minutes from the time of the seizure—probably the result of embolism of the heart or lungs—he was a corpse. I shall not soon forget the feeling which overwhelmed me at the sad and unexpected news.

Meigs was a member of numerous societies, native and foreign. For nearly a quarter of a century he was one of the leading men of the Academy of Natural Sciences of Philadelphia, whose Transactions bear testimony to his untiring zeal and industry as a worker and contributor. He was for a long time a Fellow of the College of Physicians of Philadelphia; and in 1871 was President of the Philadelphia County Medical Society.

RICHARD OSWALD COWLING.

1839–1881.

THE saying, "Death loves a shining mark," has seldom been more painfully exemplified than in the case of Dr. Richard Oswald Cowling, who expired after a brief illness at his residence in Louisville on Saturday, April 2d, 1881, at the age of forty-two years. I had known him from his boyhood; and in later years, when he became a medical student, I followed him with the interest with which an anxious father follows the steps of a beloved son. A warm friendship, founded upon mutual affection and respect, had sprung up between us, and continued until his life's end. The telegram which brought me the news of his death was a shock, for I had heard nothing of his illness.   No one outside of his family could have watched his professional career with a kindlier regard than I; no one had a truer conception of his manly attributes, of his social qualities, of his mental endowments, or of his promise as a surgeon and a teacher.   During his attendance upon our lectures in 1867 he was a frequent visitor at my house, and hardly a Sunday passed in which he did not occupy a seat at my table.   We were all fond of him.   He was always cheerful, and his conversation mirth-provoking. He was an earnest student, passed an excellent examination, and left us in high spirits for his home in Kentucky, the scene of his future labors.   I met him several times afterwards at the sessions of the American Medical Association.   I saw him for the last time in May, 1879, at the dedication of the monument erected in honor of Ephraim McDowell at Danville, Kentucky.   It was at this meeting that he presented to me, at the request of the Kentucky State Medical Society, in a brief but eloquent address, the knocker which had so long hung upon the front door of the Father of Ovariotomy.

The manner in which Cowling became a convert to medicine is curious.   He had been sick; and while confined to his room chance threw in his way a copy of Sir Thomas Watson's Practice of Medicine.   Its style, so unusual in a work of this kind, charmed him, as it has charmed thousands of others; and Blackstone and Kent were cast aside.   Business was at first slow in coming to the young practitioner.   Louisville was crowded with good physicians and surgeons; and Cowling was too independent to seek with undue haste what he felt he would be sure in time to get.   Long before his death he had a fair share of the practice of the city, and not a few patients came from a distance to seek his advice.   After his return from Philadelphia he became Demonstrator of Anatomy in the University of Louisville.   He made anatomy for many years a special study. Dr. Bayless, the Professor of Surgery, was compelled by ill health to relinquish a part of his chair. Cowling, at his request, was appointed his adjunct; and when, before the opening of another session, death had vacated the chair, the adjunct became the full professor. As a teacher he was popular and instructive; his fine form and presence, his familiarity with the subject under discussion, and the magnetism of his manners enabled him to command the respect and attention of his pupils. What he lacked in the graces of a finished speaker he made up in force of delivery and in power of expression. As an operator he was cool and deliberate, and ever ready for an emergency.

Cowling was the founder of the Louisville Medical News, a weekly journal, now in the twelfth year of its existence. He had witnessed, as many others had, the shame of the medical profession of Louisville, brought about by factions connected with ill-organized and ill-conducted schools, which, in their rivalry for securing large classes, did not hesitate to malign certain professors and to create a state of feeling at once disreputable to the country and at variance with true scientific progress. It was with a view of putting an end to this condition of things that the News was started; and how well it subserved its purpose every one acquainted with Louisville medical politics knows. At first it met with much abuse; but it had been established only a short time when a marked change became visible, and long before its founder's death it had fully accomplished its mission. Every issue contained a spicy article, full of irony and biting sarcasm; and yet the editor never indulged in improper personalities. What he said went straight to the mark. "Throughout this entire controversy," says Professor D. W. Yandell, who has written a beautiful and touching memoir of him, "Dr. Cowling never lost his temper, and," as he truly said, "in the face of the rudest assertions and grossest personal abuse ad-

ministered correction in the pleasantest possible manner.''
Cowling made the medical atmosphere of Louisville purer
than it had ever been, and he thus established a claim to
the gratitude and affection of his professional brethren.
He wielded not only a caustic, but a ready pen, ever
prompt to uphold the right and to denounce the wrong.
His chirography was generally so crabbed as to cause the
printer great trouble to decipher it. On one occasion, after
the lapse of only a few days, he himself could not read it.
He was fond of children, and not a few of his best articles
were penned in sympathy for them in the suffering to
which they are ignorantly and cruelly subjected by their
parents during the hot summer months, when infantile
mortality in this country is everywhere so great.

He was of English descent, and was born in South Carolina in 1839. Early in life his parents moved to Louisville,
where his father was engaged for many years in mercantile
pursuits. His academic education was received at Trinity
College, Hartford, Connecticut. The President of the institution said of him that he was a good student, was
very fond of his books, and was a fair classical scholar.
He was fully six feet in height. His broad chest and
shoulders were surmounted by a large head. His eyes
were of a light blue, shaded by expressive brows; and his
hair fell in heavy locks over his temples. His mouth was
large, and his voice strong and resonant.

John William Draper.

1811–1882.

The present century, I am sure, has scarcely produced
an abler man on this continent in his particular line of inquiry than John W. Draper. With a mind of great grasp,
he had a natural fondness for original investigation. His

name is associated with many discoveries and improvements in chemistry and natural philosophy which have added lustre to the scientific reputation of our country. His researches in spectral analysis, which were among the earliest of the kind, are especially worthy of mention. For many years his chemical laboratory was the scene of his labors. He did not content himself with the experiments of his predecessors and contemporaries, but he struck out into many paths in which he shed fresh light, while in not a few he developed new truths.

Draper was born near Liverpool in 1811, and came to this country in 1833. His classical education was obtained at the London University; and his medical degree in the University of Pennsylvania in 1836. He had scarcely left the lecture-room when he was appointed Professor of Chemistry and Physiology in Hampden Sidney College, Virginia, from which, in a few years, he was called to the corresponding chair in the University of New York. He was transferred to the Medical Department of the University when it was organized in 1841, in which he remained until a comparatively recent period. In consequence of increasing occupations he relinquished his chair in favor of his son, Dr. John C. Draper, who like himself was an able chemist and an original investigator. In 1839 Professor Draper took the first photographic portrait ever taken from the life. His writings have had a wide circulation, and have received the highest encomiums from competent critics. His Physiology met with marked success, passed rapidly through many editions, and was distinguished for its originality and scientific character. In 1863 appeared the History of the Intellectual Development of Europe, which brought him prominently before the public both at home and abroad. That such a work, written in a liberal spirit, exposing with an unsparing hand what he supposed to be the errors and misdeeds of bygone days, should be keenly criticized and censured is what might have been expected. Inconsiderate theologians severely denounced it, and charged Dr. Draper with atheism. When, some years later, the learned author published his famous treatise entitled Conflict between Religion and Science, the whole Church, Catholic and Protestant, regarded it as the offspring of an unsound mind, perverting the Scriptures, and substituting science for religion. The essence of this book is found in the Intellectual Development of Europe. Both works comprise a vast amount of historical matter, discussed in the genuine spirit of philosophy, in language at once clear, vigorous, and full of imagery. I know of no two treatises published during the present century in the United States of which I would rather be the author. Buckle and Lecky have penned no finer sentences or more graphic descriptions than are to be found in the works which I have named. The American Civil War was published in 1867–'68, in three volumes. Dr. Draper is also the author of numerous monographs on scientific subjects.

Dr. Draper was a man of medium stature ; he had broad shoulders, large forehead, and a fine face with a thoughtful expression. His general appearance, as well as his voice, denoted the characteristics of an Englishman rather than those of an American. Much of his time was passed at his country villa on the banks of the Hudson, amidst books and flowers and enchanting scenery.

JOSEPH PANCOAST.

1805–1882.

THE name of Joseph Pancoast will live in connection with anatomical teaching and operative surgery, in both of which he played a prominent part for more than forty years. He was born near Burlington, New Jersey, November 23d, 1805, and was only four months my junior. He was a graduate of the University of Pennsylvania. I became acquainted with him in 1828, soon after we settled in practice, he on North Fourth Street, and I at the corner of Library and Fifth Streets, next door to the Philadelphia Dispensary. We met one bright Sunday in April at the house of the late Dr. Moehring, on Race Street above Ninth. We examined minutely and with intense interest the surgical work of Bierowski, which was illustrated by beautiful colored plates; and we talked and talked until, when the time for leave-taking arrived, we had become warm friends. After this we occasionally met; and in 1830 I left the city. With two exceptions, I saw no more of him until we were colleagues in the autumn of 1856. I have often thought that our careful study of the magnificent plates of the work of Bierowski had much to do in stimulating our ambition, as well as in directing our tastes, although both of us had had strong surgical proclivities. His Operative Surgery, published quite early in life, illustrated as it was by numerous plates of operations and apparatus, was evidently an outgrowth of that interview, which so firmly impressed itself on our minds that we often talked of it in after life.

Pancoast had a natural taste for anatomy, which was heightened by the lessons of Professor Horner, who was a good surgeon as well as anatomist. Of this man the young Jerseyman was a favorite pupil, who lost no time in making himself master of the structure of the human body. Soon after he took his degree he commenced a course of lectures on Anatomy. He hired for this purpose the rooms situated on Chant Street, in the rear of the old University buildings, originally in the occupancy of Dr. John D. Godman, the anatomist and naturalist, and, at a later period, in that of Dr. James Webster, afterwards a Professor in the Medical College at Geneva, New York. Pancoast was an excellent dissector, and, with his winning manners and enthusiastic declamation, he rapidly drew around him large classes of admiring students. What lent interest to his prelections was the intermixture, if I may so express myself, of surgical and anatomical knowledge; in other words, whenever it was possible he made a practical application of anatomy—a plan which he invariably followed in his college lectures, and which rendered his teaching so successful. He knew how to infuse life into the cadaver; how to wake up the bones and muscles and nerves and viscera, and make them respond to the diagnosis and treatment of disease and accident. His knowledge of topographical anatomy was profound, and few surgeons ever wielded a knife more gracefully, more boldly, or with greater accuracy and skill. The reputation which he acquired in these obscure rooms was not lost upon him. The Trustees of the Jefferson Medical College, watching his rising reputation, unanimously called him, in 1838, to the chair made vacant by the retirement of Dr. George McClellan—a chair which he filled with marked ability until the reorganization of the Faculty in 1841. He was then transferred to the chair of Anatomy, which he occupied with equal distinction until his resignation in 1872. How much he added to the reputation of the school is too well known to require any illustration from me. During the period of our colleagueship we energetically worked together for the good of the College, and few teachers were ever more popular, respected, or beloved by their pupils than Pancoast. They all felt his worth as a man and as a teacher; they knew how thoroughly he was acquainted with anatomy—general, descriptive, and surgical—and were conscious of the pains he took to instruct them. He made anatomy so plain that the dullest pupil, if at all attentive, could not fail to be enlightened.

Pancoast was an excellent clinical teacher; he was perfectly familiar with the art of diagnosis and the treatment of diseases and accidents. If he had any defect, it was as a pathologist; but even here he was rarely at fault. He possessed all the attributes of a great operator—quickness of perception, unflinching courage, and rare presence of mind. It may truly be said of him that his hand never trembled and that his eye never winced. His success was commensurate with his skill. He was the author of a number of operative processes which are identified with his name. As a hospital surgeon he enjoyed exceptional opportunities for widening the range of his knowledge. Not long after he received his degree he was made Physician-in-Chief of the Children's Hospital; and subsequently he served for a number of years on the surgical staff, first, of the Philadelphia, and afterwards for seven years, if I mistake not, on that of the Pennsylvania Hospital.

His first literary effort was a translation of Lobstein's celebrated treatise on the Sympathetic Nerve, originally published in Latin. He edited, successively, Quain's Anatomical Plates, and Caspar Wistar's Anatomy, which he enriched with numerous additions, chiefly of an histological character. The latter work was for a long time used as a text-book by the students of the Jefferson Medical College, and it lost its hold on their esteem and affection only after the appearance of Erasmus Wilson's excellent manual, which in its turn gave way to the abler treatise of Gray. His Operative Surgery was originally issued in a thick quarto volume, profusely illustrated by lithographic plates. The work, although savagely criticized by the American and British press, soon passed into a second edition, and added greatly to his fame as a surgeon. He also contributed numerous papers to the medical journals. During the last fifteen years of his life writing had no charms for him, and when spoken to on the subject he said he thought that he had done enough of that kind of work. He was a capital shot, and took much delight in duck and quail shooting. He loved pictures and pretty landscapes, and was fond of a good anecdote. Much of his leisure in his later years was spent in light reading.

I knew Pancoast intimately, and I formed a high estimate of his character. He was a man of decided convictions, professional, moral, and political; a kind husband and father, a warm friend, and an upright citizen. Few surgeons have done more to ennoble and dignify our profession. Long before he died he was the possessor of a large fortune, the result of the labors of an honest and virtuous life. He died March 7th, 1882, in the seventy-seventh year of his age, beloved and honored by all who knew him.

B. H. HILL.

1823–1882.

B. H. HILL died on August 16th, 1882. From small beginnings he rose to be one of the most prominent statesmen of his day, an able expounder of our Constitution, and an intrepid champion of the rights of the people.

I saw Senator Hill for the first time on the 19th of July, 1881, while I was at Cape May in pursuit of recreation from hard work. "I have come," said he, "to consult you professionally. I am just from New York, where I saw Dr. Bayard, the homœopathist, and several prominent surgeons; but I am not satisfied, and I desire your advice. My trouble is a sore on the left side of my tongue which has annoyed me more or less for the last four years. When I first noticed it, it was not larger than an ordinary pin's head, and I think it must have been caused by a roughness on one of the molar teeth. Bayard says it is a specific sore, not cancerous, although I assured him that I never had any such disease. I had consulted him repeatedly, and he always adhered to his opinion despite my assertion.'' Such was Mr. Hill's statement of his case. I found an ulcer on the edge of the tongue extending a distance of more than an inch from behind forward, but not to any considerable depth, and at once, at his own request, informed him of its malignant character. "It is an epithelioma," I said, "and nothing else." "What is the remedy?" Mr. Hill asked. "The knife." "Will that effect a cure?" "That I cannot affirm; you must run the risk; the tendency of all such diseases, especially in neglected cases, is to recur." I made no promises whatever. I explained to the Senator everything—the risk of the operation, and the strong probability of a relapse. As his general health was excellent, and as there was no appreciable involvement of the lymphatic glands at the base of the jaw, I saw no reason why an operation should not afford at least temporary relief; and with this understanding it was performed two days after our interview. As I had made my arrangements to go to the Isles of Shoals in the latter part of July, Mr. Hill, in the absence in Europe of my son Dr. S. W. Gross, was left in charge of Professor William H. Pancoast, and he progressed so well that he left Philadelphia within a few weeks in excellent health and spirits. A second operation, more extensive than the first, but not bloody or painful, was performed; and then a third, which was solely directed to the removal of diseased glands. But at no time, during my treatment of the case, did I hold out to him any hope of final recovery.

A few weeks after the last operation, under the conviction that a change of air and scene was required, he was taken to Atlantic City, much exhausted and depressed by his suffering and by his inability to take food on account of the difficulty of swallowing. After a sojourn there of several weeks he returned unrelieved, and with every indication that he was wholly beyond the reach of surgery. As a last resort he went, at the earnest solicitation of his family,

to the Eureka Springs in Arkansas, erroneously invested
with curative powers in cancerous affections. His appetite
and general health improved somewhat under the use of the
water and the change of air, but the local disease steadily
progressed; his sufferings could be assuaged only by large
doses of anodynes; he became excessively emaciated; and
death finally relieved him in little more than a year after I
took charge of his case.

It is gratifying to me to know that Mr. Hill retained his
confidence in and friendship for me during the remainder of his life. The last letter he probably ever wrote
was addressed to me, consisting of a few crooked lines,
evidently penned with great difficulty, and expressive of
his kindly feeling for me. I had become warmly attached
to him. He was patient in suffering, uncomplaining, and
ever ready to adopt any suggestions offered for his relief.
He was a noble man, a loving husband and father, with
a big heart, in strong sympathy with human nature; a
hater of immorality, of crime, and of oppression; a devout
Christian; a genial and refined gentleman.

Mr. Hill was the son of a farmer, and performed farm
labor until after he was fifteen years of age; he was then
sent to college, studied hard, and on Commencement day
received the first honors in his class. "He took," says his
biographer, "his earnest temperament and gentleness from
his mother, and to her careful and loving training was indebted for the basis of what is best in his character."
How often the son inherits his greatness from the mother
history abundantly shows. Mr. Hill in due time studied
law, was sent to the Legislature, became conspicuous in
politics, and was finally elected to the Senate of the United
States. When the Rebellion broke out he exerted all his
power and genius to keep Georgia in the Union; but,
failing in this, he earnestly espoused the Southern cause.
When the war was over, he mounted the stump and
used his influence in resisting the efforts of those who

were swarming through the State and setting the colored people in hostile array against their late masters. Naturally aggressive, he threw his whole soul into the campaign; and, although he did not accomplish all he had wished, he succeeded in attracting the attention of the General Government to what were regarded as flagrant outrages, and did his best to secure for the Southern States a favorable basis of reconstruction. The people of Georgia loved Mr. Hill; and this affection was cordially shared by the Southern people generally. They were proud of him as an upright citizen; as a patriot and a statesman; as an eloquent orator and a spirited debater. In the Senate of the United States he was justly noted for his fearless exposure of evil practices among his opponents, for his unscathing rebukes, and for his uncompromising hostility to everything that savored of corruption in high places. He was a tower of strength in his party. Apart from the pangs inseparable from leaving his devoted family, his regret that he had not completed his mission was the only regret which haunted him in his last hours. But a few months before his death he said to me, "I am not afraid to die; still I should like to live a few years longer to do some useful work which has long occupied my thoughts and affection."

Mr. Hill was a noble-looking man, tall, erect, well proportioned, a ready talker, an eloquent speaker, with a mind well stored with general knowledge, and a heart full of love and as tender as that of a woman. His eyes were of a bluish color, and soft and gentle in repose, but capable, when his mind was ruffled by anger, or engaged in chastising an enemy or an offender against decency or public morality, of emitting the lightning's flash.

INDEX.

427

438 *INDEX.*

THE END.

Medicine & Society In America

An Arno Press/New York Times Collection

Alcott, William A. **The Physiology of Marriage.** 1866. New Introduction by Charles E. Rosenberg.

Beard, George M. **American Nervousness:** Its Causes and Consequences. 1881. New Introduction by Charles E. Rosenberg.

Beard, George M. **Sexual Neurasthenia.** 5th edition. 1898.

Beecher, Catharine E. **Letters to the People on Health and Happiness.** 1855.

Blackwell, Elizabeth. **Essays in Medical Sociology.** 1902. Two volumes in one.

Blanton, Wyndham B. **Medicine in Virginia in the Seventeenth Century.** 1930.

Bowditch, Henry I. **Public Hygiene in America.** 1877.

Bowditch, N[athaniel] I. **A History of the Massachusetts General Hospital:** To August 5, 1851. 2nd edition. 1872.

Brill, A. A. **Psychanalysis:** Its Theories and Practical Application. 1913.

Cabot, Richard C. **Social Work:** Essays on the Meeting-Ground of Doctor and Social Worker. 1919.

Cathell, D. W. **The Physician Himself and What He Should Add to His Scientific Acquirements.** 2nd edition. 1882. New Introduction by Charles E. Rosenberg.

The Cholera Bulletin. Conducted by an Association of Physicians. Vol. I: Nos. 1–24. 1832. All published. New Introduction by Charles E. Rosenberg.

Clarke, Edward H. **Sex in Education;** or, A Fair Chance for the Girls. 1873.

Committee on the Costs of Medical Care. **Medical Care for the American People:** The Final Report of The Committee on the Costs of Medical Care, No. 28. [1932].

Currie, William. **An Historical Account of the Climates and Diseases of the United States of America.** 1792.

Davenport, Charles Benedict. **Heredity in Relation to Eugenics.** 1911. New Introduction by Charles E. Rosenberg.

Davis, Michael M. **Paying Your Sickness Bills.** 1931.

Disease and Society in Provincial Massachusetts: Collected Accounts, 1736–1939. 1972.

Earle, Pliny. **The Curability of Insanity:** A Series of Studies. 1887.

Falk, I. S., C. Rufus Rorem, and Martha D. Ring. **The Costs of Medical Care:** A Summary of Investigations on The Economic Aspects of the Prevention and Care of Illness, No. 27. 1933.

Faust, Bernhard C. **Catechism of Health:** For the Use of Schools, and for Domestic Instruction. 1794.

Flexner, Abraham. **Medical Education in the United States and Canada:** A Report to The Carnegie Foundation for the Advancement of Teaching, Bulletin Number Four. 1910.

Gross, Samuel D. **Autobiography of Samuel D. Gross, M.D.,** with Sketches of His Contemporaries. Two volumes. 1887.

Hooker, Worthington. **Physician and Patient;** or, A Practical View of the Mutual Duties, Relations and Interests of the Medical Profession and the Community. 1849.

Howe, S. G. **On the Causes of Idiocy.** 1858.

Jackson, James. **A Memoir of James Jackson, Jr., M.D.** 1835.

Jennings, Samuel K. **The Married Lady's Companion, or Poor Man's Friend.** 2nd edition. 1808.

The Maternal Physician; a Treatise on the Nurture and Management of Infants, from the Birth until Two Years Old. 2nd edition. 1818. New Introduction by Charles E. Rosenberg.

Mathews, Joseph McDowell. **How to Succeed in the Practice of Medicine.** 1905.

McCready, Benjamin W. **On the Influences of Trades, Professions, and Occupations in the United States, in the Production of Disease.** 1943.

Mitchell, S. Weir. **Doctor and Patient.** 1888.

Nichols, T[homas] L. **Esoteric Anthropology:** The Mysteries of Man. [1853].

Origins of Public Health in America: Selected Essays, 1820–1855. 1972.

Osler, Sir William. **The Evolution of Modern Medicine.** 1922.

The Physician and Child-Rearing: Two Guides, 1809–1894. 1972.

Rosen, George. **The Specialization of Medicine:** with Particular Reference to Ophthalmology. 1944.

Royce, Samuel. **Deterioration and Race Education.** 1878.

Rush, Benjamin. **Medical Inquiries and Observations.** Four volumes in two. 4th edition. 1815.

Shattuck, Lemuel, Nathaniel P. Banks, Jr., and Jehiel Abbott. **Report of a General Plan for the Promotion of Public and Personal Health.** Massachusetts Sanitary Commission. 1850.

Smith, Stephen. **Doctor in Medicine** and Other Papers on Professional Subjects. 1872.

Still, Andrew T. **Autobiography of Andrew T. Still,** with a History of the Discovery and Development of the Science of Osteopathy. 1897.

Storer, Horatio Robinson. **The Causation, Course, and Treatment of Reflex Insanity in Women.** 1871.

Sydenstricker, Edgar. **Health and Environment.** 1933.

Thomson, Samuel. **A Narrative, of the Life and Medical Discoveries of Samuel Thomson.** 1822.

Ticknor, Caleb. **The Philosophy of Living;** or, The Way to Enjoy Life and Its Comforts. 1836.

U.S. Sanitary Commission. **The Sanitary Commission of the United States Army:** A Succinct Narrative of Its Works and Purposes. 1864.

White, William A. **The Principles of Mental Hygiene.** 1917.